Handbook of Reconfigurable Computing

Volume I

Handbook of Reconfigurable Computing
Volume I

Edited by **Akira Hanako**

CLANRYE INTERNATIONAL

New Jersey

Published by Clanrye International,
55 Van Reypen Street,
Jersey City, NJ 07306, USA
www.clanryeinternational.com

Handbook of Reconfigurable Computing: Volume I
Edited by Akira Hanako

International Standard Book Number: 978-1-63240-288-2 (Hardback)

Printed in the United States of America.

Contents

Preface

A reconfigurable system is any system whose sub-system configurations can be changed or modified after fabrication. Reconfigurable computing is generally used to allocate computers whose memory units, processing elements, and interconnections can transform function and spatial configuration after manufacturing and fabrication, before or during the run-time of a particular program or as part of such a program. This field uses the knowledge of computer architecture combined with the high performance of hardware and the flexibility of software by processing with very flexible high speed computing fabrics. One can say that its prime feature is the ability to execute computations in hardware to increase performance, while retaining most of the flexibility of software solution at the same time. In the late 20th century, one can see that there was resurgence in this area of research with many proposed future reconfigurable architectures developed in industrial and academic arenas. Reconfigurable computing has now fast established itself as a major technical discipline that encompasses numerous subjects including computing science and electronic engineering. There is vast potential in reconfigurable computing with the chance to greatly speed up a wide variety of applications. This ensures that reconfigurable computing has become the focus of a great deal of research.

This book is an attempt to compile and collate all available research on reconfigurable computing under one cover. I am grateful to those who put their hard work, effort and expertise into these research projects as well as those who were supportive in this endeavor.

Editor

Using Partial Reconfiguration and Message Passing to Enable FPGA-Based Generic Computing Platforms

Manuel Saldaña,[1] Arun Patel,[1] Hao Jun Liu,[2] and Paul Chow[2]

[1] *ArchES Computing Systems, 708-222 Spadina Avenue, Toronto, ON, Canada M5T 3A2*
[2] *The Edward S. Rogers Sr. Department of Electrical and Computer Engineering, University of Toronto, 10 King's College Road, Toronto, ON, Canada M5S 3G4*

Correspondence should be addressed to Manuel Saldaña, ms@archescomputing.com

Academic Editor: Marco D. Santambrogio

Partial reconfiguration (PR) is an FPGA feature that allows the modification of certain parts of an FPGA while the rest of the system continues to operate without disruption. This distinctive characteristic of FPGAs has many potential benefits but also challenges. The lack of good CAD tools and the deep hardware knowledge requirement result in a hard-to-use feature. In this paper, the new partition-based Xilinx PR flow is used to incorporate PR within our MPI-based message-passing framework to allow hardware designers to create *template bitstreams*, which are predesigned, prerouted, generic bitstreams that can be reused for multiple applications. As an example of the generality of this approach, four different applications that use the same template bitstream are run consecutively, with a PR operation performed at the beginning of each application to instantiate the desired application engine. We demonstrate a simplified, reusable, high-level, and portable PR interface for X86-FPGA hybrid machines. PR issues such as local resets of reconfigurable modules and context saving and restoring are addressed in this paper followed by some examples and preliminary PR overhead measurements.

1. Introduction

Partial reconfiguration (PR) is a feature of an FPGA that allows part of it to be reconfigured while the rest of it continues to operate normally. PR has been the focus of considerable research because of the many potential benefits of such a feature. For example, it allows the implementation of more power-efficient designs by using hardware on-demand, that is, only instantiate the logic that is necessary at a given time and remove unused logic. PR also allows the virtualization of FPGA resources by time sharing them among many concurrent applications. Alternatively, a single large application may be implemented even if it requires more logic resources than what a single FPGA can provide as long as the logic resources are not required simultaneously. Fault-tolerant systems and dynamic load-balancing are also potential benefits of PR. All these features make PR attractive for applications in the fields of automotive and aerospace design, software radio, video, and image processing, among other markets.

However, there are many challenges for PR to be more widely accepted, for example, dynamic changing of logic adds an extra level of difficulty to verification performance overheads in terms of designed target frequency and higher resource utilization complex design entry tools and PR CAD flows. A PR design requires the partitioning and floor-planning of the entire FPGA into static regions (SRs) and reconfigurable regions (RRs). The SR does not change during the execution of an application, and RRs may be dynamically reconfigured during the execution of the application. This partitioning has added another layer of complexity to FPGA design. To cope with this increased complexity, Xilinx has released a new partition-based ISE 12 solution that simplifies PR design [1].

By looking at Xilinx documentation and comparing the resources in Virtex-E and Virtex 7 devices, we can see that in about ten years, FPGAs have increased their resources roughly over 18-fold in LUTs, 14-fold in Flip-Flops, and 31-fold in BRAMs. Furthermore, the number of configuration bits for the XC7V2000T FPGA is just under 54 MB. At this rate, handling partial bitstreams may become more practical than handling entire bitstreams. As FPGA sizes continue to increase, new use case models that were not possible before will now start to emerge, and PR can be an enabling technology of such models.

In this paper, we extend previous work [2] on partial reconfiguration to explore new use cases for FPGAs by using PR within a message-passing system to provide generic, predesigned and prerouted computing platforms based on template designs, where the user can dynamically populate the RRs with application cores. These generic templates can then be modified as needed for a particular application and still be released as application-specific templates. The goal is to relieve the user from the burden of having to design the communications infrastructure for an application and focus solely on application cores. Equally important is to do this in a portable manner across platforms. To this end, we add PR capabilities to the ArchES-MPI framework [3, 4], which provides a communication abstraction layer that enables point-to-point communications between high-end X86 and embedded processors, and hardware accelerators.

The rest of the paper is organized as follows: Section 2 mentions some related work in PR and Section 3 introduces the concept of PR within our message-passing framework. Section 4 describes the synchronization process suggested to perform PR, how to store and restore the current status, and how to generate necessary resets. Section 5 shows the hardware platform used to run the tests. Section 6 explains the software flow to create and handle partial bitstreams. Experimental results are shown in Section 7. Section 8 describes an example where four applications reuse the same template bitstream. Finally, Section 9 presents some concluding remarks.

2. Related Work

There has been abundant research on PR in the last decade with much of it focusing on specific aspects of PR such as CAD flows [5], scheduling [6], communications [7], configuration time evaluation frameworks [8], and core relocation [9]. Our long-term goal is to use PR to implement an entire, practical and generic framework that allows hardware designers to create generic and application-specific template platforms that follows a higher-level parallel programming model that is easier to understand by software developers. This paper presents a step in that direction, providing a working framework that includes the software interface, CAD flow, network-on-chip (NoC), and message-passing layer. Future work will focus on adding and optimizing different aspects of the PR framework.

One of the PR aspects is the state store and restore capability before and after PR takes place. An approach for doing this is by reading back parts of the FPGA configuration memory as described in [10]. However, this approach

assumes deep knowledge of the bitstream format and it is strongly dependent upon the FPGA architecture, which is too low level for most developers. Additionally, unnecessary data is read back, which increases the storage overhead and the time to perform the context switch. Our approach is to let the user decide what to store and restore using the message-passing infrastructure making the solution more portable and higher-level at the expense of some additional design effort. Research has been done to provide platform-independent PR flows [11]. Similarly, our goal is to achieve more portable PR systems by using our existing MPI infrastructure.

The BORPH research project [12] follows similar goals with our work in the sense that it aims at simplifying the use of FPGAs by inserting high-level and well-known abstractions. PR has been added to BORPH as a way to dynamically configure a hardware engine at runtime and treat it as an operating system process. Communication with the engine is achieved via file system calls, such as open, read, write, and close. In our work, we treat the hardware engines as MPI processes (not operating system processes) and communication is achieved via MPI function calls, such as MPI_Send and MPI_Recv. Our approach is more suitable for parallel programming as it is based on a standard designed specifically for such a purpose.

In most prior art in this field, the configuration controller is an embedded processor (MicroBlaze or PowerPC) using a fixed configuration interface (ICAP or SelectMAP) [13] and the controller also generates the local reset pulse after PR. In our framework, the X86 processor controls the configuration and the actual configuration interface is abstracted away from the user, who does not need to know which interface is used. Also, in our approach, an embedded processor is not necessary to issue the local reset, rather it is generated by using the underlying messaging system already available.

3. Message Passing and PR in FPGAs

The MPI standard [14] is a widely used parallel programming API within the high-performance computing world to program supercomputers, clusters, and even grid applications. Previous work presented TMD-MPI [4] and proved that a subset implementation of the MPI standard can be developed targeting embedded systems implemented in FPGAs. TMD-MPI was initially developed at the University of Toronto and now it is supported as a commercial tool known as ArchES-MPI. It allows X86, MicroBlaze, and PowerPC processors as well as hardware accelerators to all exchange point-to-point messages and work concurrently to solve an application. By using MPI as a communications middleware layer, portability across multiple platforms can be achieved easily. In particular, platforms that include FPGAs have extra benefit from a portability layer as hardware can change all the time, either because of the nature of the FPGA itself or due to changes in the boards that FPGAs are placed on. But most importantly, ArchES-MPI provides a unified programming model and proposes a programming paradigm to the developer that facilitates the implementation of heterogeneous, multicore, multiaccelerator systems.

The use of PR within our message-passing framework is to allow the creation of predesigned and prerouted platforms that can be distributed as templates to the end users with the purpose of simplifying the system-level design process. By using PR it is possible to create an array of RRs that can be populated with user application cores, known as reconfigurable modules (RMs) at run time. Figure 1 shows some examples of these generic designs for one, four, and eight RRs. Application cores can also be placed in the SR and the ArchES-MPI infrastructure transparently handles the communication between the cores regardless of the region they are placed in.

A typical MPI program has multiple software processes, each with a unique ID number known as the rank. In ArchES-MPI there are software ranks running on processors and hardware ranks running as hardware engines. One MPI hardware rank can have multiple RMs. This means that the rank number assigned to it does not change during the execution of the entire application, just its functionality depending on the RM currently configured. There is another situation (not covered in this paper) where a new RM requires a change in the assigned rank number, which requires the NoC routing tables to be updated dynamically.

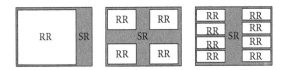

FIGURE 1: Layout of template-based, generic bitstreams for one, four, and eight reconfigurable regions (RRs) and the static region (SR).

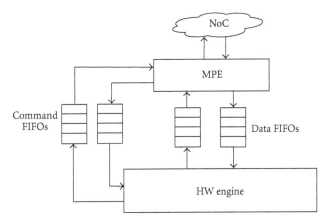

FIGURE 2: Connection of the application hardware engine and the MPE.

3.1. Message-Passing Engine and Reconfigurable Regions. To processors, ArchES-MPI appears as a software library that provides message-passing capabilities. Hardware engines must use a hardware block called the MPE (message-passing engine), which encapsulates in hardware some of the MPI functionality. The MPE provides the hardware equivalent to MPI_Send and MPI_Recv to a hardware engine in the FPGA. It handles unexpected messages, processes the communication protocol, and divides large messages into smaller size packets to be sent through the NoC. As shown in Figure 2, the MPE is connected between the hardware engine and the NoC. The MPE receives the message parameters and data from the hardware engine, such as the operation (whether it is sending or receiving a message), the destination node id (rank of the process in the MPI environment), the length of the message, and an identification number for the message (the Tag parameter in a normal MPI send/receive operation). After this, the MPE will handle the communications through the NoC with the destination rank. The hardware engine and the MPE form a single endpoint in the message-passing network. The interfaces between the MPE and the hardware engine are four FIFOs (two for commands and two for data), making integration easy. These FIFOs can be asynchronous allowing the hardware engine to operate at different frequencies than its associated MPE.

Based on where the MPE is placed relative to the RR, we can have three possible scenarios. Figure 3(a) shows the MPE placed outside the RR, and it is connected to a user wrapper that controls the MPE and the actual RM through control signals. The RM is a block instantiated within the wrapper. The RM block can be thought of as the main computational pipeline and the wrapper as a higher-level,

application-specific controller. One of the wrapper's duties is to control the PR synchronization process (described in the next section). In Figure 3(b), the MPE is also placed outside the RR but with no wrapper (or a very small and generic wrapper) and it is connected directly to the RR. This means that the entire RR is reserved for a single and self-contained RM that must directly control the MPE and handle its own PR synchronization process. This self-contained scenario is more generic than the wrapper-based scenario because it does not contain an application-specific wrapper that may not work with a different application. From the implementation point of view, the user can still design a specific wrapper for a particular application but it would have to be placed in the RR and not in the SR. Finally, Figures 3(c) and 3(d) show the scenario where there is no MPE in the SR. This scenario gives the user the opportunity to implement a sub-NoC that may contain many more ranks or user-defined bridges for off-chip communications such as an Ethernet-based bridge. For brevity, in this paper we only focus on the first two scenarios.

4. Partial Reconfiguration Synchronization

Certain applications may need a way to store the current status of registers, state machines, and memory contents before PR takes place and restore them once the RM is configured back again. This is analogous to pushing and popping variables to a stack before and after a function call. A local reset pulse may also be required to initialize the newly partially reconfigured module to drive registers or state machines to their quiescent state; the global reset cannot be used for this.

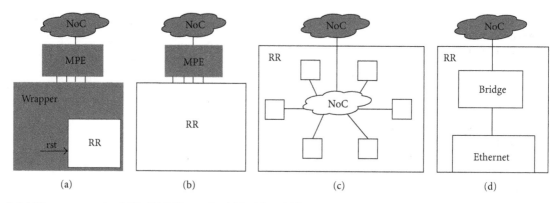

FIGURE 3: (a) Wrapper-contained RR, (b) Self-contained RR, (c) and (d) no-MPE RRs. (Gray means static and white means dynamic).

4.1. Status Store and Restore. The requirement to store and restore the current status of an RM is solved by sending explicit messages between the configuration controller (a rank within the MPI world) and the rank that is going to be partially reconfigured. Since any rank in MPI can initiate a message, there can be two options to start the PR process based on the initiating entity: the *processor-initiated PR* and the *RM-initiated PR*. This is shown in Figure 4. In the processor-initiated PR, the X86 processor (Rank 0) acts as a master and initiates the reconfiguration synchronization by sending an explicit message ("cfg") to RM_A (Rank 1), which acts as a slave waiting for this message and reacting to it. RM_A then sends an "OK-to-configure" message back to Rank 0 when it is safe to perform the configuration process. The payload of this "OK-to-configure" message can be used to save the current status of RM_A. When Rank 0 receives the "OK-to-configure" message it stores the status (if any) in memory and proceeds with the partial configuration process of RM_B (also Rank 1). Once this is done, a "configuration-done" message is sent to the newly configured module RM_B with the previously stored status data (if any), which is received and used by RM_B to restore its state prior to PR.

The second synchronization option is when the RM is the master and the X86 is the slave. In this case, when a certain condition is met, RM_A sends a "request-to-configure" message along with the status data to Rank 0, which stores the status data and proceeds with the reconfiguration of RM_B. After this is done, Rank 0 sends the "configuration-done" message to the newly configured RM_B along with the status data to restore its state. The user-defined condition that triggers the PR entirely depends on the application.

4.2. Local Reset. The reset issue can be handled easily in the wrapper-contained scenario mentioned in Section 3.1. Since the wrapper controls the MPE it knows when the PR synchronization messages are sent and received and it can assert the reset signal of the RR while PR takes place and release it after the "configuration-done" message is received. In the wrapper-contained scenario the wrapper is placed in the SR and it is aware of when PR has occurred. In contrast, in the self-contained scenario all the application logic is in the RM and it is all being configured, therefore, a

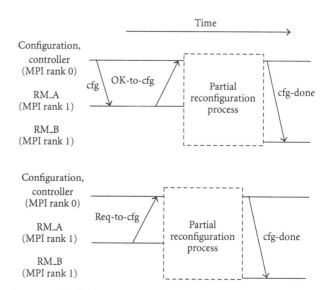

FIGURE 4: Explicit message synchronization between PR controller and RMs.

different reset mechanism must be implemented. In multi-FPGA systems this is an inherently distributed situation where the RR might be in a different FPGA than where the configuration controller (e.g., embedded processor) is located. Everything has to be done at the endpoints using messagepassing otherwise a reset signal might need an off-chip wire between FPGAs, and as many wires as there are RRs per FPGA, which is not practical.

Previous work [2] suggested that a possible way to auto-generate a local reset is by using an LUT configured as shift register (SRL) in each RM with all the bits initialized to the reset value (1's if reset is active high) and its input tied to the global system reset signal. The output of the SRL is used to reset the RM. This way, as soon as the RM is configured the RM will be in the reset state and the clock will start shifting the current value of the global reset signal, which should be deasserted assuming the rest of the system is currently running. Eventually, after a given number of cycles (length of the shift register, e.g., 16 cycles) the SRL output will be deasserted and the RM will come out of reset. This process is repeated every time the RM is configured.

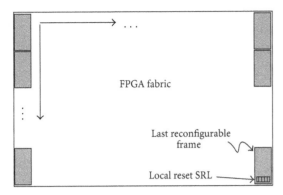

FIGURE 5: Placement of the reset SRL within the RR.

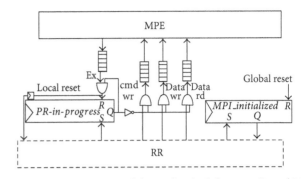

FIGURE 6: Static registers and decoupling logic between SR and RR.

However, a problem with the approach is that it will not work if the SRL placement is not properly constrained. We believe that partial reconfiguration of an entire RR does not happen atomically, which means that not all the logic of an RM is configured at once, but frame by frame. A PR frame is the smallest reconfigurable building block. A PR frame is 1 CLB wide by 16, 20, or 40 CLBs high for Virtex 4, 5, and 6, respectively. If the reset SRL is configured before the rest of the RM logic is configured then the local reset will be applied to old logic from the previous RM. The actual time it takes to complete PR depends on how fast the partial bitstream is transferred from host memory to the ICAP or SelectMAP interfaces, which in turn depends on what communication mechanism is being used (PCIe, FSB, Ethernet, etc.). In any case, a good solution should not rely on configuration time to be correct.

A possible solution to this problem is to force the CAD tools to place the SRL in the last LUT of the last frame within the RR to be configured as shown in Figure 5. This way we ensure that all the logic from the RM has been configured before the reset SRL and that the local reset will apply to the new RM logic. However, the caveat of this approach is, that to the best of our knowledge, there is no official documentation from Xilinx regarding how PR is done over the RR. For example, Figure 5 assumes that PR follows a top-down and left-right approach, but it could be otherwise.

To avoid the previous problems, the approach used to generate a local reset is to take advantage of the existing message-passing capability and the MPE to produce an external signal to the RM. This approach has the added benefit being platform independent. After an RM receives the configuration message ("cfg") and before PR takes place, the current RM can instruct the MPE to be ready to receive the "configuration-done" message, which will come eventually. The RM's FSM then goes into an idle state waiting for PR to occur. After PR is done and the new RM has been completely configured, the X86 processor sends the "configuration-done" message, which the MPE is already expecting. This causes the MPE to inform the RM of the newly arrived message by writing a control word to the command FIFO between the MPE and the RM. The exists signal (Ex in Figure 6) of the command FIFO is then used to generate the reset pulse for the new RM. After coming out of reset

the RM can dequeue the control word and start running, or resume its operation by restoring its previous status (if any) as mentioned in Section 4.1.

There is an additional requirement for RMs that use ArchES-MPI when coming out of reset. The MPI_Init function must be called only once by all ranks at the beginning of the application. This function initializes the MPI environment and in the case of a hardware rank the function initializes the MPEs. This means that after coming out of reset an RM must know whether it is the first time the application is running, and therefore the MPE needs to be initialized, or if the MPE has been initialized already by a previous RM. In the later case the RM must not go through the initialization process again. Instead, it must continue its execution and restore its status (if any) using the "configuration-done" message.

A simple solution for this is to add a set-reset flip-flop to the SR that indicates that the MPE has been initialized. This flag, shown as *MPI_Initialized* in Figure 6, must be set by the first RM to run in the FPGA during the initialization process after global reset. Successive RMs should check this flag to know whether or not to do the initialization process. This flag is analogous to a static variable within a software function that is initialized only once during the first time the function is called.

4.3. Decoupling Logic. Another consideration when using PR is the decoupling between SR and RR logic because the outputs of the RR may be undefined during PR. This may cause undesired reads or writes to FIFOs with invalid data. To this end, the synchronization messages can be used to set and clear a flag to gate the outputs of the RM as shown in Figure 6. When the RM receives the PR message ("cfg" in Figure 4) it sets the *PR-in-progress* flag, which is a set-reset flip-flop placed in SR that will disable the RR outputs during PR. After PR is done, the flag is cleared when the "configuration-done" message is received. This is the same message used to generate the local reset as previously discussed. The decoupling logic occupies very little resources: 158 flip-flops and 186 LUTs per RR. With one RR this means less than 1% of the resources available in the XC5VLX330 FPGA.

5. Development Platform

Portability is one of the benefits of using a communications abstraction layer such as ArchES-MPI, hence adding partial reconfiguration must be done in a portable way as well. ArchES-MPI has been used in a variety of platforms, but the focus here will be on the one shown in Figure 7 as it provides a heterogeneous platform. It is based on a quad-socket motherboard with one Intel Quad-core Xeon processor and the other sockets have Nallatech FSB-socket accelerator modules [15]. The accelerator module consists of a stack of up to three PCB layers. The first layer (bottom-up) contains the base FPGA (XC5VLX110) and it is reserved as a connection interface between the front side bus (FSB) and the upper layers. The second and third layers contain two XC5VLX330 FPGAs each. The FPGAs are directly connected by LVDS buses. Figure 7 also shows a Xilinx evaluation board XUPV5LX110T with a PCIe-x1 link.

The FPGA on the FSB base module drives the SelectMAP interface of the FPGAs in the upper layers to perform PR. In contrast, the PCIe board uses the ICAP port as there is only one FPGA. The FSB_Bridge and PCIe_Bridge are hardware components that are used by the NoC to handle the communications over their respective interfaces and move data packets from the FPGA to shared memory and vice-versa. The bridges are also in charge of receiving the partial bitstreams and writing them to the appropriate configuration interface: ICAP or SelectMAP.

6. Software Flow

For the purposes of this paper, which is to incorporate PR into our existing MPI infrastructure, a standard Xilinx flow is followed with some extensions to it. However, any other PR flow that can generate and handle full and partial bitstreams could potentially be used as well.

There are two parts of the CAD flow shown in Figure 8: the first flow is used to create the template bitstreams by partitioning the design into static and reconfigurable regions. The second part of the flow allows the end user to reuse the prebuilt, prerouted template design. The Xilinx EDK/ISE 12.1 suite is used to implement and synthesize the system-level design including the NoC and message-passing infrastructure (system components). The netlists are then used in PlanAhead to layout the RRs, which requires certain expertise. With the new Xilinx Partition-based flow there is no need to explicitly implement bus macros. PlanAhead will automatically insert LUT1 elements where they are required. Finally, the full template bitstream is created and can be distributed to users. Additionally, the partial bitstream of a placeholder RM can also be created. The placeholder (or bootloader RM) is discussed in Section 8.1.

The end user can implement hardware engines as Xilinx pcores in an EDK project. The engines can be coded as HDL or via C-to-Gates tools and synthesize them. The resulting netlist can then be integrated into the PlanAhead project where the predesigned SR is reused and it is only necessary to place and route the RMs and generate user partial bitstreams. The end user does not have to do any

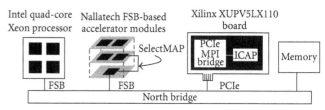

FIGURE 7: Development platform with FSB and PCIe-based FPGA boards.

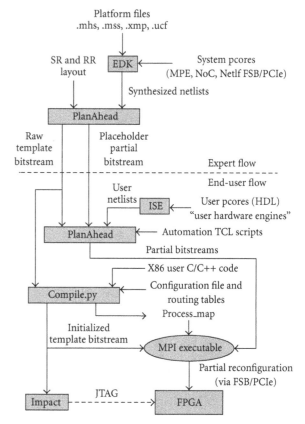

FIGURE 8: Expert and end-user software flows to generate template bitstreams, partial bitstreams, and the message-passing executables.

layout, but PlanAhead is still necessary to generate the partial bitstreams. However, additional automation TCL scripts can help in simplifying the task of using PlanAhead. The last step is to run an ArchES-MPI Python script (compile.py in Figure 8) to compile the MPI code for all the processors (X86, MicroBlaze, PowerPC) and initialize the BRAMs for those embedded processors in the FPGA. The script also initializes the routing tables for the NoC and generates a hosts file required to run the application.

This host file (process_map in Figure 8) in a typical MPI implementation is known as a machine host file and it is used to specify the host, the type of processor and the executable binary assigned to each MPI rank. The ArchES-MPI library uses a similar concept but it is extended to use bitstreams. This file has two sections, the first section assigns each rank to a host, a processing element, and a binary to execute. If it is a processor, then the binary to execute is an

```
main()
MPI_Init(···);//implicit config. of SRs and initial RMs
···
MPI_Send(···, destRank, CFG_MSG_TAG···);
MPI_Recv(statusData_RM_A,..., destRank,OK_TO_CFG_TAG,···);
ARCHES_MPI_Reconfig(RM_B.bit,boardNum,fpgaNum);
MPI_Send(statusData_RM_B,..., destRank, CFG_DONE_TAG,···);
···
```

FIGURE 9: Partial reconfiguration code snippet.

ELF file generated by the compiler (e.g., gcc) for X86, or cross-compiler for embedded processors (e.g., mb-gcc). If it is a hardware engine, the binary to execute is the partial bitstream file generated by PlanAhead. The second section assigns the full template bitstreams (as opposed to partial bitstreams) to the FPGAs available in the platform.

The template bitstreams must be downloaded first. For multi-FPGA systems such as the Nallatech FSB-based accelerator modules, there can be many template bitstreams and they all can be downloaded at runtime via FSB. For the PCIe board, JTAG or Flash memory are the only options to configure the FPGA at boot time. Once the template bitstreams are in place, the partial bitstreams can be downloaded as many times as necessary using the FSB or PCIe link without the need to reboot the host machine.

The ArchES-MPI library parses the configuration file at runtime and during the execution of the MPI_Init() function the template bitstreams (if there are more than one) are downloaded to the FPGAs. This is completely transparent to the user. After this, the user can explicitly download partial bitstreams by calling the ARCHES_MPI_Reconfig() function (as shown in Figure 9) within the source code. This function uses three parameters: the partial bitstream filename, the FPGA board number (if there are multiple FPGA boards), and the FPGA number (in case a given board has many FPGAs). The partial bitstream file includes information that determines which RR to use. In addition, the user can send and receive the synchronization messages described in Section 4. The code uses MPI message tags (user defined) to distinguish the configuration messages from the application messages. Note that the same code can be used regardless of the type of communication interface (PCIe or FSB) or the type of configuration interface (ICAP or SelectMAP); it is all abstracted away from the user.

7. The Vector Engine Example

The overall performance of a parallel application programmed using message passing depends on many different factors, such as communication-to-computation ratio, memory access times, and data dependencies, among others. When using PR, additional factors must be included, such as the partial bitstream size, the number of RRs, and the PR granularity of the application, which is the ratio between the amount of computation per PR event. It is beyond the scope of this paper to provide a complete evaluation of PR overhead by exploring all the possible parameters. Instead,

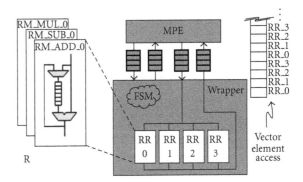

FIGURE 10: Vector Engine with 4 functional units (RRs) and three RMs.

we focus on measuring the PR overhead relative to the PR granularity. A simple vector engine example is used to verify that PR works in real hardware and to provide initial overhead measurements; it is not intended to be a fast vector operation accelerator.

This is an example of a wrapper-contained scenario (see Figure 3) because application logic is placed in the static region. The vector engine core is shown in Figure 10. The vector elements are distributed across the four functional pipelines of the engine (i.e., stride access of four). Each pipeline is an RM that can dynamically change the operation to perform (add, subtract, or multiply). Also, each pipeline includes an FIFO to store the vector elements.

The wrapper issues Send and Receive commands to the MPE and the data goes directly in and out of the pipelines. The wrapper decodes commands sent as messages from the master rank (Rank 0), which is the X86 processor; the vector engine is Rank 1. The vector commands can be LOAD (load a vector into the accumulator), ACC (perform the operation and store the results back into the accumulator), and STORE (flush the accumulator and send it back to the master rank). The wrapper controls the pipeline via control signals (e.g., enable, done, command, and vector_size).

There are four RRs and only one Vector Engine (i.e., one slave rank). The partial bitstream size is 130872 bytes per RR, and the vector size is set to 4000 floating point numbers. The experiment consists of performing 100 LOAD-ACC-STORE (LAS) cycles and performing PR every certain number of cycles. This setup allows us to control the amount of communication and computation per PR event. Note that the point of the experiment is to measure the overhead for a given setup and not to compare FSB and PCIe performance. The results are shown in Table 1. The worst-case scenario is when PR is performed every LAS cycle (i.e., fine PR granularity) with a degradation of 425-fold for PCIe and 308-fold for FSB compared to the case where no PR is performed at all. The best-case scenario is when PR is performed only once (i.e., coarse PR granularity) for the entire run with an overhead factor of 5 and 4 for PCIe and FSB, respectively. From those numbers, only 0.5% of the time is spent in the synchronization messages, the rest is spent in

TABLE 1: PR overhead at different PR event granularities.

Num of PR events	PCIe		FSB	
	Exec. time (s)	Times slower	Exec. Time (s)	Times slower
100	18.695	425	6.466	308
10	1.912	43	0.666	32
1	0.231	5	0.085	4
no PR	0.044	—	0.021	—

transferring the partial bitstreams. Note that there are four of them, one for each pipeline (RR).

These numbers are important to measure further improvements to the PR infrastructure, but they are not representative of the performance degradation expected of any application that uses this PR framework. Even for the same application, the overhead is less for a smaller partial bitstream, which is proportional to the size of the RR. The RR was drawn to an arbitrary size and the pipeline only uses 13% of LUTs and FFs, and 25% of BRAMs and DSPs of the RR. There was no attempt to minimize the RR size or to compress the partial bitstream. The MPE, NoC, and other infrastructure use 11044 LUTs (15%), 15950 FFs (23%), 80 BRAMs (54%), and 3 DSPs (4%) of the static region on the XC5VLX110.

The FSB-based board has less runtime overhead than the PCIe-based board because the FSB has less latency and more bandwidth than the PCIe-x1 link. Also, the FPGA in the FSB board runs at 133 MHz while the FPGA on the PCIe board runs at 125 MHz.

8. Generic Computing Platform Example

The vector accumulator is an application-specific template example because the wrapper implemented in the SR is part of the application. This section presents an example of a generic template bitstream that can be reused by four different applications, therefore, no application-related logic can be placed in the SR. In any case, the objective is not to show hardware acceleration but to prove functionality and that the same template bitstream is reused by four different applications. All of this is done without the user having to design the communications infrastructure or dealing with low-level hardware details.

Figure 11 shows the analogy between software and hardware binaries. The software binaries (.elf files) are loaded by the operating system and executed by X86 processor cores, and the partial bitstreams (.bit files) are loaded by the ArchES-MPI library and *executed* by the FPGA fabric within the RRs. In this case, PR is used to download the corresponding hardware engine to the FPGA at the beginning of each application. Figure 11 shows four RRs, this means that we could instantiate up to four hardware engines of the same application. Technically, it is also possible to have hardware engines of different applications in different RRs. However, our goal is to test that the same RR can be reused by different hardware engines.

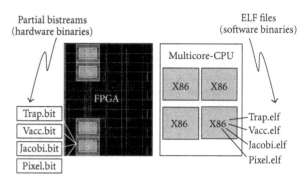

FIGURE 11: Mapping binaries to a generic template bitstream and X86 multicore CPU.

The first application is the same vector accumulator discussed in Section 7 but now in a self-contained form. This means the wrapper is now also in the RR, not in the SR as before. This implies some minor changes to the wrapper's FSM, basically it was necessary to remove the functionality to generate the local reset to the floating point pipelines. Now the reset is generated as described in Section 4.2, external to the wrapper using the MPE and messages. Now the wrapper itself needs to be reset as well. The same reset mechanism is used for all four different application engines. The vector accumulator is hand coded in VHDL.

The second application computes the area under the curve for a given function using the trapezoidal method. This application is based on the software MPI parallel implementation presented in Pacheco [16]. Impulse-C [17], a C-to-Gates compiler, is used to generate the hardware engine. With the addition of some macros introduced in previous work [18], it is possible to translate MPI calls in the C code to MPE commands in VHDL. This application requires at least two ranks but is designed to use more. In this case, one software rank and one hardware rank; both ranks perform the same computation on different data.

The third application is a simple Jacobi iteration method for approximating the solution to a linear system of equations to solve the Laplace equation with finite differences. The implementation of this application is based on previous work [19], and it was written in C and MPI for embedded processors. This application uses three ranks, one master and two slaves. The master and one slave are software ranks, and the other slave is a hardware rank. Again, Impulse-C is used to generate the hardware engine with commands to the MPE.

Finally, the fourth application is another simple MPI program written in C to invert pixels from image frames coming from a webcam or a file stored in the host's hard drive. This application uses OpenCV [20], an open source library for computer vision that provides an easy way to access the Linux video device and to open, read, and write video and image files. This application uses three ranks, Rank 0 (X86) captures the frames and send them to Rank 1 (hardware engine) where the pixels are inverted and then it sends the processed frame to Rank 2 (X86) where the frame is stored in a file or displayed on the screen. The hardware engine is hand coded in VHDL.

Although there has not been any attempt to optimize the size and placement of the RRs, the FPGA in Figure 11 has been partitioned following an educated guess. This guess comes from the experience of having to design the low-level LVDS communication interface for the FSB-based platform (See Figure 7), which is the one used in this example. The FPGA in this platform has abundant LVDS I/O logic to communicate with other FPGAs above, sideways, and below. This logic is placed and concentrated towards the middle of the chip closer to specific I/O banks. Therefore, placing the RR around the middle of the chip would complicate timing closure because the RR would displace the LVDS logic creating longer paths and delays. Additionally, the XC5VLX330 FPGA only has two columns of DSP blocks on the left side of the chip—it is not symmetrical, therefore, there are no RRs on the right side for this particular template. A different template may include DSP-enabled and non-DSP-enabled RRs. In any case, these are exactly the kind of decisions that the end user, that is, the application developer, should not need to worry about. The place where the I/O banks or DSPs are located is completely irrelevant to the trapezoidal method or the Jacobi algorithm. Instead, the template bitstream has already been created by a hardware engineer familiar with the platform who can layout the RRs for the user to work with.

The four applications were compiled, implemented, and run on the FSB-based platform and all the output results were correct for each application. The RR itself occupies 6.8% of LUTs and FFs, 4.9% of BRAMs, and 16.6% of DSPs available in the XC5VLX330 FPGA. The partial bitstreams for the four application RMs have the same size (477666 bytes), although they do not require the same resources. Table 2 presents the utilization percentage with respect to the RR not the entire FPGA. In this case, all the engines fit within that RR. If this would not have been the case then another template with a larger RR would have been selected. The decision of what template bitstream to use from a collection of them can be done by a higher-level tool that matches the resources required by an application and resources available in a template. This is an optimization problem that can be addressed in future research.

8.1. Boot Loader Reconfigurable Module. When a template bitstream is downloaded to an FPGA each RR must have an initial RM configured. The question is what RM should be placed at the beginning. In our generic platform a simple placeholder RM has been created to be the initial RM. This placeholder is in fact a small bootloader for partial bitstreams that merely follows the synchronization steps described in Section 4. It instructs the MPE to receive a PR message ("cfg" message in Figure 4) indicating that a new RM is going to be configured. The bootloader RM will then issue another receive command to the MPE for the eventual "configuration-done" message, then it disables all the outputs from the RR by setting the *PR-in-progress* flag and finally it will go to an idle state waiting for PR to occur. Once the application RM is configured and out of reset the application begins. Just before the application is about to

TABLE 2: Resource utilization of four application hardware engines (Percentages are relative to the RR).

	RR	Pixel	Trapezoidal	Vector acc	Jacobi
LUTs	9920	154 (2%)	6397 (65%)	1476 (20%)	5271 (54%)
FFs	9920	112 (2%)	3993 (41%)	1553 (16%)	4460 (45%)
DSPs	32	0	32 (100%)	8 (25%)	13 (41%)
BRAM	16	0	0	4 (25%)	2 (13%)

finish, during the call to the MPI_Finalize function (all ranks must call it) the bootloader RM is restored in all the RRs to set the FPGA ready for the next application. This last step is analogous to a software process that finishes and returns the control of the processor to the operating system. Similarly, when the application RM finishes it returns the control of the MPE to the bootloader RM.

9. Conclusions

The main contribution of this paper is the concept of embedding partial reconfiguration into the MPI programming model. We have presented an extension to the ArchES-MPI framework that simplifies the use of PR by abstracting away the hardware details from the user while providing a layer of portability. Such layer allows PR to be performed regardless of the configuration interface (ICAP or SelectMAP) and independent of the communication channel used (PCIe or FSB) to communicate with an X86 processor, which is used as a configuration controller. Also, we demonstrated a method to generate local resets without the need of an embedded processor, and provided an alternative to actively store and restore the status of reconfigurable modules via explicit messages. Very little additional logic and code were required on top of the existing message-passing infrastructure to enable PR. In addition, the concept of template-based bitstreams was introduced as a way to use this PR framework to create reusable and generic computing platforms. Four different applications were actually implemented and executed consecutively reusing the same template bitstream. An approach like this simplifies and speeds up the design process of creating multiaccelerator-based computing systems by allowing third-party hardware experts to provide prebuilt accelerators, I/O interfaces, NoC, and memory controllers, letting the designer focus on the actual value-added application logic. The initial performance overhead numbers obtained set a reference point to measure future improvements to the PR framework.

Acknowledgments

The authors acknowledge the CMC/SOCRN, NSERC, Impulse Accelerated Technologies, and Xilinx for the hardware, tools, and funding provided for this paper.

References

[1] Xilinx, Inc., "Partial Reconfiguration User Guide," http://www.xilinx.com/support/documentation/sw_manuals//xilinx 12_2/ug702.pdf.

[2] M. Saldaña, A. Patel, H. J. Liu, and P. Chow, "Using partial reconfiguration in an embedded message-passing system," in *Proceedings of the International Conference on Reconfigurable Computing and FPGAs (ReConFig '10)*, pp. 418–423, December 2010.

[3] ArchES Computing, Inc., http://www.archescomputing.com.

[4] M. Saldaña, A. Patel, C. Madill et al., "MPI as an abstraction for software-hardware interaction for HPRCs," in *Proceedings of the 2nd International Workshop on High-Performance Reconfigurable Computing Technology and Applications (HPRCTA '08)*, pp. 1–10, November 2008.

[5] P. Lysaght, B. Blodget, J. Mason, J. Young, and B. Bridgford, "Invited paper: enhanced architectures, design methodologies and CAD tools for dynamic reconfiguration of Xilinx FPGAS," in *Proceedings of the International Conference on Field Programmable Logic and Applications (FPL '06)*, pp. 1–6, August 2006.

[6] O. Diessel, H. ElGindy, M. Middendorf, H. Schmeck, and B. Schmidt, "Dynamic scheduling of tasks on partially reconfigurable FPGAs," *IEE Proceedings: Computers and Digital Techniques*, vol. 147, no. 3, pp. 181–188, 2000.

[7] C. Bobda, A. Ahmadinia, M. Majer, J. Teich, S. Fekete, and J. van der Veen, "DyNoC: a dynamic infrastructure for communication in dynamically reconfigurable devices," in *Proceedings of the International Conference on Field Programmable Logic and Applications (FPL '05)*, pp. 153–158, August 2005.

[8] K. Papadimitriou, A. Anyfantis, and A. Dollas, "An effective framework to evaluate dynamic partial reconfiguration in FPGA systems," *IEEE Transactions on Instrumentation and Measurement*, vol. 59, no. 6, pp. 1642–1651, 2010.

[9] C. Rossmeissl, A. Sreeramareddy, and A. Akoglu, "Partial bitstream 2-D core relocation for reconfigurable architectures," in *Proceedings of the NASA/ESA Conference on Adaptive Hardware and Systems (AHS '09)*, pp. 98–105, August 2009.

[10] H. Kalte and M. Porrmann, "Context saving and restoring for multitasking in reconfigurable systems," in *Proceedings of the International Conference on Field Programmable Logic and Applications (FPL '05)*, pp. 223–228, August 2005.

[11] D. Koch and J. Teich, "Platform-independent methodology for partial reconfiguration," in *Proceedings of the 1st Conference on Computing Frontiers (CF '04)*, pp. 398–403, ACM, New York, NY, USA, 2004.

[12] H.-H. So, A. Tkachenko, and R. Brodersen, "A unified hardware/software runtime environment for FPGA-based reconfigurable computers using BORPH," in *Proceedings of the 4th International Conference on Hardware/Software Codesign and System Synthesis (CODES+ISSS '06)*, pp. 259–264, October 2006.

[13] L. Möller, R. Soares, E. Carvalho, I. Grehs, N. Calazans, and F. Moraes, "Infrastructure for dynamic reconfigurable systems: choices and trade-offs," in *Proceedings of the 19th Annual Symposium on Integrated Circuits and Systems Design (SBCCI '06)*, pp. 44–49, ACM, New York, NY, USA, 2006.

[14] The MPI Forum, "MPI: a message passing interface," in *Proceedings of the ACM/IEEE Conference on Supercomputing*, pp. 878–883, ACM, New York, NY, USA, November 1993.

[15] Nallatech, http://www.nallatech.com/.

[16] P. S. Pacheco, *Parallel Programming with MPI*, Morgan Kaufmann, 1997.

[17] Impulse Accelerated Technologies, http://www.impulseaccelerated.com/.

[18] A. W. House, M. Saldaña, and P. Chow, "Integrating high-level synthesis into MPI," in *Proceedings of the 18th IEEE International Symposium on Field-Programmable Custom Computing Machines (FCCM '10)*, pp. 175–178, May 2010.

[19] M. Saldaña, D. Nunes, E. Ramalho, and P. Chow, "Configuration and programming of heterogeneous multiprocessors on a multi-FPGA system using TMD-MPI," in *Proceedings of the IEEE International Conference on Reconfigurable Computing and FPGA's, (ReConFig '06)*, pp. 1–10, September 2006.

[20] G. Bradski, "The OpenCV Library," *Dr. Dobb's Journal of Software Tools*, 2000.

Novel Dynamic Partial Reconfiguration Implementation of K-Means Clustering on FPGAs: Comparative Results with GPPs and GPUs

Hanaa M. Hussain,[1] **Khaled Benkrid,**[1] **Ali Ebrahim,**[1] **Ahmet T. Erdogan,**[1] **and Huseyin Seker**[2]

[1] *School of Engineering, University of Edinburgh, King's Buildings, Mayfield Road, Edinburgh EH9 3JL, UK*
[2] *Bio-Health Informatics Research Group, Centre for Computational Intelligence, De Montfort University, Leicester LE1 9BH, UK*

Correspondence should be addressed to Hanaa M. Hussain, h.hussain@ed.ac.uk

Academic Editor: René Cumplido

K-means clustering has been widely used in processing large datasets in many fields of studies. Advancement in many data collection techniques has been generating enormous amounts of data, leaving scientists with the challenging task of processing them. Using General Purpose Processors (GPPs) to process large datasets may take a long time; therefore many acceleration methods have been proposed in the literature to speed up the processing of such large datasets. In this work, a parameterized implementation of the K-means clustering algorithm in Field Programmable Gate Array (FPGA) is presented and compared with previous FPGA implementation as well as recent implementations on Graphics Processing Units (GPUs) and GPPs. The proposed FPGA has higher performance in terms of speedup over previous GPP and GPU implementations (two orders and one order of magnitude, resp.). In addition, the FPGA implementation is more energy efficient than GPP and GPU (615x and 31x, resp.). Furthermore, three novel implementations of the K-means clustering based on dynamic partial reconfiguration (DPR) are presented offering high degree of flexibility to dynamically reconfigure the FPGA. The DPR implementations achieved speedups in reconfiguration time between 4x to 15x.

1. Introduction

Current technologies in many fields of studies have been utilizing advanced data collection techniques which output enormous amount of data. Such data may not be useful in their collected form unless they are computationally processed to extract meaningful results. Current computational power of General Purpose Processors (GPPs) has not been able to keep up with the pace at which data are growing [1]. Therefore, researchers have been searching for methods to accelerate data analysis to overcome the limitation of GPPs, one of which is the use of hardware in the form of Field Programmable Gate Arrays (FPGAs).

K-means clustering is one of the widely used data mining techniques to analyze large datasets and extract useful information from them. Previously, we have implemented the K-means clustering on FPGA to target Microarray gene expression profiles and reported encouraging speedups over GPPs [2]. However, the implementation was limited to single dimension and eight clusters only. An extended work on FPGA implementation of the K-means algorithm is presented in this work which includes a highly parameterized architecture, a novel single, and a multicore dynamic partial reconfiguration of the K-means algorithm. Although the proposed design is meant to target Microarray gene expression profiles, it can be adopted for use in other applications such as image segmentation. In this work we also compare our parameterized implementation with other FPGA implementation of the K-means algorithms. Furthermore, we will compare the performance of our design with one that has been recently implemented on Graphics Processing Units (GPUs), a technology that has been gathering a lot of interest in the computing community because of its high performance and relatively low cost.

The remainder of this paper is organized as follows. In Section 2 an overview about the K-means clustering algorithm is given. In Section 3, related works on K-means clustering acceleration are summarized which include both FPGA and GPU methods. In Section 4 the hardware implementation of the parameterized K-means clustering is presented. Then in Section 5 three novel implementations of the K-means clustering based on dynamic partial reconfiguration are given: the first is based on reconfiguring the distance kernel within the algorithm with different distance metrics, the second is based on reconfiguring the K-means core using Internal Configuration Access Port (ICAP), and the last one is based on reconfiguring multiple K-means cores also using ICAP. In Section 6 implementations results are presented and analyzed. Finally, in Section 7 summary of findings, discussion and conclusion are presented along with some remarks on future work.

2. K-Means Clustering

K-means clustering is one of the unsupervised data mining techniques used in processing large datasets by grouping objects into smaller partitions called clusters, where objects in one cluster are believed to share some degree of similarity. Clustering methods help scientists in many fields of studies in extracting relevant information from large datasets. To arrange the data into partitions, at first one needs to determine the number of clusters beforehand and initialize centers for each cluster from the dataset. There are several ways for doing this initialization, one way is by randomly assigning all points in the overall dataset to one of these clusters, then calculate the mean of each cluster and use the results as the new centers. Another way is to randomly select cluster centers from the whole dataset. The distance between each point in the dataset and every cluster center is then calculated using a distance metric (e.g., Euclidean, Manhattan). Then, for every data point, the minimum distance to all cluster's centers is determined and the point gets assigned to the closest cluster. This step is called cluster assignment and is repeated until all of the data points have been assigned to one of the clusters. Finally, the mean of each cluster is calculated based on the accumulated points and the number of points in that cluster. Those means become the new cluster's centers, and the process iterates for a fixed number of times, or until points in each cluster stop moving across to different clusters; Figure 1 illustrates the steps of the K-means algorithm.

The Euclidean metric given in (1) is widely used with K-means clustering and one that results in better solutions [3]:

$$D(P, C) = \sqrt{\sum_{i}^{M} (P_i - C_i)^2},$$ (1)

where P is the data point, C is the cluster center, and M is the number of features or dimensions. On the other hand, Euclidean distance consumes a lot of logic resources when implemented in hardware due to the multiplication operation used for obtaining the square operation. Therefore,

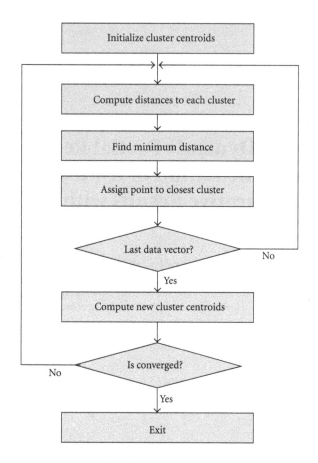

FIGURE 1: The K-means algorithm.

previous groups working on hardware implementation of the K-means clustering for image segmentation have used the Manhattan distance shown in (2) as an alternative to the Euclidean distance:

$$D(P, C) = \sum_{i}^{M} |P_i - C_i|,$$ (2)

where P is again the data point, C is the cluster center, and M is the number of features. Their results showed that it performed twice as fast as that obtained by Euclidean distance [3–9].

Distance computation is the most computationally demanding part and where most of the K-means processing time occurs. Therefore, accelerating K-means algorithm can be achieved by mainly accelerating the distance computation part, which is achieved using hardware.

3. Related Works on the Acceleration of K-Means Clustering

K-means has already been implemented in hardware by several groups; most were to target applications in hyperspectral imaging, or image segmentation. The following review will cover some of the work done on K-means clustering acceleration using FPGA and GPUs.

Novel Dynamic Partial Reconfiguration Implementation of K-Means Clustering on FPGAs: Comparative Results with GPPs and GPUs

13

3.1. K-Means Clustering Acceleration on FPGAs. In 2000, Lavenier implemented systolic array architecture for K-means clustering [6]. He moved the distance calculation part to FPGA while keeping the rest of the K-means tasks on GPP. The distance computation involved streaming the input through an array of Manhattan distance calculation units of numbers equal to the number of clusters and obtaining the cluster index at the end of the array. The disadvantage of this approach was the communication overhead between the host and the FPGA. Lavenier tested his design on several processing boards, and one of the relevant speedups obtained compared to GPP was 15x [6, 7]. In addition, he found that the speedup of the systolic array was the function of the number of clusters and transfer rated between the host and the FPGA.

Between 2000 and 2003, Leeser et al. reported several works related to K-means implementation on FPGA, based on a software/hardware codesign approach [3–5]. Their design was partitioned between FPGA hardware and a host microprocessor, where distance calculation and data accumulation were done in hardware in purely fixed point while new means were calculated in the host to avoid consuming large hardware resources. They achieved a speedup of 50x over pure GPP implementation. Their design benefited from two things: the first was using Manhattan distance metric instead of the commonly used Euclidean metric to reduce the amount of hardware resources needed, and the second was truncating the bit width of the input data without sacrificing accuracy [8].

In 2003, Bhaskaran [9] implemented a parameterized design of the K-means algorithm on FPGA where all the K-means tasks were done in hardware, except the initialization of cluster centers which was done on a host. This design implemented the division operation within FPGA hardware to obtain the new means, using dividers from Xilinx Core Generator. However, this design was tested only on three clusters and achieved a speedup of 500x over Matlab implementation including I/O overhead [9].

3.2. K-Means Clustering Acceleration on GPUs. Several implementations of K-means clustering using Graphics Processing Units (GPUs) have been reported in the literature. In 2008, Fairvar implemented K-means on GPU and achieved speedup of 13.57x. (The GPU implementation took 0.724 s compared to 9.830 s on GPP) when clustering 1 million points into 4000 clusters using Nvidia's GeForce 8600 GT and a 2-GHz GPP host [10]. Another group [11] presented good results when implementing K-means using two types of GPUs. The speedups they achieved when clustering 200 K to 1 M on the Nvidia's GeForce 5900 were between 4x to 12x more than a Pentium 4, 1.5 GHz CPU, and up to 30x when using Nvidia's GeForce 8500 and Pentium 4, 3 GHz CPU. They also found that GPU performance was less affected by the size of the dataset as compared to GPPs. Another result reported by this group was related to the effect of the number of clusters on speedup, where achieved speedups were between 10x and 20x for clusters less than 20 using the Nvidia's GeForce 5900 GPU and more than 50x when there

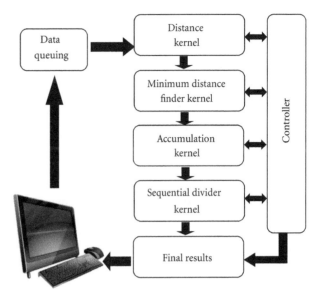

Figure 2: The main blocks of the K-means hardware design.

were more than 20 clusters. For 32 clusters, they reported a speedup of 130x on the Nvidia's GeForce 8500 GPU.

In 2010, Karch reported a GPU implementation of K-means clustering for accelerating color image segmentation in RGB space [12]. We compared the results published in [12] with our FPGA implementation and shall present this comparison in the results section. Furthermore, Choudhary et al. reported another GPU implementation using Nvidia's GeForce 8800 GT, which achieved speedups between 9x and 40x for datasets ranging from 10,000 to one million points when they were clustered into 20 partitions [13]. The group also reported that speedups of GPUs over GPPs increase as datasets grow largely in depth. From the above studies, it can be stated that GPUs outperform GPPs when datasets are large or when the number of clusters is large.

4. FPGA Hardware Design of the K-Means Clustering

In this work, a highly parameterized hardware design of the K-means algorithm is presented, which aims to carry all K-means tasks in hardware. The architecture of the whole design consists of a number of blocks which execute kernels within the K-means algorithm. The design generates the required hardware resources and logics based on the parameters entered by the user at compile time. These parameters are the wordlength of the input (B), number of clusters (C), number of data points (N), and dimensions of the input data (M). The design was captured in Verilog HDL language. Figure 2 summarizes the main kernels of the K-means clustering, which will be used to form a modular architecture. The design intends to perform all the K-means steps within the FPGA, including the division operation, and avoids directing any task to an offchip resource although this capability can be exploited when needed. In the following sections an overview about each block will be presented along with the timing of each block.

4.1. Distance Kernel Block. This block receives streaming input data stored in onchip Block RAMs or from an off-chip memory, along with the initialized or updated cluster's centers, and computes the distances between each data point and all clusters simultaneously. The hardware resources inferred by the synthesis tool to generate multiple distance processors (DPs) are based on the number of clusters and the number of dimensions of the dataset. Each DP is responsible for the computation of the distance between all the input dimensions and one of the cluster centers. Thus one DP is required for each cluster. The DPs work simultaneously such that the distances between every point to all clusters are computed in a few clock cycles, hence fully exploiting the parallelism associated with the distance calculation kernel. In this work, both the Euclidean and the Manhattan distance metrics were implemented; however, the Manhattan distance is chosen often times to simplify the computation and save logic resources; thus, the reported results are based on the Manhattan distance implementation. The datapath of this block depends on the number of dimensions (M) in the dataset as given by

$$\text{datapath of distance kernel} = \text{ceil}\left[\log_2(M)\right], \quad (3)$$

which corresponds to the stages needed to compute the distances between all the dimensions of the input and the clusters' centroids. Accordingly, the computation time for a single pass through the whole dataset is a function of the number of data points (N) in the set and the datapath, as shown in

$$\text{distance computation time} = \text{ceil}\left[\log_2(M)\right] + N. \quad (4)$$

This kernel has a throughput of 1 data point per clock cycle and a latency of $\text{ceil}[\log_2(M)]$ clock cycles, which is the same as the datapath of the distance kernel, this latency is one clock cycle only for the case of single dimension. Since there are C DPs working simultaneously, the total outputs of this block are C distances, each corresponding to the sum of distances between all the dimensions of one point vector and one cluster center resulting from a single DP.

4.2. Minimum Distance Finder Kernel Block. This block has the role of comparing the C distances received from the previous block to determine the minimum distance and the associated index which correspond to the ID of the closest cluster to the data point. The block consists mainly of a comparator tree as shown in Figure 3, which has number of stages dependent on the number of clusters (C) as given by

$$\text{datapath of min. dist. finder kernel} = \text{ceil}\left[\log_2(C)\right]. \quad (5)$$

This block is pipelined to have throughput of one result per clock cycle, with latency equivalent to (5). The combined execution time of the above two blocks consisting of the distance computation and the minimum distance finder can be summarized in (6):

$$\text{min. distance computation time} = \text{ceil}\left[\log_2(M)\right] + \text{ceil}\left[\log_2(C)\right] + N. \quad (6)$$

4.3. Accumulation Kernel Block. This block is responsible for accumulating the data points in the accumulator corresponding to a specific cluster index and incrementing the corresponding counter, keeping track of the number of points in each cluster along with the values of these points. The block receives the data point under processing along with the index of the cluster having the minimum distance, which was obtained from the previous block, and performs the accumulation and counting accordingly. The number of accumulators inferred by the HDL code is as shown in (7):

$$\text{accumulator numbers} = C \times M, \quad (7)$$

such that each cluster has M number of accumulators associated with it. As for the inferred number of counters, it is equal to the number of clusters only, so that each cluster has a counter associated with it. Since a fixed point arithmetic is used in this work, extra care was taken in choosing the appropriate wordlength (B) for the distance, accumulator, and counter results to minimize hardware resources and avoid data overflow. The latter is achieved through error and range analysis of data in all blocks. Based on the B of the input selected initially to represent the data and the number of points in the dataset to be processed, the accumulator and counter B's were calculated as follows, respectively:

$$B_{\text{Accumulator}} = \log_2\left[\left(\text{Max. range of } B_{\text{Input}}\right) \times N\right], \quad (8)$$

$$\text{counter size} = \log_2[N]. \quad (9)$$

In the case of Microarray datasets for instance, data usually do not exceed 25,000 points for Human. Hence, 15 bits are found to be sufficient for each counter and 32 bits for each accumulator given that the input point is represented by 13 bits. In general, a program was written in Matlab to automate the range and error analysis to make the process of selecting the best wordlengths easy and efficient.

4.4. Sequential Divider Kernel Block. The divider kernel block is responsible for receiving results from the accumulation kernel and calculating the new cluster centers. The divider itself was generated using Xilinx Core Generator tool, which was found to be faster due to high pipelining when compared to other dividers. In the case of Microarray data, for instance, the generated divider uses 32 bits for the dividend and 15 bits for the divisor. These values were chosen based on the results of the accumulator/counter blocks as the role of the divider is to divide each accumulator result over the corresponding counter to obtain the new cluster centers. Once signaled to start, this block starts scheduling the data received to be serviced by the divider core serially as illustrated in Figure 4. The number of divisions that needs to be performed is the same as the number of clusters specified in the design parameters. After all the divisions are completed, results are packed to the output port of the divider block. The number of clock cycles taken by the divider to complete its work is a

Novel Dynamic Partial Reconfiguration Implementation of K-Means Clustering on FPGAs: Comparative Results with GPPs and GPUs

15

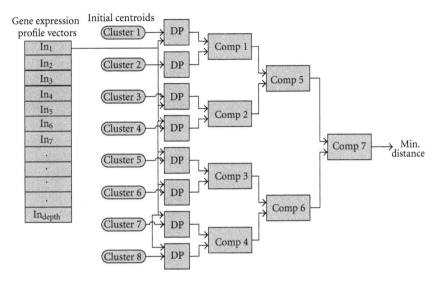

FIGURE 3: Block diagram of the minimum distance finder.

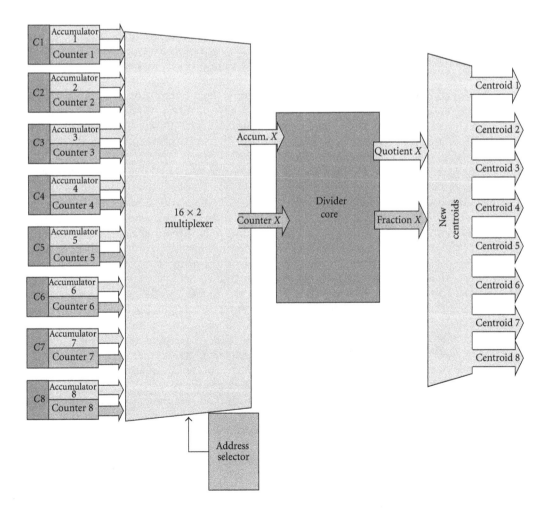

FIGURE 4: Sequential Divider Pipeline.

function of the divider latency and the number of clusters (C) as well as the number of dimensions (M) as shown in (10):

$$\text{divider time} = (\text{core latency}) + (C \times M), \qquad (10)$$

where the core latency was 84 clock cycles based on the selected sizes of the dividend and divisor; however the remaining part will be subject to change as per the initial parameters entered by the user for C and M.

The choice of using the pipelined divider from the core generator as opposed to a serial divider is that when comparing the performance of both in terms of area and timing, the serial divider was found to process one bit of the information at a time; thus, for a 32 bit dividend and 8 clusters the number of clock cycles needed was 256 as compared to 92 for the pipelined divider, based on single dimensional data only. This timing difference amplifies when the dimensions increase; for example, using 10 dimensions and 8 clusters causes the serial divider to take 2560 clock cycles while the pipelined divider takes only 164 clock cycles. On the other hand, the number of slices consumed by the serial divider is a lot less than the pipelined divider, where the latter consumed 1389 slices compared to 91 slices for the serial divider, when using Xilinx Virtex 4 FPGA. Since one of the project's aims was to accelerate the K-means algorithm, the pipelined divider was favored. However, other implementations based on multiple serial dividers are possible when FPGAs area is limited.

5. Novel Dynamic Partial Reconfiguration of the K-Means Clustering

The dynamic partial reconfiguration capability (DPR) of modern Xilinx FPGAs allows for better exploitation of FPGA resources over time and space. DPR allows for changing the device's configuration (i.e., functionality) partially and on the fly, leading to the possibility of fully autonomous FPGA-based systems. Therefore, DPR allows for the alteration of specific parts of the FPGA dynamically without affecting the configuration of other tasks placed onto the FPGA. This capability offers wider spectrum of applications for the K-means clustering serving different purposes which are explored here for the first time. For instance, DPR is useful in cases where users want to have the option to select specific distance metric when performing the K-means clustering or want to look at clustering results performed with different distance metrics since the choice of the distance metric affects the clustering performance. Another useful application of DPR with K-means is to use it for the implementation of server solution, where multiple K-means cores are configured on demand to work on different data as required by multiple users. A server solution is defined here as an application which allows a large FPGA to cater for the requirements of multiple users in a network whereby each user owns specific K-means core receiving streaming data and set with different parameters, for example, number of clusters. However, introducing changes to any of the K-means cores allocated onto the chip by a single user requires interrupting the operation of other K-means cores to

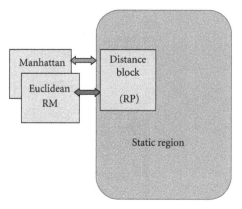

Figure 5: Illustrative diagram of the DPR implementation of the K-means core based on a reconfigurable distance kernel.

reconfigure the FPGA. As such, the use of DPR to reconfigure specific K-means core within a multicore server solution system is investigated here to overcome the limitation of having to reconfigure the full chip and discover other advantages of DPR such as effect of the DPR on reconfiguration time. In addition, the multicore application of the K-means clustering can also be used in ensemble clustering. The latter is based on combing the results of repeated clustering using the same distance metric or alternative distances. Combing clustering results from repeated runs was found to improve the clustering accuracy when performed in GPP according to the work reported in [14]. However, running K-means several times is time consuming when done in GPP especially for large datasets. Consequently, implementing ensemble clustering on FPGA using multicore DPR approach will benefit from fast execution. In the following subsections, three different implementations of the K-means clustering algorithm based on DPR are presented.

5.1. DPR Based on Reconfigurable Distance Kernel. To provide a solution to a user who wants to alter the distance metric kernel only without changing other blocks in the design or interrupting other running tasks on the FPGA, a DPR implementation of the K-means clustering based on setting the distance kernel as reconfigurable partition (RP) is proposed in this work. The RP can be configured with one of two possible Reconfigurable Modules (RMs), which correspond to the variations of the logic within the RP region. The two RMs correspond to the logic resources required to implement the distance kernel with either the Manhattan distance or the Euclidian as illustrated in Figure 5. More RMs could be created corresponding to other distance metrics such as the Hamming, Cosine, Canberra, Pearson, or Rank correlation coefficients; however, only the Manhattan and Euclidean distances are considered in this work due to their popularity with K-means clustering and to demonstrate a proof of concept.

The logic resources of the two distance metrics implemented in this work were found to be comparable in terms of the number of CLB slices and LUTs when synthesized, with the exception that the Euclidean metric required DSP48 blocks to implement the multiplication operation, which

Novel Dynamic Partial Reconfiguration Implementation of K-Means Clustering on FPGAs: Comparative Results with GPPs and GPUs

17

were not required for the Manhattan distance. However, this additional requirement was possible to cater for in this implementation and is not expected to impose serious shortage in resources as most modern FPGAs nowadays come with heterogeneous hardware resources that usually include DSP blocks. Furthermore, for the case when DSPs are not abundantly available or not available at all, the multiplication operation could still be performed using more of the CLB slices and LUTs, but this will increase the size of the RP region when compared with the case of using dedicated DSP blocks. The proposed DPR implementation is based on the case when the multiplication operation of the Euclidean distance metric is performed with DSP48 blocks.

To estimate the area requirement for the proposed DPR implementation, a non-DPR implementation based on using eight clusters, 13 bits wordlength (B), 2905 points (N), and single dimension (M) was first run using the two distance metrics. The place and route results showed that the CLB slices utilized for the Manhattan distance block were 277 as compared to 246 for the Euclidean distance both occupying only 4% of the total Xilinx XC4VFX12 floor area, with the Euclidean distance requiring eight DSP48 blocks only. The location of the RP region may be different depending on the FPGA used as different FPGAs have different number of DSP blocks and arrangements; consequently, one must make sure that enough of those blocks are included inside the RP region in order for the implementation to be successful. The above analysis of the area requirement for each of the two distances was necessary to evaluate the candidacy of this application for DPR implementation. In the case of the two areas being completely different, the DPR implementation would not have been feasible due to the significant loss of CLB slices within the RP regions causing the cost of the implementation to be considerable. In addition, if the RP is made so big, the partial reconfiguration time would be close to the full configuration losing the advantage of time saving when using DPR.

5.2. DPR Implementation Based on Reconfigurable Single K-Means Core Using ICAP. In this implementation, the K-means clustering core presented in Section 4 was modified to decrease the size of the core for simplicity; the modification was based on removing the divider since it was the kernel occupying the largest area while needed for short time during the clustering. This step is not expected to affect the remaining kernels, and future implementations would utilize larger FPGAs that can accommodate the complete core including the divider, or to perform the division operation using embedded processors. In the mean time, the new K-means implementation which excludes the divider is used and referred to as the K-means core.

This implementation is based on setting the aforementioned K-means core as a reconfigurable partition (RP) and reconfiguring it internally using Internal Configuration Access Port (ICAP). The latter has been used to access the FPGA configuration memory quickly with a bandwidth of 3.2 Gbps. To experimentally perform the DPR, an Internal Reconfiguration Engine (IRE) has been designed and tested by a colleague at the SLIg group in Edinburgh University.

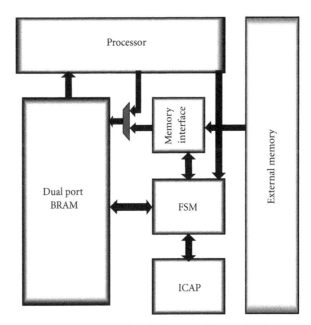

FIGURE 6: The architectural block diagram of the Internal Reconfiguration Engine (IRE) used to dynamically reconfigure the K-means core.

The block diagram of the IRE system used to dynamically reconfigure the K-means core is illustrated in Figure 6. The processor used in the IRE was based on Picoblaze soft-core processor and an external ZBT SRAM memory module.

Once the ICAP controller is enabled, the IRE starts the reconfiguration process of the K-means core using the partial bitstream. The processor passes the address of K-means partial bitstream in the external memory to the FSM which controls the ICAP signals and the flow of the partial bitstream data to the ICAP through a high speed dual port BRAM primitive used as a buffer. The main advantage of using this IRE is the fast reconfiguration time of the FPGA, which allows the variations of the K-means core to be implemented dynamically, those variations correspond to different internal memory contents, different parameters such as number of clusters or data wordlength. In addition, the IRE has an advantage of making the K-means core relocatable, which allows the system to maintain the operation of the K-means core when a fault occurs in the original location of the FPGA fabric hence providing small degree of fault tolerance; or when other processes need to be added to the FPGA hence providing a degree of flexibility in allocating the K-means core with respect to the newly introduced tasks. The latter is a particularly applicable in server solution applications.

5.3. DPR Implementation Based on Reconfigurable Multiple K-Means Cores Using ICAP. Based on the previous implementation, three K-means' cores were used to form a multicore DPR implementation, which can be reconfigured using the IRE. The IRE is capable of quickly reconfiguring each one of the cores at a time, and of relocating any of them within the same FPGA. In addition to the advantages mentioned in

TABLE 1: Performance results.

GPP (ms)	Hardware (ms)	Speedup
27.47	0.523	~53x

TABLE 2: Implementation results.

Compare	Xilinx XCV1000 [4]	Xilinx XC4VFX12
Slices	8884/12288	5107/5549
LUTs	17768	10216
Max. clock frequency	63.07 MHz	100 MHz
Single loop processing time	0.17 s	~0.07 s

the previous subsection, this implementation is particularly useful for server solution where cores are configured on demand upon request from multiple users. This feature allows the K-means cores allocated onto the FPGA to remain in operation while another core is being reconfigured elsewhere on the chip. Furthermore, DPR allows each user to exercise full control on the configuration of the owned task; thus, access to full chip reconfiguration can be granted to system administrator only to avoid frequent interruptions of operations. In this implementation, three cores were used only as proof of concept; additional cores could be added depending on the available resources and the application requirement.

6. Implementation Results

Each block in the design was implemented and tested on the Xilinx ML403 platform board, which houses the XC4VFX12 FPGA chip. The K-means design was captured in Verilog, simulated, synthesized, placed, and routed using Xilinx ISE 12.2 tool. Finally, a bitstream file was generated and downloaded to the board for testing. In the following subsections, performance results of our design, as well as comparison with GPP, FPGA, and GPU implementations are presented. Then results of the three DPR implementations of the K-means clustering will be presented.

6.1. Comparison with GPP. Implementation results when clustering a dataset of 2905 points and one dimension with input wordlength of 13 bits to 8 clusters showed that the complete design consumed 2985 slices (740 CLBs) and achieved a maximum clock frequency of 142.8 MHz. When comparing the runtime of this hardware implementation with an equivalent GPP implementation based on Matlab (R2008a) Statistical Toolbox running on 3 GHz Intel Core Duo E8400 GPP with 3 GB RAM, running Windows XP Professional operating system, the speedup results obtained are as shown in Table 1. Note that the Matlab Toolbox was chosen because it contains an optimized K-means function, and that it allows for converting data to fixed point easily before running the clustering using Matlab's Fixed-point Toolbox. The GPP time shown in Table 1 is the average time of 10,000 runs, with the initial clusters' centroids given as inputs to the algorithm; thus, the GPP implementation was made as close as possible to the FPGA implementation to ensure fair comparison. Note that the GPP implementation converged at 27 iterations while the hardware at 25.

6.2. Comparison with Other FPGA Implementation. In general, it is difficult to compare similar FPGA implementations because of the use of different FPGA families and chips, as well as different design parameters. Nonetheless, we have attempted a comparison here with the closest FPGA

implementation to ours, namely, the one reported in [4]. Here, we compare our parameterized core design excluding the divider to make it compatible with the FPGA implementation reported in [4] which performed the division operation on a host. Both implementations were based on data size of 1024 × 1024 with 10 dimensions, 12 bits data, and 8 clusters. In both cases, data were stored offchip and streamed on to the FPGA. Comparative results are shown in Table 2. Obviously, our implementation is faster because it is based on a more recent FPGA technology, but it is also more compact using normalized slice/LUT count. More importantly, it is more flexible as it has a higher degree of parameterization compared to the implementation reported in [4].

6.3. Comparison with GPUs. When comparing the performance of our FPGA K-means clustering implementation to a recent GPU implementation presented in [12] for an image processing application, the FPGA solution was found to outperform the GPU in terms of speed as shown in Table 3. The results shown were based on two different datasets, one was 0.4 Mega Pixel (MPx) in size and the other was 6.0 MPx. Both datasets were processed for 16, 32, and 64 clusters, and both were for a single dimension. The GPP and GPU results were based on 2.2 GHz Intel Core 2 Duo, with 4 GB memory and Nvidia GeForces 9600 M GT graphics card, running Microsoft Windows 7 Professional 64 bits. On the other hand, the targeted FPGA device was Xilinx XC4VSX35; the design used 13 bits to represent the dataset and could run at a maximum clock frequency of 141 MHz. The Virtex device used in this comparison is not a high end FPGAs, the latter can achieve higher speeds but we tried to limit the choice to a reasonable size that can accommodate the design and be reasonable for comparing with the above GPU. Both of images were too large to be stored within the FPGA, therefore, offchip memory was needed to store data which were streamed onto the FPGA pixel by pixel, and one data point was read every clock cycle. The processing times reported in [12] do not include the initialization of cluster's centers and the input/output stage, and similarly with the FPGA times reported in Table 3.

The speedup results of our FPGA implementation over the GPP and GPU results reported in [12] are shown in Figure 7. From the FPGA/GPP curve shown in Figure 7(a), it is clear that there is a linear relationship between the number of clusters and the attained acceleration. Similar observation was found when comparing GPU with GPP. Both observations confirm that FPGA and GPU outperform GPP as the number of clusters is increased. On the other

Novel Dynamic Partial Reconfiguration Implementation of K-Means Clustering on FPGAs: Comparative Results with GPPs and GPUs

19

TABLE 3: Execution result of K-means in GPP, FPGA, and GPU, for single dimension data.

Clusters	GPP avg. time per iteration (sec.) [12]	GPP avg. time for complete execution (sec.) [12]	GPU avg. time per iteration (sec.) [12]	GPU avg. time for complete execution (sec.) [12]	FPGA per iteration (sec.)	FPGA complete execution (sec.)
0.4 MPx						
16	0.269	4.314	0.021	0.443	0.0028	0.0392
32	0.516	7.637	0.020	0.421	0.0028	0.042
64	1.004	12.78	0.023	0.508	0.0028	0.0454
6 MPx						
16	4.279	67.07	0.256	5.176	0.0425	0.723
32	8.144	110.7	0.247	4.439	0.0425	0.638
64	15.86	208.2	0.270	5.220	0.0425	0.723

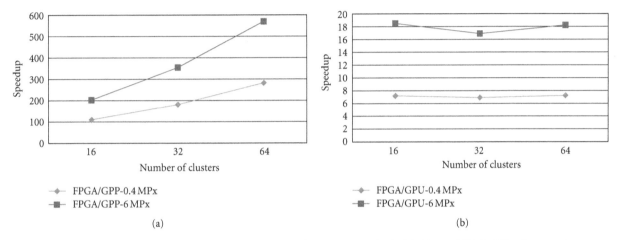

(a)

(b)

FIGURE 7: Speedup results of the FPGA implementation of K-means over both: (a) GPP and (b) GPU implementations.

hand, the FPGA/GPU curve shown in Figure 7(b) indicates that FPGA outperforms GPU in terms of execution time; this is due to higher exploitation of parallelism in FPGA. On the other hand, the FPGA/GPU acceleration is not greatly affected by the number of clusters (up to 64 clusters in our experiments) as found with GPP. As for the device utilization, the XC4VSX35 FPGA used in this comparison has 15,360 slices, which were enough to implement the logic required to accommodate the number of clusters shown in Table 3. With the 16 clusters, the implementation occupied 5,177 slices (33%), and with 32 and 64 clusters, the implementation occupied 8,055 slices (52%) and 13,859 (98%), respectively.

In addition, the effect of data dimensionality on performance of GPP, FPGA, and GPU implementations was investigated in this work based on GPP and GPU performance results reported in [15]. In [15], the authors reported the results of clustering Microarray Yeast expression profiles as shown in Table 4 where GPU achieved speedup of 7x to 8x over GPP for four and nine dimensions, respectively, while FPGA achieved 15x to 31x for the same dimensions based on dataset of 65,500 vectors, as illustrated in Figure 8 for the case of three and four clusters. When comparing the timing performance of single iteration of the K-means clustering for GPP, GPU, and FPGA implementations based

on multidimensional data, GPU and FPGA were found to outperform GPP as shown in Figure 9(a). When the performance of our FPGA implementation was specifically compared with the GPU implementation in [15], the FPGA achieved speedup between 2x to 7x over GPU [16]. Note that the results reported in Table 4, Figures 8 and 9 are all based on XC4VSX35 FPGA and Nvidia 8600 GT GPU. In addition, FPGA outperformed GPU when the dimensions of data increased (only four and nine dimensions were studied) as shown in Figure 9(b), which indicates that FPGA maintained its performance as dimensions were increased while GPU experienced a drop in performance. The drop in performance in GPU as the dimensions increased is due to the way the implementation utilizes resources within the GPU when computing specific kernels, particularly with regards to memory bottlenecks associated with GPUs as data increase in size.

Furthermore, Figure 8 also highlights the performance of five-core implementation for three and four clusters with respect to GPU, which was first reported in [2]. The five-core implementation is clearly superior to the GPUs for problems requiring small or reasonable number of clusters and dimensions that can be mapped easily onto commercially available FPGA devices [16]. This illustrates the high potentials of FPGA in parallelizing tasks.

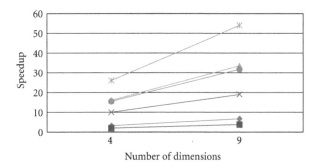

FIGURE 8: Effect of data dimensionality on the speedup of the FPGA implementation of the K-means over GPP and GPU. In addition, the performance of five-core FPGA implementation reported in [2, 16] is compared with the GPU implementation of [15].

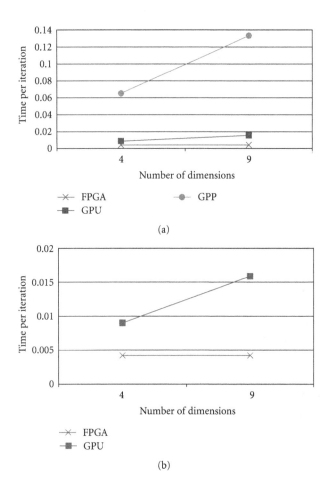

(a)

(b)

FIGURE 9: Effect of data dimensionality on the timing per iteration of the K-means clustering for (a) GPP, GPU and FPGA, and (b) GPU and FPGA only. All are based on four clusters; the GPP and GPU results are based on [15] whereby FPGA results are based on [16].

TABLE 4: Execution result of K-means in GPP, FPGA, GPU, for multidimension data.

	GPP time per iteration (sec.) [15]	GPU time per iteration (sec.) [15]	FPGA time per iteration (sec.)
Dimensions = 4			
3 clusters	0.0495	0.00623	0.0019
4 clusters	0.0652	0.00902	0.0042
Dimensions = 9			
3 clusters	0.1031	0.0125	0.0019
4 clusters	0.1333	0.01589	0.0042

TABLE 5: Comparison of power and energy of different K-means implementations.

Platform	Power (watt)	Execution time for the 0.4 MPx image, with 16 clusters (sec.)	Energy (joule)
GPP	120	4.314	517
GPU	59	0.443	26
FPGA	15	0.056	0.84

6.4. Comparison in Power and Energy Consumption. The power and energy consumption of the three K-means implementations were compared and reported in Table 5 based on the 0.4 Mpx image shown in Table 3. Both GPP and FPGA power figures were actually measured, while the GPU power was obtained from the Nvidia GeForce 9600 GT datasheet, reflecting the power rating of the device [17]. The results in Table 5 are based on using 13 bits to represent the 0.4 MPx image, 16 clusters and targeting the XC4VFX12 FPGA available on the ML 403 board with the image being stored in offchip memory. The FPGA is ~8x more power efficient than GPP and ~4x more power efficient than GPU. Consequently, the FPGA implementation is ~615x more energy efficient than the GPP and ~31x more energy efficient than the GPU as obtained from (11). Note that the FPGA implementation utilized 4909 slices (89%) of the targeted device as reported in [16].

In addition, when comparing the power consumption of the FPGA implementation of the single core K-means shown in Section 6.1 with the GPP implementation, the FPGA consumed 15 W only when actually measured as compared to 90 W in GPP; thus, the FPGA is six times more power efficient than the GPP while being 53 times faster. This has resulted in the FPGA implementation being 318 times more energy efficient than the equivalent GPP implementation as computed from (11). Note that the GPP power was measured while running the algorithm in Matlab in a loop, and GPP power was 70 W when idle

$$\text{energy efficiency} = \text{power efficiency} \times \text{speedup}. \quad (11)$$

6.5. Comparison in Cost of the K-Means Implementation. The cost of any computing platform depends on several factors, that is, purchasing cost, development cost, operating cost, and perhaps maintenance/upgrading cost. At first, purchasing any technology is associated with its technical

Novel Dynamic Partial Reconfiguration Implementation of K-Means Clustering on FPGAs: Comparative Results with GPPs and GPUs

21

TABLE 6: Purchase cost of the three computing platforms with/without host.

Platform	Purchasing cost W/O host (£)	Purchasing cost with host (£)	Normalised cost with host (£)
GPP	747.55	747.55	1
FPGA	511	1260	1.69
GPU	127	874	1.17

specifications and available resources, for example, logic resources, peripherals, hardened IP blocks, and external memory. Computing platforms are offered within a wide range of device families allowing a user to select the device having the right combination of resources for the application in hand. Table 6 reports the cost of the computing platforms used in the K-means clustering implementations which were reported in Table 5 based on using the following computing platforms:

(i) GPP-3.0 GHz Intel Core 2 Due E8400 processor and 3 GB memory;

(ii) GPU-Nvidia GeForce 9600 M GT;

(iii) FPGA-Xilinx ML403 board.

Table 6 reveals that the GPP solution was the most cost effective in terms of purchasing cost when compared with FPGA and GPU followed by the GPU solution and last by the FPGA solution. Although Table 6 implies that GPP is the most cost effective in terms of purchasing cost, followed by GPU and last by FPGA, this does not mean that GPP or GPU is more economic solutions than FPGA given that performance per dollar and performance per watt are more realistic measures for the economic viability of the technology [18]. Although it was not feasible to measure all factors leading to performance per dollar and performance per watt, the power and energy consumptions shown in Table 5 leads to estimate FPGA to have the largest performance per watt. Consequently, FPGA is the most economically viable solution.

6.6. DPR Implementation Based on Reconfigurable Distance Kernel.

The DPR implementation was created using Xilinx PlanAhead 12.2 tool following Xilinx hierarchical methodology and partial reconfiguration flow [19, 20], the distance block was set as RP as explained earlier. The actual DPR implementation shows that Euclidean distance occupied 238 slices within the RP region as opposed to 208 for the Manhattan distance; the resources were slightly different from those obtained using normal flow implementation.

Two main configurations were generated based on the two RMs and the associated full and partial bitstreams for each configuration were also generated. The full bitstream was 582 KB in size while the partial bitstream was 61 KB. In this work, JTAG cable was used to configure the FPGA, which has a bandwidth (BW) of 66 Mbps. Therefore, when fully configuring the FPGA, the configuration time was 70.55 ms as computed from (12). On the other hand, when the FPGA was partially reconfigured, the configuration time was

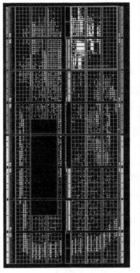 

(a) Manhattan   (b) Euclidean

FIGURE 10: The floorplan image of the DPR implementation of the K-means clustering based on reconfigurable distance metric: (a) Manhattan, and (b) Euclidean.

7.39 ms. Therefore, DPR offers significant time saving when needing to change the distance metric only leading to 10x speedup in configuration time over full device configuration. Therefore, in addition to being able to reconfigure specific part of the device without interrupting the operation of other tasks, DPR offers time saving

$$\text{configuration time} = \frac{\text{size of bitstream}}{\text{BW of configuration mode}}. \quad (12)$$

Using Internal Configuration Access Port (ICAP) as a configuration mode will offer larger bandwidth than JTAG, since ICAP have a bandwidth equivalent to 3.2 Gbps leading to small configuration time in the range of microseconds as compared to milliseconds when using JTAG. However, the speedup ratios between full and partial reconfigurations remain the same for the two configuration modes. The validity of such estimation as opposed to actual measurement will be investigated in the following subsection. Figure 10 illustrates the floorplan of the two implementations highlighting the area occupied by the RP. The image also highlights a disadvantage of the implementation which is associated with wasting some of the CLB slices within the RP region due to having to enclose enough DSP48 blocks; this issue is clearly device specific as the arrangement of DSP48 blocks affects the size of the RP region. The image shows that ~72% of the RP CLB slices are unused in the Manhattan distance case and ~69.5% for the case of the Euclidean distance.

6.7. DPR Implementation Based on Single K-Means Core and ICAP.

The design containing both the K-means core and the Internal Reconfiguration Engine (IRE) was first synthesized using Xilinx ISE 12.2 to generate the .ngc file required for creating the DPR implementation in Xilinx PlanAhead

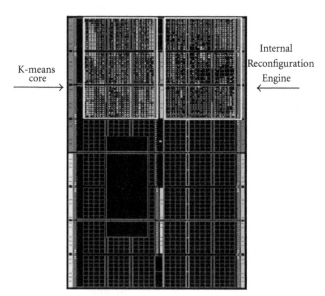

K-means core →

Internal Reconfiguration Engine ←

FIGURE 11: The floorplan image of the DPR implementation of the reconfigurable K-means core based on Internal Reconfiguration Engine (IRE).

12.2; in addition another .ngc file corresponding to the K-means core without I/O buffers was created to describe the Reconfigurable Module (RM), which corresponds to the K-means core (excluding the divider). Next, PlanAhead was used to construct the DPR implementation based on Xilinx ML 403 platform board and on setting the K-means core as a reconfigurable partition (RP).

The design was implemented, placed, and routed targeting Xilinx XC4VFX12 FPGA available in the ML403 board. The place and route results of the implementation showed that the K-means core occupied 1,178 CLB slices (~22%) of the FPGA floor area while the IRE occupied 955 CLB slices (~18%); the design was constrained to work at a 100 MHz clock speed. The implementation was run and verified, and bitstreams were created. Figure 11 illustrates the location and size of the implementation within the FPGA. The partial bitstream of the K-means core was found to be 140 KB while the full bitstream was 582 KB.

To test the DPR implementation, the partial bitstream was written to the ZBT SRAM available on board the ML403; note that the file was stored initially in a Compact Flash (CF) card which was also available on board the ML403, and that Microblaze was used to read the partial bitstream from the CF and write it to the ZBT SRAM. Second, the FPGA was fully configured using the full bitstream associated with our DPR implementation, this has invoked the K-means core and the IRE. The device by then was running the K-means clustering and was ready to be partially reconfigured upon enabling the ICAP controller in the IRE. A counter was used to measure the configuration time, which corresponds to the time in which the enable signal was asserted in the ICAP controller. Upon enabling the IRE, the partial bitstream was read from the ZBT SRAM and written to the configuration memory of the FPGA; as soon as the partial reconfiguration was finished, the IRE deasserted the enable signal, and

time was measured. The measured partial reconfiguration time was $360 \, \mu s$, as compared to $\sim 1455 \, \mu s$ for the full configuration. This shows that the DPR implementation of the single core K-means is ~4x faster than full chip configuration.

In Section 6.6, the partial configuration time was estimated from (12) based on using JTAG, while the partial configuration time in this section was actually measured. To justify the validity of the results obtained in the previous subsection, the partial configuration time of the K-mean core presented in this section was obtained using (12) based on ICAP and checked against actual measurement to see how significant the overheads are. The partial reconfiguration time was found to be $350 \, \mu s$ when applying (12), which is different from the measured time by only $10 \, \mu s$ leading to same speedup in reconfiguration time (~4x). This small difference could be attributed to the time needed to read the partial bitstream from the ZBT SRAM, time overheads result from delays in asserting or deasserting the enable signal. Therefore, estimating the configuration time gives relatively similar results to actual measurements, and one could rely on estimated results in predicting the performance of the implementation. Furthermore, the fact that the performance of the IRE was very high has led to small overhead times.

The IRE is also capable of relocating the K-means core to another location in the chip by modifying the partial bitstream to reflect the new desired location given that the new location is compatible with the original core in terms of resources, that is, Block RAMs, CLB slices, and so forth. However, due to limited resources in the available device, relocatability could not be tested on the FPGA. On the other hand, other smaller designs were successfully relocated within the FPGA using the same IRE to validate its capability in re-allocating tasks [21].

6.8. DPR Implementation Based on Multiple K-Means Cores and ICAP. The three-core DPR implementation was implemented with Xilinx XCVLX60 FPGA which has 26,624 CLB slices; thus, it was able to accommodate the three K-means' cores and the IRE as illustrated in Figure 12. The performance of this implementation was estimated based on the performance of the single core implementation, due to the unavailability of a large FPGA to actually test the implementation. The IRE system allows for one of the three cores to be partially configured at a time; thus, the partial reconfiguration time for each K-means core is the same as that of the single core being $360 \, \mu s$ as compared to $5407.5 \, \mu s$ for the full configuration. The former was measured in Section 6.6, while the latter was estimated from (12) based on a full bitstream of 2,163 KB in size and ICAP bandwidth of 3.2 Gbps. Consequently, DPR is 15x faster in reconfiguration time than full configuration when one of the K-means' cores need to be reconfigured. As for the case when the whole three cores need to be reconfigured, $1080 \, \mu s$ would be required reducing the reconfiguration speedup of this DPR implementation to 5x only. This is mainly because the ICAP has to reconfigure each core sequentially.

An important observation was made regarding the speedup in reconfiguration time relative to the size of the

Novel Dynamic Partial Reconfiguration Implementation of K-Means Clustering on FPGAs: Comparative Results with
GPPs and GPUs

23

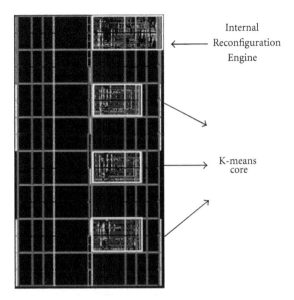

Figure 12: The floorplan image of the DPR implementation of the three K-means' cores based on Internal Reconfiguration Engine (IRE).

FPGA device. It was found that when the FPGA was large, the full bitstream would normally be large leading to longer configuration time, while the partial bitstream would be the same for the single K-means core in both the small and large FPGAs. Therefore, when the size of the FPGA is large, the speedup in configuration time is expected to be higher than that of a small device given that the size of the RP in the two devices is identical. This is particularly important for server solution as such an application is usually expected to utilize large FPGA. For instance, when XC4VFX12 FPGA was used, the speedup in reconfiguration time was 4x as compared to 15x for the XCVLX60, both based on the same PR implementation.

7. Summary and Discussion

The design and implementation of a highly parameterized FPGA core of K-means clustering were presented in this paper. This outperformed equivalent GPP and GPU implementations in terms of speed (two orders and one order of magnitude, resp.). In addition, the FPGA implementation was more energy efficient than both GPP (615x) and GPU (31x). This makes the FPGA implementation highly desirable although FPGAs still suffer from a relatively higher cost of purchase and development compared to GPPs and GPUs. The lack of standard API tools and hardware boards is a big contributor in this.

In addition, the performance of both FPGA and GPU was found to be superior to GPP when increasing the number of clusters. This is mainly attributed to the fact that FPGA and GPU scale better with the number of clusters, whereas GPPs do this computation sequentially. On the other hand, when comparing the timing performance of FPGA and GPU, the FPGA excelled the GPU's performance for the particular devices used in the comparison reported in Table 3. This

is attributed to the higher level of parallelism exploited in FPGA than in the GPU.

As for the dimensionality effect, when the number of clusters were increased for different data dimensions, the speedup of FPGA as compared to GPU was almost constant as shown in Figure 7(b), which emphasizes the fact stated earlier that the two technologies scale well as the number of clusters was increased. However, FPGA outperformed the GPU implementation when the dimensions (M) of the data were increased as reported in Table 4; this is attributed to memory bottlenecks in GPUs when the size of the data is large.

However, the above findings are device specific and could not be generalized unless fair comparison is made using higher end GPUs and FPGAs. Even then, the large variation in the size of FPGAs within the same family range makes it difficult to assess the performance of the two technologies, especially that variations in GPUs within the same family range are much smaller. Furthermore, other issues arise when high end devices are used such as the cost of purchasing the high end device, with FPGAs being more expensive than GPUs and power consumption issue where GPUs and GPPs consume more power than FPGAs [18]. Nevertheless, our comparative study was an attempt to highlight main performance bottlenecks such as memory limitations in GPUs, and issues surrounding the implementation of K-means in GPPs, GPUs, and FPGAs when number of clusters or data dimensions change, and to provide some guidelines for appropriate device selection based on the application in hand.

Another aim of the work was to investigate the benefits from using dynamic partial reconfiguration to set a specific kernel within the K-means algorithm as reconfigurable partition (RP) to serve specific applications. When setting the distance kernel as RP, the reconfiguration time was found to be 10x faster than reconfiguring the full device. The purpose of such implementation was to be able to change the type of the distance metric at run time without interrupting the operation of tasks in other parts of the FPGA and to achieve this as quickly as possible. Two distance metrics were considered in this work to demonstrate the feasibility of the concept, one was the Manhattan distance and the other was the Euclidian; however, the concept could be easily expanded to include a library of distance metrics if the application in hand requires such variability in distance metrics.

Furthermore, the results of reconfiguring a single K-means core and three K-means cores using an Internal Reconfiguration Engine (IRE) were presented; the latter was based on using ICAP to dynamically reconfigure the FPGA. The IRE illustrated true dynamic reconfiguration capability at high performance with negligible overheads. In terms of reconfiguration speedup, the single core implementation was four times fast when using small chip and 15 times fast when large chip was used. As for the three-core implementation, the speedup in reconfiguration time varies according to the number of cores to be configured at a time, for partially reconfiguring single core, two cores, and three cores the speedups were 15x, ~8x, and 5x, respectively. Consequently, it can be stated that multicore DPR has best performance in terms of configuration time when used to reconfigure one core at a time due to having short partial reconfiguration time, and this advantage becomes less or even lost as more cores get reconfigured simultaneously leading to the same performance in configuration time as non-DPR implementation (normal flow).

8. Conclusion and Future Work

A highly adaptive FPGA implementation of K-means clustering has been presented in this work which outperformed GPP and GPU in terms of speed and energy efficiency as well as scalability with increased number of clusters and data dimensions. Furthermore, the FPGA implementation was the most economically viable solution. Additionally, three novel DPR implementations of the K-means clustering were presented which allowed for dynamic partial reconfiguration of FPGA offering the advantage of reconfiguration flexibility, short partial reconfiguration time of selective tasks on chip while ensuring continuous operation of other tasks.

Future work will be centered on improving the division operation in the K-means clustering with the aim to reduce sizing and making the divider shared among multi K-means' cores by harnessing the dynamic partial reconfiguration capability to time-multiplex the divider. Additionally, considerations will be given to harnessing embedded processors to implement the division operation in conjunction with dynamic partial reconfiguration. Furthermore, applying K-means ensemble clustering in FPGA based on multicore dynamic partial reconfiguration to target Microarray data that will be implemented. Moreover, comparison with optimized multicore processor will be carried out.

Acknowledgments

The authors would like to thank the "Public Authority of Applied Education and Training" in Kuwait for sponsoring this study and to also thank "Kuwait Foundation for the Advancement in Sciences" for its contribution to this study.

References

[1] P. Kumar, B. Ozisikyilmaz, W.-K. Liao, G. Memik, and A. Choudhary, "High performance data mining using R on heterogeneous platforms," in *Proceedings of the 25th IEEE International Parallel and Distributed Processing Symposium, Workshops and Phd Forum (IPDPSW '11)*, pp. 1720–1729, 2011.

[2] H. M. Hussain, K. Benkrid, H. Seker, and A. T. Erdogan, "FPGA implementation of K-means algorithm for bioinformatics application: an accelerated approach to clustering Microarray data," in *Proceedings of the NASA/ESA Conference on Adaptive Hardware and Systems (AHS '11)*, pp. 248–255, 2011.

[3] M. Estlick, M. Leeser, J. Theiler, and J. J. Szymanski, "Algorithmic transformations in the implementation of K-means clustering on reconfigurable hardware," in *Proceedings of the ACM/SIGDA 9th International Sysmposium on Field Programmable Gate Arrays (FPGA '01)*, pp. 103–110, February 2001.

[4] M. Leeser, P. Belanovic, M. Estlick, M. Gokhale, J. J. Szymanski, and J. Theiler, "Applying reconfigurable hardware to the analysis of multispectral and hyperspectral imagery," in *Imaging Spectrometry VII*, vol. 4480 of *Proceedings of SPIE*, pp. 100–107, August 2001.

[5] M. D. Estlick, *An FPGA implementation of the K-means algorithm for image processing [M.S. thesis]*, Department of Electrical and Computer Engineering, Northeastern University, Boston, Mass, USA, 2002.

[6] D. Lavenier, *FPGA Implementation of the K-Means Clustering Algorithm For Hyperspectral Images*, Los Alamos National Laboratory, LAUR, Los Alamos, Ill, USA, 2000.

[7] M. Gokhale, J. Frigo, K. Mccabe, J. Theiler, C. Wolinski, and D. Lavenier, "Experience with a hybrid processor: K-means clustering," *Journal of Supercomputing*, vol. 26, no. 2, pp. 131–148, 2003.

[8] J. Theiler, M. Leeser, M. Estlick, and J. J. Szymanski, "Design issues for hardware implementation of an algorithm for segmenting hyperspectral imagery," in *Imaging Spectrometry VI*, vol. 4132 of *Proceedings of SPIE*, pp. 99–106, August 2000.

[9] V. Bhaskaran, *Parametrized implementation of K-means clustering on reconfigurable systems [M.S. thesis]*, Department of Electrical Engineering, University of Tennessee, Knoxville, Ten, USA, 2003.

[10] R. Farivar, D. Rebolledo, E. Chan, and R. Campbell, "A parallel implementation of K-means clustering on GPUs," in *Proceedings of the International Conference on Parallel and Distributed Processing Techniques and Applications (PDPTA '08)*, pp. 340–345, Las Vegas, Nev, USA, July 2008.

[11] S. A. A. Shalom, M. Dash, and M. Tue, "Efficient K-means clustering using accelerated graphics processors," in *Proceedings of the 10th International Conference on Data Warehousing and Knowledge Discovery (DaWaK '08)*, vol. 5182 of *Lecture Notes in Computer Science*, pp. 166–175, 2008.

[12] G. Karch, *GPU based acceleration of selected clustering techniques [M.S. thesis]*, Department of Electrical and Computer Engineering and Computer Sciences, Silesian University of Technology in Gliwice, Silesia, Poland, 2010.

[13] A. Choudhary, D. Honbo, P. Kumar, B. Ozisikyilmaz, S. Misra, and G. Memik, "Accelerating Data Mining Workloads: current approaches and future challenges in system architecture design," *Wiley Interdisciplinary Reviews*, vol. 1, pp. 41–54, 2011.

[14] M. C. P. De Souto, S. C. M. Silva, V. G. Bittencourt, and D. S. A. De Araujo, "Cluster ensemble for gene expression microarray data," in *Proceedings of the International Joint Conference on Neural Networks (IJCNN '05)*, vol. 1, pp. 487–492, August 2005.

[15] S. A. A. Shalom, M. Dash, and M. Tue, "GPU-based fast k-means clustering of gene expression profiles," in *Proceedings of the 12th Annual International Conference on Research in Computational Molecular Biology (RECOMB '08)*, Singapore, 2008.

[16] H. Hussain, K. Benkrid, H. Seker, and A. Erdogan, "Highly parametrized K-means clustering on FPGAs: comparative results with GPPs and GPUs," in *Proceedings of the International Conference on ReConFigurable Computing and FPGAs (ReConFig '11)*, pp. 475–480, 2011.

[17] Nvidia Corp., GEForce 9600 GT datasheet, 2012, http://www.nvidia.com/object/product_geforce_9600gt_us.html.

[18] K. Benkrid, A. Akoglu, C. Ling, Y. Song, X. Tian, and Y. Lue, "High perfomance biological pairwise sequence alignment: FPGA vs. GPU vs. CellBE vs. GPP," *International Journal of Reconfigurable Computing*, vol. 2012, Article ID 752910, 15 pages, 2012.

Novel Dynamic Partial Reconfiguration Implementation of K-Means Clustering on FPGAs: Comparative Results with GPPs and GPUs

25

[19] Xilinx Corp., Hierarchical Design Methodology guide, ug748, v13.3, 2011, http://www.xilinx.com/support/documentation/ sw_manuals/xilinx13_1/Hierarchical_Design_Methodology_ Guide.pdf.

[20] Xilinx Corp., Partial Reconfiguration guide, ug702, v12.3, p. 103, 2010, http://www.xilinx.com/support/documentation/ sw_manuals/xilinx12_3/ug702.pdf.

[21] X. Iturbe, K. Benkrid, T. Arslan, C. Hong, and I. Martinez, "Empty resource compaction algorithms for real-time hardware tasks placement on partially reconfigurable FPGAs subject to fault ocurrence," in *Proceedings of the International Conference on ReConFigurable Computing and FPGAs (ReConFig '11)*, pp. 475–480, November 2011.

3

Design and Implementation of an Embedded NIOS II System for JPEG2000 Tier II Encoding

John M. McNichols,[1] **Eric J. Balster,**[1] **William F. Turri,**[2] **and Kerry L. Hill**[3]

[1] *Department of Electrical and Computer Engineering, University of Dayton, Kettering Laboratory, Room 341,*
 300 College Park, Dayton, OH 45469, USA

[2] *University of Dayton Research Institute, 300 College Park, Dayton, OH 45469, USA*

[3] *Air Force Research Laboratory Sensors Directorate, Wright-Patterson Air Force Base, OH, USA*

Correspondence should be addressed to Eric J. Balster; ebalster1@udayton.edu

Academic Editor: René Cumplido

This paper presents a novel implementation of the JPEG2000 standard as a system on a chip (SoC). While most of the research in this field centers on acceleration of the EBCOT Tier I encoder, this work focuses on an embedded solution for EBCOT Tier II. Specifically, this paper proposes using an embedded softcore processor to perform Tier II processing as the back end of an encoding pipeline. The Altera NIOS II processor is chosen for the implementation and is coupled with existing embedded processing modules to realize a fully embedded JPEG2000 encoder. The design is synthesized on a Stratix IV FPGA and is shown to out perform other comparable SoC implementations by 39% in computation time.

1. Introduction

One of the most recent image compression schemes, JPEG2000, offers a wide range of features and flexibility over the existing JPEG standard [1]. A block diagram of the JPEG2000 encoder is shown in Figure 1. The encoder consists of two main parts: the discrete wavelet transform (DWT) and the embedded block coding with optimal truncation (EBCOT) coder. The wavelet transform takes an image in the spatial domain and transforms it to the wavelet domain. The wavelet domain consists of a frequency representation with the addition of spatial information as well. Once the wavelet transform is completed, the coefficients are scalar quantized if lossy compression is chosen. The quantized wavelet coefficients are then entropy encoded using EBCOT, a two-tier coding algorithm which first divides each wavelet subband into code blocks (typically 32×32 or 64×64). EBCOT is composed of Tier I and Tier II encoders. Tier I produces independent embedded bitstreams for each code block using a context-based arithmetic encoder (MQ coder), the context for which is generated by the bit-plane coder. Tier II then reorders the individual compressed bitstreams and applies rate-distortion slope optimization to form the final JPEG2000 bitstream.

While JPEG2000 offers a number of improvements and additional features over JPEG and other image encoding standards, these benefits come with much greater computational cost. JPEG2000 is approximately 4 times more computationally expensive than the original JPEG [2]. Due to these high costs, it becomes impractical to utilize JPEG2000 in applications which require real-time processing of high-resolution images, such as wide area imagery or medical imagery. To solve this problem, developers continue to turn to hardware implementations to yield the throughput necessary to meet frame rates for high-resolution imagery [3]. Hardware solutions are able to outperform software implementations through the use of parallel processing and custom designed hardware. A hardware implementation is capable of leveraging the inherent parallelism of the EBCOT block coders to achieve large increases in throughput over typical software implementations. Not only do hardware solutions offer dramatic increases in throughput over their software counterparts, but they also free host processors to handle other critical tasks.

Most embedded JPEG2000 solutions focus on performance increases in the EBCOT Tier I, either through novel architectures or simply by leveraging the parallelism of multiple block coders. Research focuses on EBCOT Tier I improvement because this is the most computationally expensive module of JPEG2000, as shown in [4, 5].

In [6, 7], architectures for the MQ coder are proposed which consume two context-data (C × D) pairs per clock cycle. Reference [4] takes a different approach, increasing performance by using column-based operation combined with pixel and group-of-column skipping techniques. A number of implementations focus on very large-scale integration (VLSI) architectures for JPEG2000. Some, such as [3], focus on high-speed VLSI implementations by utilizing pass-parallel EBCOT implementations. Others, such as [8], attempt to reduce the on-chip memory requirements for EBCOT Tier I and Tier II while also improving performance.

However, most of these implementations fail to mention the final piece of JPEG2000 which is the formation of the full bitstream, EBCOT Tier II. Generally it is not mentioned at all and assumed to be left for the host processor to handle in software. References [8, 9] propose an architecture for EBCOT Tier II which is focused on reducing memory requirements for bitstream buffering but do not offer high performance. Instead, we propose the use of a softcore coprocessor to serve as a Tier II processing module situated at the back end of an encoding pipeline to realize a fully embedded encoder. The softcore coprocessor offers more flexibility than [8, 9], due to the soft nature of the processor, while also offering adequate performance to meet the demands of high-resolution image compression.

This work couples an Altera NIOS II processor [10] with existing, efficient, and hardware implementations of the other various processing units to create a fully embedded JPEG2000 system on a chip (SoC). The hardware is designed as a tile encoding pipeline in order to efficiently encode high-resolution imagery. The NIOS II processor interfaces with a FIFO containing the independent code block bitstreams produced by a variable number of hardware block coders in order to create the final bitstream. The NIOS II processor handles all of the Tier II processing as well as transferring data back to the host processor.

While similar to [5] in the use of an Altera NIOS II processor, the proposed implementation utilizes the processor as a separate processing module as opposed to a system scheduler/device arbiter. This avoids the scheduling overhead associated with such an implementation while also preventing the other processing modules from becoming limited by the throughput of the NIOS II system. Additionally, the simplicity of using the NIOS II as a separate processing unit yields a system which is much easier to debug and test, since difficulty in debugging in [5] prevented the system from actually being implemented on an FPGA.

The rest of this paper is organized as follows. Section 2 gives a brief overview of the FPGA-based processing architectures used for the front end of the processing pipeline. Section 3 details the selected target platform and the selection of the coprocessor before giving a detailed description of the implementation of the SoC. Section 4 analyzes the performance of the implemented system and discusses the impact of increasing numbers of parallel block coders before comparing the results to other SoC implementations. Finally, Section 5 concludes the paper.

2. JPEG2000 Hardware Modules

2.1. Discrete Wavelet Transform/Quantization. The proposed system implementation uses a lossy CDF 9/7 wavelet transform [11]. The lossy wavelet transform is chosen as it offers additional compression gain over the lossless implementation while still maintaining comparable image quality at lower compression ratios. This implementation is an integer-based approach, utilizing the CDF 9/7 wavelet filter to transform integer input pixels into scaled fixed-point wavelet coefficients. These scaled fixed-point coefficients are then quantized back into integers prior to compression by EBCOT. Running at a clock rate of 100 MHz, this DWT implementation consumes two pixels per clock cycle and takes approximately 7 ms to perform a standard 5-level transform on a 1024 × 1024 tile.

2.2. EBCOT Tier I. EBCOT Tier I is comprised of two main processing modules: the bit-plane coder (BPC) and the MQ coder [1]. The BPC for the proposed implementation is a generic implementation, conforming to the standard, and operates at a clock speed of 100 MHz. While most implementations of the BPC aim to maximize throughput, this design instead focuses on reducing resource utilization and does not make use of any of the optimization techniques proposed in [3, 5–7]. Instead, minimal resource usage is achieved by consolidating the number of memory devices necessary to store code block state data. The MQ coder follows the same design principle as the BPC, with a focus on minimizing hardware resource usage. The MQ coder runs at a clock rate of 200 MHz. The design goal of both the BPC and MQ coders is to maximize the number of Tier I coders which can fit on a device. By achieving high clock rates through resource optimized designs, a Stratix IV device with over 90% resource utilization is capable of yielding throughput in excess of 180 MBytes per second when multiple parallel Tier I coders are coupled with three DWT targets.

3. Proposed System Implementation

3.1. Target Platform. The target platform for the JPEG2000 SoC is a Stratix IV PCIe ×4 development board from GiDEL [12]. The platform selected features a Stratix IV E 530 FPGA with a 512 MB DDR2 memory bank and two DDR2 SODIMMs with up to 4 GB each. The platform has two additional ports for expansion daughter cards offered from GiDEL. A block diagram of the selected platform can be seen in Figure 2. The high performance offered from a PCIe based platform coupled with the flexibility and size of an Altera Stratix IV FPGA provides an ideal platform capable of meeting the demands of a JPEG2000 SoC [12].

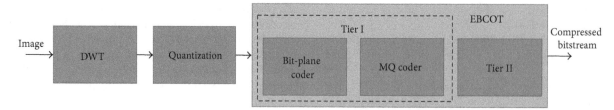

FIGURE 1: Block diagram of JPEG2000 encoder.

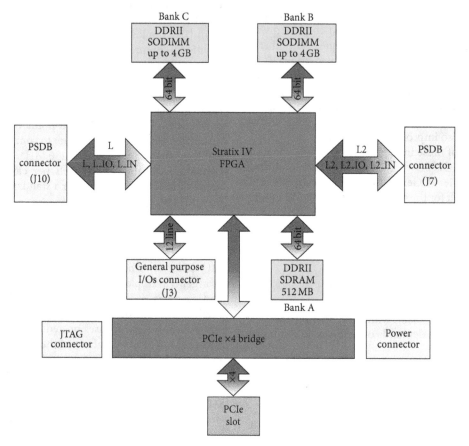

FIGURE 2: Block diagram of target platform.

3.2. Selection of Softcore Coprocessor. The softcore coprocessor chosen is the NIOS II processing core from Altera [10]. The NIOS II processor features a 32-bit reduced instruction set computing (RISC) architecture that is highly configurable, capable of supporting up to 256 custom instructions and clock speeds near 300 MHz on a Stratix IV device. The NIOS II processor system consists of a NIOS II processor core coupled with on-chip peripherals (DMA controllers, timers, and custom HW interfaces), on-chip memory as well as interfaces to off-chip memory. All of the various peripherals and memories are managed through the Avalon switching fabric which serves as an arbiter between the various masters and slaves within a system. The Avalon switching fabric allows multiple data/instruction masters to communicate directly with multiple slaves devices simultaneously, assuming no two

masters are attempting to communicate with the same slave. The NIOS II processing core is chosen given high degree of flexibility and ability to support custom peripherals as well as built-in support for embedded C/C++ development using the NIOS II software development suite [10, 13].

3.3. Hardware Implementation. In order to realize a full JPEG2000 SoC, the EBCOT Tier II processing module must reside in hardware. Most research on JPEG2000 neglects to mention the implementation of Tier II, presumably leaving it to be handled by the host processor. This paper proposes a novel solution to this gap by leveraging an embedded softcore coprocessor to serve as an embedded EBCOT Tier II processing module. While similar in nature to the proposed architecture in [5], which utilizes the NIOS II system as an

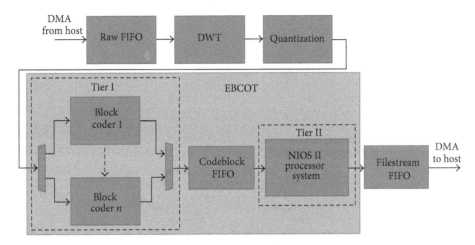

FIGURE 3: Data flow of proposed JPEG2000 SoC.

arbiter between different hardware modules, this architecture treats the coprocessor as a separate processing module.

The proposed JPEG2000 SoC is implemented on the target platform by integrating the NIOS II processing unit with existing embedded JPEG2000 processing modules. The existing design features a pipelined DWT architecture coupled with a variable number of parallel EBCOT Tier I block coders. The details of the specific architecture are given in Section 2. The coprocessor serves as the final stage of the pipeline, taking the code block streams from the block coders and forming the final JPEG2000 filestream. This eliminates the scheduling overhead associated with arbitration between the various processing modules as in [5]. The dataflow of the proposed implementation can be seen in Figure 3.

Prior to transferring the raw image to the target device, the image is padded and divided into tiles. Tiles are then sent to the target via DMA over the PCIe bus and processed sequentially. Each stage of the pipeline begins once a single tile has been received from the previous stage. Tiling the image reduces the memory requirements for each stage in the pipeline since each stage will need enough memory to store a single tile. Additionally, tile processing enables the use of distributed architectures where a single host leverages multiple target devices to process the tiles of a single image in parallel.

The NIOS II processing system creates the independent tile stream for each tile it receives from the pipeline before placing it in a FIFO for DMA back to the host via PCIe. The host system receives the tile streams from the device and applies the main headers to form a valid JPEG2000 filestream. While the NIOS II could easily be configured to add the main headers, this task is left for the host processor in order to maintain architectural flexibility in the event that more target devices are added to the system.

3.4. NIOS II System Implementation. This NIOS II processor operates within the entity created by Altera's System on a Programmable Chip (SoPC) builder [14]. This tool allows for seamless integration between the softcore processor and other hardware peripherals through the Avalon switching fabric. In addition, the SoPC builder allows for integration of multiple processing blocks running at different clock rates, with SoPC handling all of the arbitration between clock domains. The SoPC system used in the proposed design features a NIOS II fast core, running at a clock rate of 290 MHz. This NIOS II core is the fastest of the three offerings from Altera, offering high clock speeds and a number of additional features over the other two cores. A block diagram showing the implemented NIOS II system is shown in Figure 4. The clock rates and interface types of all modules shown are detailed in Table 1.

The NIOS II core is coupled with three different memory controllers. One is a DDRII SDRAM controller from Altera, running at 200 MHz, which interfaces directly with one of the two DDRII SODIMMs available on the target platform (Bank B or C) seen in Figure 2. The SDRAM serves two functions in the system. First, the SDRAM address space serves as a buffer to store incoming code blocks which are read out of the code block FIFO seen in Figure 3. Referred to as the input data buffer, code blocks are buffered in this address space prior to processing by Tier II. Second, the SDRAM address space is used to store the completed JPEG2000 filestream for each tile prior to transfer back to the host. This is referred to as the filestream buffer in subsequent sections.

Besides the off-chip SDRAM, there are also two separate on-chip memory controllers, one which controls a 50 kByte bank and the other which controls a 30 kByte bank. The 50 kByte bank is used to hold the executable code and data sections in addition to the program stack and heap during execution. The other 30 kByte bank is configured as "Tightly Coupled Data" memory. The details of this implementation are elaborated on in Section 3.5. Both of the on-chip memory banks are configured to run on the same clock as the NIOS II core.

Two custom interfaces are designed to communicate with the code block and filestream FIFOs as seen in Figure 3. These interfaces are used to couple the code block and filestream FIFOs with two DMA controllers to allow streaming of data in/out of the two FIFOs. Each DMA controller is comprised of two modules: a dispatcher and a read/write master. The

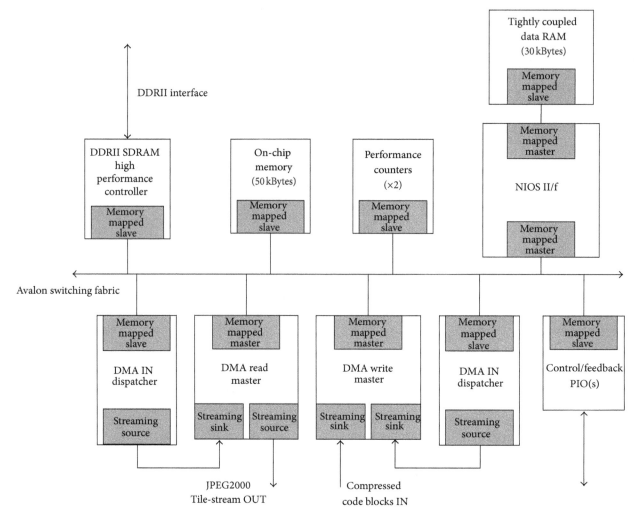

FIGURE 4: Block diagram of implemented NIOS II SoPC system.

TABLE 1: Hardware modules present in the NIOS II SoPC system.

Component	Clock (MHz)	Interface
NIOS II/f	290	Memory mapped
DDRII SDRAM controller	200	Memory mapped
On-chip RAM	290	Memory mapped
Tightly-coupled RAM	290	Memory mapped
DMA dispatcher (IN)	100	Memory mapped, streaming
DMA write master	100	Memory mapped, streaming
DMA dispatcher (OUT)	200	Memory mapped, streaming
DMA read master	200	Memory mapped, streaming
Feedback/control PIOs	100	Memory mapped
Performance counters	290	Memory mapped

dispatcher receives read/write commands from the system as a memory mapped slave. These commands are then passed to the connected read/write master which performs the memory transfer. This interaction is shown in Figure 4. Since the read/write masters are separate modules, the processor is free to complete other tasks while the data transfer is pending.

The SoPC system also has a number of parallel I/O (PIO) ports which provide direct communication with the hardware. The PIOs present in the system serve two main functions. First, PIOs enable the system to receive interrupts from the Tier I module upon completion of a tile. Second, PIOs are used to read/write registers which are in turn accessed by the host device for control or feedback. All of the PIOs operate at the same 100 MHz clock rate.

Finally, there are two performance counters, clocked at 290 MHz, present in the system. These counters are used to profile the system performance, the results of which are detailed in Section 3.5. Two counters are necessary to enable profiling of nested functions.

3.5. Optimizations.

A number of optimizations are made to the system in order to increase throughput. As the implementation couples a coprocessor with existing, optimized, and processing modules, these optimizations are focused on the NIOS II processing core. Figure 5 shows the impact of these optimizations on the processing time for a single 1024×1024 tile. Optimizations are applied on top of each other in a sequential manner to demonstrate the combined impact of all optimizations on the average processing time. Therefore, the final data point is the average processing time resulting from the combination of all of the previous optimizations. High-resolution images are compressed and the Tier II processing time is then divided by the number of tiles to yield an average Tier II processing time.

Typically, floating point operations are much more computationally expensive than integer operations. This expense is compounded when using a RISC architecture such as the NIOS II processor. While most of the Tier II algorithm is performed using integer calculations, a logarithm is required to calculate the length of a codeword segment. Codeword segments are used to signal the number of bytes contributed to a packet by a code block. The number of bits required for to store the codeword is given by

$$\text{bits} = L\text{block} + \lfloor \log_2(P) \rfloor, \tag{1}$$

where L block is the state variable for the current code block and P is the number of coding passes contributed to the current code block [1]. As this calculation is necessary for each code block, the computational cost is high. Software profiling reveals that the calculation of (1) takes over 70% of the total Tier II processing time on the NIOS II processor.

Two approaches are taken to reduce the computation cost of this calculation. The NIOS II processing core supports the addition of custom instructions, such as user created HW implementations of specific operations. Additionally, the tools include a number of premade instructions, including custom floating point (FP) instructions [10, 15]. The custom FP hardware is enabled on the NIOS II core, and significant improvement is seen in system throughput, yielding a 66% decrease in processing time. However, this calculation still takes over 35% of the total Tier II time.

To further reduce the processing burden of the binary logarithm, the standard library call is replaced with a custom implementation, referred to as a lookup table (LUT) implementation. The binary logarithm of a number can be thought of as the number of bits required to represent that number in binary. Since only the floored result is used, this calculation can be performed using only logical right shifts and addition. Pseudocode for the algorithm is shown in

Algorithm 1. The implementation described here is for a 32-bit unsigned integer and increments the result based on a series of comparisons to powers of two. First, if the input's most significant bit (MSB) is in the upper 16 bits, the output is incremented by 16, since at least 16 bits are required to represent the input. The upper 16 bits of the input are then used for subsequent comparisons by shifting the input right by 16. Then, if the MSB is contained in the upper half of the remainder, the result is incremented by 8 and the upper 8 bits are used for the next comparison. This procedure is repeated 3 more times, operating on the upper half of the remainder of the input word. Figure 5 shows that using the LUT implementation yields better performance than the custom FP hardware and is used in the final implementation in favor of the custom instructions. This implementation removes the need for costly floating point arithmetic, instead of leveraging inexpensive bit shifts and addition. The use of an LUT implementation reduces the calculation time to 3% of the total Tier II time, down from over 70%.

As mentioned in Section 3.4, the 30 kByte bank of on-chip memory is configured as "Tightly Coupled" memory (TCM). The NIOS II core can be configured to have additional data master ports for any number of TCMs, which must be on-chip. TCMs bypass the NIOS II cache and provide guaranteed low-latency memory access to specially designated instructions or data [10, 13]. These instructions or data are designated as tightly coupled through specific linker commands at compile time. In this implementation, specific data structures which are frequently accessed during Tier II are designated as tightly coupled to guarantee consistent performance. While Figure 5 shows a minor improvement in processing time, using TCMs to bypass the cache can be useful for avoiding data corruption while parallel processing is performed.

The downfall of utilizing SDRAM to serve as a tile buffer is that memory accesses to the device are considerably slower than accessing on-chip RAM. During the Tier II processing, multiple reads and writes are performed within this memory space for each code block processed. Additionally, each code block must be copied from the input data buffer to the filestream buffer. This copy alone has a detrimental impact on the overall throughput of the system. To address this issue, a third DMA controller is added to the system which masters only the SDRAM controller, allowing the system to schedule nonblocking memory copies within the SDRAM address range. The addition of this DMA controller hides the latency associated with large memory copies, allowing the processor to continue processing the next set of instructions while the transfer completes. Introduction of the third DMA controller results in a 48% decrease in processing time as shown in Figure 5 when compared to the previous implementation without the additional DMA controller. Care is taken to ensure that all pending memory copies have completed prior to writing out the completed filestream.

The final optimization made to the NIOS II system is to ensure that the system acts as a pipeline in order to maximize throughput of the system. Initially, the system is designed without the code block FIFO seen in Figure 3. Instead, the NIOS II system is directly coupled with the Tier I

```
begin
    result = 0
    if input >= 65536 then input >>= 16; result+ = 16; fi
    if input >= 256 then input >>= 8; result+ = 8; fi
    if input >= 16 then input >>= 4; result+ = 4; fi
    if input >= 4 then input >>= 2; result+ = 2; fi
    if input >= 2 then input >>= 1; result+ = 1; fi
    return result;
end
```

ALGORITHM 1: A lookup table implementation of a floored binary logarithm of a 32-bit unsigned integer.

output, reading code blocks as they become available. While a simplified approach, the downfall is that the Tier I processor must wait for the code block to be read before proceeding to the next code block. In order to eliminate this idle time, the code block FIFO in Figure 3 is added. Tier I simply writes to the FIFO and signals the Tier II module when a full tile has been buffered. Since the code block FIFO resides in SDRAM, a large 16 MByte FIFO is used which is capable of buffering multiple tiles in the event Tier II falls behind. Tier II then reads entire tiles as they become available, instead of reading each code block. Pipelining has two distinct impacts on the system throughput. First, the Tier I encoder is now free to process code blocks as fast as possible, therefore increasing the system throughput. Additionally, the interrupt latency associated with posting read requests is reduced since there is only one read request per tile, instead of one request per code block. In total, four optimizations yield a 91% reduction in Tier II processing time with the NIOS II system.

4. Analysis of Results

4.1. Performance and Analysis. The performance of the JPEG2000 SoC is measured using three 2048 × 2560 ISO test images "Café," "Woman," and "Bike." For all tests, each image is compressed and the respective processing times of all three images are averaged together. First, the overall performance of the system is measured with varying numbers of parallel block coders in order to determine the optimum number of block coders and the corresponding throughput of the system. The number of parallel block coders is increased from 1 to 20. The impact of an increased number of parallel block coders on the image processing time as well as the Tier I and Tier II times is shown in Figure 6.

The total HW time in Figure 6 shows that, as expected, additional block coders have a large impact on the average image processing time. This is especially true when the block coder count is increased from 1 to 6, resulting in a 67% drop in average processing time. Processing time continues to decrease as the block coder count is increased beyond six with a minimal processing time of 0.22 seconds achieved when 18 block coders are present. Negligible change in performance is seen with block coder counts beyond 18. The steps seen in the total HW time are attributed to lack of saturation of the DMA

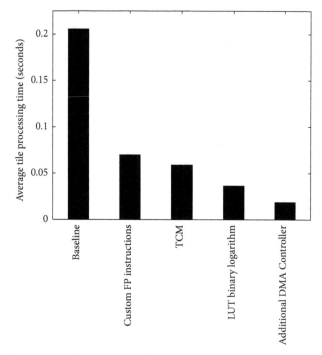

FIGURE 5: Combined impact of optimizations on average processing time for single 1024 × 1024 tile (optimizations are combined to yield lowest processing time).

controller between steps, resulting in jumps in performance when data is presented to the DMA controller at a faster rate.

The overall throughput of the system is limited by the Tier II processing time. Figure 6 shows the time spent performing Tier I and Tier II processing, as well as the total time, for a variable number of block coders. Figure 6 shows that the Tier II processing remains constant at 0.121 sec while the Tier I time decreases as more block coders are added, as expected. As the Tier I processing time approaches the Tier II time, the total processing time begins to flatten out, with little change beyond 18 block coders. Additional block coders have little impact on the total processing time since it has no impact on the Tier II processing time.

Figure 6 shows that the proposed architecture scales well with an increasing number of parallel block coders. This compares favorably with the SoC architecture presented in [5], which does not scale as well as the proposed architecture.

TABLE 2: Hardware resource comparison for a system with 4 block coders.

System	Block coders	LCs	Memory	Clock (MHz)
[5] DWT/TierI	4	15,268	622,976	50
DWT/TierI	4	13,123	637,952	100/200
DWT/TierI	18	43,690	1,417,472	100/200
TierII (NIOS)	N/A	10,996	923,008	290

Figure 7 shows a comparison between the performance of the proposed architecture and the architecture presented in [5]. The image processing time from the fastest implementation of [5] is overlaid onto the total HW time from Figure 6 for one to ten block coders, using the same set of ISO test images. Results are compared from one to ten block coders since [5] only provides results up to ten coders. It is clear that while [5] outperforms at lower block coder counts, these gains are erased once the count is increased beyond five encoders. At this point the [5] architecture has plateaued while the proposed architecture continues to improve. With 10 parallel block coders, the proposed implementation outperforms [5] by 39%. When the system is scaled to 18 block coders, the proposed design outperforms [5] by 58%. By allowing the other processing modules to operate outside the contexts of the SoPC system, the proposed architecture is able to take full advantage of multiple parallel block coders without the limitations necessarily imposed by the Avalon switching fabric. While extremely effective at integrating multiple different peripherals into a single system, the scheduling and arbitration overhead associated with the NIOS II processing system impose restrictions on the system throughput. By creating a pipelined architecture which utilizes the NIOS II processing core as a separate unit we are able to leverage the flexibility of the NIOS II system while still maintaining the speed of a pipelined encoder.

4.2. Hardware Synthesis Results.

The proposed implementation is synthesized on a Stratix IV FPGA using Altera Quartus 10.1. For the purposes of comparing the proposed design to [5], the design is synthesized with 4 parallel block coders. With this encoder count, [5] slightly outperforms the proposed system, but these gains are quickly erased with additional block coders (Figure 7). The hardware costs of the proposed system and [5] are shown in Table 2. Costs for both the 4 and 18 block encoder implementations are shown. The hardware costs for the proposed system are split into two categories: the DWT and Tier I modules and the NIOS II system which performs Tier II. The results are presented in this manner to provide an accurate comparison to [5], which only simulates the NIOS II system, so the hardware costs only reflect the DWT and Tier I modules.

Table 2 shows that the hardware resource costs of the implemented NIOS II system are minimal compared to the other processing modules, whose costs increase as more block coders are added. However, the NIOS II system does have a high memory cost. This is due to the 80 kBytes (50 kByte and 30 kByte banks) of on-chip RAM used along with the

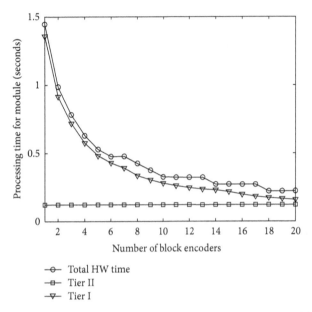

FIGURE 6: Performance profile of encoding pipeline with parallel block coders.

instruction and data caches built into the processing core. These large memory modules are necessary to run more complex code requiring larger stack and heap regions in memory. However, due to the flexibility of the NIOS II system, these costs could be shifted off-chip by utilizing more of the SDRAM. However, since the target platform utilizes a Stratix IV FPGA [12] with a large amount of on-chip memory, this is not an issue for the proposed design.

Table 2 shows that the proposed DWT and Tier I designs are comparable in cost to [5] with 4 parallel block coders. The main difference is that the proposed design is capable of higher clock speeds, with the DWT and Tier I running at 100 MHz and 200 MHz, respectively. This results in a DWT capable of processing one pixel every 7 ns as opposed to 20 ns per pixel in [5]. The higher performance of the DWT prevents the parallel block coders from becoming starved as they do in [5], which yields increased performance up to 18 block coders as opposed to [5], which peaks at 4 block coders due to starvation of the block coders. Instead, the proposed design is limited by the throughput of the NIOS II system.

5. Conclusion

This paper proposed a fully embedded JPEG2000 SoC which utilized an Altera NIOS II processor as the embedded EBCOT

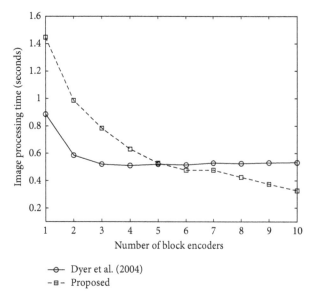

FIGURE 7: Performance comparison to other SoC implementations.

Tier II processing module. The proposed system is synthesized on a Stratix IV FPGA and yields a 39% performance increase over other JPEG2000 SoC implementations with the same number of parallel block coders. While [5] offers a more flexible and reconfigurable design, the pipelined architecture of the proposed design allows for a design capable of scaling to higher numbers of parallel block coders with comparable increases in system throughput. While limited by the performance of the NIOS II performance, future implementations could mitigate this with optimizations to the Tier II algorithm. Additional NIOS II processing cores could also be added to the system to share the processing load, assuming the availability of adequate hardware resources.

In addition to a high performance and scalable design, the proposed system also demonstrates the feasibility of utilizing an embedded softcore processor as a dedicated processing unit within a pipeline. Ease of reconfiguration and support for a variety of peripherals allowed for seamless integration of the NIOS II system into an existing encoding pipeline. The proposed design also demonstrates techniques for optimizing the performance of software running on the NIOS II through the use of custom instructions and additional peripherals.

References

[1] ISO/IEC 1. 29. 15444-1, "JPEG, 2000 Part I Final Committee Version 1. 0," 2004.

[2] D. Santa-Cruz, R. Grosbois, and T. Ebrahimi, "JPEG 2000 performance evaluation and assessment," *Signal Processing*, vol. 17, no. 1, pp. 113–130, 2002.

[3] K. Sarawadekar and S. Banerjee, "An Efficient pass-parallel architecture for embedded block coder in JPEG 2000," *IEEE Transactions on Circuits and Systems for Video Technology*, vol. 21, no. 6, pp. 825–836, 2011.

[4] K.-F. Chen, C.-J. Lian, H.-H. Chen, and L.-G. Chen, "Analysis and architecture design of EBCOT for JPEG-2000," in *Proceedings of the IEEE International Symposium on Circuits and Systems (ISCAS '01)*, pp. II765–II768, Sydney, Australia, May 2001.

[5] M. Dyer, S. Nooshabadi, and D. Taubman, "Design and analysis of system on a chip encoder for JPEG2000," *IEEE Transactions on Circuits and Systems for Video Technology*, vol. 19, no. 2, pp. 215–225, 2009.

[6] N. R. Kumar, W. Xiang, and Y. Wang, "An FPGA-based fast two-symbol processing architecture for JPEG 2000 arithmetic coding," in *Proceedings of the IEEE International Conference on Acoustics, Speech, and Signal Processing (ICASSP '10)*, pp. 1282–1285, Dallas, Tex, USA, March 2010.

[7] M. Dyer, D. Taubman, and S. Nooshabadi, "Improved throughput arithmetic coder for JPEG2000," in *Proceedings of the International Conference on Image Processing (ICIP '04)*, pp. 2817–2820, October 2004.

[8] L. Liu, N. Chen, H. Meng, L. Zhang, Z. Wang, and H. Chen, "A VLSI architecture of JPEG2000 encoder," *IEEE Journal of Solid-State Circuits*, vol. 39, no. 11, pp. 2032–2040, 2004.

[9] L. Liu, Z. Wang, N. Chen, and L. Zhang, "VLSI architecture of EBCOT Tier-2 encoder for JPEG2000," in *Proceedings of the IEEE Workshop on Signal Processing Systems—Design and Implementation (SiPS '05)*, pp. 225–228, November 2005.

[10] Altera Corporation, "NIOS II Processor Reference Handbook," 2010.

[11] E. J. Balster, B. T. Fortener, and W. F. Turri, "Integer computation of lossy JPEG2000 compression," *IEEE Transactions on Image Processing*, vol. 20, no. 8, pp. 2386–2391, 2011.

[12] GiDEL, "ProceIV Data Book," 2011.

[13] Altera Corporation, "NIOS II Software Developer's Handbook," 2011.

[14] Altera Corporation, "SOPC Builder User Guide," 2010.

[15] Altera Corporation, "NIOS II Custom Instruction User Guide," 2011.

4

An FPGA-Based Omnidirectional Vision Sensor for Motion Detection on Mobile Robots

Jones Y. Mori,[1] **Janier Arias-Garcia,**[1] **Camilo Sánchez-Ferreira,**[1] **Daniel M. Muñoz,**[2] **Carlos H. Llanos,**[1] **and J. M. S. T. Motta**[1]

[1] *Faculty of Technology, University of Brasilia, 70910-900, Brasilia, DF, Brazil*
[2] *Faculty of Gama, University of Brasilia, 72405-610, Brasilia, DF, Brazil*

Correspondence should be addressed to Jones Y. Mori, jonesyudi@unb.br

Academic Editor: Alisson Brito

This work presents the development of an integrated hardware/software sensor system for moving object detection and distance calculation, based on background subtraction algorithm. The sensor comprises a catadioptric system composed by a camera and a convex mirror that reflects the environment to the camera from all directions, obtaining a panoramic view. The sensor is used as an omnidirectional vision system, allowing for localization and navigation tasks of mobile robots. Several image processing operations such as filtering, segmentation and morphology have been included in the processing architecture. For achieving distance measurement, an algorithm to determine the center of mass of a detected object was implemented. The overall architecture has been mapped onto a commercial low-cost FPGA device, using a hardware/software co-design approach, which comprises a Nios II embedded microprocessor and specific image processing blocks, which have been implemented in hardware. The background subtraction algorithm was also used to calibrate the system, allowing for accurate results. Synthesis results show that the system can achieve a throughput of 26.6 processed frames per second and the performance analysis pointed out that the overall architecture achieves a speedup factor of 13.78 in comparison with a PC-based solution running on the real-time operating system xPC Target.

1. Introduction

Scientists predict that robots will play an important role in the future. In this scenario, robots will be able to assist humans in many tasks as domestic labors, elderly people care, cleaning, vehicles operation, and surveillance. Animals have mechanisms to interact with the environment provided by natural evolution. They are able to sense the surrounding environment and to move according to a defined objective, contouring obstacles and performing a dynamic path planning. In the robotic field, one of the major challenges is providing robots with sensorial and rational capabilities, allowing them to assist, and possibly substitute, humans in some activities requiring special skills.

Autonomous mobile robot navigation considers the execution of three stages: (a) mapping, (b) localization, and (c) decision making. The first stage uses information from sensors for creating a map of the environment. The second

one relates the map with the sensor information, allowing the robot to self-localization in the environment. The third stage considers the path-planning problem [1].

Different kinds of sensors can be used for providing environment information to the mobile robot. Such sensors are classified in two main groups: (a) interoceptive and (b) exteroceptive. The interoceptive sensors perform internal robot parameters measurements without environment dependence. Encoders, gyroscopes, and accelerometers are some examples of interoceptive sensors. On the other hand, exteroceptive sensors perform external measurements, for instance, ultrasound, radar and infrared positioning systems as well as cameras, GPS and magnetometers. In humans, the vision sense is the one which provides more quantity of information about the environment. Through the sensorial fusion (provided by our stereo vision system) we are able to estimate efficiently the localization of surrounding objects.

The use of cameras jointly with image processing algorithms for implementing sensors (e.g., distance, movement, color, and presence sensors) is suitable solution for mobile robotic applications. Additionally, cameras with embedded image processing issues are the foundations of computer vision area. Catadioptric systems are realizations of omnidirectional vision, being mainly based on specially shaped mirrors (e.g., spherical, hyperbolic, parabolic, etc.) that reflect the environment to the camera from all directions, obtaining a panoramic view. Thus, these systems can provide information from a larger area than other vision sensors [2].

The task of processing the acquired images depends on the objective of the process itself. A common problem in mobile robotics is the localization of moving objects around the robot. For that, different methodologies can be used, such as motion detection, trajectory estimation, and tracking. Since the motion detection approach makes use of simple and easily implemented algorithms, this technique is suitable for real-time embedded applications. A common technique for implementing the motion detection is the background subtraction, in which an image is acquired at the beginning of the measurement process, and then each new image is subtracted pixel by pixel from the background. This technique is largely used in surveillance systems, since it acts as an automatic intrusion detection algorithm. In robotics, the localization of the differences between the background and the new frame provides the position estimation of the moving objects around the robot.

On the other hand, distance sensors are important for solving mobile robotic localization problems (namely, local and global localization tasks), and an important issue is the use of cameras for these tasks, providing (in real time) the robot with information about the distance to an obstacle. To accomplish this, the development of a mapping process among the actual scenario and the captured image is fundamental. This aspect introduces the calibration problem, which comprises the estimation of metrological values such as accuracy and precision (that are related to systematic and random errors, resp.), apart from the calculation of calibrations curves.

Otherwise, taking into account performance points, autonomous mobile robots must be able to acquire images from the environment, processing the information and making a decision in a short period of time. In order to avoid failures, autonomous mobile robots must perform the decision process as quickly as possible. This real-time constraints require the use of high-performance computational platforms for implementing image processing algorithms. In this context, the high computational cost of the involved algorithms is the main drawback, specifically when performing operations with high accuracy and high performance.

Common robotic platforms are based on desktop solutions executing complex algorithms for robot navigation. However, desktop platforms are not tailored for embedded applications with portability and low-power consumption requirements. Field programmable gate arrays (FPGAs) are a suitable solution for implementing image processing algorithms with a high performance. FPGAs allow the involved algorithms to be mapped directly in hardware in a parallel way. In addition, FPGAs allow software RISC processors to be implemented in order to execute parts of the algorithms with low performance requirements.

In [3] the authors proposed the development of a distance sensor based on an 800×480 pixels camera connected to an FPGA, a spatial convolution filter (for edge enhancement), a hardware architecture for estimating the distance of real objects and a touch-screen display as user interface (the camera image was addressed to the screen). In that system the screen was capable to detect the coordinates of a touched point, being used for calculating the distance (in pixels) from the robot to a defined object. In this approach the calibration parameters (errors and calibration curves) were calculated by comparing the actual distances, in a particular scenario, and the pixel distance in the screen.

The main contribution of this work is the design of an integrated hardware/software sensor system for both moving object detection and distance calculation, based on background subtraction algorithm. In this approach the calibration problem has been also treated, validating a proposed calibration process, which is suitable for this kind of application. Several image processing operations as filtering, segmentation, and erosion have been implemented in the architecture. The object's position was determined by computing its center of mass coordinates. The movement detection technique was also used to automate the omnidirectional vision system (achieved in a catadioptric implementation). As a result the uncertainties related to point objects in the touchscreen were eliminated.

The proposed pipeline image processing algorithm was mapped onto a Cyclone II FPGA device. Also, in this device, a NiosII soft processor was implemented for computing the distance and orientation as well as a simple user interface. Execution time comparisons among the proposed hardware architecture and a C-code implementation show that the hardware solution speeds up by 13.78 times a pc-based solution running in an Intel Pentium IV processor at 2.2 GHz, with 2.0 GB RAM and using a real-time operating system (the xPC Target OS from MathWorks).

The remainder of this paper is organized as follows. Section 2 outlines some computational vision techniques. Section 3 presents the related work. Section 4 describes the system and the calibration procedure. Section 5 shows the FPGA hardware and software implementations, and, before concluding, Section 6 presents synthesis, validation results, and a performance analysis.

2. Background

The use of cameras is a common solution for mobile robotics applications. Different works are related to the extraction of features from images. Monocular systems are able to provide only 2D information of the environment in front of the camera. In this case, in order to extract depth information it may be necessary to analyse vanishing points or to use

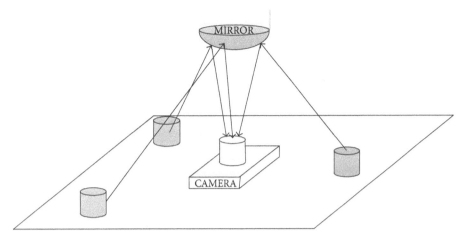

FIGURE 1: Catadioptric system.

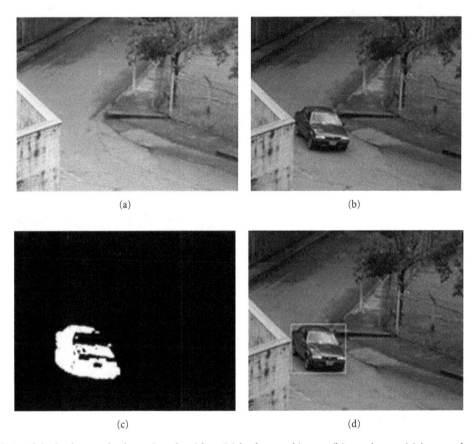

FIGURE 2: Image chain of the background subtraction algorithm: (a) background image; (b) new image; (c) image subtraction; (d) overlap of new image and object's position.

perspective models with known object shapes. The use of a pair of cameras (stereo systems) allows the depth to be estimated through the epipolar geometry. Once the objects have been identified in each camera, it is possible to compute the depth of the image using simple geometric techniques. However, similar to monocular systems, stereo cameras provide information only in front of the cameras. In order to obtain information about the surrounding environment it is necessary to turn the system 360 degrees acquiring images in all the directions [4].

Omnidirectional vision systems are a suitable alternative to view the surrounding environment from one single image. Such a system can be built in two ways: (a) using panoramic lenses, for instance, fisheye lenses and (b) using catadioptric systems. Cameras equipped with fisheye lenses acquire images directly from the environment. On the other hand,

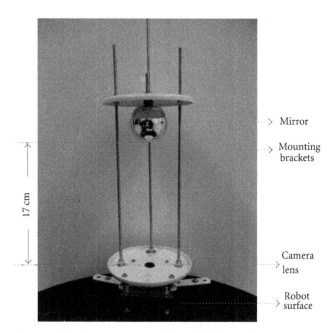

FIGURE 3: Main components of the proposed catadioptric system.

FIGURE 5: Correspondences among the omnidirectional image and the real environment.

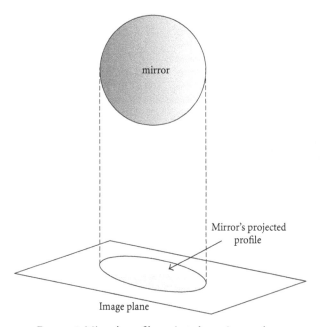

FIGURE 4: Mirror's profile projected over image plane.

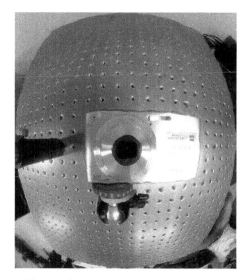

FIGURE 6: The catadioptric system mounted over a calibration board.

catadioptric systems capture the image of the environment reflected on a special geometry mirror [5].

Figure 1 shows the principles of operation of a catadioptric system. It is composed of a camera and a convex mirror. The acquired image characteristics depend on the geometry of the mirror. Thus, knowing the geometry, reflection equations can be used in order to determine the environment geometric characteristics. Commonly, omnidirectional vision systems make use of hyperbolic, parabolic, spherical, and conical mirrors [5, 6].

In our previous work [3] the object's coordinates in the image were determined using a touch screen. Thus, by touching over the object in the image, the distance in pixels was calculated. Although this procedure is easily performed, its precision depends on several factors such as parallax effect, accuracy, and lighting variations. In order to minimize the human factor, in this work we make use of an identification method based on a background subtraction algorithm which allows the object to be automatically located and identified.

Figure 2 shows an image chain demonstrating the response of the background subtraction algorithm. In this method an image without objects is acquired (background image), and then each new image (with objects) is subtracted pixel by pixel from the background. After the subtraction (Figure 2(c)), the coordinates of the center of mass are determined using (1) and used as the object location. It is important to note that the system can determine the position of only a single object in the image, since all other moving objects will be considered noise and disregarded.

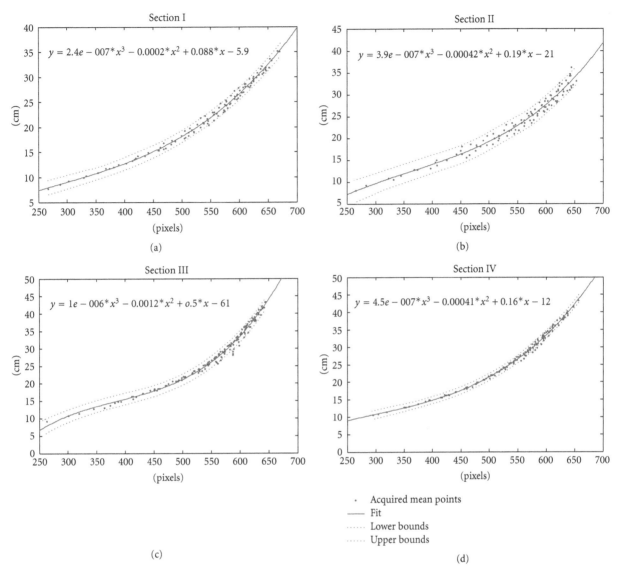

FIGURE 7: Polynomial fitting for distance estimation for sections I, II, III and IV.

Otherwise, the center of mass will be determined considering the distributed mass of all objects:

$$C(x \cdot y) = \frac{\sum_{i=0}^{M-1} \sum_{j=0}^{N-1} (i, j) \cdot B(i, j)}{\sum_{i=0}^{M-1} \sum_{j=0}^{N-1} B(i, j)}. \tag{1}$$

The construction of catadioptric systems is a complex task taking into account that there are a lot of of geometrical uncertainties that must be precisely determined in order to assure the necessary accuracy of the system. In this context, it is essential to apply a calibration process to the catadioptric system for determining the errors (namely, systematic and random ones) related to defects in the catadioptric systems (e.g., mirror defects).

3. Related Works

Several works have been developed using FPGAs for speeding up image processing tasks, mainly for embedded systems applications with real-time constraints. In [7], a biological inspired architecture for motion estimation by optical flow was implemented. This approach is suitable for implementation in both FPGA and ASIC devices, achieving a processing rate of 177 frames per second (128×96 pixels). Also, in [8] an FPGA implementation of an embedded motion estimation sensor (that uses an optical flow algorithm achieving 15 frames per second for images with 640 × 480 pixels size) is proposed.

A vision system for visual feedback applied to control a mechanical system was proposed in [9]. In this approach a matched filter by correlation is used, which also determines the object's center of mass each 4,51 ms for small images (256 × 256 pixels). In [10], a system for image

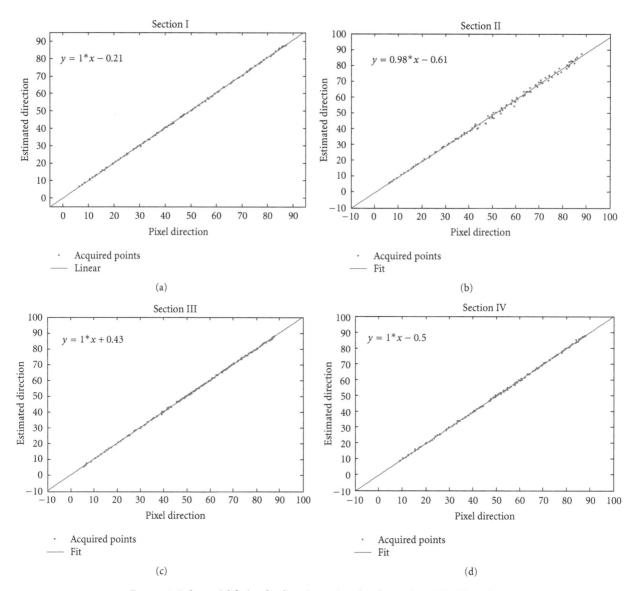

FIGURE 8: Polynomial fitting for direction estimation for sections I, II, III, and IV.

filtering and motion estimation using SAD (sum of absolute differences) is implemented using a systolic architecture suitable for estimating motion each 5 ms in images with 640×480 pixels.

The design and implementation of robust real-time visual servoing control, with an FPGA-based image coprocessor for a rotary inverted pendulum, are presented in [11]. In this approach the position of the pendulum is measured with a machine vision system whose image processing algorithms are pipelined and implemented on a FPGA device for achieving real-time constraints. Furthermore, it uses an edge enhancement algorithm to determine the center of mass of the detected object, reaching a throughput of 580 (128×101 pixels) processed frames per second.

In [12, 13] an FPGA-based video processing for surveillance systems is described. Reference [13] shows an FPGA implementation for real-time background subtraction. The implemented architecture reaches a performance of 32,8 frames per second with 1024×1024 images. In [12] a pipeline architecture for multimodal background generation algorithm is described, for colour video stream and moving objects segmentation based on brightness, colour, and textural information. In the later case, the overall throughput was about 25 frames per second, with a resolution of 720×576 pixels.

An implementation in a PC of an omnidirectional sensor for mobile robot navigation was presented in [14]. In this approach, a catadioptric system was calibrated by placing landmarks in the environment, using a polynomial interpolation to characterize the system. Additionally, the same uses an edge enhancement technique to create a polar map of the surrounding environment.

Reference [15] introduces an implementation of a framework for image processing speedup by using reconfigurable devices. Some of the most common image preprocessing algorithms were implemented achieving a high throughput.

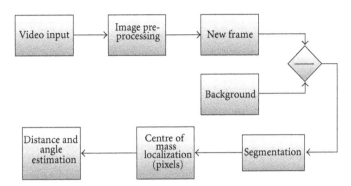

FIGURE 9: Flowchart of the general hardware architecture.

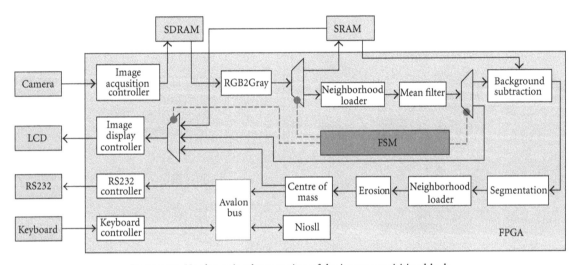

FIGURE 10: Hardware implementation of the image acquisition block.

Otherwise, [16] uses dynamic reconfiguration for color recognition and optical flow computation in FPGA, in which a throughput of 30 frames per second for 160×120 pixels images is achieved.

An approach that uses lookup tables for avoiding complex computations was proposed in [17], in which an architecture for real-time rectification of catadioptric images was implemented in FPGAs. This work has a good throughput but requires a large amount of memory block for storing all the distances, which were calculated off line.

In [18] an FPGA-based architecture (which calculates pixel by pixel the undistorted image from a polar frame) is proposed, thus providing a plane image as output. In that case, a pipeline architecture is used to organize the processing stages, achieving a throughput of one pixel per clock cycle. An FPGA for image reconstruction was used in [19]; however, differently from [17, 18], where the images are generated by an omnidirectional mirror, the system processes the images from a camera with a fisheye lens, although, in this case, the authors do not present a description of the architecture for the reconstruction process.

An architecture using a mixed FPGA/DSP to obtain large speedup factor for high-resolution images was presented in [20], while in [21] an embedded Nios II processor that makes use of several hardware coprocessors for image filtering and

tasks related to the autoadjustment of the camera focal length was described.

In [6] a complete procedure for catadioptric systems calibration using line projections is presented. In this case, the system achieves a high accuracy for paraboloid mirrors. An approach that uses calibration patterns to determine the response of hyperbolic sections on a nonrevolute hyperbolic mirror was presented in [22]. The simple idea that the external and internal boundaries of the mirror can be used as a 3D calibration pattern was proposed in [23], allowing for a high-speed self-calibration procedure. [24] which developed a complete generic camera calibration procedure by overlapping calibration grids simultaneously. It is suitable for calibrating many kinds of cameras such as fisheye lens, catadioptric cameras with spherical and hyperbolic mirrors, and also multicamera setups.

Some of the cited works use FPGAs for accelerating omnidirectional vision processing and have mainly focused on image undistortion/reconstruction/rectification tasks. However, in mobile robot applications (such as localization, navigation, and multiagent robotics), it is not always necessarily a complete image reconstruction, but the correct, appropriated, and fast measurement of distances between the robot and the different environment objects. In this context, the main contribution of this work is to provide the robot

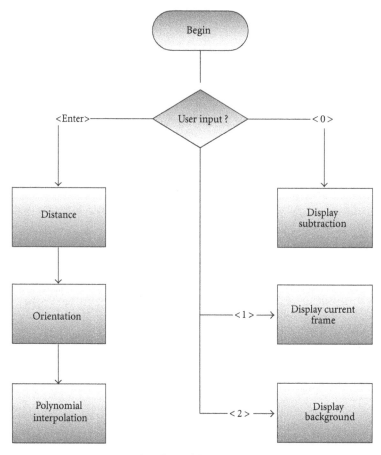

FIGURE 11: Flowchart of the NiosII coprocessor.

with a suitable and low-cost system for measuring distances automatically from the robot to the detected objects, using an appropriated image resolution (800 × 480 pixels) and achieving real-time characteristics.

4. Development of the Catadioptric System

This section describes the mechanical design of the catadioptric system as well as the calibration procedure description and its analysis.

4.1. The Proposed Catadioptric System. A catadioptric system allows the camera to capture reflected images in the mirror, obtaining a panoramic view. Figure 3 shows the system developed and its main components: (a) a convex mirror, (b) the mounting brackets, and (c) a CMOS camera with a maximum resolution of 2592 × 1944 pixels. In order to perform numerical comparisons with related works we have used a resolution of 800 × 480 pixels, which is appropriated for mobile robotics applications. The distance between the camera and the vertex of the mirror is approximately 17 cm.

In this case it is desirable that the center of the mirror is placed in a vertical line from the center of the camera lens. To achieve this, once mounted the system, an image was acquired and analyzed in order to determine (in pixels) the coordinates of the circle projected by the mirror over

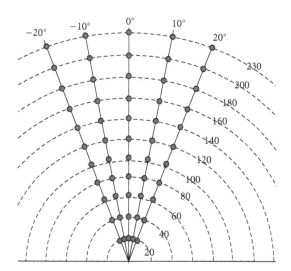

FIGURE 12: Calibration positions for a particular section in the scene.

the image plane (Figure 4 shows this idea). Otherwise, in this approach, the mirror's projection was assumed to be circular.

For mobile robot applications, the catadioptric system provides a panoramic image in which the robot occupies

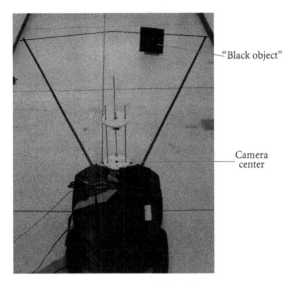

FIGURE 13: The overall system and the calibration environment.

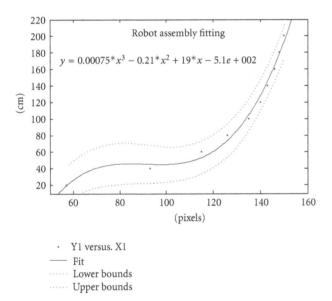

FIGURE 14: Polynomial interpolation functions.

TABLE 1: RMSE for each section.

Section	Distance RMSE	Direction RMSE
I	0.9284	0.244
II	1.038	1.110
III	0.8353	0.273
IV	0.5398	0.388

outside this area are reflected on the mirror border, and then large distortions are produced. Additional distortions in the acquired image can be produced by small errors in the optical geometry of the vision system.

4.2. Calibration Process. The quality of the data obtained from an omnidirectional vision system depends directly on several constructive parameters such as the optical geometry, curvature of the convex mirror, and quality of mirror's surface. For one to use the equations of the mirror surface profile (and afterward modeling the light reflection), the geometrical parameters of the system must be precisely characterized. However, in this work we have used a convex mirror with unknown geometry, and then it is not possible to use light reflection equations.

The proposed calibration process allows the whole vision system to be characterized providing a fitting function relating the distance in pixels with distances in world coordinates. The calibration procedure was performed by associating objects placed at measured distances with the distances estimated in the image in pixels, obtaining a polynomial fitting associated to a particular section of the convex mirror.

As in our previous work [3], the image was divided into four sections, and the same calibration procedure was executed to each one. In order to provide a better demonstration of the correctness of the calibration procedure, in this work a calibration board and a 14 megapixels camera have been used. The mounted system is depicted in Figure 6. The board used has a separation of 2,54 cm between each hole (in both horizontal and vertical directions). The catadioptric mount was positioned approximately in the center of the board, and the images are shown in Figure 6.

In this image, the holes were detected and their pixel coordinates were determined. The image was divided in four sections, and for each section the real distance and the distance in pixels were associated with a polynomial fitting. In order to allow the robot to identify the position of any object in the surrounding environment, the system was also calibrated to estimate the direction of the detected object. Figures 7 and 8 show the polynomial fitting for estimating both distances and directions, respectively, for each section of the mirror.

Table 1 shows the RMSE (root mean-square error) values of the fittings which characterize the quality of the obtained models. It can be observed that the polynomial fittings have a low value of the RMSE, which means that the calibration data can be well modeled by the polynomials.

In order to validate the precision of the measurement system, a new image (with the same assembly of Figure 6)

the center of the image. Figure 5 shows the omnidirectional image captured and the respective environment, in which the robot is positioned with some objects around it, with arrows indicating the correspondence among objects and the image.

The omnidirectional vision system provides a panoramic image, which can be processed in order to extract the distance in pixels between the center of the mirror and the identified object. Once the system has been calibrated, the actual distance can be computed by using a mathematical model (explained in the following section). Additionally, by using omnidirectional vision it is possible to estimate the direction of the surrounding objects, providing to the robot a polar representation of the environment. We assume that the robot only detects objects within its viewing area, which corresponds to a circle with a radius of 2.0 meters. Objects

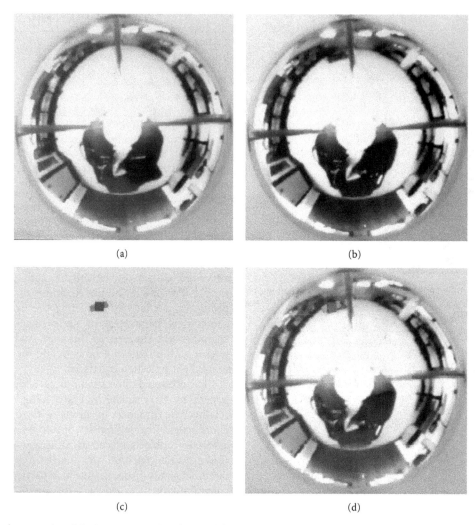

FIGURE 15: Results of the image processing chain: (a) background, (b) new frame, (c) subtraction, and (d) overlap.

was shot, and five points were picked from each section. By using the polynomial fittings (used like calibration curves), their actual positions were estimated. Table 2 shows the actual and the estimated positions of the points (distance and direction).

The validation results (shown in Table 2) demonstrate that both the calibration procedure and the polynomial fitting can be effectively used to relate distances/directions in the image (in pixels) with the actual distances/directions values.

5. FPGA Implementation

The proposed algorithms for image processing were implemented in hardware, using both VHDL and Verilog hardware description languages. Figure 9 shows the general architecture for motion detection, which is composed of several hardware components (blocks) connected in a pipeline way. The first processing step receives from the camera an RGB 800×480 pixels image with a resolution of 8 bits per color channel. At the second step, namely, *image processing*,

a gray-scale image is obtained and a *mean* filter is applied for eliminating noise. At the third step, the background subtraction is performed. To do this the background image has been previously stored in an SRAM. At the fourth step, a thresholding algorithm is applied for segmentation, obtaining a binary image (only one bit per pixel). Additionally, the obtained image is eroded in order to minimize noise. At the fifth stage the center of mass is computed, and, finally, at the sixth stage the object position (distance and orientation) is computed.

5.1. Image Acquisition and Color Conversion. The system uses a CMOS camera which provides synchronism and data signals in an RAW format. A color conversion process is performed by calculating the RGB data from RAW ones and storing it in an external SDRAM (see Figures 5 and 6).

5.2. Mean Filter Implementation. After the pixel conversion from RAW to RGB format, a gray-scale transformation is applied. Afterward, a *neighborhood loader* block provides a 3×3 neighborhood to a *mean filter*, which eliminates

FIGURE 16: Objects used for testing the overall system.

TABLE 2: Validation points.

Section	Actual distance (cm)	Estimated distance (cm)	Actual direction (°)	Estimated direction (°)
I	20.5	19.6	7.6	7.2
I	11.3	12.1	69.5	68.4
I	17.0	18.0	66.2	67.4
I	21.7	23.3	71.4	72.7
I	28.4	29.4	65.8	65.0
II	28.4	25.8	10.8	11.5
II	27.4	25.2	22.8	23.6
II	27.0	25.7	50.9	53.6
II	30.6	29.6	50.2	50.9
II	26.2	24.8	30.5	31.8
III	17.9	18.0	8.8	7.9
III	28.4	31.8	10.8	9.8
III	29.7	31.9	20.9	19.4
III	34.5	35.9	37.3	35.7
III	43.3	41.5	51.1	48.9
IV	15.5	16.1	10.3	10.2
IV	23.4	24.4	13.2	13.6
IV	29.6	30.3	32.3	32.8
IV	35.9	36.0	46.5	46.6
IV	43.3	43.7	51.1	51.8

high-frequency noises. The neighborhood loader operation requires an initial latency of 1603 clock cycles (69.62 μs) [25]. A convolution operation was used to implement the mean filter (see Figures 5 and 6), which is performed in one clock cycle by multiplying the mask with the neighborhood and then yielding the sum of the products, after an initial latency. More details on this implementation and the convolution architecture can be found in [25, 26].

5.3. The Background Storage and Image Subtraction.
The background image is stored in an external 512 Kbyte SRAM memory (chip ISSI IS61LV25616AL) of the DE2 development kit. Once the mean filter is performed, the subtraction between the current frame and background is computed, providing one output pixel per clock cycle. Afterward, the absolute value of each pixel is calculated. Finally, the segmentation operation is performed by a simple thresholding operation (see Figures 5 and 6).

5.4. The Erosion Operation.
The erosion computation is based on logic operations between the pixel of a binary image and a structuring element as shown in (2). The erosion block receives nine pixels from the neighborhood loader (f_i), as well as the structuring element (K_i) (a square mask was used like structuring element). Therefore, the e_i values are calculated in the first equation. Afterward, they are used in the next equation in order to perform a complete erosion operation. Both steps are performed in one clock cycle. In this work we have used a neighborhood of nine elements; therefore, $i = 1, \ldots, 9$:

$$e_i = \overline{K_i} \cdot \overline{f_i} + \overline{K_i} \cdot f_i + K_i \cdot f_i,$$

$$\text{Erosion} = e_1 \cdot e_2 \cdot e_3 \cdot e_4 \cdot e_5 \cdot e_6 \cdot e_7 \cdot e_8 \cdot e_9. \tag{2}$$

5.5. The Center of Mass Calculation.
In this work only the detection of a single object is performed at a time. In order to calculate the center of mass, $C(x, y)$, (1) was used, where $B(i, j)$ is a binary image and i and j are the positions of pixels on the image. Since the algorithm has to explore the overall image, the center of mass is calculated at each frame.

5.6. Distance and Orientation Estimation.
In our previous work [3] the actual and pixel distances were computed using several floating-point arithmetic libraries [27]. However, a large consumption of hardware resources was observed, specially for embedded applications. In this work we have chosen an embedded software implementation for these computations allowing for cost reduction in logic area.

A Nios II soft processor (from Altera) has been used in order to execute the following tasks: (a) receiving commands from the user through a PS2 keyboard, (b) calculating the distance in pixels and orientation values, (c) calculating the actual distance using a polynomial function obtained from the calibration data (see Figure 14), and (d) sending to the host (PC or robot computer) both the estimated distance and orientation values. The communication with the PC is done through a RS232 communication standard. The image processing architecture and a keyboard are connected to the Nios II using the Avalon Bus from Altera, as shown in Figure 10.

Figure 11 shows the flowchart algorithm implemented in the NiosII processor. The processor receives the user input

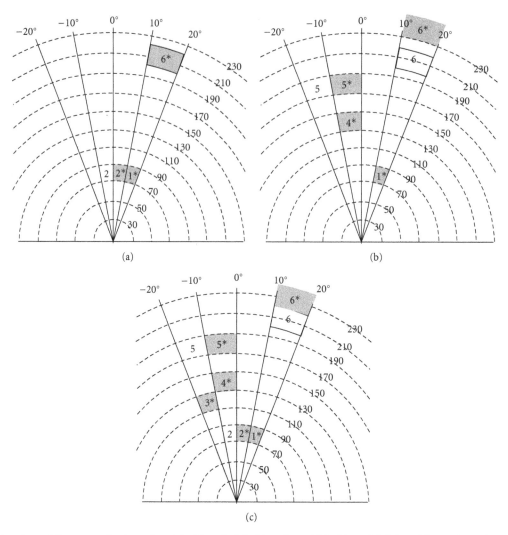

FIGURE 17: Estimation of distance and orientation. (a) object A, (b) object B, and (c) object C. White grids are the real positions and gray grids are the estimated position.

commands from a keyboard, allowing the selection of the following options.

(i) Send to the host the distance and orientation values. In this case the NiosII receives from the hardware architecture the center of mass coordinates $C(x, y)$ and computes the euclidean distance in pixels and the orientation θ using the atan() function. Finally, the polynomial interpolation is used to estimate the actual distance R, sending the polar coordinates (R, θ) to the host.

(ii) Capture a new background image. This option allows the user to upgrade the background image in the SRAM memory.

(iii) Subtract the background from current image. This option allows the user to manually execute the subtraction image step.

(iv) Display the subtraction result. This option allows the user to show the image substation result in the display.

(v) Display the current image. This option allows the user to address the current camera image to the display.

(vi) Display the background image. This option allows the user to see the stored background image in the display.

The last five commands make use of the Avalon bus to send the respective commands to the FSM (finite state machine) which controls the data flow and the LCD. The FSM was implemented in hardware for controlling the overall system operation according to the user inputs. The same controls several multiplexers for addressing the incoming pixels to the SRAM/SDRAM memories and the hardware modules previously described.

In our approach both the Euclidean distance as well as the arctangent function need to be computed (but only once time at each frame). In this case, although von Neumann-based architectures have serious restrictions (such as the NiosII case) for real-time image processing, specially for

TABLE 3: Synthesis results (chip ep2c35f672c6).

Implemented core	LC 33216	MB 483840	DSP18×18 35	Freq. 250 MHz
Entire Architecture	9953 (30.0%)	359352 (74.3%)	8 (22.8%)	10.2
Image Acquisition	2161 (6.5%)	57400 (11.86%)	0 (0%)	45.31
Gray scale Conversion	498 (1.5%)	384 (0.08%)	1 (1%)	45.31
Neighborhood Load	681 (2.05%)	16256 (3.36%)	0 (0%)	104.12
Spatial Convolution	1853 (5.0%)	16256 (3.36%)	3 (5%)	104.12
Background Subtraction	16 (0.05%)	0 (0%)	0 (0%)	250
Segmentation	15 (0.05%)	0 (0%)	0 (0%)	250
Erosion	722 (2.17%)	0 (0%)	0 (0%)	321.3
Center of mass	2521 (7.59%)	0 (0%)	0 (0%)	10.2
NiosII	3615 (10.9%)	285696 (59.0%)	4 (6%)	250.0

TABLE 4: Latency of the motion detection architecture.

Implemented core	Latency
Background Subtraction	2 clk
Segmentation	1 clk
Erostion	1603 clk
Center of mass	384.001 (1 frame)
Entire architecture	385.607

TABLE 5: Distance calibration data using mobile object detection.

Distance (cm)	Mean distance (pixels)	σ (pixels)
20	56.6	3.3
40	93.4	7.3
60	114.6	1.3
80	126.2	7.3
100	134.6	7.3
120	139.8	1.7
140	143.0	1.0
160	146.2	2.2
180	147.8	1.7
200	149.6	1.3
230	152.2	1.4

TABLE 6: Direction calibration data using mobile object detection.

Angle (°)	Mean angle (°)	σ (°)
−20	−24.8	4.8
−10	−14.4	11.6
0	−1.3	1.1
10	9.3	4.4
20	21.1	4.5

TABLE 7: Validation results (using the moving object detection technique) distance is given in cm.

Real distance	Estimated distance and error					
	A	e_A	B	e_B	C	e_C
$p_1 = 70$	70	0%	80	14%	83	19%
$p_2 = 74$	70	5%	—	—	83	12%
$p_3 = 115$	—	—	—	—	107	7%
$p_4 = 137$	—	—	132	4%	132	4%
$p_5 = 170$	—	—	170	0%	170	0%
$p_6 = 200$	200	0%	248	24%	235	17%

TABLE 8: Validation results for orientation in degrees (°), using mobile object detection.

Angle (°)	A	B	C
$p_1 = 20$	20	19	20
$p_2 = -1$	9	—	9
$p_3 = -18$	—	—	−11
$p_4 = -8$	—	−4	−3
$p_5 = -14$	—	−8	−7
$p_6 = 11$	16	15	16

embedded systems, the software implementation of these tasks attends the real-time constraints in this work.

6. Results

The proposed architectures for processing the images from the omnidirectional vision system were effectively implemented in a Cyclone II FPGA device using the Quartus II development tool.

6.1. Synthesis Results. Table 3 presents the synthesis results of the overall architecture and its main components. The cost in logic area is presented in terms of logic cells (LCs), memory bits (MBs), and embedded DSP 18×18 blocks consumption. The performance of the architectures is presented in MHz.

It can be observed that the entire architecture consumes 30% of logic cells and around 74% of the memory bits. The image acquisition block requires the largest number of memory bits due to the fact that the camera provides pixels

in an RAW format; therefore, this block needs to store several rows in order to convert the pixels to an RGB format. The neighborhood loader is composed of two line buffers, which are used for providing the 3×3 pixels for performing the neighborhood operations [25]. As described in Section 5, the spatial convolution block makes use of a neighborhood loader module leading to more memory bits consumption. As expected, the NiosII implementation requires a large

TABLE 9: Performance comparison.

Author	Year	Main algorithm	Image resolution	Frames per second	Megapixels per second
[10]	2009	Sum of absolute differences (SAD)	640×480	200	61.44
[13]	2012	Background subtraction	1024×1024	32	33.55
[9]	2006	Correlation	256×256	221	14.48
[12]	2011	Background subtraction	720×576	25	10.37
This work	*2012*	*Background subtraction*	*800×480*	*26*	*9.98*
[11]	2011	Edge enhancement	128×101	580	7.50
[8]	2008	Optical flow	640×480	15	4.61
[7]	2008	Optical flow	128×96	177	2.17
[15]	2007	Optical flow	160×120	30	0.58

amount of memory bits for storing the program memory and its hardware architecture.

The background subtraction block is based on a pixel by pixel operation. The segmentation block operates using a comparator and a multiplexer. The erosion block is based on simple logic operations. Therefore, these blocks have a small hardware resources consumption.

It can be observed that the entire architecture operates at a maximum frequency of 10.2 MHz. Taking into account that the system is based on a pipeline architecture and the images resolution is 800×480 pixels, the system achieves a performance of 26.6 frames per second.

It is important to point out that the selected FPGA chip is not the largest device from the Cyclone II family; therefore, one can expect a performance improvement when using modern FPGA devices with more hardware resources.

Since the proposed system is based on a pipeline architecture, it is necessary for several clock cycles (*latency time*) before computing the first result (center of mass). According to Table 4 the latency of the proposed architecture is around 385.607 clock cycles. Note that the center of mass has the largest latency due to the fact that the entire image must be analyzed for computing the area.

6.2. The Calibration of the Overall System Using the Moving Object Detection Technique (Figure 13). The process of using a polynomial fitting for associating distances in pixels with actual distances was validated in Section 4. However, in real environments, mobile robots commonly operate with large uncertainties associated to the odometry sensors and nonholonomic restrictions. Therefore, we have again calibrated the catadioptric system including the mobile robot, using a precision lower than shown in Section 4. To do that, the moving object detection technique implemented in the FPGA has been used for calibration tasks. In this case, several objects were introduced in the scene, and the detection system automatically defined the distance between the robot and the detected object. The calculated distances can be compared with the actual ones in the scene, yielding new polynomial functions.

For this case, the mirror was divided into sections of 40° (nine sections cover the whole mirror surface). In the scene, a grid of radial distances were chosen to vary from 20 cm to 230 cm around all sections in a circle. Figure 11 shows the calibration positions for a particular section in the scene. A black object was positioned over the red dots. The calibration environment is shown in Figure 12, in which the robot, the catadioptric system, and the object are presented. It is important to point out that the environment does not suffer from natural light variations; only artificial illumination was used, and the white floor allows for a high contrast with the black object.

Tables 5 and 6 show a statistical analysis of the experimental data. According to Figure 4, each object located in the scene had its projected position on the image calculated (in pixels) for 5 different orientations in the chosen section, in the form of mean distance and its standard deviation, summing up 55 positions in a section.

As expected in Section 5, the interpolation function has a monotonically increasing behavior. It is important to notice that, as an effect of the reflection characteristics of this system, for greater distances the objects appear smaller than in common acquisition systems (e.g., nonomnidirectional ones). That occurs due to the reflection angle for objects placed far away from the mirror. In this case, it can be observed that the variance values for each distance do not follow the monotonic behavior. This is because the error in distance estimation is not a function of the distance but is mainly determined by mirror's surface quality.

The direction of the detected object is determined by calculating the arctangent function using the estimated coordinates of the center of mass (of the detected object). Notice that the uncertainty in direction estimation is related to the uncertainty in object detection. To calculate the direction, the values in pixels have been used; therefore, both the distance estimation and direction estimation are independent tasks.

Figure 14 depicts the behavior of the pixel/centimeter transformation by using a polynomial interpolation for each one of the regions.

6.3. Validation Results. In order to demonstrate the system running in an actual scene, Figure 15 shows an example of the processing chain, in which Figure 15(a) represents the background image. Figure 15(b) shows an object around the mobile robot. Figure 15(c) depicts the background subtraction and the position of the center of mass. Finally, Figure 15(d) overlaps the current image and the detected center of mass.

Several experiments have been performed so as to evaluate the accuracy of the implemented system. To do that, three different objects (namely, A, B, and C) which corresponds to (a) a small cylindrical robot, (b) a pioneer mobile robot, and (c) the calibration object, respectively, were placed at different positions in front of the robot. Figure 16 depicts the objects used for testing the overall system. The distances and orientation between the center of the camera and the objects have been previously measured (the actual values) in the arena. Additionally, both the estimated distances and orientation were sent to the host (via RS 232 interface) and compared with the actual values.

Table 7 presents the location results and respective errors for each object. It can be observed that the proposed architecture achieves more accurate results when detecting the object A. It can be explained because the size and shape of the cylindrical robot produce a small shadow, leading to a better accurate. As expected, large approximation errors were achieved for large distances. For instance, results for localization of objects B and C show the largest errors (around 24% and 17%, resp.). This fact is explained given that the spherical mirror produces large distortions to the light rays reflected from the uppermost surface of the mirror. This distortion is produced by a compression effect, as the farther the object is, the smaller is its projection on the mirror surface.

Table 8 presents the orientation estimation for each object. Figure 17 uses occupation grids in a polar graph form for summarizing the achieved results of distance and direction estimation. The gray grid represents the estimated position of the object. As expected, the system produces large errors for large distances (see point 6 for objects B and C).

One can conclude that the omnidirectional system performs better for estimating distances than orientation. Notice that the calibration data (see Table 8) show large errors for orientation values. As explained in Section 4 the system requires a large contrast between background and objects. Therefore, when the system operates with a low contrast, some errors in the object borders are introduced. However, these errors can be overcome by using more efficient techniques for motion segmentation (e.g., optical flow).

6.4. Performance Analysis. Additionally, the same algorithm for motion detection was implemented in a PC, running at 2.2 GHz, 2.0 GB RAM using a real-time xPC Target OS from MathWorks. The average elapsed time for processing a 10×10 pixel image was around $138.1\,\mu s$, (value of the average TET (task execution time)). Thus, an output pixel is processed in $1.381\,\mu s$. Therefore, the proposed hardware architecture, operating at 10.2 MHz, achieves a speedup factor of 13.78 in comparison with the real-time software solution.

As cited in Section 3, several works have been developed to solve the problem of object's position estimation for real-time applications. Table 9 shows the comparison among some works and our approach. Each proposal uses different algorithms and image resolutions, leading to difficulty in the comparison task. Therefore, we have used the overall throughput (megapixels per second) as a comparison metric.

It is important to note that all systems listed in Table 9 have as output the estimated position of an object in the image. In this case, all listed systems have implemented FPGA-based hardware architectures to process the image and determine object's position.

7. Conclusions

This work has presented a FPGA-based omnidirectional vision system for mobile robotic applications. It takes advantage of a pipeline approach for processing the polar image, using a background subtraction algorithm. The overall latency of the motion detection architecture is 385.607 clock cycles, and after this latency, the system has a throughput of 26 frames per second (running at 10.2 MHz). The proposed architecture is suitable for robot localization, allowing to compute the distance between the robot and the surrounding objects.

The architectures were described in VHDL and Verilog and successfully implemented in a Cyclone II FPGA device. Synthesis results have demonstrated that the proposed hardware achieves an operational frequency around 10.2 MHz. In addition, the pipelined architecture allows the image to process one pixel per clock cycle after an initial delay. This fact demonstrated acceleration of 13, 78 times in comparison with the same algorithm in C using a xPC Target OS from MathWorks implementation running on a common desktop platform.

This work has also addressed several calibration problems related to omnidirectional vision systems (based on a catadioptric implementation) of mobile robotic applications, especially the application of a technique for detection of mobile objects for mirror calibration tasks. Experimental results show that the results are consistent with the expected ones.

Concerning our future work we intend to analyze the power consumption of the proposed architecture. It is an important issue in order to validate the effectiveness of the implemented algorithms for real-time image processing in portable applications.

Acknowledgments

The authors would like to thank CAPES Foundation and National Council of Scientific and Technological Development of Brazil-CNPq (processes 133501/2010-8 and 142033/2008-1) for the financial support of this work. Special thanks are to Altera Corp. for providing Quartus II Licenses and to DHW Engenharia e Representação for the partnership.

References

[1] R. Siegwart and I. Nourbakhsh, *Introduction to Autonomous Mobile Robots*, MIT Press, Cambridge, Mass, USA, 2004.

[2] L. Spacek and C. Burbridge, "Instantaneous robot self-localization and motion estimation with omnidirectional

vision," *Robotics and Autonomous Systems*, vol. 55, no. 9, pp. 667–674, 2007.

[3] J. Yudi Mori, D. Mũoz Arboleda, J. N. Arias Garcia, C. Llanos Quintero, and J. Motta, "FPGA-based image processing for omnidirectional vision on mobile robots," in *Proceedings of the 24th Symposium on Integrated Circuits and Systems Design*, pp. 113–118, João Pessoa, Brazil, 2011.

[4] E. Trucco and A. Verri, *Introductory Techniques for 3-D Computer Vision*, Prentice Hall, 1998.

[5] K. Daniilidis and C. Geyer, "Omnidirectional vision: theory and algorithms," in *Proceedings of the 15th International Conference on Pattern Recognition*, vol. 1, pp. 89–96, 2000.

[6] C. Geyer and K. Daniilidis, "Catadioptric camera calibration," in *Proceedings of the 17th IEEE International Conference on Computer Vision (ICCV '99)*, vol. 1, pp. 398–404, September 1999.

[7] G. Botella, M. Rodriguez, A. Garca, and E. Ros, "Neuromorphic configurable architecture for robust motion estimation," *International Journal of Reconfigurable Computing*, vol. 2008, Article ID 428265, 9 pages, 2008.

[8] Z. Wei, D. Lee, N. Brent, J. Archibald, and B. Edwards, "FPGA-based embedded motion estimation sensor," *International Journal of Reconfigurable Computing*, vol. 2008, Article ID 636145, 9 pages, 2008.

[9] K. Shimizu and S. Hirai, "CMOS+FPGA vision system for visual feedback of mechanical systems," in *Proceedings of the IEEE International Conference on Robotics and Automation (ICRA '06)*, pp. 2060–2065, May 2006.

[10] G. Saldaña-González and M. Arias-Estrada, "FPGA based acceleration for image processing applications," in *Image Processing*, 2009.

[11] Y. Tu and M. Ho, "Design and implementation of robust visual servoing control of an inverted pendulum with an FPGAbased image co-processor," *Mechatronics*, vol. 21, no. 7, pp. 1170–1182, 2011.

[12] T. Kryjak and M. Gorgoń, "Real-time implementation of moving object detection in video surveillance systems using FPGA," *Computer Science*, vol. 12, pp. 149–162, 2011.

[13] R. Rodriguez-Gomez, E. Fernandez-Sanchez, J. Diaz, and E. Ros, "FPGA implementation for real-time background subtraction based on horprasert model," *Sensors*, vol. 12, pp. 585–611, 2012.

[14] R. Chojecki and B. Siemiatkowska, "Mobile robot navigation based on omnidirectional sensor," in *Proceedings of the European Conference on Mobile Robots (ECMR '03)*, pp. 101–106, Radziejowice, Poland, September 2003.

[15] M. A. Vega-Rodríguez, A. Gómez-Iglesias, J. A. Gómez-Pulido, and J. M. Sánchez-Pérez, "Reconfigurable computing system for image processing via the internet," *Microprocessors and Microsystems*, vol. 31, pp. 498–515, 2007.

[16] F. Nava, D. Sciuto, M. D. Santambrogio et al., "Applying dynamic reconfiguration in the mobile robotics domain: a case study on computer vision algorithms," *ACM Transactions on Reconfigurable Technology and Systems*, vol. 4, no. 3, 2011.

[17] L. Chen, M. Zhang, B. Wang, Z. Xiong, and G. Cheng, "Real-time FPGA-based panoramic unrolling of high-resolution catadioptric omnidirectional images," in *Proceedings of the International Conference on Measuring Technology and Mechatronics Automation (ICMTMA '09)*, pp. 502–505, Hunan, China, April 2009.

[18] A. Gardel, A. Hernández, R. Miota, I. Bravo, and R. Mateos, "Correction of omnidirectional camera images using reconfigurable hardware," in *Proceedings of the 32nd Annual Conference on IEEE Industrial Electronics*, pp. 3403–3407, Paris, France, November 2006.

[19] B. Zhang, Z. Qi, J. Zhu, and Z. Cao, "Omnidirection image restoration based on spherical perspective projection," in *Proceedings of the IEEE Asia Pacific Conference on Circuits and Systems*, pp. 922–925, Macao, China, December 2008.

[20] T. Shu-ren, Z. Mao-jun, X. Zhi-hui, L. Le, and C. L. Dong, "Design and implementation of high-resolution omnidirectional vision system," *Chinese Journal of Video Engineering*, vol. 10, no. 1, pp. 1–6, 2008.

[21] A. Maeder, H. Bistry, and J. Zhang, "Towards intelligent autonomous vision systems—smart image processing for robotic applications," in *Proceedings of the IEEE International Conference on Robotics and Biomimetics (ROBIO '07)*, pp. 1081–1086, Sanya, China, December 2007.

[22] R. Benosman, E. Deforas, and J. Devars, "A new catadioptric sensor for the panoramic vision of mobile robots," in *Proceedings of the IEEE Workshop on Omnidirectional Vision*, pp. 112–116, 2000.

[23] J. Fabrizio, J.-P. Tarel, and R. Benosman, "Calibration of panoramic catadioptric sensors made easier," in *Proceedings of the 3rd Workshop on Omnidirectional Vision*, pp. 45–52, 2002.

[24] S. Ramalingam, P. Sturm, and S. K. Lodha, "Towards complete generic camera calibration," in *Proceedings of the IEEE Computer Society Conference on Computer Vision and Pattern Recognition (CVPR '05)*, vol. 1, pp. 1093–1098, June 2005.

[25] J. Y. Mori, C. Sánchez-Ferreira, D. M. Munoz, C. H. Llanos, and P. Berger, "An unified approach for convolution-based image filtering on reconfigurable systems," in *Proceedings of the 7th Southern Conference on Programmable Logic (SPL '11)*, pp. 63–68, Crdoba, Argentina, April 2011.

[26] J. Mori, *Implementação de técnicas de processamento de imagens no domínio espacial em sistemas reconfiguráveis*, M.S. thesis, Universidade de Brasília, Brasília, Brazil, 2010.

[27] D. M. Muñoz, D. F. Sanchez, C. H. Llanos, and M. Ayala-Rincón, "Tradeoff of FPGA design of a floating-point library for arithmetic operators," *Journal of Integrated Circuits and Systems*, vol. 5, no. 1, pp. 42–52, 2010.

5

HwPMI: An Extensible Performance Monitoring Infrastructure for Improving Hardware Design and Productivity on FPGAs

Andrew G. Schmidt,[1] Neil Steiner,[1] Matthew French,[1] and Ron Sass[2]

[1] *Information Sciences Institute, University of Southern California, 3811 North Fairfax Drive, Suite 200, Arlington, VA 22203, USA*
[2] *Reconfigurable Computing Systems Lab, ECE Department, UNC Charlotte, 9201 University City Boulevard, Charlotte, NC 28223, USA*

Correspondence should be addressed to Andrew G. Schmidt, aschmidt@isi.edu

Academic Editor: René Cumplido

Designing hardware cores for FPGAs can quickly become a complicated task, difficult even for experienced engineers. With the addition of more sophisticated development tools and maturing high-level language-to-gates techniques, designs can be rapidly assembled; however, when the design is evaluated on the FPGA, the performance may not be what was expected. Therefore, an engineer may need to augment the design to include performance monitors to better understand the bottlenecks in the system or to aid in the debugging of the design. Unfortunately, identifying what to monitor and adding the infrastructure to retrieve the monitored data can be a challenging and time-consuming task. Our work alleviates this effort. We present the Hardware Performance Monitoring Infrastructure (HwPMI), which includes a collection of software tools and hardware cores that can be used to profile the current design, recommend and insert performance monitors directly into the HDL or netlist, and retrieve the monitored data with minimal invasiveness to the design. Three applications are used to demonstrate and evaluate HwPMI's capabilities. The results are highly encouraging as the infrastructure adds numerous capabilities while requiring minimal effort by the designer and low resource overhead to the existing design.

1. Introduction

As hardware designers develop custom cores and assemble Systems-on-Chip (SoCs) targeting FPGAs, the challenge of the design meeting timing, fitting within the resource constraints, and balancing bandwidth and latency can lead to significant increases in development time. When a design does not meet a specific performance requirement, the designer typically must go back and manually add more custom logic to monitor the behavior of several components in the design. While this performance information can be used to better understand the inner workings of the system, as well as the interfaces between the subcomponents of the system, identifying and inserting infrastructure can quickly become a daunting task. Furthermore, the addition of the monitors may change the original behavior of the system, potentially obfuscating the identified performance bottleneck or design bug.

In this work, we focus on an extensible set of tools and hardware cores to enable a hardware designer to insert a minimally invasive performance monitoring infrastructure into an existing design, with little effort. The monitors are used in an introspective capacity, providing feedback about the design's performance under real workloads, while running on real devices. This paper presents our Hardware Performance Monitoring Infrastructure (HwPMI), which is designed to ease the identification, insertion, and retrieval of performance monitors and their associated data in developed systems.

The motivation for the creation and evaluation of this infrastructure stems from the inherent need to insert monitors into existing designs and to retrieve the data with minimal invasiveness to the system. Over the last several years we have been assembling a repository of performance monitors as new designs are built and tested. To increase a designer's productivity, we have put together a suite of software tools aimed at profiling existing designs and recommending and/or inserting performance monitors and the necessary hardware and software infrastructure. This work also leverages existing open-source work by including Torc (Tools for Open Reconfigurable Computing) to provide an efficient backend for reading, writing, and manipulating designs in EDIF format [1].

Included in HwPMI are the specific monitors, such as timers, state-machine trackers, component utilization, and so forth, along with a sophisticated monitoring network to retrieve each monitor's data all while requiring little user intervention. To evaluate HwPMI, three use cases show how existing designs can utilize HwPMI to quickly integrate and retrieve monitoring data on running systems. Moreover, HwPMI is flexible enough to support both high performance reconfigurable computing (HPRC), running on the Spirit cluster as part of the Reconfigurable Computing Cluster (RCC) [2] project at the University of North Carolina at Charlotte, and embedded reconfigurable systems running on a single board with limited compute resources. Several interesting results are discussed which support the importance of such a monitoring infrastructure. Finally, the tools and hardware cores presented here are being prepared for an open-source release in the hope of increasing and diversifying the types of monitors and the systems that will be able to utilize HwPMI.

The remainder of this paper is organized into the following sections: in Section 2 the background and related works are discussed. Section 3 details HwPMI's design and implementation, while the results and experiences of integrating the system into three applications are discussed in Section 4. Finally, in Section 5 the conclusion and future work are presented.

2. Background and Related Work

As FPGA resources increase in number and diversity with each device generation, researchers are exploring architectures to outperform previous implementations and to investigate new designs that were previously limited by the technology. Unfortunately, a designer trying to exploit the inherent parallelism of FPGAs is often faced with the nontrivial task of identifying system bottlenecks, performance drains, and design bugs in the system. The result is often the inclusion of custom hardware cores tasked with monitoring key locations in the system, such as interfaces to the network, memory, finite-state machines, and other resources such as FIFOs or custom pipelines.

This is especially true in the rapidly growing field of High Performance Reconfigurable Computing (HPRC). There are several research projects underway that investigate the use of multiple FPGAs in a high-performance computing context: RAMP, Maxwell, Axel, and Novo-G [3–6]. These projects and others, like the RCC Spirit cluster, seek to use many networked FPGAs to exploit the FPGA's potential on-chip parallelism, in order to solve complex problems faster than before.

2.1. Productivity and Monitoring Tools. Tools of some form are needed to help the designer manage the complexities associated with hardware design, such as timing requirements, resource limitations, routing, and so forth. FPGA

vendors provide many tools beyond synthesis and implementation that reduce development time, including component generators [7] that build mildly complex hardware cores, that is, single-precision floating point units and FIFOs. System generator tools like the Xilinx Base System Builder (BSB) Wizard [8] and the Altera System-on-Programmable-Chip (SoPC) Builder [9] help the designer construct a customizable base system with processors, memory interfaces, buses, and even some peripherals like UARTs and interrupt controllers. There are even tools that can help a designer debug running hardware in the same manner as with logic analyzers in a microelectronics lab [10, 11]. However, these virtual logic analyzers do not provide runtime feedback on the system's performance, and furthermore require specialized external equipment. In the case of ChipScope, each FPGA must be connected to a computer through JTAG. This limits its use in large scale designs, where debugging hundreds to thousands of FPGAs is a daunting task. While JTAG can support multiple devices in a single chain, there is additional latency as the number of devices in the chain increases. Of course, if JTAG were the only option, HwPMI could be inserted into the JTAG chain; at this time no such integration has been performed.

There are also several projects investigating ways to monitor FPGA systems. The Owl system monitoring framework presented in [12] uses hardware monitors in the FPGA fabric to snoop system transactions on memory, cache, buses, and so forth. This is done to avoid the performance penalty and intrusiveness of software-based monitoring schemes. Along similar lines [13] presents a performance analysis framework for FPGA-based systems that automates application-specific run-time measurements to provide a more complete view of the application core's performance to the designer. Source level (HDL) instrumentation is used to parse code and insert logic to extract desired data at runtime. The University of Florida proposed CARMA [14] as a framework to integrate hardware monitoring probes in designs at both the hardware and software layer. TimeTrial [15, 16] explores performance monitoring for streaming applications at the block level, which keeps it language agnostic and suitable for dealing with different platforms and clocks. FPGAs have also been used to emulate and speed up netlist level fault injection and fault monitoring frameworks to build resilient SoCs [17].

2.2. Tools for Open Reconfigurable Computing. Torc (Tools for Open Reconfigurable Computing) is a C++ open-source framework designed to simplify custom tool development and enable new research [18]. Torc's capabilities are built upon industry standard file formats, including EDIF and XDL, and come with support for a broad range of Xilinx devices. Research into reconfiguration or CAD tools with Torc can be validated in hardware or compared to mainstream tool performance. Developing and debugging these capabilities from scratch would take a significant amount of effort, but Torc provides them for free. Furthermore, the user can pick and choose the parts of Torc that are of interest to them, and ignore the rest. In fact, Torc was developed for precisely the kinds of research purposes that HwPMI is

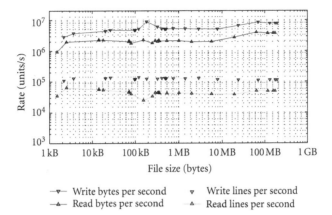

FIGURE 1: Torc's Generic Netlist API I/O Performance. This log-log plot shows reasonably linear I/O performance for EDIF file sizes ranging from 1 KB to 175 MB. On a 2.8 GHz quad-core Xeon, the API reads 45-thousand lines per second, and 2.3 Megabytes per second on average. The largest of these files contains over 150,000 instances and over 200,000 nets. Shape differences between the two curves are most likely due to different name lengths in the EDIF files.

aimed at addressing—situations in which the mainstream tools could not provide the required functionality.

Torc consists of four core Application Programming Interfaces (APIs) and a collection of CAD tools built upon them. The APIs are the Generic Netlist API, the Physical Netlist API, the Device Architecture API, and the Bitstream Frames API. The main CAD tools are the router and placer. For HwPMI, the appeal of Torc's generic netlist is that it allows us to insert performance monitors without having to modify the design's HDL source. The Generic Netlist API supports netlists that are not mapped to physical hardware and provides full EDIF 2.0.0 reading, writing, and editing capability. The internal object model is flexible enough to support other netlist formats, if parsers and exporters are provided. Because the Generic Netlist API supports generic EDIF, it is usable for Xilinx FPGAs, non-Xilinx FPGAs, ASICs, or even circuit boards.

Early versions of HwPMI interacted with VHDL source to identify and insert performance monitors and the necessary infrastructure into existing designs. Torc is being added to expand beyond VHDL and to ensure that the original source remains unmodified after it has been profiled and evaluated—only the resulting synthesized netlists are modified. Another reason for migrating to Torc is its efficiency and scalability: a plot of EDIF read and write performance is provided in Figure 1. Using Torc to interact with EDIF has been shown to be far more efficient than using VHDL parsing and insertion tools.

Another well-established CAD tool for reconfigurable computing is VPR [19, 20], a place-and-route tool that remains widely used more than a decade after its inception, and now forms the base of the broader VTR [21]. However, VPR has traditionally not supported EDIF, XDL, or actual device architectures. Some of those pieces—EDIF in particular—are available from Brigham Young University (BYU), albeit in Java rather than C++. More recently, BYU developed an open-source Java tool named RapidSmith that fully supports XDL and Xilinx device databases [22].

3. Design

The performance monitoring infrastructure assembled as part of this work builds upon our previous research in the area of resilient high-performance reconfigurable computing. In [23] a System Monitoring Infrastructure was developed and a proof-of-concept was presented to address the question: "how do we know when a node has failed?" In [24] the System Monitor functionality was significantly improved, adding a Context Interface (CIF) along with dedicated hardware cores for checkpoint/restart capability of both the processor and hardware core's state. In addition, a framework for performance monitoring was presented in [25], which this work extends to provide a designer with the capability of inserting specific performance monitors into an existing hardware design. Specifically, this article extends our previous works with a more thorough design and evaluation of HwPMI and further discusses how Torc is incorporated for efficient netlist manipulations.

Unlike conventional approaches where a designer must manually create and insert monitors into their design, including the mechanisms to extract the monitored results, this work analyzes existing designs and generates the necessary infrastructure automatically. The result is a large repository of predesigned monitors, interfaces, and tools to aid the designer in rapidly integrating the monitoring infrastructure into existing designs. This work also provides the designer with the necessary software infrastructure to retrieve the performance data at user defined intervals during the execution of the system.

3.1. Hardware Performance Monitor Infrastructure. The HwPMI tool flow, which will be discussed within this section, consists of several stages, as depicted in Figure 2. In addition to the tools, the monitoring infrastructure consists of several hardware cores that, for the high-performance reconfigurable computing (HPRC) system, spans a variety of elements both in the system and across the cluster. The infrastructure to support the HPRC monitoring system is

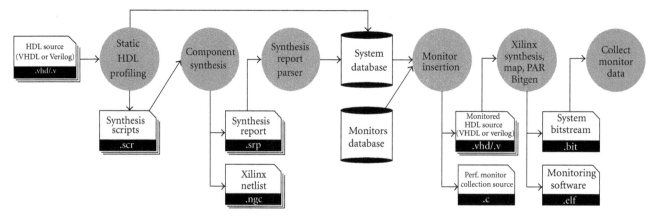

FIGURE 2: Hardware Performance Monitoring Infrastructure's Tool Flow.

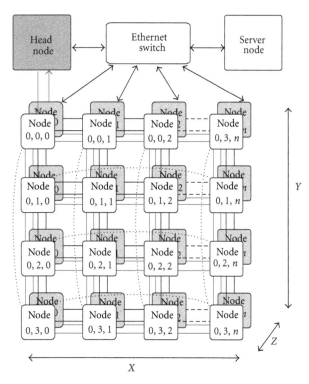

FIGURE 3: Block diagram of Spirit cluster's HwPMI.

comprised of three types of nodes and two networks, as illustrated in Figure 3. Node types include a server node, a head node, and many worker nodes. With the exception of the server, all nodes are Xilinx ML410 development boards with Virtex4 FX60 devices. 64 FPGAs are connected via six direct-connect links to configure the Spirit cluster's primary network as a custom high-speed 3-dimensional torus [26]. Two more links on the custom network board are used to form the sideband network, which is used by the HwPMI to send and receive performance monitoring commands and data. More details regarding the networks are presented in [24].

Each worker node is running an application-specific SoC which includes the HwPMI hardware cores. These cores can

be seen in Figure 4 as the System Monitor Hub, HwPMI Interfaces, Context Interface, Performance Monitor Hub, and Performance Monitor Cores. The System Monitor Hub acts as an intermediary to decode incoming requests for performance data. Each hardware core connects to the System Monitor Hub via a software-generated Context Interface (CIF). The CIF connects to the Performance Monitor Hub which in turn aggregates all of the performance monitor core data within the hardware core.

Initial HwPMI development was targeted to support high-performance reconfigurable computing systems, such as Spirit. However, the tools and techniques are also easily adapted to support more traditional embedded system development with FPGAs. In fact, the sideband network can be replaced with a bus interface to give an embedded system access to its own performance monitoring data. While this introspective monitoring does add to the runtime overhead of the system, designers can now specify the interface mechanism to HwPMI. PowerPC 405, PowerPC 440, and MicroBlaze systems are supported through interfaces with the Processor Local Bus. An embedded system example is shown in Figure 5, where a separate SoC provides independent monitoring of hardware cores. In this case, resources are required for the extra soft-processor, buses, and peripheral IP cores, in addition to the monitoring infrastructure. The benefit of this approach is that no modifications are necessary in the original Device Under Test (DUT)—no changes to the software running on the DUT's processor— so the performance overhead is minimized.

3.2. Static HDL Profiling. The process of identifying performance monitors to be inserted into an existing design begins with Static HDL Profiling, shown in Figure 2. To start, HwPMI parses the existing hardware design's HDL files in order to collect information pertaining to the construction of the system. This includes not only the design's modular hierarchy, but also the specific interfaces between components. For example, a hardware core may consist of several FIFOs, BRAMs, and finite-state machines, as well as a slave interface to the system bus. The Static HDL Profiler identifies these components and interfaces in order to assemble a list of recommended performance monitors to be inserted.

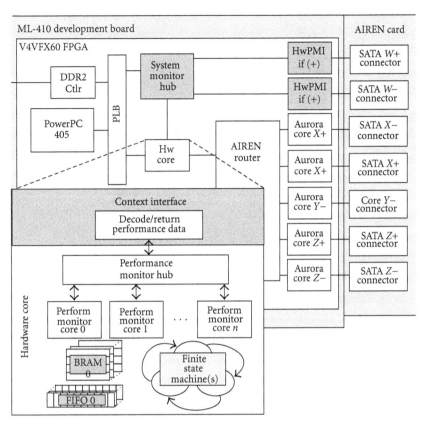

FIGURE 4: Block diagram of FPGA node's HwPMI.

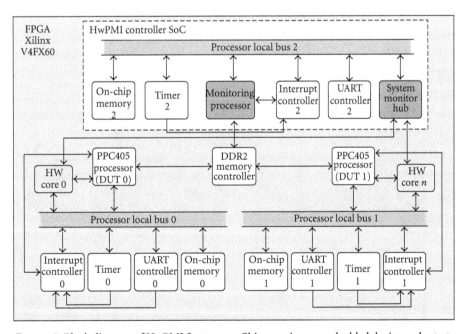

FIGURE 5: Block diagram of HwPMI System-on-Chip running on embedded device under test.

Static HDL profiling is similar in principle to software profiling (i.e., gprof) in that all of the critical information is collected in advance, and the system runtime performance information is captured during execution.

The Static HDL Profiler is comprised of three software tools written in Python, to more autonomously profile the original design. Presently, HwPMI supports the Xilinx Synthesis Tool (XST) and designs written in VHDL; however, work is underway to extend beyond XST and VHDL through the use of Torc. The first tool, HwPMI Core Parser, provides parsing capabilities for VHDL files. The designer invokes the parser on the specific design through the command

```
Collatz_core_0_wrapper:
   Interfaces:
      (1) plb_slave
   Components:
      (1) plb_slave_attachment
      (2) user_logic
      (3) collatz_kernel
            Registers (collatz_kernel):
               64-bit register for signal <n>
               32-bit register for signal <steps_i>
            FSMs:
               <FSM_0> for signal<fsm_cs >
   Signals:
      (1) PLB IPIC Signals
```

FIGURE 6: Sample output of HwPMI System Analyzer tool on the Collatz Design, identifying the components, registers, statements, and interfaces to the core.

```
Recommended Performance Monitors:
Top-Level Entity: collatz_core
collatz_core:
   plb46_slave_single_i
      NONE
   user_logic
      Utilization Monitor
      Interrupt Timer Monitor
      PLB SLV IPIF Monitor
   collatz_kernel
      Finite State Machine Profiler
```

FIGURE 7: Sample output of performance monitor recommendation tool.

line and can specify a specific VHDL source to evaluate. The parser identifies the entity's structure in terms of ports, signals, finite-state machines, and instantiated components. The parser works by analyzing the VHDL source file and uses pattern matching to decompose the component into its basic blocks. The parser is only responsible for the identification of the VHDL component's structure. The results are then passed into a Python Pickle for rapid integration with the remaining tools.

Next, the HwPMI System Analyzer tool iteratively parses the design to identify the different interfaces, such as bus slaves, bus masters, direct memory access, and Xilinx LocalLink. This is done at a higher level than the HwPMI Core Parser which more specifically analyzes individual IP Cores. Figure 6 shows the output of the HwPMI System Analyzer for one of the systems evaluated in this work, the Collatz Design. More commonly a designer would use the System Analyzer because it can support iterating through an entire design, once given a list of all of the source files. On the command line the designer invokes the tool with a project file that lists all of the VHDL source file locations. The user also specifies the top-level entity for the design.

To support Xilinx Platform Studio (XPS) IP core development, the HwPMI Parse PCORE tool is used to parse Xilinx PCORE directory files: The Microprocessor Description (MPD), Peripheral Analysis Order (PAO), and Black Box Description (BBD) files, along with any Xilinx CoreGen (XCO) project files. This enables a designer to migrate profiled cores to other XPS systems with minimal effort. Furthermore, monitors can be written based on the Xilinx CoreGen project files to provide monitoring of components such as generated FIFOs, memory controllers, or floating point units, if so desired.

3.3. Component Synthesis. The next stage is Component Synthesis where the original hardware design is synthesized prior to any insertion of performance monitors. The purpose of synthesizing the design at this point is to retrieve

additional design details from the synthesis reports including subcomponents, resource utilization, timing requirements, and behavior. This leverages the synthesis tool output to supplement the Static HDL Profiling stage by more readily identifying finite state machines and flip-flops in the design. All of the configuration information and synthesis results are available for performance monitor recommendation/ insertion.

Three tools have been developed to specifically support the designer in the Component Synthesis stage. These tools automatically synthesize, parse, and aggregate the individual component utilization, resource utilization, and timing information data for the designer. The first tool is the Iterative Component Synthesis tool which runs the synthesis scripts for each of the components in the design. The second tool is the Parse Component Synthesis Reports tool: it runs after all of the system components have been synthesized, and collects a wealth of information about each component from the associated synthesis report file (SRP). This information includes the registers, FIFOs, Block RAMs, and finite-state machines (FSM), in addition to all subcomponents. The third tool is the Aggregate System Synthesis Data tool which is used to aggregate all of the data collected as part of the Parse Component Synthesis Reports tool. These tools collectively identify the system's interconnects, processors, memory controllers, and network interfaces, in addition to the designer's custom compute cores.

3.4. Insertion of Performance Monitors. At this point the design has been analyzed in order to recommend specific performance monitors for insertion. The designer can choose to accept any number of these recommendations, from a report like that shown in Figure 7 The monitors are stored in a central repository which can be augmented by the designer if a specific monitoring capability is not available. The monitors all are encapsulated by a Performance Monitor Interface, shown in Figure 8, which connects the monitor to the Performance Monitor Hub and includes a finite-state machine to retrieve the specific performance monitor data and forward it to the hub. To aid in the insertion of HwPMI into existing hardware designs, a software tool has been

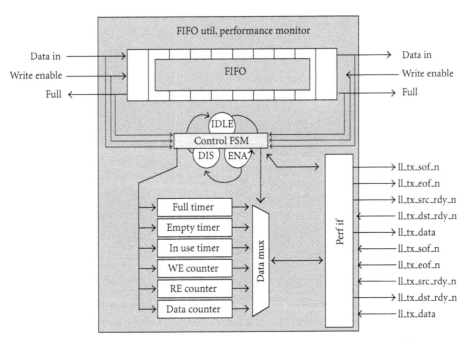

FIGURE 8: Block diagram of performance monitor interface connecting to a simple configurable timer monitor.

developed, the HwPMI System Insertion tool. The purpose of this tool is to insert the System Monitor Hub and Sideband Network Interface cores into the top-level design. The tool inserts the monitors directly into the VHDL source, prior to synthesis, MAP, and PAR.

It is important to emphasize that the HwPMI flow does not intelligently insert a subset of monitors when the available resources are depleted. Future work is looking into ways to weight monitors such that HwPMI can insert more important monitors; however, presently HwPMI recommends the available monitors that can be inserted into the design and it is up to the designer to choose the subset that will provide the best feedback versus resource availability trade-off.

When a performance monitor is created there is a set of criteria that must also be included to allow the recommendation to take place. For example, there is a PLB Slave Interface performance monitor which specifically monitors reads and writes to the hardware core's slave registers. All signals are identified during profiling, but until these signals are matched against a list of predetermined signals, there is no specific way to identify when those signals are being written to. Another example considers finite-state machines: once an FSM has been identified by the system, it is trivial for the respective performance monitor to be recommended for insertion. The actual insertion of the performance monitors is done at the HDL level. Each performance monitor's entity description and instance are automatically generated and inserted in the HDL.

3.5. Torc Netlist Modifications. The initial development of HwPMI focused on parsing designs written in VHDL and inserting monitors directly into the VHDL source. The advantage of this approach is the portability of the monitored design. However, by leveraging tools such as Torc, the

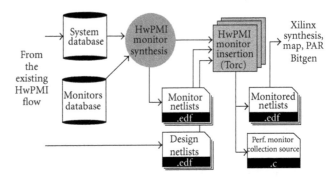

FIGURE 9: Insertion of Torc into Hardware Performance Monitoring Infrastructure's Tool Flow.

insertion can be performed at the netlist level. The HwPMI tool flow has now been augmented to support inserting the monitoring infrastructure into either the VHDL source or into synthesized netlists, based on a user parameter. Continued work is underway to perform the netlist profiling with Torc instead of relying on the HDL parsing tools. Specifically, Torc inserts the monitors into the EDIF design. Figure 9 illustrates how Torc is currently used in the HwPMI flow to avoid modifying the VHDL source. The HwPMI flow remains identical throughout the initial stages, but once the monitors have been selected for insertion, Torc is used to merge them into the synthesized netlists. Torc provides a fast and efficient mechanism to generate modified design netlists with the monitoring infrastructure inserted.

3.6. Retrieval of Monitored Data. Once the design is running, it is necessary to retrieve the performance monitoring data with minimal invasion to the system. This is accomplished through the use of the sideband network in the HPRC system

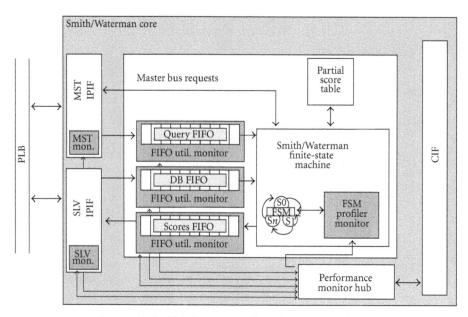

FIGURE 10: Smith/Waterman core's performance monitors.

or the HwPMI SoC in an embedded system. The head node issues requests to retrieve data from a node, core, or a specific hardware monitor anytime the application is running. To aid in the retrieval, the Performance Monitor Collection tool assembles the entire system's performance monitoring data structure for the head node to use for runtime data collection. This data is stored in a *C* struct that is generated for the specific design. Also available are subroutines for the head node to automatically collect and report each monitor's data back to the designer. Presently, the data that is retrieved must be manually evaluated by the designer to make design modifications, if deemed necessary. In HPRC systems this monitoring data can be fed into SDAflow, a tool developed in [27] to reallocate the resource utilization along with memory and network interfaces.

4. Results

Three applications are used to demonstrate our HwPMI tool flow: single precision matrix-matrix multiplication, a hardware implementation of the Smith/Waterman `FLOCAL_ALIGN()`, and a hardware implementation of the Collatz Conjecture core. This section will highlight different use cases of HwPMI in these applications.

4.1. Matrix-Matrix Multiplication. Matrix-Matrix Multiplication (MMM) is a basic algebraic operation where two matrices, *A* and *B*, are multiplied together to form the resultant matrix *C*. This operation is highly parallel but is very demanding upon the memory hierarchy. During Static HDL Profiling the MMM hardware core successfully identified the following subcomponents: `plb_slave_ipif`, `user_logic`, `mac_array`, thirty-two `mac_units`, and eighteen 32-bit × 512 deep FIFOs. From these components the static HDL parser correctly identified 25 software-addressable registers that were connected via the PLB's

IPIF by tracing from the PLB's address and data signals to the core's registers set and accessed by these signals. These registers are used partly for control and also for data inputs and outputs which can be monitored via HwPMI to provide processor and hardware accelerator interface efficiency.

Three sets of performance monitors were selected and inserted into the MMM core: Firstly, for the PLB slave IPIF, to monitor the efficiency of the transfers from the processor. Secondly, for the eighteen FIFOs to monitor capacity and determine if more buffer resources should be allocated in the future to improve performance. And thirdly, for the utilization of the core itself, to monitor performance and determine how much time the core spends on actual computation versus I/O. The results indicate the largest bottleneck in the current design is the PLB slave IPIF. The processor spends over 98% of the total execution time transferring the matrix data and results into and out of the MMM hardware core. Furthermore, the results for the FIFOs showed very low overall utilization, which indicates that the FIFO depth can be reduced.

4.2. Smith/Waterman. The second design evaluated with HwPMI is a hardware-accelerated implementation of the Smith/Waterman algorithm, commonly used in protein and nucleotide sequence alignments [28]. The particular implementation on the FPGA was developed as a proof of concept [29] for accelerating the `FLOCAL_ALIGN()` function of the *SSEARCH* program—an implementation of the Smith/Waterman algorithm from the *FASTA35* code package [30].

From the Static HDL Profiling and Component Synthesis stages, six performance monitors were identified for inclusion into the Smith/Waterman hardware core. Figure 10 shows a high-level block diagram of the performance monitors in their locations relative to the Smith/Waterman hardware core.

TABLE 1: Performance monitor results for PLB SLV IPIF.

Register	Original		Modified	
name	# Reads	# Writes	# Reads	# Writes
Control_reg	0	186	0	186
Core_status	29540	0	29540	0
aa1	0	2095745	0	2095745
n1	0	2095838	0	93
n0	0	2095838	0	93
GG	0	2095838	0	93
HH	0	2095838	0	93
f_str_waa_s	0	2095838	0	93
score	186	0	186	0
ssj	0	2095838	0	93
Counter_idle	186	0	186	0
Counter_work	186	0	186	0

```
ssearch->aa1 = *aa1p;
if (only_once == 0) {
    ssearch->n1 = n1;
    ssearch->n0 = n0;
    ssearch->GG = GG;
    ssearch->HH = HH;
    ssearch->f_str_waa_s = PWA_BASE;
    ssearch->ssj = SS_BASE;
    /* ADDED MISSING GUARD HERE: */
    only_once = 1;
}
```

FIGURE 11: Modification made to original dropgsw2.c.

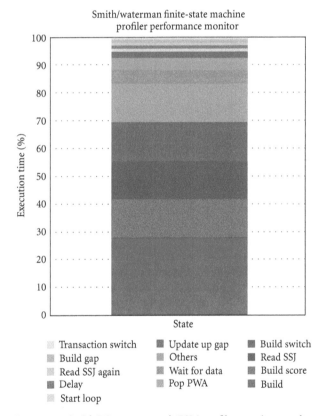

FIGURE 12: Smith/Waterman core's FSM profiler monitor results.

The first performance monitor identifies the number of writes to the software-addressable registers in the Smith/Waterman hardware core via the PLB Slave interface (PLB SLV IPIF), the results of which are listed in Table 1. In addition to the register name, number of reads and number of writes, Table 1 also presents these reads and writes when run in Original and Modified modes. The performance monitoring data indicated that several software registers were being written to unnecessarily, and the modified version of the application eliminates these extra writes. This demonstrates the benefit of HwPMI for debugging: the results quickly revealed that the software application was missing a guard, as shown in Figure 11.

Also identified by HwPMI were additional performance monitors to evaluate the PLB Master interface (PLB MST IPIF), which identified that only off-chip memory transactions were performed by the core. Moreover, the off-chip memory transactions were 118,144 read-only requests, which is a significant number of transfers and warrants the evaluation of a DMA interface. The designer could also adapt the core to leverage an alternative interface, such as the Native Port Interface (NPI), to reduce memory access latency, increase bandwidth, and reduce the PLB contention.

An FSM profiler performance monitor was added that provides feedback in the form of a histogram, to identify the percentage of time each FSM state is active. Figure 12 presents the breakdown of the time in each state. This shows that BUILD is the longest running state, accounting for 27.67% of the execution time. The next four states, BUILD_SCORE, READ_SSJ, BUILD_SWITCH, POP_PWAA, each occupies ~13.8%. Thirteen of the remaining states account for less than 1% each, and have been group together in the OTHERS category. Overall, this profiling data should

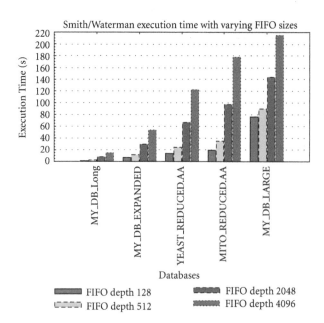

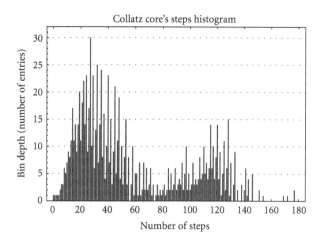

FIGURE 14: Collatz core's histogram of steps.

FIGURE 13: Smith/Waterman's performance with varying FIFO depths.

more quickly focus the designer's attention on the BUILD state, to determine if there is a more efficient way to implement this state.

Another useful feature of HwPMI is its ability to evaluate designs with different resource utilizations. Designers often find themselves adding buffers or FIFOs into designs without knowing a priori how large they should be. In these cases, HwPMI can collect run-time data as a designer modifies the FIFO depth. Sometimes these modifications can reveal interesting design tradeoffs, such as those shown in Figure 13, where a design utilizing smaller parallel buffers runs more efficiently than one using fewer larger buffers. In order to collect this data, a designer simply modifies the FIFO depth, and HwPMI collects the information at user defined intervals.

4.3. Collatz Conjecture. The third application used in our HwPMI evaluation is Collatz. The Collatz Conjecture states that given a natural number, it is possible reduce that number to one, by either dividing by two when even, or multiplying by three and adding one when odd [31]. For even numbers the resulting calculation reduces the size in half; however, for odd numbers the new number produced is greater than the original number. Thus, it is not obvious that it will converge to one. For example, given a small number such as $n = 3$, seven iterations are required to reduce n to one.

The performance monitor data is collected with the assistance of HwPMI. In addition to the utilization and interface performance monitors, an additional monitor was added that yielded a highly beneficial result. This is an example of supplemental data collection. When a designer needs to collect additional information, HwPMI offers the ability to add custom monitors without the need to augment how the system will retrieve the data. This can be especially

useful for quick one-off data that might only be useful for a short period of time. Rather than manually adding the infrastructure to the original core, only to remove it later—or retain it and waste resources—HwPMI can collect the data quickly and efficiently. Figure 14 shows a histogram of the number of steps taken for each input number to be reduced to one.

Another interesting monitor is the processor interrupt monitor. For latency sensitive applications with processor-to-hardware core communication, an interrupt is often used. However, configuring the interrupt or optimizing the interrupt service routines is critical. In the case of Collatz the time for the processor to respond to a single interrupt was measured as $\approx 11.12\,\mu s$.

4.4. Resource Utilization. Finally, we present the resource utilization of HwPMI. Our goal is to be minimally invasive both in terms of processing overhead and resource utilization overhead. Listed in Table 2 are some of the performance monitor cores that have been used in the three applications. This includes varying sizes of the monitors to show the overall scalability. While the individual monitor's utilization is heavily dependent on the function of the monitor, we show that with very low overhead HwPMI can be added to a design. Especially when compared to a design that requires the addition of a bus interface to a hardware core for performance data retrieval, HwPMI offers an attractive alternative. Furthermore, the overhead of the hardware monitor interface, which is 34 Slice FFs and 74 4-input LUTs on the V4FX60 FPGA, makes the standard monitor infrastructure of HwPMI very appealing compared to custom monitoring cores.

5. Conclusion

The Hardware Performance Monitoring Infrastructure (HwPMI) presented in this work expedites the insertion of a minimally invasive performance monitoring networks into existing hardware designs. The goal is to increase designer

TABLE 2: Example of HwMPI's resource utilization on V4FX60.

Component	Configuration	FFs (%)	LUTs (%)
Performance monitor hub	1 port	14 (0.03%)	70 (0.14%)
Performance monitor hub	2 ports	17 (0.03%)	78 (0.15%)
Performance monitor hub	4 ports	21 (0.04%)	153 (0.30%)
Performance monitor hub	8 ports	21 (0.04%)	250 (0.49%)
Performance monitor hub	16 ports	23 (0.05%)	419 (0.83%)
Timer monitor	1 32-bit timer	37 (0.07%)	96 (0.19%)
Match counter monitor	1 64-bit counter	67 (0.13%)	109 (0.22%)
Match counter monitor	2 64-bit counters	132 (0.26%)	207 (0.41%)
Match counter monitor	16 64-bit counters	1034 (2.05%)	1593 (3.15%)
FIFO monitor	1 32-bit FIFO	402 (0.80%)	594 (1.17%)
Histogram monitor	512 Bins	20 (0.04%)	3207 (6.34%)
Finite state machine monitor	12 states	775 (1.53%)	1266 (2.50%)
Finite state machine monitor	64 states	4116 (8.14%)	6332 (12.52%)
System monitor hub	1 port (1 Hw Core)	212 (0.42%)	513 (1.01%)
System monitor hub	2 ports (2 Hw Cores)	213 (0.42%)	565 (1.12%)
System monitor hub	4 ports (4 Hw Cores)	216 (0.43%)	691 (1.37%)
System monitor hub	8 ports (8 Hw Cores)	224 (0.44%)	911 (1.80%)
System monitor hub	16 port (16 Hw Cores)	230 (0.45%)	1369 (2.71%)

productivity by analyzing the existing design and automatically inserting monitors with the necessary infrastructure to retrieve the monitored data from the system. As a result of HwPMI the designer can focus on the development of the hardware core rather than trying to include front-end application support to monitor performance. Toward this goal, a collection of hardware cores have been assembled, and a series of software tools have been written to parse the existing design and recommend and/or insert hardware monitors directly into the source HDL.

HwPMI also integrates with an existing sideband network to retrieve the performance monitor results in High Performance Reconfigurable Computing without requiring modifications to the original application. Embedded systems can leverage HwPMI through a dedicated System-on-Chip controller which reduces run-time overhead on existing processors in the system. This work demonstrated HwPMI's capabilities across three applications, highlighting several unique features of the infrastructure.

This work also leverages Torc to provide netlist manipulations quickly and efficiently, in place of the original HDL modifications [25] which were limited to VHDL and were less efficient. Future work will integrate Torc more fully into the tool flow, replacing the static HDL analysis in favor of netlist analysis. In addition, HwPMI is being prepared for an open-source release which includes the tool flow and hardware IP core repository of both the monitoring infrastructure and performance monitor cores.

Acknowledgments

This material is based upon work supported by the Defense Advanced Research Projects Agency (DARPA) under Contract No. HR001-11-C-0041. Any opinions, findings and conclusions or recommendations expressed in this material are those of the author(s) and do not necessarily reflect the views of the Defense Advanced Research Projects Agency (DARPA). DARPA Distribution Statement A. Approved for Public Release, Distribution Unlimited.

References

[1] "Torc: Tools for Open Reconfigurable Computing," 2012, http://torc.isi.edu/.

[2] R. Sass, W. V. Kritikos, A. G. Schmidt et al., "Reconfigurable Computing Cluster (RCC) project: investigating the feasibility of FPGA-based petascale computing," in *Proceedings of the 15th Annual IEEE Symposium on Field-Programmable Custom Computing Machines (FCCM '07)*, pp. 127–140, IEEE Computer Society, April 2007.

[3] D. Burke, J. Wawrzynek, K. Asanovic et al., "RAMP Blue: implementation of a Manycore 1008 Processor System," in *Proceedings of the Reconfigurable Systems Summer Institute 2008 (RSSI '08)*, 2008.

[4] R. Baxter, S. Booth, M. Bull et al., "Maxwell—a 64 FPGA supercomputer," in *Proceedings of the 2nd NASA/ESA Conference on Adaptive Hardware and Systems (AHS '07)*, pp. 287–294, August 2007.

[5] P. P. Kuen Hung Tsoi, A. Tse, and W. Luk, "Programming framework for clusters with heterogeneous accelerators," in *International Workshop on Highly-Efficient Accelerators and Reconfigurable Technologies*, 2010.

[6] NSF Center for High Performance Reconfigurable Computing (CHREC), "Novo-g: Adaptively custom research supercomputer," April 2005.

[7] Xilinx, Inc., "Xilinx CORE Generator System," July 2011, http://www.xilinx.com/tools/coregen.htm.

[8] Xilinx, Inc., *Embedded System Tools Reference Manual EDK 10.1*, 2010.

[9] Altera Corporation, *System-on-Programmable-Chip (SOPC) Builder User Guide (UG-01096-1.0)*, 2010.

[10] Xilinx, Inc., "ChipScope Pro and the Serial I/O Toolkit," http://www.xilinx.com/tools/cspro.htm.

[11] Altera Corporation, "Design Debugging Using the SignalTap II Embedded Logic Analyzer," http://www.altera.com/literature/hb/qts/qts_qii53009.pdf.

[12] M. Schulz, B. S. White, S. A. McKee, H.-H. S. Lee, and J. Jeitner, "Owl: next generation system monitoring," in *Proceedings of the 2nd Conference on Computing Frontiers*, pp. 116–124, ACM, May 2005.

[13] S. Koehler, J. Curreri, and A. D. George, "Performance analysis challenges and framework for high-performance reconfigurable computing," *Parallel Computing*, vol. 34, no. 4-5, pp. 217–230, 2008.

[14] R. A. Deville, I. A. Troxel, and A. D. George, "Performance monitoring for run-time management of reconfigurable devices," in *Proceedings of the 5th International Conference on Engineering of Reconfigurable Systems and Algorithms (ERSA '05)*, pp. 175–181, June 2005.

[15] J. M. Lancaster, J. D. Buhler, and R. D. Chamberlain, "Efficient runtime performance monitoring of FPGA-based applications," in *Proceedings of the IEEE International SOC Conference (SOCC '09)*, pp. 23–28, September 2009.

[16] J. M. Lancaster and R. D. Chamberlain, "Crossing timezones in the timetrial performance monitor," in *Proceedings of the Symposium on Application Accelerators in High Performance Computing*, 2010.

[17] A. Pellegrini, K. Constantinides, D. Zhang, S. Sudhakar, V. Bertacco, and T. Austin, "Crash test: a fast high-fidelity FPGA-based resiliency analysis framework," in *Proceedings of the 26th IEEE International Conference on Computer Design (ICCD '08)*, pp. 363–370, October 2008.

[18] N. Steiner, A. Wood, H. Shojaei, J. Couch, P. Athanas, and M. French, "Torc: towards an open-source tool flow," in *Proceedings of the 19th ACM/SIGDA International Symposium on Field Programmable Gate Arrays (FPGA '11)*, pp. 41–44, March 2011.

[19] V. Betz and J. Rose, "VPR: a new packing, placement and routing tool for FPGA research," in *Proceedings of the 7th International Workshop on Field-Programmable Logic and Applications*, W. Luk, P. Y. K. Cheung, and M. Glesner, Eds., vol. 1304 of *Lecture Notes in Computer Science*, pp. 213–222, Springer, 1997.

[20] J. Luu, I. Kuon, P. Jamieson et al., "VPR 5.0: FPGA CAD and architecture exploration tools with single-driver routing, heterogeneity and process scaling," in *Proceedings of the 7th ACM SIGDA International Symposium on Field-Programmable Gate Arrays (FPGA '09)*, pp. 133–142, February 2009.

[21] J. Rose, J. Luu, C. W. Yu et al., "The VTR project: architecture and CAD for FPGAs from verilog to routing," in *Proceedings of the 20th ACM/SIGDA International Symposium on Field-Programmable Gate Arrays*, pp. 77–86, 2012.

[22] C. Lavin, M. Padilla, P. Lundrigan, B. Nelson, and B. Hutchings, "Rapid prototyping tools for FPGA designs: Rapid-Smith," in *Proceedings of the 2010 International Conference on Field-Programmable Technology (FPT '10)*, pp. 353–356, December 2010.

[23] B. Huang, A. G. Schmidt, A. A. Mendon, and R. Sass, "Investigating resilient high performance reconfigurable computing with minimally-invasive system monitoring," in *Proceedings of the 4th International Workshop on High-Performance Reconfigurable Computing Technology and Applications (HPRCTA '10)*, pp. 1–8, November 2010.

[24] A. G. Schmidt, B. Huang, R. Sass, and M. French, "Checkpoint/restart and beyond: resilient high performance computing with FPGAs," in *Proceedings of the 19th IEEE International Symposium on Field-Programmable Custom Computing Machines (FCCM '11)*, pp. 162–169, May 2011.

[25] A. G. Schmidt and R. Sass, "Improving design productivity with a hardware performance monitoring infrastructure," in *Proceedings of the 6th Annual International Conference on Reconfigurable Computing and FPGAs*, 2011.

[26] A. G. Schmidt, W. V. Kritikos, R. R. Sharma, and R. Sass, "AIREN: a novel integration of on-chip and off-chip FPGA networks," in *Proceedings of the IEEE Symposium on Field Programmable Custom Computing Machines (FCCM '09)*, pp. 271–274, April 2009.

[27] A. G. Schmidt, *Productively scaling hardware designs over increasing resources using a systematic design analysis approach [Ph.D. thesis]*, The University of North Carolina at Charlotte, 2011.

[28] T. F. Smith and M. S. Waterman, "Identification of common molecular subsequences," *Journal of Molecular Biology*, vol. 147, no. 1, pp. 195–197, 1981.

[29] S. Ganesh, *Implementation of the smith-waterman algorithm on fpgas [Ph.D. thesis]*, University of North Carolina at Charlotte, 2009.

[30] W. R. Pearson, "FASTA Sequence Comparison at the University of Virginia," July 2011, http://fasta.bioch.virginia.edu/fasta_www2/.

[31] J. C. Lagarias, "The 3x+1 problem and its generalizations," *American Mathematical Monthly*, pp. 3–23, 1985.

6

A Coarse-Grained Reconfigurable Architecture with Compilation for High Performance

Lu Wan,[1] Chen Dong,[2] and Deming Chen[1]

[1] *ECE Illinois, University of Illinois at Urbana-Champaign, Urbana, IL 61801-2918, USA*
[2] *Magma Design Automation, Inc., San Jose, CA 95110, USA*

Correspondence should be addressed to Deming Chen, dchen@illinois.edu

Academic Editor: Kentaro Sano

We propose a *fast data relay* (FDR) mechanism to enhance existing CGRA (*coarse-grained reconfigurable architecture*). FDR can not only provide multicycle data transmission in concurrent with computations but also convert resource-demanding inter-processing-element global data accesses into local data accesses to avoid communication congestion. We also propose the supporting compiler techniques that can efficiently utilize the FDR feature to achieve higher performance for a variety of applications. Our results on FDR-based CGRA are compared with two other works in this field: ADRES and RCP. Experimental results for various multimedia applications show that FDR combined with the new compiler deliver up to 29% and 21% higher performance than ADRES and RCP, respectively.

1. Introduction and Related Work

Much research has been done to evaluate the performance, power, and cost of reconfigurable architectures [1, 2]. Some use the standard commercial FPGAs, while others contain processors coupled with reconfigurable coprocessors (e.g., GARP [3], Chimaera [4]). Meanwhile, *coarse-grained reconfigurable architecture* (CGRA) has attracted a lot of attention from the research community [5]. CGRAs utilize an array of pre-defined *processing elements* (*PEs*) to provide computational power. Because the PEs are capable of doing byte or word-level computations efficiently, CGRAs can provide higher performance for data intensive applications, such as video and signal processing applications. In addition, CGRAs are coarse grained so they have smaller communication and configuration overhead costs compared to fine grained field programmable gate arrays (FPGAs).

Based on how PEs are organized in a CGRA, the existing CGRAs can be generally classified into linear array architecture and mesh-based architecture. In linear array architecture, PEs are organized in one or several linear arrays. Representative works in this category are RaPiD [6] and PipeRench [7]. RaPiD can speed up highly regular, computational intensive applications by deep pipelining the application on a chain of RaPiD cells. PipeRench provides speedup for pipelined application by utilizing PEs to form reconfigurable pipeline stages that are then interconnected with a crossbar.

The linear array organization is highly efficient when the computations can be linearly pipelined. With the emergence of many 2D video applications, the linear array organization becomes less flexible and inefficient to support block-based applications [8]. Therefore, a number of mesh-based CGRAs are proposed. Representative works in this category include KressArray [9], MATRIX [10], and MorphoSys [8].

The KressArray was one of the first works that utilized 2D mesh connection in CGRA. KressArray uses *reconfigurable data path units* (rDPUs) as basic computation cell. These rDPUs are connected through local *nearest neighbor (NN)* links and global interconnection [9]. To accommodate high volume of communications between function units, the MATRIX [10] proposed a 3-level network connecting its *basic function unit* (BFU) including NN connection, length-4 bypassing connections and global lines. Finally, Morphosys [8] used an 8×8 PE array, divided into four 4×4 quadrants, as the coprocessor for a RISC host CPU. Each PE is directly connected with any PE in the same row/column within the same quadrant and its NN regardless of the quadrants. Morphosys also exploits a set of buses called *express lanes* to link PEs in different quadrants.

Two interesting CGRAs are recently proposed: ADRES [11] and RCP [12]. ADRES belongs to mesh-based architecture. It utilizes Morphosys' communication mechanism and resolves resource conflict at compile time using modulo scheduling. RCP belongs to linear array architecture. It proposes an architecture with ring-shaped buses and connection boxes. One unique feature of RCP is that it supports concurrent computation and communication [12]. However, its hardware and software only support this feature in one dimension, which may limit RCP performance. Another representative architectural work is RAW [13], which pioneered the concept of concurrent computation and communication using MIPS processor array. However, due to the complexity of MIPS processor as a PE, RAW may not be an efficient platform to accelerate kernel code used in embedded applications. On the compiler side, a recent work is SPR [14], which presents an architecture-adaptive mapping tool to compile kernel code for CGRA. Their compiler targets an FPGA-like CGRA, and it supports architectures with a mix of dynamically multiplexed and statically configurable interconnects.

Some recent studies [15–18] show that further exploiting instruction level parallelism (ILP) out of ADRES architecture can cause hardware and software (compiler) inefficiency. This is mainly because ADRES utilizes heavily ported global register file and multi-degree point-to-point connections [18]. In particular, to implement communication pattern that broadcasts shared data on ADRES is challenging [15]. Using integer linear programming to find better code schedule may incur prohibitive long runtime [16]. Given the difficulty of further pushing for ILP performance, [17] turned to exploit thread-level parallelism in MT-ADRES.

In this work, to exploit ILP performance further, we propose a new mechanism, named *fast data relay* (FDR), in CGRA. This proposed FDR architecture replaces the heavily ported global register file with distributed simple register files (Section 2.2). It also replaces the point-to-point connections with simple wire-based channels (Section 2.3). The main features of FDR include (1) fast data links between PEs, (2) data relay where communication can be done in multiple cycles as a background operation without disturbing computations, and (3) source operand that can have multiple copies with longer lifetimes in different PEs so that a dependent PE can find a local copy in its vicinity. We name the proposed new architecture *FDR-CGRA*. These FDR mechanisms are generic and could also be incorporated into ADRES architecture to enhance the ILP performance. To utilize FDR efficiently, we propose new compiler techniques to map kernel code onto FDR-CGRA leveraging its unique hardware features.

In the following, we provide the motivation and the architecture support of FDR-CGRA in Section 2. In Section 3, we introduce our CAD-based compiler support for the efficient use of FDR. The experimental results will be discussed in Section 4, and we conclude this paper in Section 5.

2. Motivation and Architectural Support for *FDR*

With the shrinking of CMOS technology, more and more devices can be integrated into a single die. The granularity of CGRA has also gradually been raised from 4 bit to 16 bit or even 32 bit. The ADRES uses 32 bit ALU as its basic computation unit and is one of the representative modern CGRA architectures for mesh-based designs. It couples a VLIW processor with an array of PEs. Each PE consists of a predicated ALU, local register file, and I/O multiplexers. The functionality of each ALU can be configured dynamically through the *context SRAM* (CS). A unified *global register file* (GRF) is used to provide data exchange among PEs and the host VLIW processor. The interconnection of ADRES exploits the communication mechanism similar to Morphosys. Its compiler uses modulo scheduling algorithm to resolve resource conflict at compile time.

The research in [18] extensively studied how the configuration of register files impacts the performance of ADRES. It showed that the unified GRF is a severe performance bottleneck. In ADRES, each PE connected to the GRF has dedicated read and write ports to the GRF. In a 64-PE ADRES baseline configuration organized as 8 rows and 8 columns, eight PEs on the top row are connected to the GRF. The study in [18] showed that even this baseline configuration needs a highly complicated 8-read and 8-write GRF with significant area penalty. And at the same time, allowing only 8 simultaneous reads and 8 simultaneous writes to this GRF seriously limited the performance (IPC < 14) of 64-PE ADRES. It is also shown in [18] that to achieve an IPC above 23 on the original 64-PE ADRES architecture, the global register file needs to support >40 sets of read and write ports, which is, if not impossible, very challenging and costly for physical implementation. Also, their study pointed out that increasing the number of registers in GRF and each PE local register file can only contribute to performance marginally. Due to this limitation, the performance of ADRES can barely take advantage of the growing budget given by ever-shrinking modern CMOS technology.

RCP is a representative architecture for linear array-based design. But linear array architecture may not be able to accommodate block-based applications as well as mesh-based designs. To study this, we will also compare our results with RCP. In the rest of this section, we propose several architectural enhancements for the mesh-based architecture to improve the performance. Then, in the section afterwards, we will propose several compiler techniques for better utilizing these new hardware features. As will be shown in the experimental result section, these hardware changes as well as the new compiler techniques can exploit higher instruction level parallelism (ILP) comparing to ADRES and RCP.

The architectural changes are summarized into a single term named fast data relay (FDR), which includes three main features: *bypassing registers*, *wire-based companion channels*, and the use of *non-transient copies*. In the following subsections, we will first introduce the overall architecture of FDR-CGRA. Then, each of the aforementioned three features will be explained in detail, respectively.

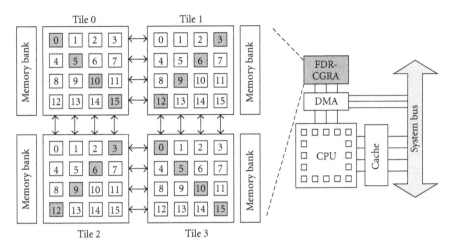

FIGURE 1: FDR-CGRA system overview.

2.1. Architectural Overview. Similar to existing reconfigurable computing platforms surveyed in [2], we assume that a host CPU initializes the kernel computation on our FDR-CGRA and is in charge of system-level dataflow via DMA. We assume filling data via DMA can be done in parallel with CGRA computations using double buffers (Ping-Pong buffers). Thus, FDR-CGRA can focus on accelerating time-consuming kernels. Figure 1 provides a conceptual illustration of the overall FDR-CGRA system. In FDR-CGRA, the basic computation units are PEs (Section 2.2) organized in tiles, and a wire-based communication layer (Section 2.3) glues PEs together.

FDR-CGRA adopts the tile-based design philosophy, like that of existing commercial FPGAs, for design scalability. Considering that memory banks have limited bandwidth, we restrict that only the shadowed PEs can access memory banks with load/store instructions (Figure 1).

To exploit more instruction level parallelism, it is desirable to exchange data for operations on non-critical paths without intervening with critical computations. Fast data relay is such a mechanism. It is capable of routing data from one PE to another in multiple cycles in parallel with computations by utilizing the bypassing registers (Section 2.2) and companion channels (Section 2.3). It is an enhancement over ADRES point-to-point communication. The philosophy of concurrent computation and communication was exploited in the RAW microprocessor [13]. However, instead of using switches that route data dynamically, FDR-CGRA uses wire-based channels. Communication within a tile is faster in FDR-CGRA than in RAW. The detailed analysis can be found in Section 2.3.

2.2. Processing Element and Bypassing Registers. As shown in Figure 2, each PE has a dedicated computation data path (left) similar to the PE used in ADRES and a communication bypassing path (right) that can be used for FDR. This dedication is essential to enable simultaneous computation and communication. Similar to ADRES, each ALU is driven by traditional assembly code and its functionality can be configured dynamically through the *context SRAM* (*CS*). The CS stores both the function specification of the ALU and the communication information that provides cycle-by-cycle reconfiguration of channels among PEs. The communication information includes control bits for the input multiplexers (1, 2, and B) on the top of the PE and output multiplexers at the bottom (3 and 4).

One key hardware feature of FDR-CGRA is the use of distributed bypassing register file (marked as BR in Figure 2): in addition to the normal local register file (marked as LR), which is used to store intermediate data for ALU, our PE includes a bypassing register file, through which multicycle data communication can be carried out. A leading PE can deposit a value in the bypassing register of a leading PE and a trailing PE can fetch it later on without disturbing computations on the leading PE. Such multicycle data communication is an effective way to reduce communication congestion, because it can detour communication traffic for non-critical operations to uncongested area. Note that the way our compiler utilizes the bypassing registers is different from the way the PipeRench compiler utilized its passing registers. In PipeRench, the passing registers were solely used to form virtual connections when a connection needs to span multiple stripes. And due to the greedy nature of the PipeRench compiler [19], whenever a path is unroutable due to resource conflict, a NOOP is inserted as the solution. As we will point out in Section 3.2 and in the experimental results, our compiler will use the bypassing registers as a powerful resource to solve routing congestions and exploit more ILP from application.

The bypassing register file associated with each PE provides a way for information exchange among PEs without incurring the same design complexity as in ADRES. As pointed out in [20, 21], central register file with a large number of read/write ports involves considerable complexity from multiplexing and bypassing logic, resulting in area penalty and timing closure challenges. The authors of [20] advocated to use distributed register files for media processing instead of using a heavily ported monolithic central

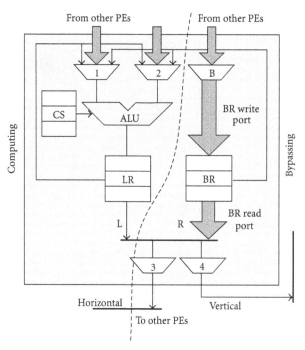

FIGURE 2: Architectural support for fast data relay at the PE level.

register file. Following this approach, in our FDR-CGRA, the distributed bypassing registers replace the unified GRF used in ADRES and its descendants [11, 15, 22]. To further simplify the register file design, we restrict the number of simultaneous accesses to the bypassing register file to 2 reads and 2 writes (2R2W). This constraint is explicitly modeled, and our tool can honor it during operation scheduling, mapping, and routing. By distributing the unified data storage in ADRES into small pieces as bypassing registers, we can exploit more ILP out of applications and gain larger programming flexibility over the original ADRES. However, at the same time, they pose some challenges for our compiler. This will be discussed in Section 3.

2.3. Wire-Based Companion Channels. In FDR-CGRA, inter-tile communication is simply through direct connections between PEs on the tile boundaries, as shown in Figure 1, while intratile communication is implemented with companion channels (Figure 3). Each PE owns two private companion channels: a vertical channel and a horizontal channel. Within a tile, the owner PE can send data via its private vertical (horizontal) channel to any PE in the same column (row) in a time-multiplexing way. Note that a vertical/horizontal channel can only be used by its owner for sending (not receiving) data. In this sense, these vertical (horizontal) channels are *unidirectional*. In Figure 3, for example, the companion channels owned by PE12 are PE12V and PE12H. All other PEs have similar sets of companion channels: there are four *unidirectional* vertical channels for each column of PEs and four *unidirectional* horizontal channels for each row of PEs. Note that vertical/horizontal channels span only across the PEs within the same tile for

scalability reasons. Comparing to the 3-level interconnections used in Morphosys and ADRES where each PE has a set of dedicated links connecting to all PEs in the same row and column within a quadrant, our organization of companion channels is simpler because each PE only has one vertical and one horizontal channel and both are unidirectional. Initialized by the sender PE, scalar data can be deposited onto either horizontal or vertical channel through the output multiplexer. In the same cycle, the receiver PE can fetch the scalar data from its corresponding input multiplexer. The control bits of the output multiplexer and input multiplexer are determined at compile time and stored in the Context SRAM.

Comparing with multipoint point-to-point connection used in other tile-based architecture [8, 11, 15], utilizing the proposed simple wire-based companion channels may have some benefits when it comes to area cost. Firstly, the regularity of these proposed companion channels makes them easier to be implemented on top of PEs in metal layers without complicated routing to save routing area. Secondly, for intra-tile communication, the proposed companion channels can actually save configuration bits. Multi-point point-to-point interconnection needs several bits to specify a destination PE out of several connected neighbors. Using the companion channels, to specify either the vertical or the horizontal channel requires only one configuration bit.

Each PE in our architecture is a simple programmable predicated ALU similar to the PE defined in ADRES with the goal of accelerating the program kernel. ADRES assumed that in a single hop (a single cycle) a signal can travel across 5 PEs [11]. RCP assumed that one hop can travel across 3 PEs because of the complexity of its crossbar-like *connection*

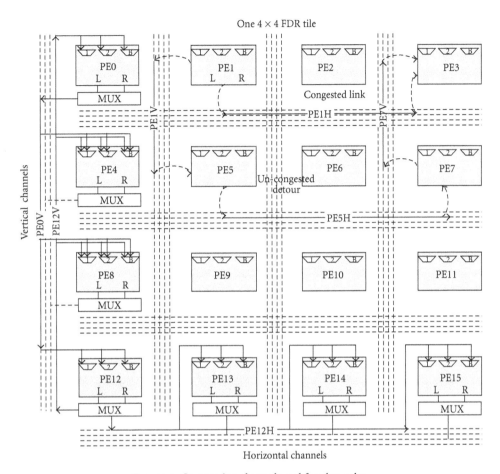

FIGURE 3: Companion channels and fast data relay.

box design [12]. RAW used complex MIPS core as PE, thus one hop can only travel across 1 PE [13]. Given the similarity of our enhanced PE to PE used in ADRES, we assume that one hop of data transmission can travel across 4 PEs. As a result, our wire-based companion channels enable a corner-to-corner transmission in a 4×4-tiled FDR architecture to finish in 2 cycles (PE0 → PE12 → PE15) via PE0 vertical channel (PE0V) and PE12 horizontal channel (PE12H) as shown in Figure 3.

It should be noted that ADRES connects PEs with dedicated point-to-point links without the capability of multi-cycle routing and buffering as proposed in our FDR-CGRA. The bypassing registers and the companion channels enable us to do data communication in a more flexible way. The right upper corner of Figure 3 illustrates a possible scenario to do multi-cycle communication if data needs to be sent from PE1 to PE3 and the compiler finds the horizontal channel PE1H connecting from PE1 to PE3 is congested, then it can decide to use a multi-cycle detour through PE5 and PE7 by utilizing their bypassing registers and companion channels PE1V, PE5H, and PE7H to avoid the congestion. Comparing with RCP, FDR-CGRA supports 2D communication, rather than the 1D ring-shape communication in RCP. Furthermore, the companion channel also allows shared data to be sent concurrently to multiple PEs in the same

row/column. These capabilities help alleviate the data route congestion problem experienced in other works (e.g., [15]).

Each communication link used in FDR involves three components: sender PE, companion channel, and receiver PE. We call such a communication path *inter-PE link*. It is desirable to reduce the total amount of inter-PE communication to reduce the latency and power. Next, we introduce the concept of non-transient copy to mitigate the inter-PE link usage in our solution.

2.4. Non-transient Copy. All PEs on the multi-cycle communication path except the sender are called *linking PEs*. During the multi-cycle FDR, the source scalar data will be transmitted to a receiver PE through linking PEs. Along the transmission, all linking PEs can possess a local copy of the origin data. Because our PEs contain bypassing register files, multiple local copies from different source PEs can coexist in the bypassing register file simultaneously. Furthermore, we can classify these local copies into two categories: *transient copy* and *non-transient copy*. Here we use "transient" to refer to a software property of a value hold in registers. We call a value a transient copy if the register holding the value will be recycled immediately after the value being fetched by the first trailing-dependent operation. In contrast, a non-transient

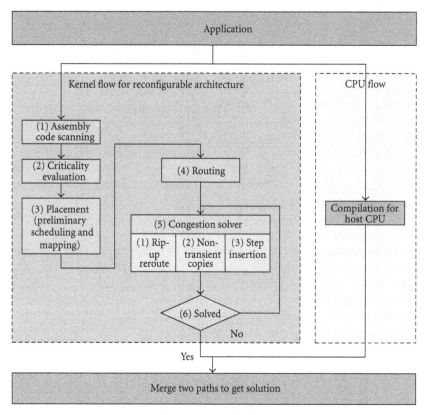

FIGURE 4: Overall flow.

copy will stay in the register until no more operations depend on it. Note that physically there is no difference between transient copy and non-transient copy since they both reside in the bypassing register file. Conceptually, the compiler treats them differently at compile time according to how they will be utilized. Since ADRES and RCP do not have bypassing register files to hold multiple copies, they need to recycle registers as soon as possible.

As will be shown in our experimental results, using non-transient copies can significantly benefit applications where some source data need to be reused by multiple dependent operations. Because it in effect distributes a source operand to several PEs and keeps them alive as non-transient copies, a dependent operation can probably find a local copy in its vicinity, instead of getting it from the origin PE. This can decrease the number of inter-PE links used.

From now on, we call those linking PEs that can provide local copies *identical start points*. Whether to keep the scalar data in linking PEs bypassing register files as a transient copy or a non-transient copy is decided at the routing stage (Section 3.2).

3. Supporting Compiler Techniques

Because FDR-CGRA is intended to accelerate the kernel code of an application, the overall design flow shown in Figure 4 can branch into two separate paths. On the right, the non-kernel code is compiled in a traditional manner targeting the host CPU. On the left is the flow to map kernel code

operations onto the FDR-CGRA, which is the focus of our study.

First, we choose *low level virtual machine* (LLVM) [23] to compile the computation-intensive kernel code in C into assembly code. LLVM has its own architecture-independent virtual instruction set, and it can extensively rename registers during compilation, which is essential to avoid hitting the unnecessary IPC wall due to the limited number of registers that can be used by a compiler targeting specific processor architecture [24]. The assembly code of the kernel function generated by LLVM with the optimization option "−O3" is then scanned by a parser to identify data dependencies, and a directed acyclic graph (DAG) representing the data dependency among operations in the kernel code is constructed in step 1 of Figure 4. Step 2 will evaluate the criticality of each node in the DAG. This will be discussed in detail in Section 3.1.

Later on, steps 3–6 are used to find a valid operation mapping honoring resource constraints. Step 3 provides a preliminary placement for operations. Steps 4 and 5 refine it by doing routing and solving congestions. The problem of mapping kernel code onto FDR-CGRA can be formulated as follows: given a DAG representing the data dependency among operations, find a valid scheduling, mapping, and data communication scheme of all operations on the *routing region* so that all data dependency is satisfied and no resource conflict exists, where the routing region is constructed as shown in Figure 5 by the following steps: (1) line up all PEs in the two-dimensional computation grid along the *x* axis. The PEs on the grid are marked as PE(m, n), where m is the PE ID and n is this PE schedule step. (2) Duplicate the PE row L times along the time axis (the y axis) to form a routing region, where L is achieved through a list scheduling algorithm honoring the resource constraint. (3) Add edges between any nearby PE rows to reflect the available connectivity among PEs according to the connectivity specification in the architecture, that is, companion channels specified in Section 2.3. Figure 5(b) shows a sample routing region for a small group of PEs specified in Figure 5(a). The solid lines indicate inter-PE connections and the dash lines indicate intra-PE communication. Such a routing region incorporates all the feasible connections between PEs along the scheduling steps and provides a working space to carry out the compilation tasks.

Figure 5(c) is a DAG representing data dependency among operations. In this DAG, (1) solid edges represent single-cycle data dependency and (2) the dashed edge represents multi-cycle dependency, which requires FDR. Our compilation process consists of two phases: *placement frontend* and *routing backend*. The placement frontend produces an operation mapping solution in the routing region and leaves the detailed resource conflict problems to be resolved in the routing backend. This is similar to the physical design stages where a placer determines the location of cells and the routing determines the detailed wiring of the cells. In our case, each cell would be an operation. Figure 5(d) shows a placement and routing result for the DAG in Figure 5(c). In cycle 1, nodes 1 to 4 are mapped to PEs 0 to 3, respectively. In cycle 2, node 5 is mapped to PE 1 and node 6 to PE 3. Note that the output of node 2 is kept in PE 1 bypassing register file, which is then used by node 8 in cycle 3.

We would like to emphasize that explicitly using a dedicated routing phase to solve congestion can enable us to achieve higher ILP performance than modulo scheduling used in CGRA compilers from [11, 12, 14]. When resource conflict due to the competition for the same resource by consecutive iterations in a loop cannot be resolved, modulo scheduling algorithm resorts to increasing the *iteration interval* (II), which has negative impact on ILP performance. Meanwhile, although modulo scheduling is commonly used to optimize loops with arbitrary large number of iterations, the performance could suffer from the unsaturation of operations during the wind-up and wind-down phases. This problem is particularly severe for a compact loop body with small number of iterations. Unfortunately, many applications demonstrate this property because of the popularity of partitioning large kernels into small pieces for data localization. In contrast, our two-phase procedure can virtually discard the II constraints by unrolling the whole loop and explicitly resolving resource conflicts during the backend data routing stage. Considering that the routing algorithm we borrowed from the physical design automation field can typically handle hundreds of thousands of instances, this dedicated routing phase enables us to work on the fully unrolled kernel loops efficiently.

3.1. Placement Frontend for FDR

A criticality evaluation needs to be done first for all nodes in the DAG to guide placement. Note that we will use the term node and operation interchangeably from now on. The node criticality is evaluated as *slack* defined as

$$slack(op) = ALAP\_level(op) - ASAP\_level(op).$$

ALAP_level (*ASAP_level*) is the as-late-as-possible scheduling level (as-soon-as-possible scheduling level) for an operation computed by the ALAP (ASAP) scheduling algorithm [25]. If the slack is zero, there is no margin to delay the execution of the operation. If the slack is a positive value, the operation can be delayed accordingly without hurting the overall schedule length.

The placement frontend carries out operation scheduling and operation-to-PE mapping. We perform a list scheduling [25] guided by operation criticality such that critical operations will be placed on PEs that are directly connected with companion channels and noncritical operations will be placed on PEs without direct companion connecting them.

Algorithm 1 outlines the algorithm. First of all, every unprocessed node (operation) whose dependency is satisfied (i.e., its predecessor nodes, including PI nodes, are already scheduled and mapped) in the DAG is collected into *ReadyNodeSet*. Given the *ReadyNodeSet*, *FreePESet* (available PEs) and the current schedule step S as inputs, the algorithm maps the nodes from *ReadyNodeSet* to PEs in *FreePESet* and output a *MappedNodeSet*. Two constraints are considered here (lines 2–12 of Algorithm 1).

3.1.1. Functionality Constraint.

This is to make sure that the candidate PE has the ability to perform the required computations because the PEs could be heterogeneous. For example, not all ALUs can perform memory load/store operations as explained in Section 2.1. We use *CapablePESet(n)* to identify the set of PEs that are capable of performing the operation n (line 3).

3.1.2. Routability Constraint.

Although detailed routing scheme is determined at routing backend, a hint of routability is still used to help Algorithm 1 to determine mapping of nodes by calling *RoutableSet(p, l)* (line 8-9). Recall that FDR may need multiple steps to send data from a source PE to a destination PE. Given a PE p, the l-step reachable set of p is defined as all the PEs which can be reached within at most l hops starting from p. Then the candidate PEs are filtered out by taking the intersection of candidate sets generated according to functionality constraints, routability constraints, and availability constraints (line 10).

As an example, assume operation node b has two source operands: one is on PE1, and other is on PE2. Assume we have

$$CapablePESet(b) = \{PE0\ PE2\ PE4\ PE8\},$$
$$RoutableSet(PE1, l) = \{PE4\ PE5\ PE7\},$$
$$RoutableSet(PE2, l) = \{PE3\ PE4\ PE9\}.$$

The intersection of the above three sets is PE4, indicating that PE4 is the only mapping candidate for node b. If PE4 turns

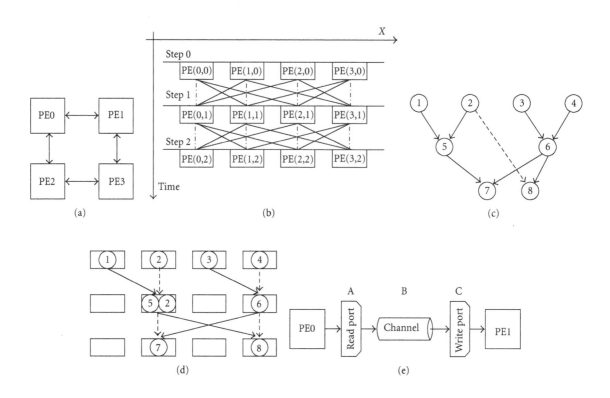

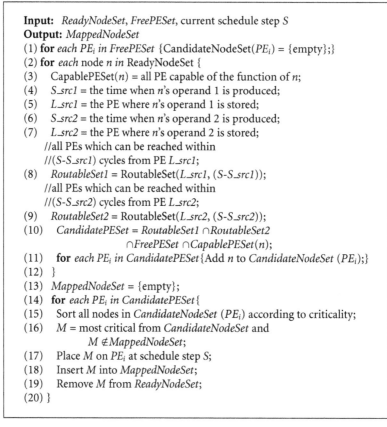

FIGURE 5: (a) A 2 × 2 PE array, (b) the routing region, (c) the DAG, (d) the mapping and routing solution, and (e) constraint model

Input: *ReadyNodeSet, FreePESet*, current schedule step *S*
Output: *MappedNodeSet*
(1) **for** *each PE_i in FreePESet* {CandidateNodeSet(PE_i) = {empty};}
(2) **for** *each* node *n in* ReadyNodeSet {
(3)   CapablePESet(*n*) = all PE capable of the function of *n*;
(4)   *S_src1* = the time when *n*'s operand 1 is produced;
(5)   *L_src1* = the PE where *n*'s operand 1 is stored;
(6)   *S_src2* = the time when *n*'s operand 2 is produced;
(7)   *L_src2* = the PE where *n*'s operand 2 is stored;
        //all PEs which can be reached within
        //(S-S_src1) cycles from PE *L_src1*;
(8)   *RoutableSet1* = RoutableSet(*L_src1*, (S-S_src1));
        //all PEs which can be reached within
        //(S-S_src2) cycles from PE *L_src2*;
(9)   *RoutableSet2* = RoutableSet(*L_src2*, (S-S_src2));
(10)   *CandidatePESet = RoutableSet1 ∩RoutableSet2*
                     ∩FreePESet ∩CapablePESet(n);
(11)   **for** *each PE_i in CandidatePESet*{Add *n* to *CandidateNodeSet* (PE_i);}
(12)   }
(13)   *MappedNodeSet* = {empty};
(14)   **for** *each PE_i in CandidatePESet*{
(15)   Sort all nodes in *CandidateNodeSet* (PE_i) according to criticality;
(16)   *M* = most critical from *CandidateNodeSet* and
            M ∉MappedNodeSet;
(17)   Place *M* on PE_i at schedule step *S*;
(18)   Insert *M* into *MappedNodeSet*;
(19)   Remove *M* from *ReadyNodeSet*;
(20) }

ALGORITHM 1: Placement frontend (simultaneous scheduling and mapping).

out to be already occupied (PE4 not free), node *b* cannot be mapped in this schedule step and will fall to later schedule steps.

If there are more than one candidate nodes to map into a PE as indicated in *CandidateNodeSet*, the node with higher criticality will have a privilege over those with lower criticality for mapping (line 13–19). Those successfully mapped nodes will be moved to the *MappedNodeSet* (line 18), while the unmapped nodes will still remain in the *ReadyNodeSet* to be processed in scheduling steps thereafter. This procedure will continue until all nodes are processed.

3.2. Routing Backend for FDR. The routing backend is used to solve resource conflict in detail. We use an algorithm inspired by global maze routing [26] to find inter-PE communication schemes that can efficiently utilize bypassing registers introduced in Section 2.2. Our algorithm also determines which operands stay in bypassing registers as non-transient copies and which are not.

Each operand used in the DAG is identified with its own ID and its associated location in the routing region in the format of PE[m, n], where m stands for the ID of PE that hosts the operand and n stands for the schedule step in which the operand is ready for R/W (read/write). The inputs to the routing procedure are a list of routing requirements represented as (*src → dest*) pairs, where *src* and *dest* are in the above format. Figure 6 shows an example. Assume three operations op1, op2, and op3 all need an operand *M* from PE [1, 1] as indicated in Figure 6(a) with 3 routing requirements:

op1: M, PE[1, 1] → PE[2, 4],

op2: M, PE[1, 1] → PE[0, 4],

op3: M, PE[1, 1] → PE[3, 5].

3.2.1. Solve Routing Congestion with Rip-Up and Reroute. An initial routing solution usually has congestion. We improve the quality of routing solutions iteratively. A commonly used way to solve congestion is by rip-up and reroute [26] as shown in Algorithm 2: (1) pick a routed path (line 4); (2) rip-up (or break) the path by deallocating all the resources (i.e., channels and ports) taken by this path except the source PE and the destination PE (line 8); (3) based on the existing congestion information of the routing region, find an uncongested detour and reroute the path (line 11–14). These steps are iterated for all paths until the congestion is eliminated or it stops when no improvement can be achieved. After rip-up and reroute, a routing solution for the previous problem is shown in Figure 6(b), in which four inter-PE links (solid arrows) are used.

3.2.2. Detail Route for Each Inter-PE Communication Path. To detail route for each communication path, a maze routing procedure "route_path" in line 11 of Algorithm 2 is called to find routing solution for each requirement entry. Note that a set of special data structures used for CGRA is used to provide routing guidance for "route_path." First, we apply *channel constraints*, which are channel capacities on vertical and horizontal companion channels and apply *port constraint* which is an upper bound on the number of total simultaneous accesses to the read/write ports of bypassing register files in PEs to reflect the bandwidth constraint of a physical register file (Figure 2). Second, each inter-PE communication link is modeled as a cost function of three parts (Figure 5(e)): read port, channel, and write port. Whenever an inter-PE link is used, the capacity of the affected channel and ports will decrease and the cost of using this link will increase proportional to the congestion on it. Third, each PE has a PE score recording the cost of the cheapest path (with least congestion) from the source PE.

At the beginning of "route_path," a queue contains only the source PE. Starting from the source PE by popping it up from the queue, multiple-directional scores are calculated for its trailing PEs, that is, directly connected neighboring PEs. PE scores for those trailing PEs may be updated to record the changes for the cheapest paths leading to them. Any PE whose PE score is updated will be pushed into the queue for further exploration. The process is quite similar to wave front propagation, and the router stops when the queue is empty. After wavefront propagation is done by "route_path," a "backtrace" procedure (line 13) starts from the end point and backtraces along the cheapest direction at each backtrace step in the routing region "cost_grid" until reaching the start point. This backtraced path "new_p" is reported as the cheapest path.

3.2.3. Utilize Non-Transient Copies. What differentiate our algorithm from ordinary routing algorithm is that we integrate the utilization of features of non-transient copy in the routing algorithm.

In the example of Figure 6(b), after the first route from *M* on PE[1, 1] to op1 on PE[2, 4] is established via the path PE[1, 1] → PE[3, 2] → PE[2, 3] → op1. Both PE2 and PE3 have once possessed a copy of *M* during this procedure. In fact, the copy in PE3 can be reused by op3 later on at step 5, as long as the register holding value *M* in PE[3, 2] will not be reclaimed immediately after PE[2, 3] fetches it. This is achieved by marking the copy of *M* in PE[3, 2] as a non-transient copy. In contrast, for the copy of *M* in PE[2, 3], except op1 no other operation needs it. Therefore register holding *M* in PE2 can be marked as transient and reclaimed immediately after op1 consumes it to save register usage. To decide whether a copy should be transient or non-transient, a special data structure "regDuplicatorLst" is used in Algorithm 2 to help making the decision. "regDuplicatorLst" is implemented as a lookup table storing the identical start points for each origin source operand. The index to the table is the origin source operand, and the contents pointed by the index are all identical start points organized as a list. This lookup table is updated (line 15) every time after the cheapest path is found by the backtrace procedure by inserting all new identical start points into the entry of their associated origin source operands. An example of a "regDuplicatorLst" entry is shown below. After the first route to op1 in Figure 6(b) is found by "backtrace," the origin source *M* may be found in three different places:

M: PE[1, 1], PE[3, 2], PE[2, 3].

```
Input: &routingPathLst // routingPathLst stores routing requirements
Output: a new less congested routing solution stored in routingPathLst
1       for (i = 0; i < iMax; i++) {
2           regDuplicatorLst.clear(); // clear regDuplicatorLst before new iteration
3           newRoutingPathLst.clear();
4           for each path p in routingPathLst {
5               src = p.origin;    // get start_point of p
6               dest = p.destination;    // get end_point of p
7               //step 1: ripup
8               ripup_path(p);        // ripup p by release all resources used by p
9               end_step = getReadyStep(dest);
10                //step 2: reroute
11                cost_grid = route_path(src, end_step, &regDuplicatorLst);
12                //step 3: backtrace
13                new_p = backtrace(dest, &src, cost_grid);
14                add(new_p, newRoutingPathLst);
15                update(regDuplicatorLst, new_p);
16          }
17          routingPathLst = newRoutingPathLst;
18  }
```

ALGORITHM 2: ripup_reroute.

As we pointed out before, an identical start point can serve as an alternative source for the same operand. To take this into consideration, procedure "route_path" of Algorithm 2 is modified accordingly to push all identical start points for the origin source into the queue at the beginning of the routing. As a result, the wavefront propagation can actually start from multiple sources. But only one source that produces the cheapest route found by "backtrace" will be used as actual start point. If this actual start point is different from the origin source, it means this data relay route actually reuses an operand that is deposited by another route before. To allow this reusing, this start point is marked as a non-transient copy.

In the simple example of Figure 6(c), by maintaining the identical start points in "regDuplicatorLst," the backtrace for op3 is able to find the cheapest route solution, which is to reuse the value M once stored in the bypassing register, for example, BR[2], of PE[3, 2]. Then BR[2] is declared as nontransient copy thus can be kept untainted in PE[3, 2] for future reuse by op3 without establishing a physical inter-PE link from the origin of M in PE[1, 1]. With non-transient copies, the solution can make less use of inter-PE links, for example, in Figure 6(c) only three inter-PE links are used while four are used in Figure 6(b). Moreover, during the routing for op2, with the "regDuplicatorLst," Algorithm 2 will find it can get a copy of M from either PE[1, 3] or PE[2, 3] in Figure 6(c). With more choices, the router in Algorithm 2 can effectively select the least crowded communication scheme to avoid congestion.

Non-transient copies usually have longer life cycles than transient copies and serve as data origins for multiple trailing-dependent operations. Our compiler can trace the last access to a non-transient copy at the compile time and decide to reclaim this non-transient copy after this last usage.

3.2.4. Schedule Step Relaxation. In some cases, applying the above techniques still cannot resolve all the congestions, and *schedule step relaxation* (SSR) will then be invoked as the last resort. SSR utilizes a well-known fact that routing sparsely distributed nodes on a larger routing region will result in less congestion. SSR in effect increases the size of the routing region along the time axis by inserting extra steps into the most congested regions. Trading area for routability guarantees that congestion will be reduced to zero. As the last resort, a greedy algorithm is used to do SSR as follows: starting from the most congested step, insert an extra *relaxation step*, then redo rip-up and reroute on the extended routing region, and continue doing so until all congestions are solved. The side effect of SSR is the increased schedule length.

4. Experimental Results

Experiments are performed on an architecture configuration shown in Figure 1. The reconfigurable array consists of 4 tiles. Each tile has 16 PEs organized in a 4 × 4 mesh. The PEs in a single tile communicate with each other as specified in Section 2.3. The data relay ports on the bypassing register for read and write are bounded by 2, respectively, to reflect the physical register file bandwidth constraint. Similarly, load/store operations are limited to be performed only by PEs on the diagonal line to reflect memory bandwidth constraint. Other computational operations can be performed by any PEs. The latency of each operation is set to 1. LR has 16 entries. To explore the best performance that can be achieved using BR, the size of BR is not fixed. However, as the results shown in Section 4.3, a fairly small amount of BR is used, thus practical. The architecture in Figure 1 can be configured in two ways: (1) *large Cfg.*, all 64 PEs can be used to map

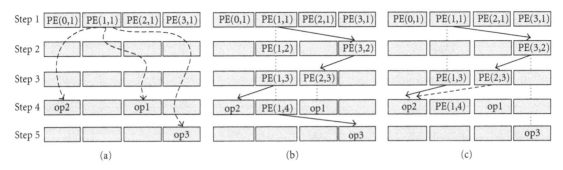

FIGURE 6: (a) Initial routing requirements, (b) data relay solution, and (c) solution of data relay with register duplication.

a benchmark program, (2) *small Cfg.*, a benchmark program is limited to be run on a single tile, but four independent programs can run concurrently on four tiles. Each Cfg. has its own merit to be explained in Section 4.2.

Benchmarks are extracted from two open source applications: xvid 1.1.3 and JM 7.5b. xvid [27] is an open source package consisting of various codecs for various video formats. JM v7.5b [28] is a reference implementation of the H.264 video codec. Five subroutines are extracted from the xvid package: idct_row, idct_col, interpolation8 × 8_avg4_c, interpolate8 × 8-_halfpel_hv_c, and SAD16_c. IDCT is a fixed-point inverse discrete cosine transformation working on rows and columns of the 8 × 8 pixel blocks. This is the same as that used in [11] and [12]. Interpolation8 × 8_avg4_c and interpolate8 × 8_halfpel_hv_c are subroutines to calculate pixel values for 8 × 8 blocks by interpolating pixels from neighbor image frames. SAD16_c is used in motion estimation to calculate the similarity of two 16 × 16 pixel blocks. Another four subroutines are extracted from the H.264 reference implementation JM v7.5b: getblock(V), getblock(H), getblock(HV), and getblock(VH). They calculate the pixel values for a 4 × 4 block by interpolating from neighbor image frames.

We should point out that the number of loop iterations in media applications is bounded by fine-grained partitioned data set, usually for better image quality. For instance, each H.264 loop typically operates on a 4 × 4 or 8 × 8 pixel block. This type of usage gives rise to the opportunity to exploit ILP within loops by fully unrolling, which fits perfectly to FDR-CGRA typical usage.

4.1. Execution Trace. Our compiler implemented in C++ can dump a placed and routed execution trace for the kernel code. Then a simulator implemented in PERL is used to validate the result. We use PERL because it supports text array very well, and text arrays are used to represent instruction, channel, and port configurations in our code. The simulator not only simulates the data flow on FDR-CGRA but also verifies on the fly for the satisfaction of three sets of resource constraints: channel constrains, port constraints and resource constraints. Table 4 shows an abbreviated execution trace for idct_row scheduled on an architecture depicted in Figure 1. To save space, only operations on one tile are shown and the other three

tiles are omitted. 16 PEs in the tile are numbered from 0 to 15. Operations are represented as parenthesized letters. Round bracket ones are of one unrolled iteration (ite1), while square bracket ones are of another iteration (ite2). Operations from the same iteration can be scheduled across tiles when necessary. Both iterations start at the first cycle. In our approach, iterations compete for PE resource and also complement each other when the other is waiting for data: for example in Table 4, nine ops are from ite1 in cycle 5, while six ops are from ite2, while in cycle 6, five ops are from ite1 and ten ops are from ite2. In addition, we can see that the result respects the resource constraints by (1) only allowing PE0, 5, 10, 15 to perform load/store operations (L) due to memory bandwidth constraint (2) and only allowing at most 2 reads and 2 writes to each PE bypassing register file due to the port constraint (2R2W) we set. In Table 4, the "write (read) requests" column shows, for each PE, how many write (read) requests are served at each cycle. Each single digit from left to right in a row corresponds to the number of write (read) requests on PE0 to PE15, respectively. Each column of these digits reflects the write (read) requests for its corresponding PE over time. The "Communication Vol.," where each * represents an inter-PE link usage, shows the amount of inter-PE link usage at each cycle. It is clear that computation and communication are indeed concurrently executed every cycle due to dedication of bypassing register, except cycle 1, 7, 10, 12, where extra relaxation steps are used to solve routing congestion.

4.2. Performance Analysis. Modulo scheduling-based code scheduling approaches [11, 15] have advantage to handle loops with a large number of iterations because they can reuse the scheduled code on PEs throughout the iterations. However, the inflexibility of modulo scheduling may limit its performance for a class of applications that have a special communication pattern. This type of applications, represented by video applications, usually "broadcast" shared data from one PE to multiple receiving PEs. As reported in [15], an edge centric modulo scheduling does not perform well for H.264 if an CGRA does not provide complex routing schemes including using diagonal channels.

The performance of benchmark programs on FDR-CGRA, as well as on ADRES and RCP, is shown in Tables 1 and 2. The benchmark programs are mapped on

TABLE 1: Large configuration results.

Arch.	App.	Large Cfg.: 4 tiles, each tile has 4 × 4 PEs				
		Ops	Cycles	Avg. IPC	Perf. gain	Efficiency
ADRES	idct_row(8 × 8)	—	—	27.7	—	43%
FDR-CGRA	idct_row(8 × 8)	857	24	35.7	29%	56%
ADRES	idct_col(8 × 8)	—	—	33.0	—	52%
FDR-CGRA	idct_col(8 × 8)	1185	33	35.9	9%	56%
FDR-CGRA	Interpolate 8 × 8_avg4_c	1193	40	29.8	—	47%
FDR-CGRA	Interpolate 8 × 8_halfpel_hv_c	1295	38	34.1	—	53%
FDR-CGRA	sad16_c(16 × 16)	3441	106	32.5	—	51%

TABLE 2: Small configuration results.

Arch.	App.	Small Cfg.: 1 tile, 4 × 4 PEs each tile				
		Ops	Cycles	Avg. IPC	Perf. Gain	Efficiency
RCP	idct(row+col)	—	—	9.2	—	57%
FDR-CGRA	idct(row+col)	2042	184	11.1	21%	69%
FDR-CGRA	interpolate8 × 8_avg4_c	1193	136	8.8	—	55%
FDR-CGRA	interpolate8 × 8_halfpel_hv_c	1295	135	9.6	—	60%
FDR-CGRA	sad16_c(16 × 16)	3441	339	10.2	—	63%
ADRES	get_blocks (64 PEs)	—	—	29.9(64 PEs)	—	47%
FDR-CGRA	get_block(H)	340	38	8.9	—	56%
FDR-CGRA	get_block(V)	296	37	8.0	—	50%
FDR-CGRA	get_block(V+H)	899	93	9.7	—	60%
FDR-CGRA	get_block(H+V)	900	95	9.5	—	59%
FDR-CGRA	Adjusted Avg. (4 tiles)	—	—	36.1(4 tiles)	21%	56%

both a large and a small Cfg's. In the large Cfg., our approach achieves an average IPC of 35.7/35.9 for idct_row/idct_col, outperforming 8 × 8-FU ADRES architecture reported in [11] by 29% and 9%, respectively. In the small Cfg., we compare our results with 16-issue RCP reported in [12]. Our result of IDCT scheduled on a single tile (16 PEs) outperforms the 16-issue RCP IPC = 9.2 by 21%. As to the get_blocks, we observed that some modes—get_block(H) and get_block(V)—have significant fewer ops than other benchmark programs. Spreading a small number of ops on a large number of PEs would artificially introduce many multi-hop routing requirements. Given that each get_block can indeed work independently of others, a more efficient way is to schedule each get_block on a single tile and allow four instances of different get_block's to run concurrently. With this 4x adjustment to the get_block's average IPC in Table 2, the final average IPC for get_block is larger than 36, which is better than the "in-house" optimized results (avg. IPC = 29.9 for ADRES) in [22]. Note that the IPC values for ADRES and RCP are directly quoted from their published results. No data is reported for the interpolation and SAD benchmarks from either ADRES or RCP.

In the rightmost column of Tables 1 and 2, efficiency of a schedule is defined as the quotient of average IPC divided by total number of PEs. It can be observed that for the same application the large Cfg. has the smallest latency (under the *cycles* column) because it can use more resources, while the small Cfg. always has higher efficiency. This is because scattering operations on large Cfg. may introduce more operation "bubbles", where no useful work is actually done by a NOP operation for dependency or communication reasons. This fact suggests that the large Cfg. can be used when reducing execution latency is the sole goal, while the small Cfg. is suitable for applications where efficiency and performance are both important.

We should point out that one important reason that the proposed FDR-CGRA outperforms ADRES is the use of companion channels and non-transient copies. When necessary, the wire-based companion channel naturally allows "broadcast" of a datum to multiple PEs in the same row or column. At the same time, non-transient copies not only allow reusing of datum that needs to be shared by multiple PEs but also increase the path choices during routing.

The comparison with RCP is also interesting because RCP also allows concurrent data routing and computations. However, it is limited to one dimension. The experimental results demonstrate that our proposed compiling technique effectively exploits the performance potential of FDR 2D concurrent data routing and computations.

TABLE 3: Bypassing register usage profile and effects of using non-transient copy on a single tile (16 PE) configuration.

| | Bypassing register usage profile: per PE per cycle | | | | | Performance impact | | | | | |
| | Average | | Peak | | % Nontransient | Amount of inter-PE links | | | IPC | | |
	Disable	Enable	Disable	Enable	Enable	Disable	Enable	Delta	Disable	Enable	Delta
idct(row+col)	2.8	2.3	19	20	45%	2357	2245	−5%	10.9	11.1	2%
interpolate8 × 8_avg4_c	4.8	3.1	21	14	58%	1707	1333	−22%	6.4	8.8	38%
interpolate8 × 8_halfpel_hv_c	3.7	3.9	19	16	45%	1835	1621	−12%	8.3	9.6	16%
sad16_c(16 × 16)	1.0	0.8	6	5	54%	4752	4000	−16%	9.8	10.2	4%
get_block(horizontal)	1.0	0.9	6	5	22%	455	438	−4%	8.1	9.0	10%
get_block(vertical)	1.6	1.0	8	5	52%	513	400	−22%	5.7	8.0	41%
get_block(V+H)	4.2	2.2	18	10	45%	1469	1150	−22%	7.9	9.7	23%
get_block(H+V)	3.1	2.3	13	8	43%	1455	1148	−21%	8.4	9.5	13%
Average								−15%			18%

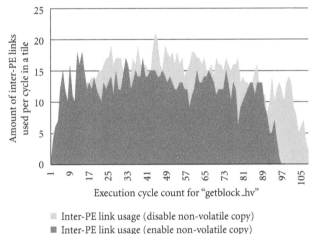

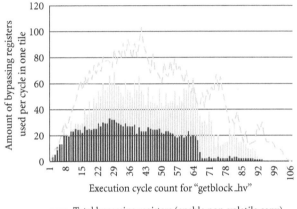

(a) Inter-PE link usage for each execution cycle with nontransient copy enabled and disabled

(b) Bypassing register usage for each execution cycle with nontransient copy usage breakdown

FIGURE 7: Performance impact of nontransient copies.

4.3. Effect of Non-Transient Copies. To test the effect of using non-transient copies, we rerun all the applications in Table 2 without using non-transient copies for a single tile configuration. The experimental results in Table 3 indicate that our algorithm produces solutions that only use an affordable amount of bypassing registers. On average, each PE only uses several bypassing registers at each cycle (column 2-3) and the peak bypassing register usage of a single PE ranges from 5 to 21 depending on applications. When non-transient copy usage is enabled, 22–58% of the total bypassing registers hold non-transient copies.

Table 3 also shows the performance impact of enabling non-transient copy. We can view its effects from three perspectives: (1) the primary goal of using it is to mitigate data relay congestion by allowing data reusing. With less congestion, the applications can finish sooner. (2) Distributing non-transient copies across a tile enables a PE to find a local copy in its vicinity and thus can reduce the usage of resource-and-power-consuming inter-PE links. (3) With less usage of inter-PE links, the total number of bypassing registers required can actually be reduced, although those non-transient copies do not recycle as fast as transient copies. These three effects are reflected in Figure 7 for application "getblock_hv." The usage for inter-PE links and usage for bypassing registers are plotted for every cycle. Obviously in Figure 7(a), non-transient copies enable the application to finish earlier and use less inter-PE links in total. It can be seen in Figure 7(b), with non-transient copy enabled, the proportion of non-transient copies to total bypassing registers is close to 1 in the first few cycles ranging from cycle 1 to 12 that correspond to loading input values from a reference image block. It means most of these loaded input values will be reused later on. Correspondingly, in Figure 7(a) the inter-PE link usage is also higher in the first a few cycles because non-transient copies need to be distributed across the tile as soon as possible for further reusing. But interestingly the total amount of bypassing registers used can still be kept lower with non-transient copy enabled. This is because that by reusing non-transient copies, the compiler does not need to allocate as many fresh

TABLE 4: Execution trace of IDCT (row).

Legend:
"L": load
"S": store
"P": getptr
"C": cast
"M": mul
"A": add
"B": sub
"H": shl
"R": shr

	PE 0	1	2	3	4	5	6	7	8	9	10	11	12	13	14	15	Communication Vol.	Write requests	Read requests
Cycle 0:	(L)	—	—	—	—	[L]	—	—	—	—	—	—	—	—	—	—		0000000000000000	1000010000000000
Cycle 1:	—	—	—	—	—	—	—	—	—	—	—	—	—	—	—	—	* *	0010000000000000	1100100000000000
Cycle 2:	(P)	(P)	—	—	[P]	[P]	[P]	—	—	—	—	—	—	—	—	—	* * * *	0011001000000000	0111111000000000
Cycle 3:	(L)	—	(C)	(C)	(C)	(L)	(C)	(C)	—	—	(L)	(C)	—	—	—	(L)	* * * * * *	0000011110100001	1000121100200002
Cycle 4:	(C)	(C)	(C)	(C)	(C)	[L]	(C)	(C)	—	—	[L]	(C)	—	—	—	[L]	* * * * * * * * * *	0111111100110001	2222122110210002
Cycle 5:	(A)	(A)	[C]	[C]	(M)	(M)	(M)	(M)	(M)	[C]	[L]	[C]	(M)	—	(M)	(H)	* * * * * * * * * * * * * * * * * *	2211222112111011	0111201002221001
Cycle 6:	(M)	(M)	[C]	[M]	[M]	(A)	[M]	(A)	[C]	[A]	[M]	[M]	(H)	[C]	[C]	—	* * * * * * * * * * * * * *	0011111111111111	1101001101111111
Cycle 7:	—	—	[C]	[M]	[M]	(A)	[M]	[C]	[C]	[M]	[M]	[M]	—	[C]	[C]	—	* * * * * * * * * * * *	0121101111101001	0101101101000011
Cycle 8:	(B)	(B)	(B)	(A)	[A]	(M)	[M]	—	[M]	[M]	[H]	(A)	[H]	—	—	(B)	* * * * * * * * *	1111101000110001	1122122110010011
Cycle 9:	(B)	(B)	(B)	(A)	[B]	[M]	(A)	(B)	[A]	[B]	[A]	—	—	—	—	—	* * * * * * * * * * * *	2112111111020011	1101111111111001
Cycle 10:	(B)	—	(C)	(B)	[B]	[A]	(A)	(B)	(A)	[B]	[A]	[A]	—	—	—	—	* * * * * * * * * *	1111111111110100	1010011111120111
Cycle 11:	(B)	(A)	(C)	(B)	[B]	[A]	(A)	(B)	(A)	[B]	(A)	[A]	—	—	—	—	* * * * * * * *	1001011112221001	1011100111111000
Cycle 12:	—	—	—	—	—	—	—	—	—	—	—	—	—	—	—	—	* * * * * *	1010110101101101	1010211101110000
Cycle 13:	(M)	(M)	(C)	(C)	[B]	[B]	(C)	[B]	(C)	(C)	[B]	[A]	[A]	[A]	—	[A]	* * * * * * * * * * * *	0001100100121111	0012100122110111
Cycle 14:	(A)	(A)	(B)	[C]	[B]	[A]	[C]	[C]	(B)	[C]	(A)	[C]	[C]	—	[C]	[A]	* * * * * * * * * * * * * *	0111111112210111	0102001101122001
Cycle 15:	(R)	(R)	(C)	(R)	[M]	[M]	[R]	(C)	(C)	[B]	[A]	[A]	—	—	—	[B]	* * * * * * * * * *	0011101111210002	0011001110010001
Cycle 16:	(C)	(C)	(R)	[C]	[A]	[A]	(C)	(C)	(C)	[C]	[R]	—	—	—	—	—	* * * * * * * *	2111001100100011	2211101100100000
Cycle 17:	(B)	(B)	(A)	(A)	[R]	[R]	(C)	[R]	(R)	[R]	[R]	[R]	—	—	[C]	(S)	* * * * * * * * * *	0000011111020010	0010002111010010
Cycle 18:	(C)	(C)	(R)	(R)	[C]	[C]	[C]	[C]	[C]	(S)	(S)	—	—	—	—	[S]	* * * * * * * *	0000111110200011	0000221010000010
Cycle 19:	(R)	(R)	(C)	(C)	[B]	[B]	[C]	[A]	(C)	(R)	(S)	—	—	—	—	(S)	* * * * * *	0000111100200001	0011001100000000
Cycle 20:	(C)	(C)	[R]	[R]	[C]	[C]	[A]	—	—	(S)	(S)	—	—	—	—	(S)	* * * * *	0011000001000001	0100011100000000
Cycle 21:	(S)	[R]	[C]	[R]	[R]	(S)	—	—	—	—	[S]	—	—	—	—	[S]	* * * *	0100010000100001	0011100000000000
Cycle 22:	[C]	[C]	—	—	—	—	—	—	—	—	—	—	—	—	—	—	* *	1000000000100001	0100100000000000
Cycle 23:	[S]	—	—	—	[S]	[S]	—	—	—	—	—	—	—	—	—	—	* *	1000010000000000	0000000000000000

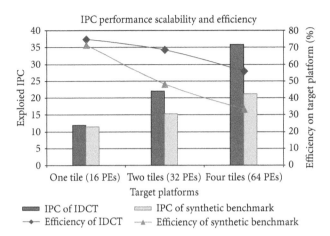

FIGURE 8: Performance scalability for IDCT and a synthetic benchmark.

bypassing registers that are dedicated to data relay as it does with non-transient copy disabled.

Table 3 compares the performance results for other applications with the feature of non-transient copy on and off. On average, using non-transient copy can improve the IPC by 18%. Two special cases where the IPC does not improve much are idct and sad16_c. This is because these two algorithms are designed in the manner of "in-place-update," in which an instruction replaces the source register with the new result immediately after computation. With this special coding style, registers are used very locally and few operands can be reused. In contrast, the other applications make significant reuse of operands. For example, the computation of two adjacent pixels usually can share a large amount of reference pixels. As a result, distributing the shared reference pixels to multiple PEs as non-transient copies helps for data reusing, and the performance improves significantly.

From Table 3, we can also observe that the total usage of inter-PE links is reduced by 15% on average, which can directly be translated into power saving. Moreover, for most of the applications, both the average and peak bypassing register usage are smaller when non-transient copy is enabled.

4.4. Performance Scalability Study. It can be observed from the results in Section 4.2 that the benchmark applications achieved high IPC on both small configuration and large configuration. Actually these video applications can achieve very good performance scalability because of the weak data dependency between each of their kernel iterations. This is illustrated in Figure 9(a), where intra-iteration data dependency is strong while inter-iteration data dependency is weak. As a result, these almost independent iterations can be scheduled across the whole reconfigurable array without incurring much performance penalty. However, it would be interesting to study the performance scalability if an application does not possess this weak inter-iteration property. Unfortunately, good kernels are more than often written in loop fashion with weak inter-iteration data dependency. So we have to create a somewhat contrived

synthetic benchmark to simulate what would happen if a kernel has strong inter-iteration dependency. This is done by generating instructions with data dependency with each other for the synthetic benchmark. In order to compare the performance scalability difference between a typical IDCT (row+col) with weak inter-iteration dependency and the synthetic benchmark, we produce the synthetic benchmark to contain the same number of instructions of the IDCT and similar level of instruction-level parallelism but with strong inter-iteration dependency as illustrated in Figure 9(b).

The performance results are plotted in Figure 8 for compiling these two applications on three configurations: one tile, two tile, and four tiles. It is clear that when the target platform has more PEs, IDCT scales better than the synthetic benchmark though they both get performance boost with more available PEs. Specifically, in four-tile configuration where 64 PEs are available, >35 IPC can be achieved in the case of IDCT, but only 21 IPC can be achieved for the synthetic benchmark. Another interesting point about the CGRA efficiency can be observed from Figure 8. Both applications experience efficiency drop when the number of available PEs becomes larger. This is because scattering an application across a large CGRA tends to introduce more operation "bubbles" in the final execution trace. Therefore, the efficiency may degrade with the increasing of PE numbers.

For the synthetic benchmark, not only that the performance does not scale as well as IDCT but also that the efficiency drops more than IDCT. We think this is mainly due to the difference between the data dependency patterns in these two applications. Since IDCT has weak inter-iteration dependency the operations only need to talk to other operations in the same iteration on neighboring PEs locally. In contrast, the strong inter-iteration data dependency pattern in the synthetic benchmark requires more global communication from one PE to another in a different tile. Therefore, the larger the scale of the PE array, the longer distance for transferring data between remote PEs. Consider a scenario in Figure 9(c) for the synthetic benchmark. Assume M is the computation grid (analogous to a metropolis area) and N is a subgrid within M (the downtown). Two routing requirements are shown. There can be chances that the path connecting node 1 and node 2 will also make use of channels in the subgrid N (downtown). Accumulating the effects, the N (downtown) could have heavy communication (traffic) jam. To avoid congestion, the long routing path will probably be dispersed to the outskirt area. Since long distance across multiple tiles may need more routing cycles, the overall performance will be dragged down by this *downtown effect*.

This suggests that it may not be always a good practice to scatter an application to as many available PEs as possible. For certain applications, instead of having the whole computational array to be mapped for a single application kernel, it is preferable to partition the tile-based FDR-CGRA into several regions. Each region carries out one application and run multiple parallel applications simultaneously. In the synthetic benchmark case, compiling it onto one tile and save the other tiles for other tasks may yield the highest efficiency.

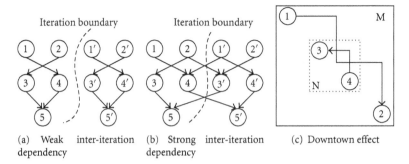

(a) Weak   inter-iteration   (b) Strong   inter-iteration   (c) Downtown effect
dependency   dependency

FIGURE 9: Different benchmark DFGs and downtown effect.

5. Conclusions

In this paper, we proposed FDR (fast data relay) to enhance existing coarse-grained reconfigurable computing architectures (CGRAs). FDR utilizes multicycle data transmission and can effectively reduce communication traffic congestion, thus allowing applications to achieve higher performance. To exploit the potential of FDR, a new CAD inspired compilation flow was also proposed to efficiently compile application kernels onto this architecture. It is shown that FDR-CGRA outperformed two other CGRAs, RCP and ADRES, by up to 21% and 29%, respectively.

References

[1] S. Hauck and A. DeHon, Eds., *Reconfigurable Computing: The Theory and Practice of FPGA-Based Computation (Systems on Silicon)*, Morgan Kaufmann, Boston, Mass, USA, 2007.

[2] T. J. Todman, G. A. Constantinides, S. J. E. Wilton, O. Mencer, W. Luk, and P. Y. K. Cheung, "Reconfigurable computing: architectures and design methods," *IEE Proceedings—Computers and Digital Techniques*, vol. 152, no. 2, article 193.

[3] J. R. Hauser and J. Wawrzynek, "Garp: a MIPS processor with a reconfigurable coprocessor," in *Proceedings of the 5th Annual IEEE Symposium on Field-Programmable Custom Computing Machines*, pp. 12–21, April 1997.

[4] Z. A. Ye, A. Moshovos, S. Hauck, and P. Banerjee, "Chimaera: a high-performance architecture with a tightly-coupled reconfigurable functional unit," in *Proceedings of the The 27th Annual International Symposium on Computer Architecture (ISCA '00)*, pp. 225–235, June 2000.

[5] R. Hartenstein, "Coarse grain reconfigurable architecture (embedded tutorial)," in *Proceedings of the 16th Asia South Pacific Design Automation Conference (ASP-DAC '01)*, pp. 564–570, 2001.

[6] C. Ebeling, D. C. Cronquist, and P. Franklin, "RaPiD—reconfigur-able pipelined datapath," in *Proceedings of the 6th International Workshop on Field-Programmable Logic, Smart Applications, New Paradigms and Compilers (FPL '96)*, 1996.

[7] S. C. Goldstein, H. Schmit, M. Budiu, S. Cadambi, M. Matt, and R. R. Taylor, "PipeRench: a reconfigurable architecture and compiler," *Computer*, vol. 33, no. 4, pp. 70–77, 2000.

[8] H. Singh, M. H. Lee, G. Lu, F. J. Kurdahi, N. Bagherzadeh, and E. M. Chaves Filho, "MorphoSys: an integrated reconfigurable system for data-parallel and computation-intensive applications," *IEEE Transactions on Computers*, vol. 49, no. 5, pp. 465–481, 2000.

[9] R. W. Hartenstein and R. Kress, "Datapath synthesis system for the reconfigurable datapath architecture," in *Proceedings of the Asia and South Pacific Design Automation Conference (ASP-DAC '95)*, pp. 479–484, September 1995.

[10] E. Mirsky and A. DeHon, "MATRIX: a reconfigurable computing architecture with configurable instruction distribution and deployable resources," in *Proceedings of the IEEE Symposium on FPGAs for Custom Computing Machines (FCCM '96)*, pp. 157–166, April 1996.

[11] B. Mei, S. Vernalde, D. Verkest, and R. Lauwereins, "Design methodology for a tightly coupled VLIW/reconfigurable matrix architecture: a case study," in *Proceedings of the Design, Automation and Test in Europe Conference and Exhibition (DATE '04)*, pp. 1224–1229, February 2004.

[12] O. Colavin and D. Rizzo, "A scalable wide-issue clustered VLIW with a reconfigurable interconnect," in *Proceedings of the International Conference on Compilers, Architecture, and Synthesis for Embedded Systems (CASES '03)*, pp. 148–158, November 2003.

[13] M. B. Taylor, W. Lee, J. Miller et al., "Evaluation of the raw microprocessor: an exposed-wire-delay architecture for ILP and streams," in *Proceedings of the 31st Annual International Symposium on Computer Architecture (ISCA '04)*, pp. 2–13, June 2004.

[14] S. Friedman, A. Carroll, B. Van Essen, B. Ylvisaker, C. Ebeling, and S. Hauck, "SPR: an architecture-adaptive CGRA mapping tool," in *Proceedings of the 7th ACM SIGDA International Symposium on Field-Programmable Gate Arrays (FPGA '09)*, pp. 191–200, February 2009.

[15] H. Park, K. Fan, S. Mahlke, T. Oh, H. Kim, and H. S. Kim, "Edge-centric modulo scheduling for coarse-grained reconfigurable architectures," in *Proceedings of the 17th International Conference on Parallel Architectures and Compilation Techniques (PACT '08)*, pp. 166–176, October 2008.

[16] G. Lee, K. Choi, and N. D. Dutt, "Mapping multi-domain applications onto coarse-grained reconfigurable architectures," *IEEE Transactions on Computer-Aided Design of Integrated Circuits and Systems*, vol. 30, no. 5, pp. 637–650, 2011.

[17] T. Suzuki, H. Yamada, T. Yamagishi et al., "High-throughput, low-power software-defined radio using reconfigurable processors," *IEEE Micro*, vol. 31, no. 6, pp. 19–28, 2011.

[18] Z. Kwok and S. J. E. Wilton, "Register file architecture optimization in a coarse-grained reconfigurable architecture," in *Proceedings of the 13th Annual IEEE Symposium on Field-Programmable Custom Computing Machines (FCCM '05)*, pp. 35–44, April 2005.

[19] S. Cadambi and S. C. Goldstein, "Efficient place and route for pipeline reconfigurable architectures," in *Proceedings of*

the International Conference on Computer Design (ICCD '00), pp. 423–429, September 2000.

[20] S. Rixner, W. J. Dally, B. Khailany, P. Mattson, U. J. Kapasi, and J. D. Owens, "Register organization for media processing," in *Proceedings of the 6th International Symposium on High-Performance Computer Architecture (HPCA '00)*, pp. 375–386, January 2000.

[21] R. Balasubraamonian, S. Dwarkadas, and D. H. Albonesi, "Reducing the complexity of the register file in dynamic superscalar processors," in *Proceedings of the 34th Annual International Symposium on Microarchitecture (ACM/IEEE '01)*, pp. 237–248, December 2001.

[22] B. Mei, F. J. Veredas, and B. Masschelein, "Mapping an H.264/AVC decoder onto the adres reconfigurable architecture," in *Proceedings of the International Conference on Field Programmable Logic and Applications (FPL '05)*, pp. 622–625, August 2005.

[23] C. Lattner, "Introduction to the LLVM Compiler Infrastructure," in *Itanium Conference and Expo*, April 2006.

[24] J. L. Hennessy and D. A. Patterson, *Computer Architecture: A Quantitative Approach*, chapter 3, Morgan Kauffmann, Boston, Mass, USA, 4th edition, 2006.

[25] G. D. Micheli, *Synthesis and Optimization of Digital Circuits*, McGraw-Hill, 1994.

[26] R. Nair, "A simple yet effective technique for global wiring," *IEEE Transactions on Computer-Aided Design of Integrated Circuits and Systems*, vol. 6, no. 2, pp. 165–172, 1987.

[27] Xvid video codec, http://www.xvid.org/.

[28] Opensource H.264 reference code, http://iphome.hhi.de/suehring/tml/.

7

Implementation of Ring-Oscillators-Based Physical Unclonable Functions with Independent Bits in the Response

Florent Bernard, Viktor Fischer, Crina Costea, and Robert Fouquet

Laboratoire Hubert Curien, CNRS, UMR5516, Université de Lyon, 42000 Saint-Etienne, France

Correspondence should be addressed to Florent Bernard, florent.bernard@univ-st-etienne.fr

Academic Editor: Kris Gaj

The paper analyzes and proposes some enhancements of Ring-Oscillators-based Physical Unclonable Functions (PUFs). PUFs are used to extract a unique signature of an integrated circuit in order to authenticate a device and/or to generate a key. We show that designers of RO PUFs implemented in FPGAs need a precise control of placement and routing and an appropriate selection of ROs pairs to get independent bits in the PUF response. We provide a method to identify which comparisons are suitable when selecting pairs of ROs. Dealing with power consumption, we propose a simple improvement that reduces the consumption of the PUF published by Suh et al. in 2007 by up to 96.6%. Last but not least, we point out that ring oscillators significantly influence one another and can even be locked. This questions the reliability of the PUF and should be taken into account during the design.

1. Introduction

Security in integrated circuits (ICs) became a very important problem due to high information security requirements. In order to assure authenticity and confidentiality, cryptographic keys are used to encrypt the information. Several solutions were proposed for key generation, each with their upsides and downsides.

Confidential keys can be generated using True Random Number Generators (TRNGs) and stored in volatile or nonvolatile memories. Saving the confidential key in a nonvolatile memory inside the device ensures that the key will never be lost and that it will not be disclosed in case of passive attacks. On the other hand, nonvolatile memories are easy targets for invasive attacks [1]. Volatile memories are typical for Field Programmable Gate Arrays (FPGAs). Storing the confidential key in a volatile memory permits to erase the memory contents in case of invasive attack detection. This implies the use of a communication channel to transmit the key after device configuration [1]. Communication channels are usually easy to corrupt and information can be easily intercepted. The confidentiality and authenticity of designs are therefore compromised.

A solution is backing up the embedded volatile memory block with a battery. However, it was proved that battery-backed RAMs content can be read after a long period of storage [2–5] even if the memory is not powered any more. Thus, the need of generating secret keys inside the IC became obvious.

An alternative to TRNG for key generation is the Physical Unclonable Function (PUF). PUFs are functions that extract a unique signature of an IC, based on randomness during the manufacturing process. This signature can be used as device-dependent key or device identification code. The main advantage of this principle introduced by Pappu et al. in [6, 7] is the fact that the key does not need to be stored in the device and it is thus harder to disclose. Based on intrinsic physical characteristics of circuits obtained during the manufacturing process, the extracted signature is impossible to reproduce by a different IC or by an attacker. PUFs work on challenge-response pairs. The challenge is usually a stimulus sent from outside the device, and the response is the signature of the circuit.

The quality of a PUF is determined mainly by its uniqueness and its reliability. To quantify these properties of a PUF, two types of response variations: intra- (for reliability)

and inter- (for uniqueness) chip variations [8] are used. The intrachip variation refers to the responses of the same PUF (the same device) at the same challenge, regardless of environmental changes (e.g., temperature, voltage). In the ideal case, this variation should be 0. This means that the response of the PUF for a given challenge should always be the same. The intrachip variation measures the reproducibility of the response. The function must be able to reproduce the same response over and over again, especially in the case of reconfigurable devices.

The interchip variation refers to the responses of different PUFs (different devices) at the same challenge. Ideally, this variation should be of 50%, meaning that every bit is equally likely to be zero or one. If this variation is close to 50% then the uniqueness of the responses is guaranteed.

In this paper, we focus on PUF implementation issues in reconfigurable devices and on the independency of bits in the response. Reconfigurable devices are intensively used for implementing cryptographic algorithms on hardware due to the "reconfigurable" property of such circuits. Thus we have to deal with two objectives: to keep the reconfigurable property of FPGAs and to guarantee the uniqueness and reliability of a PUF. In other words, if the PUF response changes when the device is reconfigured, the uniqueness and reliability of a PUF are questionable. We analyze and propose some enhancements of the concept introduced in 2007 by Suh and Devadas [8]. This principle is a ring-oscillators-based PUF (RO-PUF). It was chosen for our experiments because it is one of the most suitable for implementation in FPGAs, independently from the technology. The PUF uses a relatively high number of ring oscillators in order to emphasize the intrinsic characteristics of ICs and extract the signature. The principle is based on the fact that the frequency of ROs depends on gate and routing delays determined partially in an uncontrolled way by the manufacturing process.

In the first part of our work, we had to deal with implementation issues related to the mapping of the PUF to various FPGA technologies. We found out that, contrary to what original authors stated [8], the placement and routing constraints play a very important role (even when ROs are identically laid out) in the design of the function, especially if one wants to obtain sufficient inter-chip variability. The precise control of the initial phase of ROs and careful design of frequency comparators is another important issue that determines the precision of the function and thus reduces intrachip variations. This was not discussed before. Furthermore, in the response there are bits that are dependent on each others. We propose a method justified by mathematical means in order to identify which pairs of ROs we have to select to ensure independency of bits in the response. The main disadvantage of the original design is the high power consumption. We propose a simple modification enabling significant power economy. Finally, during our experiments we observed a very important phenomenon that has a significant impact on the generated results and that was completely neglected in the original design: the existence of a mutual dependence between the ROs can lead sometimes to their mutual locking in FPGAs. It is essential to take into account this unavoidable behavior of ROs in the PUF design.

The paper is organized as follows. In Section 2 we present related work on PUFs implementation and metrics used to measure the quality of a PUF. Section 3 deals with PUF design issues and with the first problem stated: the need of manual placement and routing of the design. Then we remark that some bits in the response might be dependent due to an inappropriate selection of ROs. An example of such a situation and a model of RO pair selection is proposed in Section 4 and a method to identify pairs that will give independent bit in the response is provided. Section 5 presents results of implementation of the RO PUF in main FPGA technologies and analyzes the quality of the PUF in relationship to the selected technology and the quality of the evaluation board. It also evaluates the impact of the mutual dependence of rings on the reliability of the PUF. Section 6 proposes some important enhancement of the function and finally, Section 7 concludes the paper.

2. PUF Background

2.1. Source of Noise in Electronic Devices. From its manufacturing to its usage, an electronic device is faced with many sources of noise coming from different processes and having different signification from one to another. We can distinguish at least three classes of sources of randomness.

(i) In manufacturing process: this noise is due to variation in the silicon layers during the manufacturing process. Once the device is manufactured, it contains these informations which are specific to each integrated circuit. An ideal PUF should be built to extract the maximum amount of this manufacturing noise in order to identify a circuit.

(ii) Local noise: this noise appears when the circuit is working. It is due to the random thermal motion of charge carriers. This noise is very suitable for random number generation but inappropriate for PUF. It should be reduced compared to manufacturing noise to decrease the intrachip variation.

(iii) Global environmental noise: this noise comes from environmental condition (e.g., global temperature and voltage) when the circuit is working. This noise can disrupt the PUF response and increase the intrachip variation making a circuit identification more difficult to perform. Furthermore, this source of noise can be easily manipulated from outside. Therefore, PUFs must be developed in order to reduce the influence of this global environmental noise.

2.2. Related Works and PUF Evaluation. Several concepts of PUF and implementation in reconfigurable devices have already been introduced until now. In [9], the random initialization of SRAM cells in FPGAs is used to generate a specific signature. But in recent FPGAs, manufacturers tend to initialize SRAM cells to a known value that make SRAM cells-based PUF difficult to use. A similar idea is used on FPGA flip-flops and is based on their initial unstable states

[10]. Other PUFs are based on differences in the silicon layers of the device leading to differences between delay paths [8, 11, 12]. The main difficulty in these last designs is to guarantee a perfect symmetry on delay paths in order to exploit the slight differences due to the manufacturing process. Furthermore the placement and routing must be done carefully to exploit the noise due to manufacturing process.

In most of these PUFs, delay paths are implemented with ROs (RO-PUFs). In [13], a new approach is studied in order to use RO-PUF. The so-called *Compensation Method* permits to reduce the influence of unsuitable source of noise on the PUF response. It is realized with Configurable ROs (CROs). One disadvantage pointed by the authors is the reduction of the maximum number of independent bits that can be extracted from such a PUF leading to an increase in the number of ROs that should be used.

As mentioned in introduction, PUF quality is evaluated by its uniqueness and its reliability. In [13], authors proposed two metrics. These metrics cannot directly give the characterization of interdie variation process which can only be estimated based on PUF responses. Thus it depends greatly on how the PUF is implemented to extract the maximum amount of manufacturing noise.

Let (i, j) be a pair of chips with $i \neq j$ and R_i (resp., R_j) the n-bit response of chip i (resp., chip j). The first metric is the *average interdie Hamming Distance (HD)* among a group of k chips and is defined as

$$\overline{\text{Inter} - d_{\text{HD}}}(k) = \frac{2}{k(k-1)} \sum_{i=1}^{k-1} \sum_{j=i+1}^{k} \frac{\text{HD}(R_i, R_j)}{n} \times 100\%. \tag{1}$$

This distance should converge to 50% in the case of an ideal PUF.

The second metric introduced by the authors of [13] is used to ensure the reliability of a PUF. An n-bits response is extracted from chip i (R_i) at normal operating conditions. Then at a different operating condition (different temperature or different voltage), x samples $(R'_{i,y})_{y \in \{1,...,x\}}$ of the response of the same PUF at this operating conditions are extracted. The *average intradie HD* over x samples for the chip i is defined as

$$\overline{\text{Intra} - d_{\text{HD}}}(x, i) = \frac{1}{x} \sum_{y=1}^{x} \frac{\text{HD}(R_i, R'_{i,y})}{n} \times 100\%. \tag{2}$$

This distance should be close to 0% to ensure reliable responses from the PUF in a given chip at various operating conditions.

In [14], a deeper analysis on a special PUF (the Arbiter PUF that was originally proposed in [12]) evaluation lead the author to consider 4 indicators on the evaluation of the intrachip variation (randomness, steadiness, correctness, and diffuseness). For the inter-chip variation the metric used is also the uniqueness (expressed differently than in [13]). Even if measurements of uniqueness and reliability seem sufficient to qualify a PUF, it can be interesting to go further

(especially in the case of an unexpected high intrachip variation).

3. PUF Design Issues

3.1. Principle of the PUF and Its Implementation in FPGA. In the principle of the PUF published in [8] that was selected for our experiments, N identically laid-out ROs are placed on the IC. Slight differences between their frequencies will appear because of the unavoidable differences in the silicon layers of the semiconductor device caused by the manufacturing process. Pairs of oscillators are chosen one after another and their frequencies compared. The response of the PUF is equal to 1 if the first RO is faster and 0 otherwise.

The RO PUF in Figure 1, as not many details were given by the authors in [8], is realized using 32 ROs controlled by an enable signal for all selected technologies (ALTERA, XILINX, and ACTEL). Two counters are used to define the winner of the race by counting N periods of the two generated clock signals: if one of the two counters (the winner of the race) reaches a predefined value N, the arbiter stops the race and saves its result in the shift register. The principle of the race arbiter is depicted in Figure 2. Once one of counters reached the maximum value N, it sets its output signal "finished" to 1. This value causes that the "done" signal of the winning counter is also set to 1 and it blocks the "done" signal of the second counter, which cannot be set any more. This means that the race can have only one winner, pointed out by the OR gate (0 for counter 2, 1 for counter 1). Once the race result was obtained and saved, the oscillation and counter could restart using the same control signal (enable).

When compared with the original principle published in [8], the proposed principle is more precise; it can recognize differences that are smaller than 1-bit, so the counting period can be shorter and the PUF response faster. In our experiments, we used 10-bit counters and the most significant bit was used as the output signal (signal "finished") of the counter.

The output of the PUF presented in Figure 1 is 1-bit wide. In order to obtain a wider response, we use a shift register with a 16-bit output. To get more responses at once, the challenge generator is included in the design. It is a simple 8-bit counter-incremented after each race. For each value of the challenge generator, two different oscillators are chosen for comparison. They are separated in two groups of 16 (group A and group B). The output of the counter is divided in two parts: 4 Least Significant Bits (LSB) selecting one of 16 ROs in group A and 4 Most Significant Bits (MSB) selecting one of 16 ROs in group B. Thus, every oscillator in group A is compared to all oscillators in group B. This way, we obtain $16 \times 16 = 256$ different challenges thus 256 responses of 1 bit for each device. For simplicity, we consider that each IC delivers 256-bit responses. The generated bit streams are sent to the PC using a USB interface. For this reason, a small USB module featuring a Cypress EZ-USB device was connected to the evaluation board containing

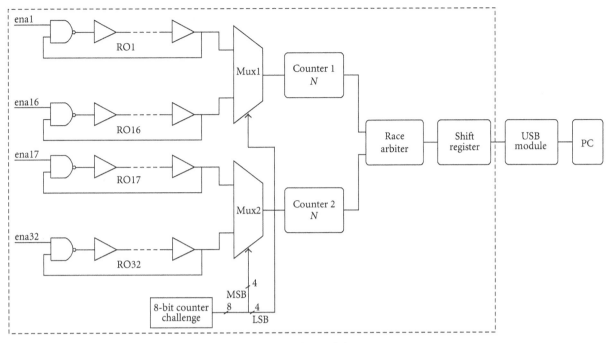

FIGURE 1: RO PUF Scheme.

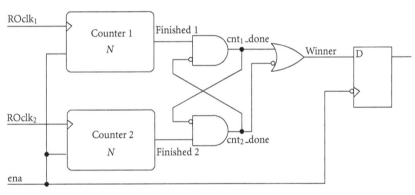

FIGURE 2: Principle of the race arbiter.

FPGA. A 16-bit communication interface with this module was implemented inside the FPGA. A Visual C++ application running on the PC reads the USB peripheral and writes data into a text file. For both ALTERA and XILINX technology, delay elements of the ROs are implemented using Look-Up Tables (LUTs). Finally, one NAND2 gate that is necessary to obtain oscillations, close the loop, and provide the structure with an enable signal. This configuration allows the use of either an odd or even number of delay elements. Thus, the ROs used in the design are made of 7 delay elements and one NAND2 gate in order to fit the ring into one LAB. In ACTEL technology, the oscillators employ 7 AND2 gates as delay elements and a NAND2 gate as a control gate.

3.2. Implementation Results and Tests. As resources in FPGAs have increased in volume and performances, integrated development environments (IDEs) are charged with automatic placement and routing. This is very convenient in common applications. The design can be translated into a significant number of logic elements, thus with automatic placement and routing, the user gains time and the surface of the IC is used at its maximum capacity. The compiler used by these environments calculates the optimal disposition of logic cells.

The RO PUF presented in [8] exploits, as any other PUF, the intrinsic characteristics of an IC. By definition, the position of the PUF on the IC determines the set of challenge-response pairs. RO placed in LAB A will most probably not oscillate at the same frequency as RO placed in LAB B. In order to use this PUF for the authentication process or as a secret key generator, one must be sure that the response of the PUF will be the same under any environmental conditions and even more important, after each reconfiguration of the device.

The first tests were conducted on ALTERA DE1 boards including Cyclone II EP2C20F484C7N FPGA. We used the PUF to authenticate the devices available in the laboratory. It allowed us to identify a given IC between the 13 available.

TABLE 1: RO PUF responses for three projects implemented in the same device (ROs were constrained but not the race arbiter).

Response no. 1 (only the PUF)	031f031f031f0005573f031f031f471f 573f031f011fd73ff7bf431f0117031f
Response no. 2 (PUF and counter)	010000004df20000000045a04de245e0 45a0fff70000000045e0fff745e045e0
Response no. 3 (only the PUF and an extra output)	0007600f7eef7eef200ffffff724f704f 600f0007600f7eef0005000772ef0007

TABLE 2: RO PUF responses for three projects implemented in the same device (ROs and race arbiter were constrained).

Response no. 1 (only the PUF)	ea09ebf9ea09ebfbea09e**b**59ebfbeb79 ea09ebfbffffbffeb79ea49ebfb0001
Response no. 2 (PUF and counter)	ea09ebf9ea09ebfbea09ea**6**9ebfbeb79 ea09ebfbffffbffeb79ea49ebfb0001
Response no. 3 (only the PUF and an extra output)	ea09ebf9ea09ebfbea09ea59ebfbeb79 ea09ebfbffffbffeb79ea**1**9fbfb0001

As expected, we were able to perform this operation on all the devices: both inter- and intrachip variations were in normal ranges. However, authors insisted that the design needed no further placement and routing constraints in [8], page 3: "[· · ·] there is no need for careful layout and routing. For example, the paths from oscillator outputs to counters do not need to be symmetric." While it is clear that ROs must be identically laidout (which is achieved thanks to a macro in [8]), it is questionable that extra logic around the ROs (e.g., the race arbiter) needs no placement and routing constraints. We can imagine the next scenario: in order to control royalties, the IP vendor wants to use a PUF for linking the IP licence to a concrete FPGA device. However, a while later, he needs to make an upgrade of his IP function, still related to the same device and the same PUF response. This means that he needs that the response of the PUF block will be independent of the rest of the design.

We evaluated the impact of the changes in surrounding logic on the PUF response. First, we added a new counter-block module. Since it was independent of the PUF, it should not change the PUF response. Contrary to all expectations, instead of obtaining almost the same response of the PUF (i.e., obtaining small intrachip variation), the device gave completely different response so that presumably low intrachip variation after addition of the additional logic was almost as high as an ideal inter-chip variation: 48,8% of the response bits changed. We have to stress here, that the placement and routing of ROs was constrained, but not the structure of the arbiter.

In the next experiment, we kept initial PUF and sent its output, as before, towards the USB module and additionally towards a 7-segment display available on ALTERA DE1 board. While we were still maintaining the placement and routing for ROs, we got another (the third) response of the PUF for the same device! The responses for three projects including the same PUF in the same device are depicted in Table 1.

3.3. Imposing Placement and Routing Solution for Response Stabilization. The above-mentioned results show that the optimization performed by the compiler implies different placement and routing for the race arbiter after each recompilation.

As we need to have the minimal intrachip variation even for project upgrades, this is of extreme importance. Different placement of the race arbiter implies different PUF and different intrinsic characteristics that are explored. In both targeted processes (authentication and key generation) this is not acceptable. Therefore, imposing placement and routing constraints on the whole PUF block is mandatory in order to obtain a response independent from architecture modifications in a reconfigurable device.

Once placement and routing constraints were applied on both ROs and arbiter structure, the PUF provided excellent and expected responses. Table 2 presents results of three projects including the same PUF in the same device. Only few differences exist (printed in bold).

4. Bit Dependency in the PUF Response

In Section 3.1, we presented the way we selected pairs of oscillators to obtain a 256-bit response. We have to evaluate how many bits are independent in the PUF response. For example, consider 2 ROs a, b in group 1 and two other ROs c, d in group 2. The comparisons are (a, c), (a, d), (b, c), and (b, d), giving 4 possible bits in the response. But if $a > c$, $c > b$, $b > d$, then we can predict $a > d$, so there are only 3 bits of information instead of 4 in this example.

In the following, we propose to compute how many bits in the response are independent. This could help RO-PUF designers to select pairs of ROs.

4.1. Generalization. Let $(a_1, \ldots, a_n)$ be the first group of ROs and $(b_1, \ldots, b_n)$ be the second group of ROs. We use the relation $x > y$ when RO x is faster than RO y. In most of cases, ROs in group 1 (resp., in group 2) are not sorted thanks to the relation $>$. However it exists a permutation $\sigma \in \mathcal{S}_n$ (resp., $\sigma' \in \mathcal{S}_n$) such as $a_{\sigma(1)} > a_{\sigma(2)} > \cdots > a_{\sigma(n)}$ (resp., $b_{\sigma'(1)} > b_{\sigma'(2)} > \cdots > b_{\sigma'(n)}$).

We define the matrix of all comparison results between one RO in group 1 and one RO in group 2. Matrix rows are indexed by $(a_{\sigma(1)}, \ldots, a_{\sigma(n)})$ and matrix columns are indexed by $(b_{\sigma'(1)}, \ldots, b_{\sigma'(n)})$

$$\text{Comp}_n = \begin{pmatrix} c_{1,1} & c_{1,2} & \cdots & c_{1,n} \\ c_{2,1} & c_{2,2} & \cdots & c_{2,n} \\ \vdots & \vdots & \ddots & \vdots \\ c_{n,1} & c_{n,2} & \cdots & c_{n,n} \end{pmatrix}, \tag{3}$$

$$\text{where } c_{i,j} = \begin{cases} 0 & \text{when } a_{\sigma(i)} \leq b_{\sigma'(j)} \\ 1 & \text{when } a_{\sigma(i)} > b_{\sigma'(j)}. \end{cases}$$

Because $(a_{\sigma(i)})_i$ and $(b_{\sigma'(j)})_j$ are sorted, if $a_{\sigma(i)} \leq b_{\sigma'(j)}$, then for all $k \geq i$, $a_{\sigma(k)} \leq b_{\sigma'(j)}$ because $a_{\sigma(i)} > a_{\sigma(k)}$. In other words if $c_{i,j} = 0$ then for all $k \geq i$, $c_{k,j} = 0$.

Similarly, if $a_{\sigma(i)} > b_{\sigma'(j)}$, then for all $l \geq j$, $a_{\sigma(i)} > b_{\sigma'(l)}$ because $b_{\sigma(j)} > b_{\sigma(l)}$. In other words, if $c_{i,j} = 1$ then for each $l \geq j$, $c_{i,l} = 1$.

Among the 2^{n^2} possible matrices, only matrices with general term $c_{i,j}$ following the two rules,

(1) if $c_{i,j} = 0$ then for all $k \geq i$, $c_{k,j} = 0$,

(2) if $c_{i,j} = 1$ then for each $l \geq j$, $c_{i,l} = 1$,

can be obtained when comparing pairs of ROs. The others denote antagonist comparisons that cannot appear (e.g., $a > c$, $c > b$, $b > d$ and $a < d$ which is impossible).

4.2. Number of Possible Matrices.

Let $M_{m,n}$ be the number of possible matrices $\mathcal{M}_{m,n}$ with m rows and n columns. By symmetry of the role played by $(a_i)_i$ and $(b_j)_j$ it is obvious that $M_{m,n} = M_{n,m}$.

By convention, we set for all $n \in \mathbb{N}$, $M_{0,n} = 1 = M_{n,0}$, thus we have the following recursive relation giving $M_{m,n}$ ($m \leq n$):

$$M_{m,n} = \sum_{i=0}^{m} M_{i,n-i} \times M_{m-i,i}. \tag{4}$$

To prove this relation, we write the matrix with four blocks for i from 0 to m:

$$\mathcal{M}_{m,n} = \left(\begin{array}{c|c} A_{i,n-i} & B_{i,i} \\ \hline C_{m-i,n-i} & D_{m-i,i} \end{array} \right) \tag{5}$$

with block $B_{i,i}$ necessarily filled with 1s and block $C_{m-i,n-i}$ necessarily filled with 0 s. This can be explained by building first matrices.

For example, for $i = 0$ we have

$$\mathcal{M}_{m,n} = (C_{m,n}) = \begin{pmatrix} 0 & \cdots & 0 \\ \vdots & \ddots & \vdots \\ 0 & \cdots & 0 \end{pmatrix}. \tag{6}$$

Then the only location to set a one in the matrix is the upper right corner. Indeed, if we set a 0 instead then the last column will be filled with 0 s according to rule (1). In this case, it is impossible to set a 1 elsewhere in a line of the matrix because according to rule (2), it would force a 1 in the last column in the same line which is impossible. For $i = 1$ we have

$$\mathcal{M}_{m,n} = \left(\begin{array}{c|c} A_{1,n-1} & 1 \\ \hline \begin{matrix} 0 & \cdots & 0 \\ \vdots & \ddots & \vdots \\ 0 & \cdots & 0 \end{matrix} & D_{m-1,1} \end{array} \right) \tag{7}$$

with $M_{1,n-1}$ matrices for $A_{1,n-1}$ and $M_{m-1,1}$ for $D_{m-1,1}$ for a total of $M_{1,n-1} \times M_{m-1,1}$ possible matrices in this configuration. The next configuration is obtained with a 1 in the upper right corner of block $C_{m-1,n-1}$ and following rules (1) and (2) the 2×2 block $B_{2,2}$ is necessarily filled with 1 s. So the next configuration will be the study of all possible matrices of the shape

$$\mathcal{M}_{m,n} = \left(\begin{array}{c|c} A_{2,n-2} & \begin{matrix} 1 & 1 \\ 1 & 1 \end{matrix} \\ \hline \begin{matrix} 0 & \cdots & 0 \\ \vdots & \ddots & \vdots \\ 0 & \cdots & 0 \end{matrix} & D_{m-2,2} \end{array} \right) \tag{8}$$

then for $i = 3$ possible matrices with a 1 in the upper right corner of block $C_{m-2,n-2}$, and so on until $i = m$ where the last possible matrice has the form:

$$\mathcal{M}_{m,n} = \begin{pmatrix} 1 & \cdots & 1 \\ \vdots & \ddots & \vdots \\ 1 & \cdots & 1 \end{pmatrix}. \tag{9}$$

Thus for i from 0 to m we count all the possible matrices $A_{i,n-i}$ and $D_{m-i,i}$ following the two previously mentioned rules. For each i, there are $M_{i,n-i}$ possible matrices for $A_{i,n-i}$ and $M_{m-i,i}$ matrices for $D_{m-i,i}$. Thus, there are $M_{i,n-i} \times M_{m-i,i}$ possible matrices for a given i. The sum over i gives the formula in (4).

Using this formula in our context (two groups with the same number n of ROs), there are $M_{n,n}$ possible matrices. Then $\log_2(M_{n,n})$ gives the number of independent comparisons we can perform to get independent bits in the response.

For $n = 16$ ROs in each group, we got (only) $M_{16,16} = 601080390$ authorized matrices among the 2^{256} possible. Then only a mean of $\log_2(M_{16,16}) \approx 29$ comparisons leads to 29 independent bits in the PUF response (instead of 256). We can deduce that we should have $n = 135$ ROs in each group to get a PUF response with 256 independent bits.

4.3. Example.

In the next example, we use the response in Table 2. Due to intrachip variation, some bits change in the response. To have only one representation of the response, we use a mean over 64 PUF responses with the same challenge and we obtain ea09ebf9ea09ebfbea09eb59ebfbeb79ea09ebf-bfffffb ffeb79ea49ebfb0001. If we analyze the response, we can see repetitive patterns (e.g., ea09, ebf9, etc.) meaning that there are dependent bits in the response.

We can be more precise and give, in this configuration, the number of bits that are independent in the PUF response.

We rewrite the PUF response column by column in a 16×16 matrix, with rows from top to bottom $a_1, \ldots, a_{16}$ and columns from left to right $b_1, \ldots, b_{16}$

$$
\begin{pmatrix}
1 & 1 & 1 & 1 & 1 & 1 & 1 & 1 & 1 & 1 & 1 & 1 & 1 & 1 & 1 & 0 \\
1 & 1 & 1 & 1 & 1 & 1 & 1 & 1 & 1 & 1 & 1 & 1 & 1 & 1 & 1 & 0 \\
1 & 1 & 1 & 1 & 1 & 1 & 1 & 1 & 1 & 1 & 1 & 1 & 1 & 1 & 1 & 0 \\
0 & 0 & 0 & 0 & 0 & 0 & 0 & 0 & 0 & 0 & 1 & 1 & 0 & 0 & 0 & 0 \\
1 & 1 & 1 & 1 & 1 & 1 & 1 & 1 & 1 & 1 & 1 & 1 & 1 & 1 & 1 & 0 \\
0 & 0 & 0 & 0 & 0 & 0 & 0 & 0 & 0 & 0 & 1 & 0 & 0 & 0 & 0 & 0 \\
1 & 1 & 1 & 1 & 1 & 1 & 1 & 1 & 1 & 1 & 1 & 1 & 1 & 1 & 1 & 0 \\
0 & 1 & 0 & 1 & 0 & 1 & 1 & 1 & 0 & 1 & 1 & 1 & 1 & 0 & 1 & 0 \\
0 & 1 & 0 & 1 & 0 & 0 & 1 & 0 & 0 & 1 & 1 & 1 & 0 & 0 & 1 & 0 \\
0 & 1 & 0 & 1 & 0 & 1 & 1 & 1 & 0 & 1 & 1 & 1 & 1 & 1 & 1 & 0 \\
0 & 1 & 0 & 1 & 0 & 0 & 1 & 1 & 0 & 1 & 1 & 1 & 1 & 0 & 1 & 0 \\
0 & 1 & 0 & 1 & 0 & 1 & 1 & 1 & 0 & 1 & 1 & 1 & 0 & 1 & 0 \\
1 & 1 & 1 & 1 & 1 & 1 & 1 & 1 & 1 & 1 & 1 & 1 & 1 & 1 & 1 & 0 \\
0 & 0 & 0 & 0 & 0 & 0 & 0 & 0 & 0 & 0 & 1 & 1 & 0 & 0 & 0 & 0 \\
0 & 0 & 1 & 0 & 0 & 1 & 0 & 0 & 1 & 1 & 1 & 0 & 0 & 1 & 0 \\
1 & 1 & 1 & 1 & 1 & 1 & 1 & 1 & 1 & 1 & 1 & 1 & 1 & 1 & 1 & 1
\end{pmatrix}. \tag{10}
$$

Then we have to transform this matrix with respect to the two previous rules. We count the Hamming weight of each line. Then we permute lines to obtain the Hamming weight of line $a_{\sigma(i)}$ greater than or equal to the one of line $a_{\sigma(i+1)}$ for each i see Table 5.

We obtain

$$
\begin{pmatrix}
1 & 1 & 1 & 1 & 1 & 1 & 1 & 1 & 1 & 1 & 1 & 1 & 1 & 1 & 1 & 1 \\
1 & 1 & 1 & 1 & 1 & 1 & 1 & 1 & 1 & 1 & 1 & 1 & 1 & 1 & 1 & 0 \\
1 & 1 & 1 & 1 & 1 & 1 & 1 & 1 & 1 & 1 & 1 & 1 & 1 & 1 & 1 & 0 \\
1 & 1 & 1 & 1 & 1 & 1 & 1 & 1 & 1 & 1 & 1 & 1 & 1 & 1 & 1 & 0 \\
1 & 1 & 1 & 1 & 1 & 1 & 1 & 1 & 1 & 1 & 1 & 1 & 1 & 1 & 1 & 0 \\
1 & 1 & 1 & 1 & 1 & 1 & 1 & 1 & 1 & 1 & 1 & 1 & 1 & 1 & 1 & 0 \\
1 & 1 & 1 & 1 & 1 & 1 & 1 & 1 & 1 & 1 & 1 & 1 & 1 & 1 & 1 & 0 \\
0 & 1 & 0 & 1 & 0 & 1 & 1 & 1 & 0 & 1 & 1 & 1 & 1 & 1 & 1 & 0 \\
0 & 1 & 0 & 1 & 0 & 1 & 1 & 1 & 0 & 1 & 1 & 1 & 1 & 0 & 1 & 0 \\
0 & 1 & 0 & 1 & 0 & 1 & 1 & 1 & 0 & 1 & 1 & 1 & 1 & 0 & 1 & 0 \\
0 & 1 & 0 & 1 & 0 & 0 & 1 & 1 & 0 & 1 & 1 & 1 & 1 & 0 & 1 & 0 \\
0 & 1 & 0 & 1 & 0 & 0 & 1 & 0 & 0 & 1 & 1 & 1 & 0 & 0 & 1 & 0 \\
0 & 0 & 0 & 1 & 0 & 0 & 1 & 0 & 0 & 1 & 1 & 1 & 0 & 0 & 1 & 0 \\
0 & 0 & 0 & 0 & 0 & 0 & 0 & 0 & 0 & 0 & 1 & 1 & 0 & 0 & 0 & 0 \\
0 & 0 & 0 & 0 & 0 & 0 & 0 & 0 & 0 & 0 & 1 & 1 & 0 & 0 & 0 & 0 \\
0 & 0 & 0 & 0 & 0 & 0 & 0 & 0 & 0 & 0 & 1 & 0 & 0 & 0 & 0 & 0
\end{pmatrix}. \tag{11}
$$

The same work is done with columns (Hamming weight of column $b_{\sigma'(j)}$ is less or equal than the one of column $b_{\sigma'(j+1)}$) see Table 6:

Finally, we obtain the following matrix:

$$
\begin{pmatrix}
1 & 1 & 1 & 1 & 1 & 1 & 1 & 1 & 1 & 1 & 1 & 1 & 1 & 1 & 1 \\
0 & 1 & 1 & 1 & 1 & 1 & 1 & 1 & 1 & 1 & 1 & 1 & 1 & 1 & 1 \\
0 & 1 & 1 & 1 & 1 & 1 & 1 & 1 & 1 & 1 & 1 & 1 & 1 & 1 & 1 \\
0 & 1 & 1 & 1 & 1 & 1 & 1 & 1 & 1 & 1 & 1 & 1 & 1 & 1 & 1 \\
0 & 1 & 1 & 1 & 1 & 1 & 1 & 1 & 1 & 1 & 1 & 1 & 1 & 1 & 1 \\
0 & 1 & 1 & 1 & 1 & 1 & 1 & 1 & 1 & 1 & 1 & 1 & 1 & 1 & 1 \\
0 & 1 & 1 & 1 & 1 & 1 & 1 & 1 & 1 & 1 & 1 & 1 & 1 & 1 & 1 \\
0 & 0 & 0 & 0 & 0 & 1 & 1 & 1 & 1 & 1 & 1 & 1 & 1 & 1 & 1 \\
0 & 0 & 0 & 0 & 0 & 0 & 1 & 1 & 1 & 1 & 1 & 1 & 1 & 1 & 1 \\
0 & 0 & 0 & 0 & 0 & 0 & 1 & 1 & 1 & 1 & 1 & 1 & 1 & 1 & 1 \\
0 & 0 & 0 & 0 & 0 & 0 & 0 & 1 & 1 & 1 & 1 & 1 & 1 & 1 & 1 \\
0 & 0 & 0 & 0 & 0 & 0 & 0 & 0 & 0 & 1 & 1 & 1 & 1 & 1 & 1 \\
0 & 0 & 0 & 0 & 0 & 0 & 0 & 0 & 0 & 0 & 1 & 1 & 1 & 1 & 1 \\
0 & 0 & 0 & 0 & 0 & 0 & 0 & 0 & 0 & 0 & 0 & 0 & 0 & 1 & 1 \\
0 & 0 & 0 & 0 & 0 & 0 & 0 & 0 & 0 & 0 & 0 & 0 & 0 & 1 & 1 \\
0 & 0 & 0 & 0 & 0 & 0 & 0 & 0 & 0 & 0 & 0 & 0 & 0 & 0 & 1
\end{pmatrix} \tag{12}
$$

with $\sigma = \begin{pmatrix} 1 & 2 & 3 & 4 & 5 & 6 & 7 & 8 & 9 & 10 & 11 & 12 & 13 & 14 & 15 & 16 \\ 16 & 1 & 2 & 3 & 5 & 7 & 13 & 10 & 8 & 12 & 11 & 9 & 15 & 4 & 14 & 6 \end{pmatrix}$ which is the permutation of rows and $\sigma' = \begin{pmatrix} 1 & 2 & 3 & 4 & 5 & 6 & 7 & 8 & 9 & 10 & 11 & 12 & 13 & 14 & 15 & 16 \\ 16 & 1 & 3 & 5 & 9 & 14 & 6 & 8 & 13 & 2 & 4 & 7 & 10 & 15 & 12 & 11 \end{pmatrix}$ which is the permutation of columns. Thus, $a_{\sigma(1)} = a_{16} > b_{\sigma'(1)} = b_{16}$ (upper left corner in the matrix) gives a one. Then other comparisons between $a_{\sigma(1)}$ and $b_{\sigma'(j)}$ for $j > 1$ give no additional information because we know that they will give a 1. The next comparison is between $a_{\sigma(2)} = a_1$ and $b_{\sigma'(1)} = b_{16}$ which is a zero, meaning that $a_1 < b_{16}$. Then

other comparisons between $b_{\sigma'(1)}$ and $a_{\sigma(i)}$ for $i > 1$ are useless because we know that they will give a 0. In this way, we can identify which comparisons are giving information (they are boxed in the matrix). This also gives indexes of ROs that have to be compared. In this special case, they are $(a_{\sigma(1)} = a_{16}$ and $b_{\sigma'(1)} = b_{16}, a_{\sigma(2)} = a_1$ and $b_{\sigma'(1)} = b_{16}, a_{\sigma(2)} = a_1$ and $b_{\sigma'(2)} = b_1, \ldots)$. In our case, we have 31 suitable comparisons and so 31 bits in the response that are independent (close to the theoretical mean of 29 computed).

TABLE 3: Intrachip variation for different devices in nominal conditions.

Device	Cyclone III	Spartan 3	Virtex 5	Fusion
Intrachip variation	0.92%	0.81%	3.38%	13.5%

TABLE 4: Locking of ROs depending on voltage.

Voltage (5)	Number of RO locked (over 16 ROs)
0.95–1.15	0
1.20–1.25	2
1.30	4
1.35–1.40	8

4.4. Comments on This Method. This method is useful to know how many bits are independent in the PUF response. In particular, when the PUF is used for cryptographic key generation, it indicates how many bits of entropy you can expect in the response.

However the response has still 256 bits (including dependencies) and can be used to compute inter-chip variation between many devices of the same family. Due to intrinsic parameters of each device, permutations of ring oscillators will be different from one device to another, giving different response and contributing to inter-chip variation.

For intrachip variation, it is different. Permutations of ring oscillators are related to the device and will obviously change from one device to another. The number of independent bits in the response and their positions will depend on each device and our method permits to know precisely how many independent bits are there and what are their positions. The intrachip variation must be computed on these bits.

The proposed method is used to analyze the PUF response and not to change it. It has been implemented in software in order to estimate the entropy of the generated sequence. A hardware implementation could be possible and useful for improving PUF response. This aspect was not studied in this paper.

5. Observation of the PUF in Various Technologies and Environmental Conditions

5.1. Observing the PUF in ALTERA, XILINX, and ACTEL Technologies. In order to compare different FPGA technologies, we would need a huge number of devices for all of tested families. Unfortunately, we had only cards with thirteen Altera Cyclone II and four Cyclone III devices, five Xilinx Spartan 3, three Xilinx Virtex 5 chips, and five Actel Fusion FPGAs at our disposal. For this reason, we used the biggest group of thirteen Cyclone II FPGAs to verify the inter-chip variation. We used results obtained in Section 4 (i.e., a PUF response of 31 bits in this case). The obtained value computed using (1) was 48.57% in average, which is close to the ideal value of 50%. The intrachip variation of the PUF was tested on four ALTERA Cyclone III EP3C25F256C8N ICs. These experiments were conducted under variable temperature and voltage conditions. Results have been prevailed for a temperature range from 30 to 80°

Celsius (see Figure 3) and a voltage range from 0.9 to 1.3 V for the nominal voltage of 1.2 V (see Figure 4).

In these two figures, the distribution of the number of bits (x-axis) that changed between two different responses from the same PUF is shown as a histogram. The doted line presents the binomial distribution $\mathcal{B}(n, p)$, where $n = 31$ is the number of bits of the response using the methodology presented in Section 4 and $p = \overline{\text{Intra} - d_{\text{HD}}}(64, i)$ is the average intradie Hamming distance over 64 samples for the board tested.

Experiments show that intrachip variation increases when temperature increases. Furthermore, the behavior of the PUF drifts from the binomial distribution. This is probably caused by the influence of thermal noise which is more important as temperature increases and superposes a normal distribution on the binomial distribution.

The lowest intrachip variation is obtained in the normal operating conditions, both in voltage (1.2 V) and temperature (30° Celsius).

In comparison to our previous results in [15], intrachip variations were underestimated because the mean was computed on a 256-bit response ignoring dependency between bits. According to our method, we identify 31 bits of information in the response. Thus the intrachip variation must be computed on these bits. This explains why the ratio

$$\frac{\text{intrachip variation in } [15]}{\text{intrachip variation in this paper}} \approx \frac{256}{31}. \quad (13)$$

The PUF was also tested on XILINX Spartan 3 XC3S700ANn, on XILINX Virtex 5 XC5VLX30T, and on ACTEL Fusion M7AFS600 FPGA devices. Experimental results confirm the fact that placement constraints are mandatory. Intrachip variation for these devices are presented in Table 3.

For ACTEL technology, the tests were performed on ACTEL Fusion M7AFS600 FPGA. The intrachip variation reaches 13.5%! This technology presents the highest intrachip variation which is unexploitable for IC authentication. One of the reasons for which we think the intrachip variation is higher for these boards is the fact that they present more noise than the other ones. We observed a peak at 20 MHz in the core voltage spectrum, caused probably by some internal oscillator embedded in ACTEL FPGA. Similar peak was not detected in other technologies. These results show that the quality of this PUF is strongly related to the quality of the device and the board. In this precise case, the intrinsic characteristics of the IC are overwhelmed by the noise and the results are far from being ideal.

5.2. PUF and Mutual Relationship between Rings. While studying properties of ROs, we observed that ROs influence one another sometimes to an unexpected extent. If the ROs are identically laid out, their oscillating frequencies are almost the same. The differences are caused by the intrinsic characteristics of the IC as well as by the noise. If the frequencies are so close that the current peaks caused by rising and falling edges overlap, the ROs can lock and oscillate at the same frequency, either in phase or with a phase shift.

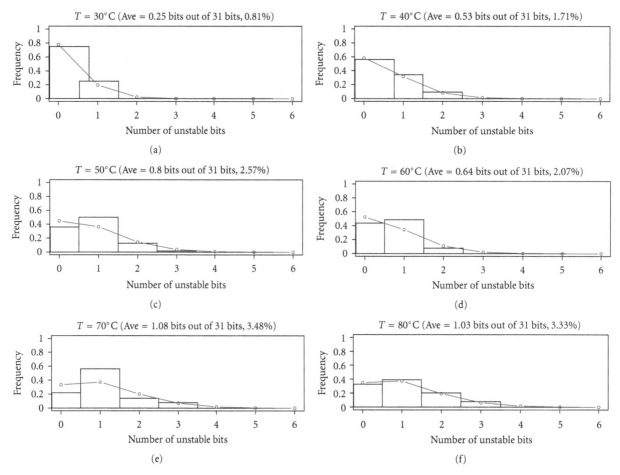

FIGURE 3: Intrachip variation on the same Cyclone III EP3C25F256C8N FPGA for various temperatures.

TABLE 5

Old line index	1	2	3	4	5	6	7	8	9	10	11	12	13	14	15	16
Number of 1	15	15	15	2	15	1	15	10	7	11	9	10	15	2	6	16
New index	2	3	4	14	5	16	6	9	12	8	11	10	7	15	13	1

TABLE 6

Column index	1	2	3	4	5	6	7	8	9	10	11	12	13	14	15	16
Number of 1	7	12	7	13	7	10	13	11	7	13	16	15	11	8	13	1
New index	2	10	3	11	4	7	12	8	5	13	16	15	9	6	14	1

Figure 5 shows output waveforms of two ROs that are locked (both waveforms are visible) and Figure 6 shows ROs that are not locked (the second waveform is not observable). Note that the oscilloscope was synchronized on the first waveform.

One can argue that the mutual dependence of rings could be caused by the FPGA input/output circuitry. In order to avoid influencing the results by outputting the signals from FPGA, we used simple circuitry permitting to detect the locking. The signals delivered by the two ROs were fed into the D flip-flop: one of them to the data input and the other to the clock input. If the output of the flip-flop is constant ("1" or "0") then the oscillators are locked.

The observation of numerous rings confirmed the fact that the mutual dependence of oscillators is big enough for them to lock and oscillate at the same frequency. We could also observe that independent oscillators at moment t_0 can become locked at moment t_1 if external conditions (temperature, voltage) present even slight changes.

If the challenge sent to the PUF selects a pair of oscillators that are locked, then the response is no longer based on intrinsic characteristics of the IC. Frequencies are identical, therefore the bit should not be valid. This depends however on the method employed for frequency measurement. In our design, if the ROs are locked with a phase shift, the rising edge of the RO with an advance will always be counted

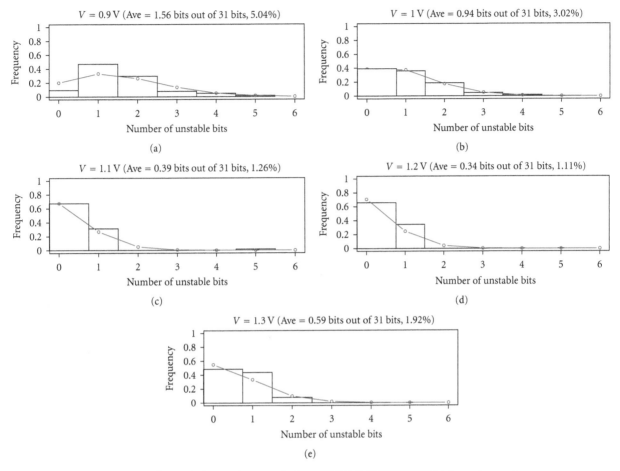

FIGURE 4: Intrachip variation on the same Cyclone III EP3C25F256C8N FPGA for various voltages.

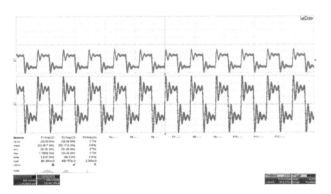

FIGURE 5: Locked ring oscillators. Trigger on top signal.

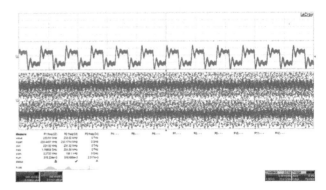

FIGURE 6: Unlocked ring oscillators. Trigger on top signal.

before the rising edge of the second RO. Thus, the result of the evaluation will always show that this RO has a greater oscillating frequency. If the oscillators are locked without a phase shift, the two counters will finish at the same time and the bit will be declared not valid.

This raises an important question on the quality of the response delivered by the PUF. If the oscillators are locked at the moment we compare their frequencies, the response is deterministic and no longer based on intrinsic characteristics of the device.

Identically laid-out oscillators request manual placement of the delay elements, as argued earlier. This means that the user will impose the position of the ROs on the device. Experimental results on the PUF showed that in certain configurations the distribution of "1"s and "0"s in the response was not uniform at all. In other configurations, the response presented a better distribution of values. Thus, we studied the locking phenomenon for ROs in certain configurations occupying the smallest area possible. These configurations were chosen because the surface of the PUF

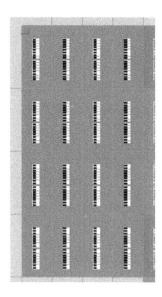

FIGURE 7: Configuration of ROs in a compact block.

FIGURE 8: Configuration of ROs in 2 columns.

should be relatively small comparing to the rest of the logic implemented in the device. Moreover, the PUF needs to be implemented in an isolated zone so that additional logic has only minimum influence on the response.

We tested two particular configurations, ROs grouped in a compact block, as presented in Figure 7 and ROs placed on two columns as presented in Figure 8. In this case one column represents one group of ROs.

Experimental results show that in the first configuration, there are more chances to have locked ROs. The most probable explanation for this phenomenon is that ROs placed close to each others are powered by the same wires. This fact has a great influence on the behavior of the oscillators. In Table 4 we present the influence of the voltage on the locking of the ROs on Cyclone III IC. Considering these experimental results, we cannot determine with precision the conditions under which ROs lock. We only observed that pairs of ROs can lock or unlock if environmental conditions change. Thus, questions rise on the reliability of the PUF and as manual placement is required, the configuration of the oscillators and the placement and routing of both ROs and arbiter must be carefully studied. In a recent publication by Maiti and Schaumont [13], the "Compensation method" used to select pairs of ROs in order to have good PUF properties indicate to choose ROs as close as possible from one to each others. Even if more investigation should be done on the locking of RO, such a method seems to be exposed to this phenomenon.

6. Further Enhancements of the PUF

Next, we propose some modifications of the PUF in order to enhance its characteristics.

6.1. Reduction of Intrachip Variations. As we observed in Session 5, changing environmental conditions (namely, voltage

and temperature) increases the intrachip variation. This is due to the fact that identically laid-out ROs have very close oscillation frequencies. Since all ROs do not have exactly the same dependence on environmental conditions, some ROs can be more affected than others, and differences in frequencies can invert. While for laboratory temperatures the intrachip variation did not exceeded 4 bits, for temperature ranges from 30 to 80° Celsius, up to 15 bits out of 256 were unstable. For device authentication this is not a problem if the inter-chip variation remains high. For key generation this fact is not acceptable. We must guarantee the uniqueness of the key generated by the device. Therefore, as proposed by Suh and Devadas, an error correcting code can be used to correct errors due to the intrachip variation.

As usual, the response should not be used directly as a key even after correcting the errors. On one hand, there are weak and periodic patterns in the response. On the other hand, after this error correcting process, the entropy of the "key" will probably be reduced. A hash function (e.g., Whirlpool [16] based on a modified AES) can be used to remove weak patterns but unfortunately it cannot solve the problem of entropy reduction.

6.2. Reduction of the Power Consumption. When dealing with the power consumption of the PUF, we used small dedicated modules made in our laboratory featuring ALTERA Cyclone III EP3C25F256C8N FPGA. We measured the static current consumption of the module and obtained 4 mA. Then we measured the consumption of the PUF using the 32 ROs and a PLL delivering the clock signal. The module consumed 24.7 mA, which is indeed considerable for a background function such as PUF. However, the PUF employs each time only two out of N ROs in order to obtain one bit of the response. Thus, we propose to stop all the $N - 2$ oscillators (30 in our case) that are currently not used for the response bit. The ROs are enabled and stopped using the enable input of the structure (Figure 1). When only two ROs were running, we measured a 13.4 mA current consumption. This is a reduction of consumption by approximately 51%.

In the next paragraph, we estimate the approximate power reduction that can be obtained in the design proposed in [8]. The total power consumption represents the sum of the static consumption (S), the consumption of the logic which is independent of the number of ROs (i.e., PLL, counters, comparators, etc.) (L) and the consumption of the logic which depends almost linearly on the number of ROs (multiplexers and ROs) denoted by $R(N) = \lambda \times N$ where N is the number of ROs and λ a constant float. We can make a simple calculus and show that the improved model would probably reduce considerably the consumption of the board.

In [8], Suh and Devadas used 1024 ROs in their design. Then, if we shut down unused ROs for each comparison, we should obtain a consumption of approximately $S + L + \lambda \times 2 = 13.4$ mA instead of $S + L + \lambda \times 1024 = 397.6$ mA. With our improved PUF control, we obtain a current consumption reduction of $1 - 13.4/397.6 = 96.6\%$. The PUF's power consumption thus becomes much more suitable for practical implementations.

Such an idea for reducing self-heating has been proposed in [17] but was not considered by Suh and Devadas in their design. However, in this paper only one ring is selected at a time. This idea cannot be used in our proposal to save more power consumption. If we want to use only one RO, we have to count its number of raising edges during one enable time, record this number, and repeat this measurement by selecting another RO during the same enable time. The main problem in such a case is the influence of the global deterministic part of the jitter on the frequency of one-ring oscillator [18]. This influence will not be the same from one measurement to another. Thus the comparison between the number of raising edges of two ROs will be suitable only if they are influenced by the same global deterministic part of the jitter in the same time.

7. Conclusions

The concept introduced in [8] is very simple, with a differential structure that presents an excellent behavior as long as the IC is not reconfigured. As this structure (the PUF) is useless if implemented alone in an IC, we analyze the influence of additional logic upon the response of the PUF. Our work proves that placement and routing constraints are required in order to maintain the quality of the PUF in FPGAs. Without any constraints, additional logic creates a completely different PUF and implicitly a completely different response. Instead of a small and acceptable intrachip variation after the IC reconfiguration, we obtained the variation 48.8% that was comparable in size to an ideal inter-chip variation (50%).

We also showed that bits in the response are dependent and propose a method to select pairs of ROs to have independent bits. Unfortunately this shortens the PUF response. The huge current consumption obtained by Suh and Devadas was also of our concern. We improved the design in order to considerably reduce the consumption. For a small PUF, (e.g., the one described in our experimental conditions with 32 ROs) the consumption was reduced by 51%. For a greater PUF, our improvement leads to an even more important reduction: we reduced the consumption of the PUF described in [8] by 96.6%.

Moreover, we showed that there are other phenomena that influence and jeopardize the integrity of the PUF. We argued why the "locking" phenomenon is affecting the response of the PUF and it is very important to notice that not all challenges can be used at any moment. Apart from the locking, our experimental results show that noisy motherboards can increase the intrachip variation for the PUF.

Acknowledgments

The work presented in this paper was realized in the frame of the SecReSoC Project n. ANR-09-SEGI-013, supported by the French National Research Agency (ANR). The work was partially supported also by the Rhones-Alpes Region and Saint-Etienne Metropole, France. The authors would like to thank Malick Boureima and Nathalie Bochard for their help with numerous experiments.

References

[1] S. Drimer, "Volatile FPGA design security–a survey," in *IEEE Computer Society Annual Volume*, pp. 292–297, 2008.

[2] R. Anderson and M. Kuhn, "Low cost attacks on tamper resistant devices," in *Security Protocols*, pp. 125–136, Springer, 1998.

[3] R. Anderson and M. Kuhn, "Tamper resistance: a cautionary note," in *2nd USENIX Workshop on Electronic Commerce*, vol. 2, 1996.

[4] S.P. Skorobogatov, "Semi-invasive attacks-a new approach to hardware security analysis," Tech. Rep., University of Cambridge, Computer Laboratory, 2005.

[5] J. A. Halderman, S. D. Schoen, N. Heninger et al., "Lest we remember: cold boot attacks on encryption keys," in *USENIX Security Symposium*, P.C. van Oorschot, Ed., pp. 45–60, 2008.

[6] R. Pappu, *Physical one-way functions*, Ph.D. thesis, Massachusetts Institute of Technology, 2001.

[7] R. Pappu, B. Recht, J. Taylor, and N. Gershenfeld, "Physical one-way functions," *Science*, vol. 297, no. 5589, pp. 2026–2030, 2002.

[8] G. E. Suh and S. Devadas, "Physical unclonable functions for device authentication and secret key generation," in *44th ACM/IEEE Design Automation Conference (DAC '07)*, pp. 9–14, June 2007.

[9] J. Guajardo, S. Kumar, G.J. Schrijen, and P. Tuyls, "FPGA intrinsic PUFs and their use for IP protection," in *Cryptographic Hardware and Embedded Systems (CHES '07)*, pp. 63–80, 2007.

[10] S. Kumar, J. Guajardo, R. Maes, G. J. Schrijen, and P. Tuyls, "Extended abstract: the butterfly PUF protecting IP on every FPGA," in *IEEE International Workshop on Hardware-Oriented Security and Trust (HOST '08)*, pp. 67–70, 2008.

[11] B. Gassend, D. Clarke, M. Van Dijk, and S. Devadas, "Silicon physical random functions," in *Proceedings of the 9th ACM Conference on Computer and Communications Security*, pp. 148–160, November 2002.

[12] D. Lim, J. W. Lee, B. Gassend, G. E. Suh, M. Van Dijk, and S. Devadas, "Extracting secret keys from integrated circuits," *IEEE Transactions on Very Large Scale Integration*, vol. 13, no. 10, pp. 1200–1205, 2005.

[13] A. Maiti and P. Schaumont, "Improved ring oscillator PUF: an FPGA-friendly secure primitive," *Journal of Cryptology*, pp. 1–23, 2010.

[14] Y. Hori, T. Yoshida, T. Katashita, and A. Satoh, "Quantitative and statistical performance evaluation of arbiter physical unclonable functions on FPGAs," in *International Conference on Reconfigurable Computing and FPGAs*, pp. 298–303, 2010.

[15] C. Costea, F. Bernard, V. Fischer, and R. Fouquet, "Analysis and enhancement of ring oscillators based physical unclonable functions in FPGAs," in *International Conference on Reconfigurable Computing and FPGAs*, pp. 262–267, 2010.

[16] P. Barreto and V. Rijmen, "The Whirlpool hashing function," in *1st Open NESSIE Workshop*, vol. 13, p. 14, Leuven, Belgium, 2000.

[17] P. Sedcole and P. Y. K. Cheung, "Within-die delay variability in 90nm FPGAs and beyond," in *IEEE International Conference on Field Programmable Technology (FPT '06)*, pp. 97–104, December 2006.

[18] V. Fischer, F. Bernard, N. Bochard, and M. Varchola, "Enhancing security of ring oscillator-based RNG implemented in FPGA," in *Proceedings of the Field- Programable Logic and Applications (FPL '08)*, pp. 245–250, September 2008.

8

Redesigned-Scale-Free CORDIC Algorithm Based FPGA Implementation of Window Functions to Minimize Area and Latency

Supriya Aggarwal and Kavita Khare

Department of Electronics and Communication Engineering, MANIT, Bhopal 462007, India

Correspondence should be addressed to Supriya Aggarwal, sups.aggarwal@gmail.com

Academic Editor: Michael Hübner

One of the most important steps in spectral analysis is filtering, where window functions are generally used to design filters. In this paper, we modify the existing architecture for realizing the window functions using CORDIC processor. Firstly, we modify the conventional CORDIC algorithm to reduce its latency and area. The proposed CORDIC algorithm is completely scale-free for the range of convergence that spans the entire coordinate space. Secondly, we realize the window functions using a single CORDIC processor as against two serially connected CORDIC processors in existing technique, thus optimizing it for area and latency. The linear CORDIC processor is replaced by a shift-add network which drastically reduces the number of pipelining stages required in the existing design. The proposed design on an average requires approximately 64% less pipeline stages and saves up to 44.2% area. Currently, the processor is designed to implement Blackman windowing architecture, which with slight modifications can be extended to other widow functions as well. The details of the proposed architecture are discussed in the paper.

1. Introduction

Window filtering techniques [1, 2] are commonly employed in signal processing paradigm to limit time and frequency resolution. Various window functions are developed to suit different requirements for side-lobe minimization, dynamic range, and so forth. Commonly, many hardware efficient architectures are available for realizing FFT [3–5], but the same is not true for windowing–architectures. The conventional hardware implementation of window functions uses lookup tables which give rise to various area and time complexities with increase in word lengths. Moreover, they do not allow user-defined variations in the window length. An efficient implementation of flexible and reconfigurable window functions using CORDIC algorithm is suggested in [6, 7]. Though they allow user-defined variations in window length, latency is a major problem. The CORDIC algorithm [8–10] inherently suffers from latency issues and using two CORDIC processors in series, as is done in [6, 7]; the overall latency of the system is hampered.

In this paper, a new area-time efficient FPGA implementation to realize Blackman window function is suggested.

We first redesign the conventional CORDIC algorithm to eliminate scale-factor compensation network and optimize its microrotation sequence identification. We then replace the linear CORDIC processors used in the existing design by shift-add tree derived using Booth multiplication. These modifications scale down the area consumption of the window architecture, with decrease in the number of pipeline stages.

The rest of the paper is structured as follows. Section 2 provides a comprehensive idea about various window functions and the conventional CORDIC algorithm. In Section 3, we propose a new CORDIC algorithm as redesigned-scale-free CORDIC. Section 4 deals with architecture for implementing the window functions. Section 5 presents the FPGA implementation and complexity issues, while Section 6 concludes the paper.

2. Background

2.1. Window Filtering Techniques. Window filtering is a well-known processing technique for limiting any signal to short-time segment in various fields, like audio or video signal processing, communication systems, and so forth. The rectangular, Gaussian, Hamming, Hanning, Blackman-Harris, and Kaiser are some of the most common available windowing techniques [2, 11]. The selection of the available windows is based on the spectral characteristics desired by the applications. Equations (1a)–(1c) explains the Hanning, Hamming, and the Blackman window family as follows:

$$W_{\text{Hann}}(n) = 0.5 + 0.5 \cos\left(\frac{2\pi n}{(N-1)}\right), \qquad (1a)$$

where N is the window length.

$$W_{\text{Hamm}}(n) = \alpha + \beta \cos\left(\frac{2\pi n}{(N-1)}\right); \qquad (1b)$$

where $\beta = 1 - \alpha$.

The values of α and β are determined to achieve maximum side-lobe cancellation. For Hamming window, the coefficients are calculated as $\alpha = 25/46$ and $\beta = 21/46$;

$$W_{\text{Blkman}}(n) = \alpha_0 + \alpha_1 \cos\left(\frac{2\pi n}{(N-1)}\right) + \alpha_2 \cos\left(\frac{4\pi n}{(N-1)}\right), \qquad (1c)$$

where $\alpha_0 + \alpha_1 + \alpha_2 = 1$.

The Blackman Harris window has three degrees of freedom which can be used to design a family of window functions having different window amplitudes, roll-off rates, and side-lobe rejections. The Blackman window with coefficients $\alpha_0 = 0.42$, $\alpha_1 = 0.5$ and $\alpha_2 = 0.08$ has side-lobe roll off rate of 18 dB/octave and the worst case side-lobe level is about 58 dB; while with coefficients $\alpha_0 = 0.4243801$, $\alpha_1 = 0.4973406$ and $\alpha_2 = 0.0782793$ the side-lobe level is 71.48 dB with side-lobe roll off rate of 6 dB/octave.

The hardware implementation of window functions invlove trigonometric computations. The primitive technique to compute trigonometric functions uses LUTs. But this approach fails to support user-defined changes in the window-length. Another popular algorithm for computing trigonometric functions is known as CORDIC (coordinate rotation digital computer) algorithm. This algorithm is used in [6, 7] for efficient window implementation in hardware and to provide application dependent changes in the window length. It uses two serially connected CORDIC processors operating in different modes, one in linear and other in circular. Inherently, the CORDIC algorithm suffers from latency issues; and the design in [6, 7] operates two CORDIC processors in series, as a result the latency is the major drawback in the existing designs of [6, 7]. Therefore, we redesign the CORDIC algorithm to minimize the number of iterations and hence reduce latency. Moreover, we replace one of the CORDIC processors with a booth multiplication shift-add tree to further minimize latency and area.

2.2. CORDIC Algorithm. The conventional CORDIC algorithm [9, 10, 12, 13] has various modes of operation and trajectories. But as window functions use CORDIC

algorithm in rotation mode following circular trajectory, we restrict our discussion to circular-rotation mode CORDIC only.

The coordinates of two vectors $\mathbf{V_A}[x_A, y_A]$ and $\mathbf{V_B}[x_B, y_B]$ separated by an angle "θ" are related as

$$\begin{bmatrix} x_B \\ y_B \end{bmatrix} = \mathbf{R_p} \cdot \begin{bmatrix} x_A \\ y_A \end{bmatrix}, \quad \mathbf{R_p} = \begin{bmatrix} \cos\theta & -\sin\theta \\ \sin\theta & \cos\theta \end{bmatrix}. \qquad (2)$$

Equation (2) forms the basic principle for iterative CORDIC coordinate calculations [8]. The key concept for realizing rotations using CORDIC algorithm is to express the desired rotation angle "θ" as an aggregation of predefined elementary angles, defined as:

$$\theta = \sum_{i=0}^{b} \mu_i \cdot \alpha_i, \qquad (3)$$

where $\mu_i \in \{-1, 1\}$, $\alpha_i = \tan^{-1} 2^{-i}$ and b is the word length.

The rotation matrix $\mathbf{R_p}$ in its original form (2) requires determining the sine and cosine values and four multiplication operations. Factoring the cosine term simplifies the rotation matrix (4) by converting the multiplication operations to shift, as the tangent of elementary angles are defined in the negative powers of two (3) as

$$\mathbf{R_p} = K_i \cdot \begin{bmatrix} 1 & -2^{-i} \\ 2^{-i} & 1 \end{bmatrix}, \quad K_i = \frac{1}{\sqrt{1 + 2^{-2i}}}. \qquad (4)$$

The rotation matrix $\mathbf{R_p}$ in (4) is applicable for anticlockwise vector rotations. To support both clockwise and anticlockwise CORDIC rotations, the rotation matrix is altered as

$$\mathbf{R_p} = K_i \cdot \begin{bmatrix} 1 & -\mu_i \cdot 2^{-i} \\ \mu_i \cdot 2^{-i} & 1 \end{bmatrix}, \qquad (5)$$

where $\mu_i = 1$ for anticlockwise rotations and $\mu_i = -1$ for clockwise rotations.

In its original form, the CORDIC algorithm suffers from major disadvantages like scale-factor compensation, latency, and optimal identification of micro-rotations. We propose a redesigned-scale-free CORDIC algorithm to overcome these disadvantages.

3. Redesigned-Scale-Free CORDIC Algorithm

The proposed CORDIC algorithm is an improved version of the conventional CORDIC algorithm in circular-rotation mode. The major ideas which lead to the proposed CORDIC algorithm are as follows: (i) redefine the elementary angles to eliminate the ROM required in conventional CORDIC algorithm to store the elementary angles, (ii) extend the Taylor series approximation of Scaling-Free CORDIC [13] to provide completely scale-free solution over the entire coordinate space, and (iii) obviate the redundant CORDIC iterations using new micro-rotation sequence identification. However, the existing scaling-free CORDIC [13] is outperformed by the conventional CORDIC beyond 20 bit implementation. But since an extensive set of applications work on word lengths up to 16 bits, our aim is to redesign the scaling-free CORDIC for word-length up to 16 bits.

TABLE 1: Mean square error in x-coordinate and y-coordinate for varying approximation orders.

Order of approximation	Mean square error	
	x-coordinate	y-coordinate
3	1.6881×10^{-7}	3.8830×10^{-7}
4	2.2539×10^{-7}	3.3926×10^{-7}
5	2.2360×10^{-7}	3.3404×10^{-7}
6	2.2343×10^{-7}	3.3413×10^{-7}

3.1. Redefining the Elementary Angles.

We redefine the elementary angles used in conventional CORDIC (3) as

$$\alpha_i = 2^{-i}. \tag{6}$$

The above definition of elementary angles obviates the ROM required by the conventional CORDIC algorithm to store the elementary angles.

3.2. Coordinate Calculation Equations.

We derive a new set of coordinate calculation equations by modifying the Taylor series expansion of sine and cosine functions used in scaling-free CORDIC [13]. Instead of using second order approximation of scaling-free CORDIC, we use third order of Taylor series approximation. It is necessary to analyze various orders of Taylor series approximation before third order is finalized for use in coordinate equations. We compare the mean square errors in the x-coordinate and y-coordinate for various orders of approximation in Table 1. The errors are calculated from the results obtained after simulating the CORDIC processors. The rotation matrix of the CORDIC processors was designed using the orders of approximation mentioned in Table 1 in $\mathbf{R_p}$ (2) and given by:

$$\mathbf{R_{pc1}} = \begin{bmatrix} 1 - \dfrac{\alpha_i^2}{2!} & -\left(\alpha_i - \dfrac{\alpha_i^3}{3!}\right) \\ \alpha_i - \dfrac{\alpha_i^3}{3!} & 1 - \dfrac{\alpha_i^2}{2!} \end{bmatrix},$$

$$\mathbf{R_{pc2}} = \begin{bmatrix} 1 - \dfrac{\alpha_i^2}{2!} + \dfrac{\alpha_i^4}{4!} & -\left(\alpha_i - \dfrac{\alpha_i^3}{3!}\right) \\ \alpha_i - \dfrac{\alpha_i^3}{3!} & 1 - \dfrac{\alpha_i^2}{2!} + \dfrac{\alpha_i^4}{4!} \end{bmatrix},$$

$$\mathbf{R_{pc3}} = \begin{bmatrix} 1 - \dfrac{\alpha_i^2}{2!} + \dfrac{\alpha_i^4}{4!} & -\left(\alpha_i - \dfrac{\alpha_i^3}{3!} + \dfrac{\alpha_i^5}{5!}\right) \\ \alpha_i - \dfrac{\alpha_i^3}{3!} + \dfrac{\alpha_i^5}{5!} & 1 - \dfrac{\alpha_i^2}{2!} + \dfrac{\alpha_i^4}{4!} \end{bmatrix}, \tag{7}$$

$$\mathbf{R_{pc4}} = \begin{bmatrix} 1 - \dfrac{\alpha_i^2}{2!} + \dfrac{\alpha_i^4}{4!} - \dfrac{\alpha_i^6}{6!} & -\left(\alpha_i - \dfrac{\alpha_i^3}{3!} + \dfrac{\alpha_i^5}{5!}\right) \\ \alpha_i - \dfrac{\alpha_i^3}{3!} + \dfrac{\alpha_i^5}{5!} & 1 - \dfrac{\alpha_i^2}{2!} + \dfrac{\alpha_i^4}{4!} - \dfrac{\alpha_i^6}{6!} \end{bmatrix}.$$

The errors are calculated for 16 bit word length, for angles lying in the range $[0, \pi/4]$, since for sine/cosine functions this range can be easily extended over the entire coordinate space using the octant wave symmetry. From Table 1, we conclude that the errors are of the same order for various orders of approximation of Taylor series expansion. Therefore, to keep the hardware complexity to minimum, we choose third order of approximation. Thus, the rotation matrix of the proposed CORDIC algorithm is given by

$$\mathbf{R_p} = \begin{bmatrix} 1 - \dfrac{\alpha_i^2}{2!} & -\left(\alpha_i - \dfrac{\alpha_i^3}{3!}\right) \\ \alpha_i - \dfrac{\alpha_i^3}{3!} & 1 - \dfrac{\alpha_i^2}{2!} \end{bmatrix}. \tag{8}$$

In order to implement the above rotation matrix using shift-add implementation, we approximate (3!) to 2^3. With this approximation, the mean square errors in the x-coordinate and y-coordinate are 1.5839×10^{-7} and 2.7664×10^{-7}, respectively. The errors are calculated for 16 bit word length, for angles lying in the range $[0, \pi/4]$ since for sine/cosine functions this range can be easily extended over the entire coordinate space using the octant wave symmetry. As these errors are of the same order as the errors in Table 1, this approximation does not affect the accuracy. Finally, the rotation matrix of the proposed CORDIC algorithm is defined as

$$\text{For } \alpha_i = 2^{-r_i}$$
$$\mathbf{R_p} = \begin{bmatrix} 1 - 2^{-(2r_i+1)} & -\left(2^{-r_i} - 2^{-(3r_i+3)}\right) \\ 2^{-r_i} - 2^{-(3r_i+3)} & 1 - 2^{-(2r_i+1)} \end{bmatrix}. \tag{9}$$

3.3. Determination of Highest Elementary Angle.

The use of Taylor series approximation imposes a restriction on the highest elementary angle being used in CORDIC iterations [13]. This restriction ensures that the higher order terms neglected due to the order of approximation used do not affect the accuracy of the processor. For third order of approximation, fourth and subsequent higher order terms should be zero after the shift operation of CORDIC so that their role in mathematical operations is obviated.

For a word length of N-bits, nth order term T_n is zero if it gets right shift by r-bits, defined as

$$T_n = \dfrac{\alpha^n}{n!}$$
$$\text{for } \alpha = 2^{-r}, \quad T_n = 2^{-(r \cdot n + \log_2 n!)}$$
$$\text{for } T_n \longrightarrow 0 \quad r \cdot n + \log_2 n! \geq N \tag{10}$$
$$\Rightarrow r \geq \dfrac{N - \log_2 n!}{n}.$$

For third order of approximation, $n = 4$, the smallest value of $r_{\min}$ and the highest permissible elementary angle are given by:

$$r_{\min} = \left\lceil \dfrac{N - \log_2 4!}{4} \right\rceil. \tag{11}$$
$$\alpha_{\max} = 2^{-r_{\min}}$$

Thus, for 16 bit word length, $r_{\min} = 2$ and the highest elementary angle permissible is $\alpha_{\max} = 0.25$ radians.

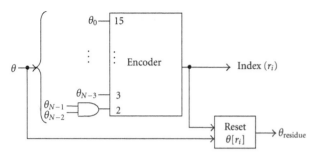

FIGURE 1: Micro-rotation sequence generator.

3.4. Micro-Rotation Sequence Identification. The proposed micro-rotation sequence generation is different from the conventional CORDIC micro-rotation identification. In conventional technique, each elementary angle is used only once; while we allow multiple micro-operations corresponding to the same elementary angle. Then, the use of every elementary angle is a must in conventional CORDIC, where as we have selective micro-rotations that depend on the angle of rotation. Further, we restrict the micro-rotations in single direction (anticlockwise) only as against bidirectional micro-rotations (clockwise and anticlockwise) in conventional CORDIC.

The micro-rotation sequence generator selects appropriate elementary angle for the current CORDIC iteration. Using the redefined elementary angles (6), the micro-rotations can be identified using the circuit shown in Figure 1. It comprises of a priority encoder and a reset circuitry. The input to the micro-rotation sequence generator is the rotation angle $\theta[N - 1 : 0]$, where N is the word length. The priorities of the encoder are hooked in the reverse order with θ_{N-1} having the highest priority and θ_0 the least. The reset circuitry resets a bit of the input rotation angle to generate the residue angle for next CORDIC iteration. Since, the micro-rotation sequence generates the shift-index r_i for one CORDIC iteration, it is required in every stage of the CORDIC pipeline (the implementation of CORDIC stage is discussed in the forthcoming sections). The micro-rotation sequence generation block handles the angles in the range $[0, \pi/4]$. This range can be extended to the entire coordinate space using the octant symmetry of sine and cosine functions [14].

3.5. Number of Iterations. The number of iterations required to realize this range $[0, \pi/4]$ of rotation angles is decided based on: (i) maximum iterations of the highest elementary angle and (ii) the iterations of the other elementary angles. The rotation angle θ is given by

$$\theta = n_1 \cdot \alpha_{\max} + \sum_{r_i}^{n_2 \text{ iterations}} \alpha_{r_i}, \tag{12}$$

where $r_i \neq r_{\min}$ and $\alpha_{r_i} = 2^{-r_i}$.

The maximum angle that can be handled by the micro-rotation sequence generator is $\pi/4 \approx 0.785$ radians. Therefore, no more than 3 iterations of highest elementary angle ($\alpha_{\max} = 2^{-2} = 0.25$ radians) is required, that is, maximum of $n_1 = 3$ iterations are required to realize any

angle of rotation in the range $[0, \pi/4]$. The rest n_2 iterations determine accuracy. To select an appropriate value of n_2, we simulate the CORDIC processor for varying n_2 iterations, the mean square error is tabulated in Table 2. After observing the errors in Table 2, we can say that the errors for $n_2 = 4$ and $n_2 = 5$ are of same order. Therefore, to minimize the number of CORDIC iterations, we select $n_2 = 4$. We require a maximum of $n_1 + n_2 = 3 + 4 = 7$ iterations for the proposed CORDIC processor.

3.6. Error Analysis. The error analysis of the proposed CORDIC algorithm is divided into two parts: (i) residue angle error and (ii) error in the coordinate values.

3.6.1. Residue Angle Error. In the proposed methodology, desired angle of rotation is expressed as

$$\theta = \sum^{\text{for } n \text{ iteration}} 2^{-r_i}, \qquad r_{\min} \leq r_i \leq (N - 1), \tag{13}$$

where $r_{\min}$ is minimum shift-index (11), N is word length.

We identify the micro-rotations by using the bit representation of the desired rotation angle. The residue angle error depends on the number of bits set in the radix-2 representation of the rotation angle and varies for different rotation angles. Therefore, we derive the worst-case angle error in the range of convergence $[0, \pi/4]$.

The maximum number of iterations is fixed for all rotation angles. The input rotation `angle` with the MSB-nibble value of 4'b1011, requires four iterations of $r_{\min} = 2$, while, three or less iterations are required for other MSB-nibble values. From second MSB-nibble onwards each bit set to 1'b1 in the radix-2 representation of the rotation angle would require one iteration; therefore, maximum four iterations are required if the second MSB nibble value is 4'b1111. Since the iteration count is seven, the worst-case error is $(2^{-7} - 2^{-16})$. This worst-case residue angle error is specific to the rotation angle of 16'b1011_1111_1111_1111, while for other rotation angles the residue angle error will be less. In the proposed 16 bit fixed point representation scheme, 16'b1011_1111_1111_1111 is 42.97°; the worst-case residue angle error is 0.4467°.

3.6.2. Error in Coordinate Values. For fixed-point implementation, the error is represented in terms of bit-error position (BEP). The BEP in x and y coordinates calculated using the proposed CORDIC processor is shown in Figure 2. For a BEP of n, the conventional CORDIC requires a word length of $n + \log_2 n + 2$-bits [15]. For a BEP of 10 bits as achieved by the

TABLE 2: Mean square error in x-coordinate and y-coordinate for varying n_2 iterations.

Number of n_2 iterations	Mean square error	
	x-coordinate	y-coordinate
3	4.3028×10^{-6}	2.9493×10^{-6}
4	1.6412×10^{-7}	2.6070×10^{-7}
5	1.0640×10^{-7}	2.1940×10^{-7}

proposed CORDIC algorithm, the conventional CORDIC will require 16 bit word length. We, therefore, compare the proposed design with the existing design using conventional CORDIC processor [7] for 16 bits.

4. Architecture for Implementing Window Functions

In this section, we focus on implementing the pipelined architecture to generate window functions. The length of the window function is selected by the user at run time. Currently, the architecture implements the Blackman window, but with slight modifications it can be extended to other window functions as well. In the proposed architecture, the output bit width is set to 16 bits.

Figure 3 shows the block diagram for generating Blackman window function. The circuit consists of theta generator unit (TGU), window coefficient multiplier (WCM), circular CORDIC processor (CCP) and FIFO. The TGU generates the two angle values ($\theta = 2\pi n/(N - 1)$) and $2\theta = 4\pi n/(N - 1)$ required in the three-term Blackman window function. WCM multiplies the input signal samples with the window constants using a shift-add tree derived from Booth multiplication algorithm. CCP is used for generating the cosine terms in the window function. The FIFO is used for proper synchronization between the window coefficients having cosine terms and constants.

4.1. Circular CORDIC Processor (CCP).
The CCP is pipelined implementation of the proposed redesigned-scale-free CORDIC algorithm discussed in Section 3. A total of seven ($n_1 = 3$ and $n_2 = 4$) iterations are required (as discussed in Section 3.5), since each pipeline stage performs one iteration, the proposed CCP-pipeline is seven stages long. Each stage (Figure 4) is a combination of three blocks (i) the coordinate calculation unit, (ii) the shift-index calculation, and (iii) the micro-rotation sequence generation. The coordinate calculation unit implements (9) using shift-add implementation. The shift-index calculation computes the necessary shifts ($(2r_i+1)$ and $(3r_i+3)$), required by the coordinate calculation unit. The micro-rotation sequence generation is shown in Figure 1.

The complexity of coordinate calculation unit is equal to six N bit logic shifters and six N bit adder/subtractor. The shift-index calculation unit requires three ($\log_2 N + P$)-bit adders, where P are the extra bits required to store the sum. Even though, the coordinate calculation unit of the proposed redesigned-scale-free CORDIC is more complex than the conventional CORDIC [8]; the overall gate count of the proposed window architecture using the proposed CCP-pipeline is reduced.

4.2. Window Coefficient Multiplier (WCM).
The WCM unit multiplies the input samples with the Blackman window coefficients (α_0, α_1, and α_2). The shift-add tree for multiplication with α_0, α_1, and α_2 is derived using the Booth multiplication algorithm. In radix-2 representation system, multiplication with 0.5 is equivalent to single right shift.

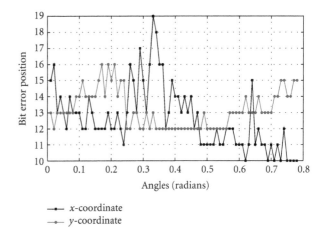

FIGURE 2: Bit error position in coordinate values calculated using the proposed CORDIC algorithm.

Therefore, multiplication with $\alpha_1 = 0.5$ is realized using a hardwired shifter. The coefficient α_0 is represented in 16 bit fixed-point format as 0001_1011_0010_0000, that requires four 16 bit adders and five hardwired shifters, while α_2 is represented as 0000_0101_0000_0010 and requires two 16 bit adders and three hardwired shifters.

The complexity of the WCM unit is equivalent to six 16 bit adders, as hardwired shifters do not incur any hardware costs.

4.3. Theta Generator Unit (TGU).
The TGU generates the two angles given by

$$\theta = \frac{2\pi n}{(N - 1)}, \qquad 2\theta = \frac{4\pi n}{(N - 1)}, \qquad (14)$$

where N is a multiple of 2 such that $N = 2^M$.

The difference between the consecutive values of θ is given by

$$\Delta\theta = \theta_{n+1} - \theta_n$$
$$\Delta\theta = \frac{2\pi}{(N - 1)}, \qquad (15a)$$

$$\text{For } N = 2^M, \quad \Delta\theta = \frac{2\pi}{(2^M - 1)}, \qquad (15b)$$

$$\Longrightarrow \Delta\theta = \frac{2\pi}{2^M} \cdot \left(1 - 2^{-M}\right)^{-1}. \qquad (15c)$$

Using binomial theorem (B.T.), we simplify (15c) to the following:

$$\text{using B.T.} (1 - x)^{-1} = 1 + x + x^2 + x^3 + \cdots$$
$$\text{B.T. of} \Longrightarrow \left(1 - 2^{-M}\right)^{-1} = 1 + 2^{-M} + 2^{-2M} + \cdots, \qquad (16a)$$

$$\Delta\theta = \frac{2\pi}{2^M} \cdot \left(1 + 2^{-M} + 2^{-2M}\right), \qquad (16b)$$

$$\Longrightarrow \Delta\theta = \frac{2\pi}{2^M} + \frac{2\pi}{2^{2M}} + \frac{2\pi}{2^{3M}}$$
$$\Longrightarrow \Delta\theta = (2\pi \gg M) + (2\pi \gg 2M) + (2\pi \gg 3M). \qquad (16c)$$

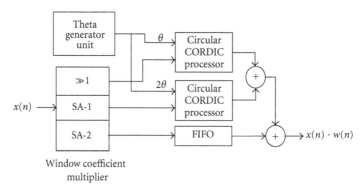

FIGURE 3: Block diagram for generating blackman window function.

Generally in most signal processing applications, not less than 16-point DFT is used which implies $N \geq 16$ and $M \geq 4$. Therefore, only three terms of binomial expansion are sufficient for 16 bit accuracy as follows:

$$\text{fourth term of B.T. in (16c) } \Delta\theta_4 = \frac{2\pi}{2^{4M}}$$
$$\implies \Delta\theta_4 = 2\pi \gg 4M. \tag{17}$$

For 16 bit word length and $M \geq 4$, the term $\Delta\theta_4$ always gets a right shift greater than or equal to 16. Therefore, $\Delta\theta_4$ is zero for 16 bit word length.

Figure 5 shows the block diagram representation of TGU. The angles in the windowing function are uniformly distributed over the entire coordinate space. The CCP unit handles angles in the range of $[0, \pi/4]$. Therefore, the TGU divides the entire coordinate space into octants, so that the input angle to CCP always lies in the range $[0, \pi/4]$. The octants are distinguished as shown in Figure 6; the TGU also generates signals for proper octant mapping of values generated by CCP.

The TGU requires three 16 bit adders, two barrel-shifters and one encoder.

4.4. Window Generation. In Figure 7, we compare the Blackman window generated using the proposed processor with that of MATLAB inbuilt function blackman() for $N = 32$.

5. FPGA Implementation and Complexity Issues

The proposed architecture is coded in Verilog and simulated and synthesized using Xilinx ISE 9.2i Design Suite to be mapped on Xilinx Virtex 2Pro (XC2VP50-6FF1148) device. For 16 bit implementation, the proposed design consumes 1800 slices and 3371 4-Input LUTs, with a maximum operating frequency of 101.284 MHz. The total delay of 9.873 nsec is distributed as 58.7% logic delay and 41.3% route delay. The total gate count of the proposed design is 34739.

5.1. Comparison with Existing Architecture. The CORDIC processor both linear and circular used in [7] is designed using conventional CORDIC algorithm. The scaling-free CORDIC [13] and enhanced scaling-free CORDIC [16] are

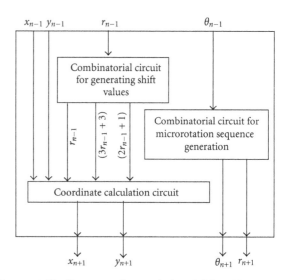

FIGURE 4: Pipeline stage of new redesigned CORDIC processor.

currently the best available hardware designs for circular CORDIC implementation. We compare our processor with three designs: (i) the existing design in [7] using conventional circular CORDIC, (ii) replace the conventional circular CORDIC in [7] with scaling-free CORDIC [13], and (iii) replace the conventional circular CORDIC in [7] with enhanced scaling-free CORDIC [16]. The area complexity and latency of the proposed design with three variants of existing design [7] mentioned above are compared in Table 3.

5.1.1. Area Comparison. The area of conventional circular CORDIC processor is calculated using Xilinx CORDIC IP v3.0. The Xilinx CORDIC Core is optimized for circular CORDIC computation with maximum pipelining for 16 bit word length. The gate count is 20122. In [13], the complexity of 16 bit scaling-free CORDIC is computed to be equivalent to 1000 1 bit full adders and 597 1 bit registers. This area complexity approximately uses 16776 gates for implementation. The SFB4C architecture of enhanced scaling-free (ESF) CORDIC [16] replaces the initial four scaling-free CORDIC iterations with conventional CORDIC iterations. Thus, the complexity of 16 bit ESF CORDIC without scale-factor compensation is equivalent to 512 1 bit full adders and 420 1 bit registers, approximately equal to 9504 gates.

TABLE 3: Complexity comparison of proposed design with existing design variants.

| Circular CORDIC | Existing design | | % Savings | |
	Area	Latency[1]	Area[2]	Latency[3]
Conventional	73585	32	52.79	68.75
Scaling-free [13]	66273	28	47.58	64.28
ESF-CORDIC [16]	51264	25	32.23	60

[1] Latency is defined in terms of number of pipelining stages required by the design.
[2] The gate count of the proposed design is 34739.
[3] The latency of the proposed design is 10.

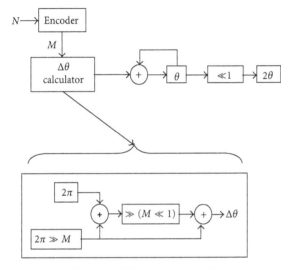

FIGURE 5: Theta generator unit.

The complexity of the 16 bit linear conventional CORDIC is equivalent to 512 1 bit full adders and 768 1 bit registers, approximately equal to 12288 gates. The other units like theta generator unit, FIFO, and adders required for realizing the window processor are common for the proposed as well as the existing design.

5.1.2. Latency. The throughput of all the designs is same, that is, one data sample per clock cycle, while the latency is different and is closely related to number of iterations in circular CORDIC and linear CORDIC processor when the designs are operating at the same clock frequency. The 16 bit linear CORDIC processor uses 16-stages long pipeline. The conventional circular CORDIC processor again uses 16-stages pipeline for 16 bit word length. For the same 16 bit word length, the scaling-free CORDIC [13] processor uses 12-stages long pipeline, while the ESF CORDIC [16] pipeline is 9 stages long. Therefore, the latency of existing design in [7] with conventional circular CORDIC is 32 stages, while with scaling-free is 28 stages and with ESF-CORDIC is 25 stages.

The new redesigned-CORDIC pipeline is 7 stages long (Section 4.1). The delay of the WCM unit (Section 4.2) is three adders in serial, which can be considered equivalent to three linear CORDIC iterations. Hence, the total latency of the proposed design is 10 stages, which is far less as compared

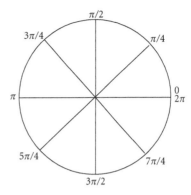

FIGURE 6: Mapping of coordinate space into octants.

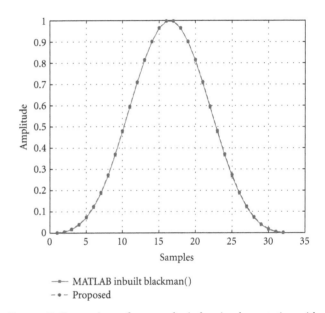

FIGURE 7: Comparison of proposed window implementation with MATLAB inbuilt blackman() function for $N = 32$.

to existing design using the best of the available circular CORDIC hardware.

5.1.3. Delay. The delay is the time required to generate one set of window coefficients for a window length of N when the design is operating at the maximum clock frequency. The critical path for the proposed design is the TGU. Since the existing design using the conventional circular CORDIC and the scaling-free circular CORDIC also work using the same TGU, while, the existing design using the ESF-CORDIC uses a slightly less complex TGU as compared to other designs. The TGU for the proposed design and the existing design using the conventional circular CORDIC and the scaling-free circular CORDIC generates angle in the range $[-\pi/4, \pi/4]$, while for existing design using the ESF-CORDIC the TGU generates angles in the range $[-\pi/2, \pi/2]$. Therefore, the maximum clock frequency for the existing design using ESF-CORDIC is 101.983 MHz and for other designs including the proposed design is 101.284 MHz. Figure 8 compares the delay for the four designs for various window lengths.

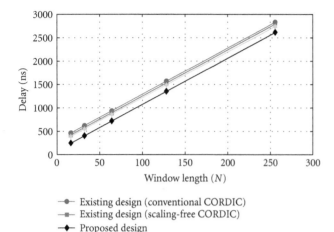

time spectral analysis," *IEE Proceedings: Circuits, Devices and Systems*, vol. 153, no. 6, pp. 539–544, 2006.

[7] K. C. Ray and A. S. Dhar, "High throughput VLSI architecture for Blackman windowing in real time spectral analysis," *Journal of Computers*, vol. 3, no. 5, pp. 54–59, 2008.

[8] J. E. Volder, "The cordic trigonometric computing technique," *IRE Transactions on Electronic Computers*, vol. 8, no. 3, pp. 330–334, 1959.

[9] J. S. Walther, "A unified algorithm for elementary functions," in *Proceedings of the 38th Spring Joint Computer Conferences*, pp. 379–385, Atlantic City, NJ, USA, 1971.

[10] P. K. Meher, J. Valls, T. B. Juang, K. Sridharan, and K. Maharatna, "50 years of CORDIC: algorithms, architectures, and applications," *IEEE Transactions on Circuits and Systems I*, vol. 56, no. 9, pp. 1893–1907, 2009.

[11] J. O. Smith III, *Spectral Audio Signal Processing*, W3K, 2011.

[12] T. B. Juang, S. F. Hsiao, and M. Y. Tsai, "Para-CORDIC: parallel CORDIC rotation algorithm," *IEEE Transactions on Circuits and Systems I*, vol. 51, no. 8, pp. 1515–1524, 2004.

[13] K. Maharatna, S. Banerjee, E. Grass, M. Krstic, and A. Troya, "Modified virtually scaling-free adaptive CORDIC rotator algorithm and architecture," *IEEE Transactions on Circuits and Systems for Video Technology*, vol. 15, no. 11, pp. 1463–1474, 2005.

[14] J. Vankka, *Digital Synthesizers and Transmitters for Software Radio*, Springer, Dordrecht, Netherlands, 2005.

[15] K. Kota and J. R. Cavallaro, "Numerical accuracy and hardware tradeoffs for CORDIC arithmetic for special-purpose processors," *IEEE Transactions on Computers*, vol. 42, no. 7, pp. 769–779, 1993.

[16] F. J. Jaime, M. A. Sánchez, J. Hormigo, J. Villalba, and E. L. Zapata, "Enhanced scaling-free CORDIC," *IEEE Transactions on Circuits and Systems I*, vol. 57, no. 7, pp. 1654–1662, 2010.

FIGURE 8: Comparison of delay of the proposed design with existing designs operating at maximum clock frequency.

6. Conclusion

In this paper, we present an area-time efficient CORDIC based processor for realizing window functions. Currently, the architecture implementing the Blackman window function, with slight modification, can be extended to other window functions as well. We also propose a circular CORDIC processor for word lengths up to 16 bits. The redesigned scale-free CORDIC processor uses third order of approximation of Taylor series to realize scale-free CORDIC iterations. However, removal of scaling factor comes with the disadvantage of complex coordinate calculations. The micro-rotation sequence generation is optimized using a priority encoder which reduces the total CORDIC processor pipeline to seven stages. A shift-add tree derived using Booth multiplication algorithm replaces the linear CORDIC processor in the original design of window architecture. The proposed Blackman window architecture saves approximately 44.2% area and drastically reduces latency with no affect on accuracy.

References

[1] K. K. Parhi, *VLSI Digital Signal Processing Systems*, John Wiley & Sons, 1999.

[2] J. G. Proakis and D. G. Manolakis, *Digital Signal Processing Principles, Algorithms and Applications*, Prentice Hall, 3rd edition, 2006.

[3] A. M. Despain, "Fourier transform computers using CORDIC iterations," *IEEE Transactions on Computers*, vol. 23, no. 10, pp. 993–1001, 1974.

[4] T. Sansaloni, A. Pérez-Pascual, and J. Valls, "Area-efficient FPGA-based FFT processor," *Electronics Letters*, vol. 39, no. 19, pp. 1369–1370, 2003.

[5] M. Ayinala, M. Brown, and K. K. Parhi, "Pipelined parallel FFT architectures via folding transformation," *IEEE Transactions on Very Large Scale Integration (VLSI) Systems*, vol. 20, no. 6, pp. 1068–1081, 2011.

[6] K. C. Ray and A. S. Dhar, "CORDIC-based unified VLSI architecture for implementing window functions for real

9

DMPDS: A Fast Motion Estimation Algorithm Targeting High Resolution Videos and Its FPGA Implementation

Gustavo Sanchez,[1] Felipe Sampaio,[2] Marcelo Porto,[1,2] Sergio Bampi,[2] and Luciano Agostini[1]

[1] Group of Architectures and Integrated Circuits (GACI), Federal University of Pelotas (UFPEL), 96010-610 Pelotas, RS, Brazil
[2] Microelectronics Group (GME), Federal University of Rio Grande do Sul (UFRGS), 90040-060 Porto Alegre, RS, Brazil

Correspondence should be addressed to Gustavo Sanchez, gustavofreitassanchez@gmail.com

Academic Editor: Michael Hübner

This paper presents a new fast motion estimation (ME) algorithm targeting high resolution digital videos and its efficient hardware architecture design. The new Dynamic Multipoint Diamond Search (DMPDS) algorithm is a fast algorithm which increases the ME quality when compared with other fast ME algorithms. The DMPDS achieves a better digital video quality reducing the occurrence of local minima falls, especially in high definition videos. The quality results show that the DMPDS is able to reach an average PSNR gain of 1.85 dB when compared with the well-known Diamond Search (DS) algorithm. When compared to the optimum results generated by the Full Search (FS) algorithm the DMPDS shows a lose of only 1.03 dB in the PSNR. On the other hand, the DMPDS reached a complexity reduction higher than 45 times when compared to FS. The quality gains related to DS caused an expected increase in the DMPDS complexity which uses 6.4-times more calculations than DS. The DMPDS architecture was designed focused on high performance and low cost, targeting to process Quad Full High Definition (QFHD) videos in real time (30 frames per second). The architecture was described in VHDL and synthesized to Altera Stratix 4 and Xilinx Virtex 5 FPGAs. The synthesis results show that the architecture is able to achieve processing rates higher than 53 QFHD fps, reaching the real-time requirements. The DMPDS architecture achieved the highest processing rate when compared to related works in the literature. This high processing rate was obtained designing an architecture with a high operation frequency and low numbers of cycles necessary to process each block.

1. Introduction

Nowadays digital video compression is really a relevant issue. It happens due to the growing development of applications that handle high definition videos, as smart phones, digital cameras, tablets, and so on. These applications would not be possible without video compression. The video bitstream must be drastically reduced to enable the transmission and storage, especially when high definition videos must be processed in real-time.

In a digital video there is a lot of redundant information, and this redundancy is explored in the current video coder standards. Neighbor blocks in a frame usually have very similar pixel colors and intensity and the intraframe prediction of the current video coders explore this type of redundancy. The transforms and quantization also contribute to reduce the intraframe redundancy, but in this case, in the frequency domain. In a set of neighbor frames, the information is also very similar among them, because the video is encoded at a frame rate of at least 24–30 frames per second, so neighbor frames tend to be very similar. This redundancy is explored by the interframe prediction operation. The redundancy on the bitstream representation is also explored by the current video coder standards through the entropy coding operation. Our work is focused on the interframe prediction.

Motion Estimation (ME) is the main operation of the interframe prediction and it represents about 80% of the total computational complexity of current video coders [1]. The ME must find the best matching in the reference frames for each block of the current frame, defining a motion vector indicating where the best matching was found. A search algorithm defines how the search is done and a similarity criterion is used to compare the candidate blocks with each original block. A search area is defined inside the reference frame around the collocated block to constrain the ME complexity. The collocated block is that block in the reference frame which is located at the same position of the original block that is currently being processed. The search for best vectors is known to be very expensive in terms of calculations and, consequentially, in terms of the processing time. The Full Search (FS) [2] algorithm explores all possibilities in a given search area, which implies in a very high computational cost, especially for high resolution videos, which requires the use of larger search areas.

The current video coding standards like MPEG2 [3] and H.264/AVC [4] and even the emerging HEVC (High Efficiency Video Coding) [5] standard do not restrict how the ME is done. Based on this fact, there is a vast space to explore new algorithm solutions for the ME. These solutions are evaluated according to the tradeoff between complexity and objective quality of the encoded digital video.

There are many fast search algorithms in scientific literature. These algorithms deal with this complexity, at different levels of impact in objective quality (PSNR). Generally, these algorithms exploit the characteristic of locality among temporal correlated blocks and they can achieve good results in terms of numbers of calculations. However, these algorithms assume that the error function decreases monotonically on the surface of the frame, in order to speed up the algorithm. This assumption does not hold true sometimes, and the search might be trapped into a local minima.

The majority of the published ME search algorithms only considers low resolution videos, as QCIF and CIF, in its experiments. However, the quality results of the ME algorithms can significantly change with the increasing of the video resolution. For low resolution videos, the quality results for FS and many other fast algorithms are very close. The great amount of pixels in high definition videos may lead the fast algorithms to choose, more frequently, local minima as the best matching. Thus, the quality losses (in comparison with FS) are significant in this scenario. Techniques to avoid local minima falls must be explored to enhance the video quality without a significant increase in the ME computational complexity.

In previous works of our group, new algorithms and hardware architectures for ME on high definition videos were presented, as [6, 7]. The Multipoint Diamond Search (MPDS) and the hardware solution targeting real-time for HD 1080 p (1920 × 1080 pixels) videos were presented in [6]. The Dynamic Multipoint Diamond Search (DMPDS) algorithm and the initial hardware design for this algorithm were presented in [7]. This paper presents detailed results related to the ME behavior on high resolution videos, showing the growth on the quality losses of the traditional fast algorithms with the increasing of the video resolution. The DMPDS algorithm is also presented and evaluated with detailed information. The results showed that the DMPDS algorithms can significantly improve the video quality when compared with traditional fast algorithms like Diamond Search (DS) [8], especially when high definition videos are considered. Finally, this paper presents the hardware design for the DMPDS algorithm, including the synthesis results

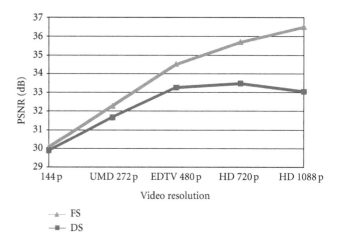

FIGURE 1: Average PSNR curves of DS and FS.

targeting an Altera Stratix 4 [9] and a Xilinx Virtex 5 FPGAs [10]. The hardware design of the DMPDS algorithm targeted real-time processing for Quad Full High Definition (QFHD) (2160 × 3840 pixels) video sequences.

The paper is organized as follows. Section 2 presents an investigation about the ME in high definition videos. Section 3 explains the MPDS and DMPDS algorithms. Section 4 shows details about the architecture presented in this paper and Section 5 presents the results and comparisons with related works. Finally, Section 6 renders the conclusions.

2. Motion Estimation in High Definition Videos

The increasing in the video resolution can directly affect the ME results. The fast ME algorithms can be affected by this characteristic, generating different results, for the same video, in different resolutions. High resolution videos tend to present very similar neighboring pixels (much more than low resolution ones) and this fact contributes to increase the occurrence of local minima falls.

Diamond Search (DS) [8] and Full Search (FS) [2] algorithms were applied to ten HD 1080 p video sequences to demonstrate the influence of the video resolution growing in the ME quality. The used video sequences were blue_sky, man_in_car, pedestrian_area, hush_hour, station2, sunflower, riverbed, rolling_tomatoes, traffic, and tractor [11]. These sequences were resized for many lower resolutions: 256 × 144 pixels (144p—which is equivalent to QCIF resolution in a 16 : 9 aspect ratio); UMD 272 p (480 × 272); EDTV 480 p (854 × 480); HD 720 p (1280 × 720) and HD 1080 p (1920 × 1080). The search areas were defined proportionally with the resolution. All the experiments in this paper will consider the average results achieved for these ten video sequences.

Figure 1 presents the average PSNR curves of DS algorithm in red and FS algorithm in blue, considering the five different resolutions. The used block size was 16 × 16 pixels, and the search area grew proportionally to the video resolution growing.

In low resolution videos, DS and FS algorithms obtained almost the same PSNR results. However, through the analysis of Figure 1 curves it is possible to notice that the difference in PSNR results between DS and FS algorithms grows significantly with the video resolution increasing. The FS continuously increases the PSNR gains with the video resolution growing. This happens because the search area also grows and the FS algorithm can explore all candidate blocks in the search area. Analyzing the DS algorithm PSNR curve, the growing in resolution does not mean that the DS quality increases. In fact, the DS got a worse quality for 1088 p than when encoding 720 p or 480 p. It is explained because the DS can easily be trapped into a local minimum. The efficiency of the DS is reduced a lot for high definition videos, because there is a lot of similar information among neighbor pixels (and blocks).

These results show that the DS algorithm is efficient for low resolution videos, since it has PSNR results which are very similar to FS results, with a significant computational cost reduction. For high definition videos, the PSNR losses become more significant, and the relevance of the algorithm is only related with computational cost reduction. This experiment demonstrates that quality results for fast algorithms in low resolution videos cannot be extrapolated for a high definition video scenario.

The increase of local minima falls in high definition videos is the main reason why the DS algorithm loses its efficiency. The increase in the search area for the DS does not present much gain because in average the DS iterates only 5 times. Also, with the increase in the search area, the ME optimum candidate block can be far away from the center of the search area. Fast algorithms, like DS, can be easily trapped in local minima, before they achieve the optimum result.

A widely used similar criterion is the Sum of Absolute Difference (SAD). To perform the SAD, the block that has been encoded is subtracted from a candidate block and the absolute value of this operation is added. SAD maps are presented in Figure 2, to illustrate the growing of the local minima occurrences in high definition videos. In Figure 2 SAD maps are presented for a search area in the sun_flower video. Each map represents the same region of the frame, with a different number of pixels. Figures 2(a)–2(e) represents the SAD maps for the resolutions 144 p, UMD 272 p, EDTV 480 p, HD 720 p, and HD 1080 p, respectively. The images represent the SAD magnitude for 16×16 blocks, where dark blue represents lower SAD values, and light orange represents higher SAD values.

In Figure 2(a) it is possible to see that good SAD results can be achieved around the center of the search area; traditional fast algorithms like DS would easily reach the global minimum. With the increase of resolution, some regions, dark blue regions, that is, good SADs results, can be found within some distance from the central block. This proves that the video resolution increase is a problem if the used search algorithm cannot deal with local minima falls. More dark regions can be seen in Figure 2(c); however, in Figures 2(a)–2(c) the global minima can be visually identified. However, in Figure 2(d) and Figure 2(e), there are a lot of dark blue regions and it is impossible to visually identify the global minima.

The analyses of the images presented in Figure 2 can explain the results presented in Figure 1. Both DS and FS algorithms choose similar candidate blocks (or even the same) at low resolution videos. As presented in Figure 2(a), there are only a few candidate blocks with good SAD results in a low resolution video, and all around the center of the search area. Even if the DS does not reach the optimal candidate block, it will choose a closer block with a similar SAD value (average difference of 0.19 dB). For high resolution videos, like HD 1080 p, the higher number of local minima significantly increases the differences between PSNR results for DS and FS algorithms (more than 3.4 dB). This DS fragility to local minima falls should be explored by new algorithms to achieve a good quality result without increasing a lot the complexity like FS would.

For a better analysis about local minima, Figure 3 presents the SAD for every candidate block in a search area of 128×128 samples in the HD 1080 p sun_flower sequence. This picture represents a 3D view of the SAD magnitude for blocks with 16x16 samples, where valleys represent lower SAD values, and peaks represent higher SAD values.

In Figure 3 it is also possible to see that there are a lot of peaks and valleys in this search area. The global minimum is the valley with the lowest SAD. This scenario is different for low resolution videos, where the number of peaks and valleys is much lower than that presented in Figure 3. In high resolution videos, fast iterative algorithms (DS for example) are unable to transpose some peaks around the center to achieve a global minimum. Then fast algorithms are easily trapped in local minima around the center of the search area.

Due to the FS algorithms complexity, their implementation for high definition videos is very computationally expensive. The performance requirements to achieve real-time processing in this kind of video are extremely high. Hardware solutions for FS algorithm must massively explore parallelism to reach real-time, increasing the hardware recourses utilization and also power consumption. Fast algorithm implementations use much lower hardware resources and achieve a much better processing rate, but at a cost of an expressive loss in quality.

The development of new fast ME algorithms, focused in high definition videos, is very important to achieve a good tradeoff between quality and computational cost. The hardware implementation is also very important, mainly for real-time applications on portable devices. Fast algorithms must be easily implemented in hardware, translating their computational cost reduction to hardware resources reduction, and also power in savings.

3. The DMPDS Algorithm

The DMPDS algorithm is based on the MPDS algorithm [6]; however, DMPDS introduces the dynamic control of the multi point search engines position. The basic engine used by the DMPDS algorithms is the well-known DS algorithm. A multi point approach is used to find the best matching in five different positions of a search area, and the dynamic control defines where the search engines will be placed, according to the video motion activity characteristics. With this strategy it is possible to reduce the local minima falls and to increase the quality results.

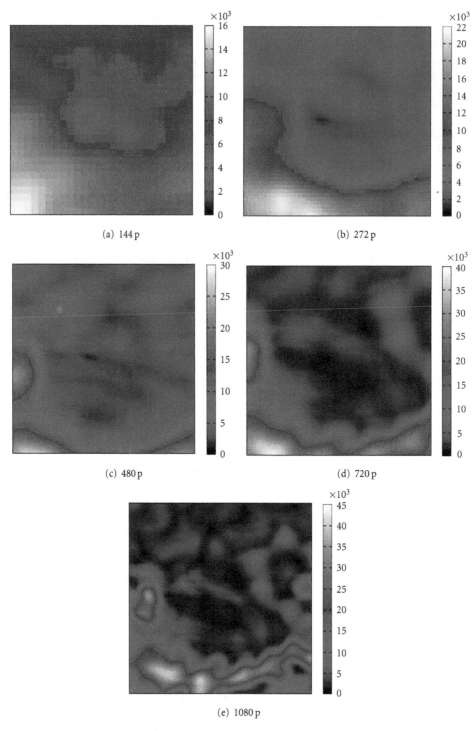

FIGURE 2: SAD maps for a sun_flower frame.

This section presents the Diamond Search and the Multipoint Diamond Search algorithms which are the basis for the Dynamic Multipoint Diamond Search proposed in this paper.

3.1. Diamond Search Algorithm. Diamond Search [8] is a fast and well-known search algorithm for ME. As previously explained, the DS achieves quite impressive results for low resolution videos; however, when dealing with high resolution videos, the quality degradation becomes higher.

The DS algorithm has two search patterns: the Large Diamond Search Pattern (LDSP) and the Small Diamond Search Pattern (SDSP) [8], as presented in Figure 4. The first used pattern is the LPDS. If a best match is found in an edge or a vertex of the LDSP, a new LDSP is formed, considering the best match of the previous LDSP as the center. This

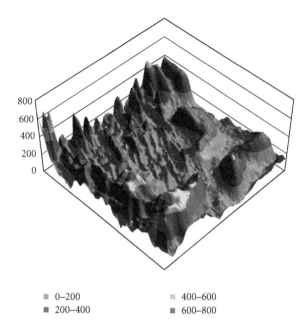

■ 0–200   ▨ 400–600
■ 200–400   ■ 600–800

FIGURE 3: 3D SAD map for a 1080 p sun_flower frame.

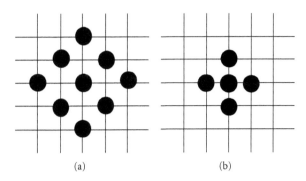

(a)   (b)

FIGURE 4: LDPS at the left and SDSP at the right [8].

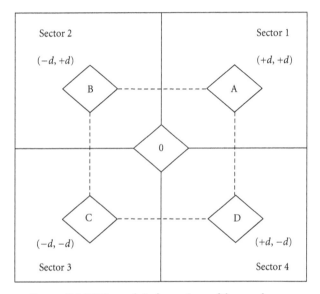

FIGURE 5: MPDS search in five regions of the search area.

process can be repeated many times. When the best match of an LDSP is found at the center, then all positions of the SDSP are evaluated to refine the result, considering the previous best result of LDSP as the center. The SDSP is applied just once while LDSP may be used many times and the best position found in the refinement is used to generate the motion vector.

3.2. Multipoint Diamond Search Algorithm.

The main motivation to develop new fast algorithms to ME is related to the behavior of the traditional approach used in fast ME algorithms which does not reach good results for high resolution videos. The single iterative approach, as the one used in DS and other algorithms, is strongly susceptible to local minima falls when processing high resolution videos. Then new approaches are mandatory if the quality increase is intended in this type of applications. The MPDS algorithm was a first solution developed in our group [6] dealing with this challenge. The MPDS algorithm intends to generate quality results close to those generated by FS with a much lower number of calculations. In low resolution videos, the DS achieves good results ruining alone; however, the MPDS increases the DS computational complexity and it is able to achieve high quality on high definition videos.

The MPDS finds the best block matching in five different positions of a search area. Each position is the start point of a DS iterative search. Beyond the central point, other four points are defined, each one inside of a sector (A, B, C, and D), as presented in Figure 5. The MPDS is not restricted to only one start point, exactly to avoid the same local minimum reached by DS. In the worst case, the MPDS algorithm will reach the same results as the DS algorithm. This multi point approach is the technique that is used by MPDS to obtain a better quality when a high definition video has been encoded.

Figure 5 describes the search positions of MPDS algorithm. Each initial search point is defined by its coordinates inside the sector. The point $(0, 0)$ is the central position and it will obtain the same vector as the DS algorithm. The search in the sectors A, B, C and D will be done according the distance parameter d. The d parameter is the distance (number of samples in X- and Y-axis) from the central point $(0, 0)$. The sector A, B, C and D starts searching, respectively, at positions (d, d), $(-d, d)$, $(-d, -d)$ and $(d, -d)$. When the search ends the MPDS algorithm selects the best result from the five applied diamonds. Pseudocode 1 describes the MPDS algorithm.

The d parameter has a high impact on the results obtained by the MPDS algorithm. If a low motion activity video has been encoded, the MPDS algorithm would achieve good results if low values of d are used since the motion would be so small that there would be good candidate blocks near the origin. On the other hand, high motion activity videos would achieve better results using the opposite (high values of d). Figure 6 shows the PSNR curves for MPDS algorithm with each one of the ten used test video sequences cited before. The curves were generated considering the variation of the d parameter value, from zero to 40, considering blocks of 8×8 pixels. One can notice that when

```
(1) Define d
(2) Frame <= 0
(3) Block <= 0
(4) Repeat
(5)    Repeat
(6)       SAD_zero <= Execute_DS (0, 0)
(7)       SAD_A <= Execute_DS (d, d)
(8)       SAD_B <= Execute_DS (−d, d)
(9)       SAD_C <= Execute_DS (−d, −d)
(10)      SAD_D <= Execute_DS (d, −d)
(11)      Lowest_SAD <= Min (zero, A, B, C, D)
(12)      Generate_Vector (Lowest_SAD)
(13)      Block ++
(14)   While (Block<Max_Blocks)
(15)   Frame ++
(16) While (Frame<Max_Frames)
```

PSEUDOCODE 1

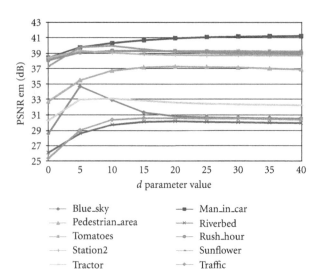

FIGURE 6: Variation of d parameter for MPDS algorithm.

$d = 0$ the MPDS applies all DS in the same position (i.e., in the correlated block) and the MPDS will obtain the same result obtained by a single DS.

From Figure 6 it is easy to notice that the MPDS algorithm obtains different results based on the d parameter value. The optimum value can significantly change according to the video motion characteristics. Low motion activity videos like blue_sky can reach best results using $d = 5$, with more than 6 dB gain in comparison to the DS algorithm. The video pedestrian_area has a lot of motion activities and reaches the best results with a $d = 20$, obtaining a quality gain superior to 4.5 dB in relation to DS algorithm.

The same experiment was made for 16×16 block sizes to identify the d value that maximize the average results of MPDS algorithm (considering the ten sequences). Using $d = 10$ the MPDS algorithm can achieve the best average gain in comparison to the DS algorithm (1.69 dB). This was the used value for d parameter on MPDS algorithm.

3.3. Dynamic Multipoint Diamond Search Algorithm.

With the analyses about the d parameter it was possible to notice that a fixed d parameter would not achieve the optimum quality result for all video sequences. The best d parameter value for the blue_sky sequence does not generate the best result for the traffic sequence, for example. It happens because these two sequences have different motion activity scenarios, which has significant influence in ME quality results. In this context, the DMPDS algorithm was developed, inserting a dynamic control of the d parameter of the MPDS algorithm. This makes the DMPDS algorithm more robust to handle videos with different motion activity scenarios.

The DMPDS defines the d parameter value dynamically. The variations of the d parameter are influenced by the characteristic of the current scene. For a low motion activity scene, the d parameter value can be dynamically reduced, resulting in better quality results. If the characteristic changes, and the motion activity is increased, the d

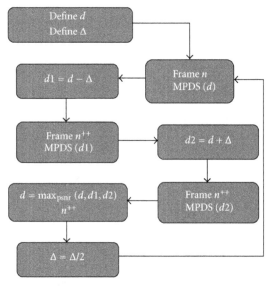

FIGURE 7: Dynamic control of the d parameter in the DMPDS algorithm.

parameter value can be dynamically increased. This dynamic adjustment enhances the robustness of the algorithm to deal with any kind of video sequences.

The algorithm to define the d parameter is presented in Figure 7. Firstly, an initial d value and a dynamic variation (Δ) are set. The first frame is processed with an original d parameter, the second frame with $d1 = d - \Delta$, and the third one with $d2 = d + \Delta$. The d used in the frame that obtains the lowest SAD becomes the new d and the dynamic variation (Δ) is divided by 2. This process is repeated until the dynamic variation reach the value 1, when the oscillation becomes 1 until the algorithm is restarted. This technique tries to approximate the optimal d for each frame using a low complexity heuristic. The start value of the dynamic parameter Δ is 5 and the start value of d is 10.

It is important to notice that the DMPDS algorithm could be executed in a parallel or in a sequential fashion. Each

TABLE 1: Quality and computational cost results for the DMPDS Algorithm.

Video	DS		MPDS		DMPDS		FS	
	PSNR (dB)	Number of ECB ($\times 10^9$)	PSNR (dB)	Number of ECB ($\times 10^9$)	PSNR (dB)	Number of ECB ($\times 10^9$)	PSNR (dB)	Number of ECB ($\times 10^9$)
Blue_sky	30.38	0.04	33.23	0.27	33.73	0.24	34.51	14.66
Man_in_car	38.15	0.03	39.41	0.22	39.60	0.24	40.34	14.66
Pedestrian_area	32.56	0.05	35.05	0.33	35.25	0.34	36.15	14.66
Riverbed	24.61	0.06	26.48	0.35	26.86	0.36	27.88	14.66
Rolling_tomatoes	37.76	0.03	38.27	0.25	38.32	0.28	38.65	14.66
Rush_hour	36.70	0.03	37.29	0.31	37.28	0.36	37.60	14.66
Station2	38.00	0.04	38.39	0.26	38.50	0.22	38.80	14.66
Sunflower	37.31	0.05	38.68	0.37	38.53	0.43	39.11	14.66
Traffic	25.10	0.06	29.05	0.38	28.81	0.39	33.38	14.66
Tractor	29.65	0.07	31.69	0.35	31.85	0.33	32.54	14.66
Average	33.02	**0.05**	**34.75**	**0.31**	**34.87**	**0.32**	35.90	**14.66**

4. Software Evaluation

The DMPDS algorithm was described in C language and evaluated in a framework containing the ME and MC (Motion Compensation) processes. The framework just contained the ME and MC because the ME algorithm can be performed in many different standards like MPGE-2, H.264/AVC, or even in the emerging HEVC. For this reason no other features were added in this framework so the ME is able to be evaluated without a specific video coding standard, since no characteristics of a standard like fractional ME [12], entropy coding tools, and others are going to be evaluated. The multi point technique is useful to reduce the local minima falls and then it will reduce the residual information improving the overall encoder efficiency.

The ten previously presented 1080 p video sequences were used in this evaluation, with a 16 × 16 block size and a search range of [−64, +64]. The results for quality and computational cost of DS, MPDS, DMPDS, and FS algorithms are presented in Table 1. The computational cost is measured in a number of Evaluated Candidate Blocks (ECB) and the quality results are presented in PSNR.

The best DMPDS result in comparison to MPDS is achieved in the *blue_sky* video, where the DMPDS obtains a PSNR gain of about 0.50 dB. The DMPDS also presents a lower number of comparisons in this video and this is a significant result since the quality result can be improved with a reduction of the computational cost.

In some videos the MPDS achieves better results than the DMPDS, for example, in the rush_hour video. It happens because the number of frames encoded in this evaluation was only 200 and the DMPDS could not converge to the optimum point for the video sequence.

In the average results, the DMPDS achieves a PSNR 0.12 dB higher than MPDS with a minimum increase of complexity (about 3% more comparisons). However, the DMPDS could achieve a higher gain for real videos because

TABLE 2: Average results for DMPDS and DS with iteration restrictions and subsampling.

Algorithm	PSNR (dB)	Number of ECB ($\times 10^9$)	Number of Comp. ($\times 10^9$)
DMPDS	34.87	0.32	81.55
DS	33.06	0.05	12.33
DMPDS 4 : 1	34.65	0.30	19.29
DS 4 : 1	32.76	0.05	2.97
DMPDS 4 : 1 and 5 iterations	33.67	0.24	15.54
DS 4 : 1 and 5 iterations	31.42	0.04	2.64

there would be more frames in the same sequence (the 200 frames in the evaluation represent less than 7 seconds of a scene).

Comparing to FS, the DMPDS achieves 1.03 dB lower PSNR; however, it is possible to reduce the number of ECBs in more than 45 times. One can notice that a good tradeoff between computational complexity and digital video quality was reached using the proposed DMPDS algorithm.

The DS algorithm does not have any limitation in the number of iterations. This is a problem if we want to design a real-time system. The proposed hardware solution should be able to guarantee that the real-time restriction should be reached, that is, at least 30 frames per second. Since the number of DS iterations is variable, and consequently the number of clock cycles are nondeterministic, an iteration limit should be set. Results targeting hardware implementation, considering the restriction in the number of iterations, are presented in Table 2. In this case, the evaluation considers a restriction of five LDSP iterations and only the DMPDS and the DS algorithms are considered with this evaluation. This restriction of five LDSP iterations was used in the hardware architecture design presented in the next section. Table 2 also presents the evaluation considering the use of 4 : 1 pixel subsampling. This is a useful technique to reduce the number of calculations with low impact in the quality results. The use

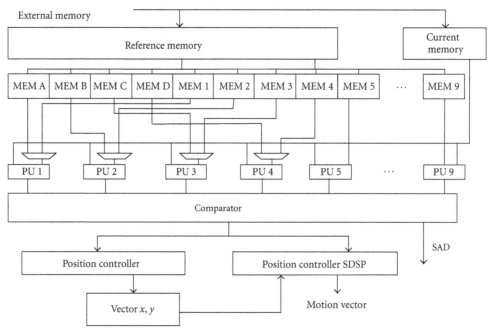

FIGURE 8: Block diagram of the DS core architecture.

of pixel subsampling is an interesting strategy especially for hardware implementations, since the internal memory and processing unities can be reduced. It helps to increase the processing rate without an impressive impact in the video quality.

The use of pixel subsampling in a 4 : 1 level together with the DMPDS algorithm reduces the number of ECBs and comparison operations about four times, as presented in Table 2. In this case, the quality losses are very small (less than 0.13 dB) and the number of comparisons is only 56.4% higher than DS without pixel subsampling, with an average PSNR gain of 1.59 dB.

The PSNR gain of the DMPDS algorithm over DS increases when the restriction in the number of iterations and the subsampling are considered. The DMPDS PSNR gain can reach 2.25 dB over DS considering the 4 : 1 subsampling and the restriction of five iterations. Another positive point is that the difference in the number of comparisons between DMPDS and DS is reduced in this scenario. In this case, the number of comparisons used by the DMPDS algorithm is six-times higher than the DS. If no iteration restriction or subsampling is considered, the DMPDS PSNR gain is of 1.81 dB and the number of comparisons is 6.4-times higher than DS.

Considering the good quality and complexity results achieved by the DMPDS algorithm with subsampling and the restriction of LDSP iterations, the designed hardware architecture considered these two simplifications, intending to reduce the hardware cost and increase its performance.

5. DMPDS Architecture

The DMPDS architecture works with a block size of 16×16 samples, and it uses a 4 : 1 pixel subsampling rate. Each one of the five DS cores is restricted to five iterations

for the reasons presented in the last section. The DMPDS architecture performance is focused on real-time processing for QFHD videos, with low consumption of the hardware resources.

The DMPDS architecture is formed by five DS cores and some additional logic to dynamically control the d parameter, to define which is the best vector among the five cores and to group these DS cores. Figure 8 presents the block diagram of the DS architecture, which is strongly based on the DS architecture presented in [13] for this module. To start the ME process, it is necessary to fill the reference memory and the current memory. The reference memory is a 34×34 bytes memory, which can store all data for five iterations and the final refinement. The current memory has 8×8 bytes and it contains the block being processed.

This first memory reading process takes 34 cycles to fill the DS reference memory. However, when this memory is being filled, this memory is also being read by the local memories (8×8 bytes), which are responsible to store the data of each possible candidate in the current iteration. During the reference memory writing process, the processing units (PUs) also start to perform the SAD computation of the available blocks. Each PU calculates the SAD between the current block and a candidate block. The PU architecture was implemented in a pipeline with five stages, as presented in Figure 9.

When the PUs finish to compute the SADs, these SADs are compared and the position is updated. The process is repeated until the comparator finds the lowest SAD in the center of the DS (in PU 5). In this case the data for the final refinement is already stored in Local Memories A–D and in Local Memory 5, then the refinement can be computed without any additional access to the external memory.

The first LDSP takes 34 cycles to be processed and the next iterations can be performed in 27 cycles each because

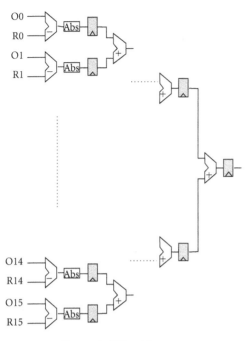

FIGURE 9: PU architecture.

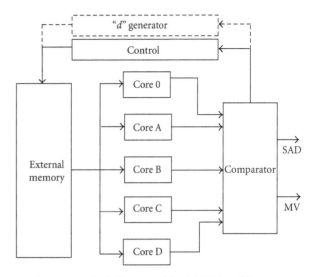

FIGURE 10: Block diagram of the DMPDS architecture.

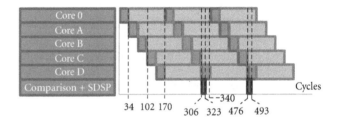

Reading memory
Processing
Comparison

FIGURE 11: Clock cycles diagram.

there is no need to fill the reference memory again. In the worst case scenario, the DS is computed in 169 cycles (five LDSP iterations plus one SDSP refinement).

The block diagram of the DMPDS architecture is presented in Figure 10. Each core in Figure 10 is composed by a DS architecture presented in Figure 8. The comparator in Figure 10 is responsible to find the best SAD among the SADs of the five cores. The DMPDS architecture basically controls where to write the data received from the external memory and it informs the external memory which data is necessary. In advance to start the ME process, the Core O (in the center) starts to receive data from the off-chip memory. It is necessary for 34 cock cycles to fill the internal memories of this core. When these memories are completely filled, this core does not read additional data from the external memory until this block is completely computed and the next one is required.

This filling process is repeated for the memories of the next cores until the memories of core D are completely filled. In this moment, it is possible to start to fill again the memories of the O core with data for the next motion vector generation. After core D computes its SAD it is possible to define the best SAD among the five cores and the final motion vector.

Figure 11 presents the clock cycles diagram of the MPDS architecture. The DMPDS architecture has a latency of 170 cycles to fill all cores' internal memories. In the worst case scenario, the core D needs more 135 cycles to finish the SAD computation and more 17 cycles are necessary to perform the refinement of Core D; the comparator decides which are the best SADs and to generate the final motion vector. After the first motion vector is generated, only more 170 cycles necessary to generate the next one. It happens because when the first vector finishes it is processing, the cores O, A, B and C are already processing the next block. The DMPDS architecture efficiently explores the used hardware maintaining the cores operating during 169 of 170 cycles after the first iteration (considering the worst case), that is, the architecture was designed to be active during 99.4% of the time. The external memory bandwidth necessary for the DMPDS architecture is 34 bytes per cycle.

The control block is responsible to implement the state machine to model the control flow presented in Figure 7 (Section 2). This step is important to define the d parameter for the next frame. Since this operation is simple, it does not imply extra clock cycles and it can be done in parallel with other operations. The control block is responsible to correctly select which core is being fed from the external memory and to inform the external memory the value of d in the current iteration. Firstly, the architecture processes one frame with $d = 10$. The second frame will be processed with $d = 5$, and the third one will be processed with $d = 15$. Then the d is updated to the value that generated the lowest SAD among these three first frames and the dynamic parameter Δ becomes 2. This process is repeated with the new d and the new dynamic parameter until $\Delta = 1$.

6. Synthesis Results and Comparisons

The DMPDS architecture was described in VHDL and synthesized to an EP4S40G2F40I2 Altera Stratix 4 FPGA and to an XC5VLX30-3FF324 Xilinx Virtex 5 FPGA. The synthesis results are presented in Table 3. The performance results considered the worst case scenario, when all cores use five iterations. The DMPDS architecture synthesis results show that it can work with an operational frequency of 187.58 MHz (Stratix 4) and 294 MHz (Virtex 5).

The high operation frequency reached in both syntheses is function of the well-balanced pipelined designed in all architectural stages. The Stratix 4 synthesis used dedicated RAM blocks and also registers. The registers were used to implement the pipeline and the block RAMs were used to implement the memory hierarchy. The Virtex 5 synthesis used only registers to implement both the memory hierarchy and the pipeline.

Considering the reached operation frequency and since the designed architecture consumes 170 clock cycles to process one 16×16 block, then the DMPDS architecture is able to process 213.2 1080 p frames per second or 53.3 QHDTV frames per second.

The comparative results for the DMPDS architecture and some related works are presented in Table 4. The DMPDS architecture was compared with the results of related works [6, 14–19]. Table 4 presents some synthesis results, like the reached operations frequency, the use of hardware resources, and the use of memory bits. The used technology for each solution is also presented.

Table 4 also shows the number of cycles necessary to process one block and the reached processing rate in frames per second considering 1080 p (1920×1080 pixels) and QFHD (2160×3840 pixels) resolutions.

Since the related works are focused in different technologies and using different algorithms, a fair comparison is not easy. But the possible comparisons are presented in the next paragraphs.

The work [6] presents a previous work about the MPDS architecture. Comparing to [6], the area and memory usage are the same and the main difference is the reached operational frequency. However, the DMPDS architecture presents an average PSNR improvement of 0.12 dB when compared to [6].

The work [14] proposes a tree-engine architecture for fractional motion estimation (FME) with a variable block size (VBSME). The work [14] cannot process QFHD videos in real-time. Our solution uses a bigger and well-organized memory hierarchy to reach a better processing rate. DMPDS architecture also uses less hardware resources, but this was expected since it does not support FME and VBSME.

The work [15] performs the Dynamic Variable Step Search (DVSS) fast ME. The architecture in [15] uses the same block size of our work and it needs 467 cycles to process a block, which is much more than our work. Comparing the area results, the architecture presented in [15] uses less internal memory. However, our solution can process QFHD videos in real-time.

TABLE 3: DMPDS synthesis results.

Device	Frequency (MHz)	Area	Memory bits (K)	Register (K)
Stratix 4	187.58	34.5 K ALUTS	46.2	44.5
Virtex 5	294.00	56.3 K LUTS	—	110.0

The architecture presented in [16] is a configurable ME architecture and it performs the following algorithms: (1) Hexagon-Based-Search (HEXBS), (2) Block Based Gradient Descent Search (BBGDS), (3) Three Step Search (TSS) algorithms. It needs 390, 437, and 680 cycles to process each block with each algorithm, respectively. The DMPDS needs fewer cycles to process a block than any configuration of [16]. Our work uses more hardware resources comparing to [16], however, we are able to process QFHD videos while [16] can only process 1080 p videos in real-time.

The work [17] presents the hardware architecture for the Fast Top-Winners Search Algorithm. Our work uses almost the double of the memory used by [17]. However, our solution reaches a much better processing rate and it is able to process QFHD videos in real-time, while [17] cannot even reach real-time for 1080 p videos.

The work [18] presents an architecture for the Multiresolution ME Algorithm (MMEA). This solution can process only 28 1080 p frames per second while our DMPDS architecture can process 34 or 53.3 QFHD frames per second, depending on the target FPGA. But, is important to notice that this solution considers two reference frames in the ME process, which improves the ME quality.

The work [19] presents the Adaptive True Motion Estimation Algorithm (ATME) and it also uses techniques for Frame Rate UpConversion (FRUP). It also evaluates the algorithm for HD 1080 p videos. The hardware designed in [19] processes a 16×16 block in 104 cycles, which is less cycles than our architecture. However, our architecture reaches a much better operating frequency, which causes a final processing rate near to two-times higher than [19].

It is difficult to compare the quality results among the related works, since almost none of them (except [6, 19]) evaluate their algorithms and architectures for HD 1080 p videos. Also [14–18] do not mention any alternatives to avoid local minima falls, so probably these architectures will process high resolution videos with a worst quality if compared with our work.

Finally it is important to emphasize that only our work and the previous version of this work [6] are able to reach a frame rate of 30 QFHD fps among all related works.

7. Conclusions

This paper presented a new ME search algorithm and its hardware design. The Dynamic Multipoint Diamond Search (DMPDS) algorithm was developed focusing on high resolution videos.

An investigation about the traditional fast ME search approach shows that this type of approach loses efficiency

TABLE 4: Synthesis results and comparisons.

Architecture	Technology	Frequency (MHz)	Area	Memory (K bits)	Cycles per block	1080 p fps	QFHD fps
Porto et al. [6]	Stratix 4	199.2	34.5 KALUTS	46.2	170	144	36
Kao et al. [14]	180 nm	154	321 KGates	9.72	631	30	7.5
Tasdizen et al. [15]	Virtex 5	130	2282 KCLBs	0.51	467	34	8.5
Vanne et al. [16]	130 nm	200	14 KGates	2.5	390/437/680	63/56/36	15.75/14/9
Lai et al. [17]	180 nm	83.3	26 KGates	28.7	1282	8	2
Yin et al. [18]	180 nm	200	260 KGates	11.3	872	28	7
Cetin and Hamzaoglu [19]	90 nm FPGA	63	33 KLUTS	8 dual-port block RAM	104 (average)	74.7	18.7
DMPDS	**Stratix 4**	**187.58**	**34.5 KALUTs**	**46.2**	**170**	**136**	**34**
DMPDS	**Virtex 5**	**294**	**56.3 KLUTs**	**—**	**170**	**213.2**	**53.3**

when the resolution is increased. The results of this investigation is presented in this paper and shows that traditional search algorithms like Diamond Search may loses more than 3 dB in PSNR when compared to Full Search if high resolution videos are considered. The explanation about why this expressive quality loss occurs is also presented in this paper where it is possible to conclude that the losses are function of a fragility in the traditional search approach which are willing to fall in a local minimum near to the search area center without finding the global minimum.

The DMPDS algorithm was developed focusing on high quality when encoding high definition videos. The DMPDS algorithm uses a multipoint approach to reduce the number of local minima choices, in comparison with traditional fast ME algorithms. To reach this objective, five DS instances are started in different positions of the same search area. The DMPDS is an evolution of a previous algorithm developed in our group called MPDS. The main new idea of the DMPDS is to dynamically adapt the distance of each DS core inside a search area. This solution caused a PSNR gain of 0.12 dB with a negligible impact in the number of calculations. The DMPDS algorithm can reach a PSNR gain of 1.85 dB in comparison with the DS algorithm and DMPDS reaches a PSNR only 1.03 dB lower than that reached by FS. The DMPDS algorithm is also able to reduce in more than 45 times the number of calculations when compared to FS, but DMPDS used six-times more calculations than DS.

Some simplifications were inserted in the DMPDS algorithm intending to reduce the cost of the hardware design. These simplifications were the restriction in the number of iterations and the use of subsampling. These simplifications were evaluated and showed good results, with the DMPDS algorithm increasing the PSNR gains and reducing the complexity loses when compared to DS. These results are also presented in this paper.

The DMPDS hardware design was focused on-high throughput for high definition videos. To reach this performance goal, five instances of a DS architecture were grouped to work in parallel. Each DS architecture was designed using an efficient memory hierarchy and a well-balanced pipeline, intending to avoid unnecessary external memory accesses and to provide a high throughput. The control efficiently schedules the external memory accesses to allow a maximum

use of the five DS cores, allowing a very high processing rate (similar to that obtained with a single instance of the DS architecture). In the worst case, the DMPDS architecture is able to process one block in only 170 clock cycles. The DMPDS architecture was synthesized targeting an Altera Stratix 4 and a Xilinx Virtex 5 FPGAs and the synthesis results shows that the DMPDS architecture was able to process up to 53.3 QFHD frames per second. This is the highest processing rates among all compared works and it is the function of the low number of cycles used to process each block and also to the high operation frequency reached.

References

[1] Y. S. Cheng, Z. Y. Chen, and P. C. Chang, "An H.264 spatio-temporal hierarchical fast motion estimation algorithm for high-definition video," in *Proceedings of the IEEE International Symposium on Circuits and Systems (ISCAS '09)*, pp. 880–883, May 2009.

[2] I. Richardson, *Video Codec Design: Developing Image and Video Compression Systems*, Wiley, 2002.

[3] ITU-T e ISO/IEC JTC1, "Generic coding of moving pictures and associated audio information—Part 2: Video," ITU-T Rec. H.262 and ISO/IEC, 13818-2 (MPEG-2), 1994.

[4] T. Wiegand, G. Sullivan, and A. Luthra, Eds., Draft ITU-T Recommendation and final draft international standard of joint video specification (ITU-T Rec.H.264—ISO/IEC, 14496-10 AVC), 2003.

[5] JCT, Working Draft 3 of High-Efficiency Video Coding, JCTVC-E603, 2011.

[6] M. Porto, G. Sanchez, D. Noble, S. Bampi, and L. Agostini, "An efficient ME architecture for high definition videos using the new MPDS algorithm," in *Proceedings of the 24th symposium on Integrated circuits and systems design (ACM SBCCI '11)*, pp. 119–124, 2011.

[7] G. Sanchez, M. Porto, S. Bampi, and Agostini, "Real time QFHD motion estimation architecture for DMPDS algorithm," in *IEEE Southern Programmable Logic Conference*, 2012.

[8] S. Zhu and K. K. Ma, "A new diamond search algorithm for fast block-matching motion estimation," *IEEE Transactions on Image Processing*, vol. 9, no. 2, pp. 287–290, 2000.

[9] Altera Corporation, "Altera: The Programmable Solutions Company," http://www.altera.com/.

[10] Xilinx, http://www.xilinx.com/.

[11] Xiph.org: Test media, 2011, http://media.xiph.org/video/derf/.

[12] M. M. Corrêa, M. T. Schoenknecht, R. S. Dornelles, and L. V. Agostini, "A high-throughput hardware architecture for the H.264/AVC half-pixel motion estimation targeting high-definition videos," *International Journal of Reconfigurable Computing*, vol. 2011, Article ID 254730, 9 pages, 2011.

[13] G. Sanchez, D. Noble, M. Porto, and L. Agostini, "High efficient motion estimation architecture with integrated motion compensation and FME support," in *Proceedings of the IEEE 2nd Latin American Symposium on Circuits and Systems (LASCAS '11)*, pp. 1–4, February 2011.

[14] C. Y. Kao, C. L. Wu, and Y. L. Lin, "A high-performance three-engine architecture for H.264/AVC fractional motion estimation," *IEEE Transactions on Very Large Scale Integration (VLSI) Systems*, vol. 18, no. 4, pp. 662–666, 2010.

[15] O. Tasdizen, A. Akin, H. Kukner, and I. Hamzaoglu, "Dynamically variable step search motion estimation algorithm and a dynamically reconfigurable hardware for its implementation," *IEEE Transactions on Consumer Electronics*, vol. 55, no. 3, pp. 1645–1653, 2009.

[16] J. Vanne, E. Aho, K. Kuusilinna, and T. D. Hämäläinen, "A configurable motion estimation architecture for block-matching algorithms," *IEEE Transactions on Circuits and Systems for Video Technology*, vol. 19, no. 4, pp. 466–476, 2009.

[17] Y. K. Lai, L. F. Chen, and S. Y. Huang, "Hybrid parallel motion estimation architecture based on fast top-winners search algorithm," *IEEE Transactions on Consumer Electronics*, vol. 56, no. 3, pp. 1837–1842, 2010.

[18] H. Yin, H. Jia, H. Qi, X. Ji, X. Xie, and W. Gao, "A hardware-efficient multi-resolution block matching algorithm and its VLSI architecture for high definition MPEG-like video encoders," *IEEE Transactions on Circuits and Systems for Video Technology*, vol. 20, no. 9, pp. 1242–1254, 2010.

[19] M. Cetin and I. Hamzaoglu, "An adaptive true motion estimation algorithm for frame rate conversion of high definition video and its hardware implementations," *IEEE Transactions on Consumer Electronics*, vol. 57, no. 2, pp. 923–931, 2011.

10

Multidimensional Costas Arrays and Their Enumeration Using GPUs and FPGAs

Rafael A. Arce-Nazario and José Ortiz-Ubarri

Department of Computer Science, University of Puerto Rico, Río Piedras, San Juan, PR 00924, USA

Correspondence should be addressed to Rafael A. Arce-Nazario, rafael.arce@upr.edu

Academic Editor: René Cumplido

The enumeration of two-dimensional Costas arrays is a problem with factorial time complexity and has been solved for sizes up to 29 using computer clusters. Costas arrays of higher dimensionality have recently been proposed and their properties are beginning to be understood. This paper presents, to the best of our knowledge, the first proposed implementations for enumerating these multidimensional arrays in GPUs and FPGAs, as well as the first discussion of techniques to prune the search space and reduce enumeration run time. Both GPU and FPGA implementations rely on Costas array symmetries to reduce the search space and perform concurrent explorations over the remaining candidate solutions. The fine grained parallelism utilized to evaluate and progress the exploration, coupled with the additional concurrency provided by the multiple instanced cores, allowed the FPGA (XC5VLX330-2) implementation to achieve speedups of up to 30× over the GPU (GeForce GTX 580).

1. Introduction

A two-dimensional Costas array (2DCA) of size N is a permutation $f : N \rightarrow N$ such that for every integer h, i, and j, where $1 \leq h \leq N-1$ and $1 \leq i, j \leq N-h$, $f(i+h) - f(i) = f(j+h) - f(j)$, implies that $i = j$. Thus, informally, a size N Costas array is defined as $N \times N$ matrix containing exactly N dots, where every row and column contain exactly one dot and the vectors joining each pair of dots are distinct. Figure 1 illustrates a Costas array of size $N = 6$, both as a matrix and a permutation. The figure also shows the array's difference triangle, which organizes the differences between the various permutation digits in $N - 1$ rows where each row corresponds to a fixed h. By definition, each row in the difference triangle of a Costas array must consist of unique numbers.

Their definition implies that Costas arrays have perfect autocorrelation (autocorrelation = 1), which makes them useful in communications where signals must be recoverable even in the presence of considerable noise. Costas arrays are useful in many security and communication applications, such as remote object recognition and optical

communications [1]. Furthermore, some special cases of Costas arrays can be used for digital watermarking [2].

Costas arrays with dimensions higher than two were introduced in 2008 by Drakakis [3]. These arrays maintain perfect autocorrelation, which broadens their applicability in optical communications, for example, 3D optical orthogonal codes [4]. Multidimensional periodic Costas arrays (MPCAs) over elementary Abelian groups, introduced by Moreno and Tirkel , add the property of being periodic over all dimensions. This extends their applicability to digital watermarking of video and combined video and audio, where higher-dimensionality codes are desired [2]. A formal definition and some of their properties are presented in Section 3. In this paper, we focus on the latter kind of multidimensional periodic Costas arrays (MPCAs) due to their richer application range.

The enumeration of 2D Costas arrays has been a topic of interest since their discovery by Costas in the 1960s [5]. With each new size enumerated, new properties and generation techniques may be discovered [6]. Ortiz-Ubarri et al. presented MPCA transformations and their first enumeration in [7]. Given their relatively new discovery, it is expected that the enumeration of MPCAs will, as with 2DCAs, help researchers improve their understanding.

Both 2DCAs and MPCAs can be generated using algebraic constructions based on finite fields like the Welch and Lempel-Golomb constructions [7]. Small sizes can be enumerated using hand computation, yet the only known method to guarantee complete enumeration is by exhaustive exploration. The search space for complete enumeration of 2DCAs grows factorially with N, thus computer-based exploration is the only practical approach for medium and large sizes. The most common approach for the enumeration of 2DCAs is to use a backtracking algorithm that incorporates symmetries and other observations to further prune the search space. This paper presents the first discussion of search space pruning techniques for MPCAs. Both the FPGA and GPU implementations utilize these methods to significantly reduce the search space. Nevertheless, the worst case timecomplexity is still factorial, requiring tremendous run times even for small cases of N and m (the dimension).

This paper discusses our implementations for the enumeration of $(m + 1)$-dimensional Costas arrays in GPUs and FPGAs and constitutes the first description of such an enumeration. We present the techniques chosen to prune the search space as well as the organization of our designs. Our FPGA implementation achieved speedups of up to 30 times faster than the GPU. Furthermore, the modules that were created as part of the design process can easily be adapted to other constraint satisfaction problems that use backtracking.

The rest of this paper is organized as follows. Section 2 presents the relevant previous work, while Section 3 defines $(m + 1)$-dimensional Costas arrays and some of their symmetries. Section 4 describes the backtracking algorithm and its use for the enumerations. Section 5 introduces several techniques that allow us to prune the search space during the enumerations. Sections 6 and 7 discuss the GPU and FPGA designs, respectively. Section 8 reports and discusses the results and Section 9 provides our conclusions.

2. Previous Work

Most recent enumerations of 2DCAs have been completed using general purpose processors [8, 9]. The latest enumerations have been achieved by deploying many computer clusters (in all, thousands of cores) to concurrently explore disjoint parts of the search space. For $N = 28$ and $N = 29$, the time per single CPU was determined to be 70 and 366.55 years, respectively.

To the best of our knowledge, the only reported FPGA-accelerated 2DCA enumerations have been [10, 11]. Devlin and Rickard implemented sizes $N = 13$ through 19 on a Xilinx Spartan-3 XC3S1000 running at 25 Mhz and extrapolated their results to sizes up to $N = 32$ using the same device as well as the Virtex-5 XC5VLX110 [10]. The extrapolated execution times for $N = 28$ and 29 were 9.26 and 48.45 years, respectively. Arce-Nazario and Ortiz-Ubarri compared the execution of 2DCA enumeration in an FPGA (Virtex 5-XC5VLX330-2) and a GPU (GeForce GTX 580). The FPGA implementation achieved speedups of up to 40×

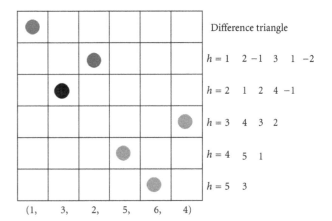

FIGURE 1: The Costas array (1, 3, 2, 5, 6, and 4), its matrix and permutation representations. The difference triangle confirms that this is a Costas array since each row h consists of unique numbers.

over the GPU and 4.44× over the fastest reported software implementation [9].

The first generalizations of Costas arrays were given by Drakakis in [12]. He defined various classes of multi-dimensional arrays by modifying the Costas property constraints and presented examples. Moreno et al. defined the $(m + 1)$-dimensional periodic Costas arrays over elementary Abelian groups [13] and described algebraic Welch Costas constructions. More recently, Ortiz-Ubarri et al. presented symmetries over the MPCAs that allow the expansion of the families discovered by Moreno [7]. They reported the first enumeration for sizes $(\mathbb{Z}_2)^2$, $(\mathbb{Z}_3)^2$, and $(\mathbb{Z}_5)^2$, yet no details are offered regarding enumeration or solution space pruning techniques.

3. $(m + 1)$-Dimensional Costas Arrays

We begin by providing the definitions of the $(m + 1)$-dimensional periodic Costas arrays over elementary Abelian groups.

Definition 1. A generic $(m + 1)$-dimensional periodic Costas array over the elementary Abelian group $(\mathbb{Z}_p)^m$ is a permutation function $f : ((\mathbb{Z}_p)^m)^* \to (\mathbb{Z}_{p^m-1})$, where A^* means $A - \{0\}$. This function has the distinct difference property: for any $h \neq 0$, $a, b \in (\mathbb{Z}_p)^m$, $f(a + h) - f(a) = f(b + h) - f(b)$ implies $a = b$, where the addition and subtraction operations are performed in the corresponding Abelian group.

Remark 2. Since, by definition, the $(m + 1)$-dimensional periodic Costas arrays over the elementary Abelian group are fully periodic; the periodic shifts of an MPCA on any of its $(m + 1)$ dimensions result in a different $(m + 1)$-dimensional periodic Costas array over the elementary Abelian group.

Example 3. The following is a grid defined over $\mathbb{Z}_3 \times \mathbb{Z}_3$:

$$\mathbf{W} = \begin{pmatrix} w_{2,0} & w_{2,1} & w_{2,2} \\ w_{1,0} & w_{1,1} & w_{1,2} \\ w_{0,0} & w_{0,1} & w_{0,2} \end{pmatrix}. \tag{1}$$

As a shorthand method, we may also enumerate the elements in a Costas array $(\mathbb{Z}_p)^m$ using the index mapping $(d_0, \ldots, d_{m-1}) \mapsto (d_0 + p \cdot d_1 + \cdots + p^{m-1} \cdot d_{m-1})$

$$\mathbf{W} = \begin{pmatrix} w_6 & w_7 & w_8 \\ w_3 & w_4 & w_5 \\ w_0 & w_1 & w_2 \end{pmatrix}. \tag{2}$$

The distinct difference property can be verified, in a manner similar to 2DCAs, by using difference matrices. The differences for a $(\mathbb{Z}_p)^m$ array are organized into $p^m - 1$ matrices. For instance, for $m = 2$, each difference matrix $h = (h_0, h_1)$ is $p \times p$ and contains at each cell (i, j) the result of $w_{i+h_0, j+h_1} - w_{i,j}$. The cells for differences that involve position $(0, 0)$ are represented using $*$.

Figure 2 shows a $\mathbb{Z}_3 \times \mathbb{Z}_3$ Costas array along with its corresponding difference matrices. For example, cell $(1, 1)$ of the difference matrix $h = (0, 1)$ contains the difference between $w_{(1+0),(1+1)} - w_{1,1} = w_{1,2} - w_{1,1} = 7 - 2 = 5$. A MPCA satisfies the distinct difference property if each of its $p^m - 1$ difference matrices contain each number in $\mathbb{Z}_{p^m-1}$-$\{0\}$ exactly once.

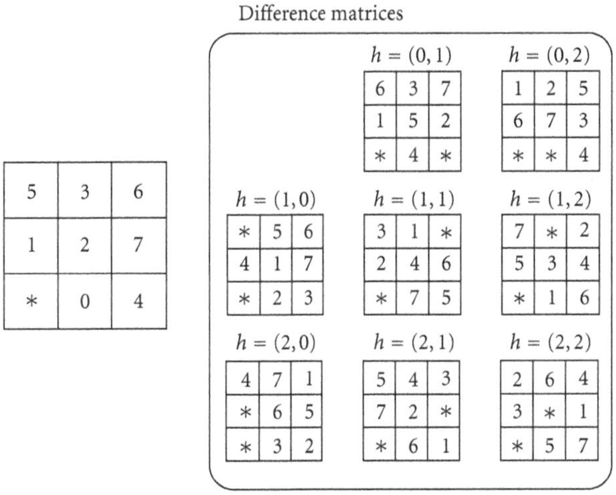

3.1. Addition and Multiplication (Modulo $p^m - 1$) Symmetries. Two algebraic symmetries introduced by Moreno et al. can be used to significantly reduce the search space for MPCA enumeration [13].

Theorem 4. *Multiplication (modulo $p^m - 1$) of a periodic Costas array by an integer less than and relatively prime to $p^m - 1$ generates a new periodic Costas array.*

Example 5. Multiplying **W**, the array in Figure 2, by $7 \equiv -1$ mod 8 yields the following MPCA:

$$\begin{pmatrix} 3 & 5 & 2 \\ 7 & 6 & 1 \\ * & 0 & 4 \end{pmatrix}. \tag{3}$$

Theorem 6. *Addition (modulo $p^m - 1$) of any integer less than $p^m - 1$ to a periodic Costas array generates a new periodic Costas array.*

Example 7. Adding 3 to **W** yields the MPCA:

$$\begin{pmatrix} 0 & 6 & 1 \\ 4 & 5 & 2 \\ * & 3 & 7 \end{pmatrix}. \tag{4}$$

4. Backtracking

Backtracking is a general algorithm for solving a computational problem by incrementally generating all possible solutions. The execution of a backtracking algorithm can be modelled as a search tree where every node is a partial solution. Moving forward corresponds to approaching a valid solution, and going backward corresponds to abandoning a partial candidate that cannot possibly generate a valid solution.

FIGURE 2: A $\mathbb{Z}_3 \times \mathbb{Z}_3$ MPCA and its difference matrices. The $*$ in the MPCA symbolizes that the mapping for $(0, 0)$ is not defined, that is, recall the mapping is $f : ((\mathbb{Z}_p)^m)^* \to (\mathbb{Z}_{p^m-1})$.

For the purpose of this discussion, we define a subpermutation $P_\ell^X = (p_1, p_2, \ldots, p_\ell)$, where $p_i \in X$. For MPCAs, $X = \mathbb{Z}_{p^m-1} + \{*\}$. The next subpermutation of size $\ell + k$ of P_ℓ^X, where $k \in \{-1, 0, 1\}$, expressed as $\aleph(P_\ell^X, \ell + k)$ is defined as the next subpermutation in lexicographical order of size $\ell + k$ that conserves the first $\ell + k - 1$ elements.

Example 8. For $X = \mathbb{Z}_{3^2-1} + \{*\}$, let $P_4^X = (*, 0, 4, 3)$, the next subpermutation of size 4, $\aleph(P_4^X, 4) = (*, 0, 4, 5)$. The next subpermutation of size 5, $\aleph(P_4^X, 5) = (*, 0, 4, 3, 1)$. The next subpermutation of size 3, $\aleph(P_3^X, 3) = (*, 0, 5)$.

Example 9. For $X = \mathbb{Z}_{3^2-1} + \{*\}$, let $P_4^X = (*, 0, 4, 7)$. $\aleph(P_4^X, 4) = \epsilon$, that is, there is no next subpermutation beginning with $(*, 0, 4)$. $\aleph(P_4^X, 5) = (*, 0, 4, 7, 1)$. $\aleph(P_4^X, 3) = (*, 0, 5)$.

Algorithm 1 illustrates the backtracking algorithm used for enumerating all MPCAs in $(\mathbb{Z}_p)^m$ given a seed permutation P_{init}. Figure 3 illustrates the steps in the computational tree of the backtracking approach, given the seed $(*, 0, 4, 1, 2, 7)$ for $(\mathbb{Z}_3)^2$.

5. Techniques for Pruning the Search Space and Efficient Evaluation of Candidate Arrays

MDCA symmetries can be leveraged to reduce the search space in their enumeration. For instance, it can be deduced from Theorems 4 and 6 that backtracking exploration must proceed only through permutations lexicographically smaller than $(*, 0, \lfloor p^m/2 \rfloor, \lfloor p^m/2 \rfloor + 1, \ldots)$.

(1) MPCAs with the $*$ in any position other than $(0, 0)$ are generated by periodic shifts of the arrays with the $*$ in position $(0, 0)$. These include all the geometric symmetries (horizontal flip, vertical flip, and 90^0 rotations) of the MPCAs.

```
Inputs: p, m: MPCA dimensions
        P_init: initial permutation
Output: Displays all MPCAs in (Z_p)^m

Perm = Perm_init
ℓ = length of Perm_init
while (ℓ >= length of Perm_init) {
    if (IsCostas (Perm) {
        if (ℓ == p^m) {
            display Perm
            do {
                ℓ − −;
            } until (Next (Perm, ℓ)!= empty)
        }
        else
            ℓ++; //explore a deeper level
    }
    else {
        // backtrack
        do {
            ℓ − −;
        } until (Next (Perm, ℓ)!= empty)
    }
    Perm = Next (Perm, ℓ);
}
```

ALGORITHM 1: Backtracking algorithm to enumerate all MPCAs in $(Z_p)^m$ beginning with permutation Perm_init.

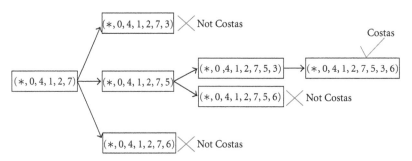

FIGURE 3: Backtracking search tree for MPCAs in $(Z_3)^2$ with $P_{init} = (*, 0, 4, 1, 2, 7)$.

(2) Any permutation starting with $*$, 0, and followed by a $\lfloor p^m/2 \rfloor$, $\lfloor p^m/2 \rfloor + 1$ can be obtained by multiplying a lexicographically smaller subpermutation by -1, that is, using Theorem 4. For example, for (Z_3), any permutation including and higher than $(*, 0, 4, 5, 1, 2, 3, 6, 7)$ can be obtained by multiplying a smaller permutation by -1, for instance, $(*, 0, 4, 5, 1, 2, 3, 6, 7)$ by multiplying $(*, 0, 4, 3, 7, 6, 5, 2, 1)$ by -1.

(3) Any permutation starting with $*$, followed by a nonzero element can be obtained by adding to a permutation that starts $*, 0$, that is, using Theorem 6. For example, $(*, 1, 5, 4, 0, 7, 6, 3, 2)$ is obtained from the addition of 1 to $(*, 0, 4, 3, 7, 6, 5, 2, 1)$.

Thus, the required exploration is reduced from $(p^2 - 1)!$ to approximately $(p^2 - 2)!/2$ permutations in the worst case.

5.1. Evaluation of Candidate Arrays. Computationally, we determine if a permutation is an MPCA by using the distinct difference property. In the backtracking algorithm, every time the algorithm moves forward by adding a new element p_k to the permutation, the new differences generated by subtracting p_k and $p_1, \ldots, p_{k-1}$ are added to the corresponding arrays. Thus, the difference arrays fill up as the permutation in the backtracking tree grows and deplete as the backtracking algorithm moves backward.

From the MPCA definition it can be deduced that only half of the difference matrices must be maintained. To understand this, let us define the negative of a distance vector.

Definition 10. Let $h = (h_0, \ldots, h_{m-1})$ be a distance vector of $(m + 1)$-dimensional periodic Costas array over the elementary Abelian group $(Z_p)^m$. The negative of the distance vector h, expressed as $-h$, is defined as $(-h_0, \ldots, -h_{m-1})$. In other words, h is a vector in the direction $(h_0, \ldots, h_{m-1})$ then $-h$ is a vector of same length in the opposite direction.

Example 11. The negative of the difference vector $h = (1, 0)$ over the elementary Abelian group $(\mathbb{Z}_3)^2$ is $-h = (-1, 0) = (2, 0)$.

The difference matrix for a distance vector $-h$ accumulates the negatives of the differences collected by the matrix for the distance vector h. This is illustrated in Figure 4. The current subpermutation being evaluated $(*, 0, 4, 1, 2, 7)$ has produced the differences shown in the matrices. Notice how the differences in $h = (0, 1)$ and $h = (0, 2)$ are the negatives of each other, for example, $-4 = 4$, $-1 = 7$, $-5 = 3$, and $-2 = 6$. The same behavior is obtained for the rest of the h and $-h$ pairs, for example, $(0, 1)$ and $(0, 2)$, $(1, 1)$ and $(2, 2)$, and $(2, 1)$ and $(1, 2)$. Therefore, we only need to keep track of either the h or $-h$ of each $h, -h$ pair, that is, the other matrix contains redundant information.

Furthermore, using the index mapping $(d_0, \ldots, d_{m-1}) \mapsto (d_0 + p \cdot d_1 + \cdots + p^{m-1} \cdot d_{m-1})$, we can demonstrate that the $(p^m - 1)/2$ matrices can be completed by computing all $w_b - w_a$, $a, b \in \mathbb{Z}_{p^m - 1}$ where $b > a$.

Theorem 12. *The differences $w_b - w_a$, $a, b \in \mathbb{Z}_{p^m - 1}$, where $b > a$ complete all the differences matrices.*

Proof. Without loss of generality, we consider $m = 2$, that is, $a, b \in \mathbb{Z}_{p^2 - 1}$. The matrix (h_0, h_1) collects all differences $f((i, j) + (h_0, h_1)) - f(i, j)$. If $(i + h_0) + p \cdot (j + h_1) > i + p \cdot j$ then $b > a$. Else, $b < a$, that is, $(i + h_0) + p \cdot (j + h_1) < i + p \cdot j$ which implies one of two cases.

(1) $j > j + h_1$. This implies that $h_1 \geq p - j$, in which case, for the negative, $h_1 < p - j$ and $j < j + h_1$. Thus, the negative of this case can be found using a difference covered by $b > a$.

(2) $j = j + h_1$ and $h_0 > i + h_0$. This implies that $h_0 \geq p - h_0$, in which case, for $-h$, $h_0 < p - i$ and $i < i + h_0$. Thus, the negative of this case can be found using a difference covered by $b > a$.   □

Example 13. For the difference matrix $h = (0, 1)$ the computation for $f((2, 2) + (0, 1)) - f(2, 2)$, that is, $f(2, 0) - f(2, 2)$ can be obtained from $-(f(2, 2) - f(2, 0))$, that is, $-(w_8 - w_6)$.

In our implementations, the difference matrices are managed as follows.

(i) A hash table of size $p^m - 1$ is used for each of the $(p^m - 1)/2$ matrices to keep track of its differences.

(ii) Whenever the permutation length increases (P_ℓ^X to $P_{\ell+1}^X$), the differences between the last added digit and the rest of the digits are computed and compared to the contents of the corresponding hash tables. A hit in any of the tables indicates a repeated difference and hence a non-Costas permutation. Otherwise, the differences are registered in the corresponding tables.

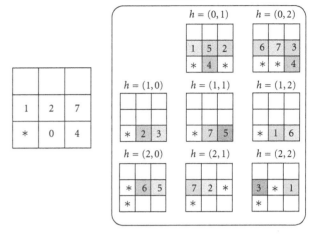

FIGURE 4: Difference matrices for a subpermutation during enumeration of $\mathbb{Z}_3 \times \mathbb{Z}_3$ MPCAs, to illustrate the behavior of h and $-h$ matrix pairs.

(iii) Whenever the permutation length decreases (P_ℓ^N to $P_{\ell-1}^X$), the differences between the dropped digit and the rest of the digits are deleted from the hash tables.

6. GPU Design

We perform our computations in a GeForce GTX 580 with 16 multiprocessors, each with 32 cores at 1.54 GHz clock rate, 1.5 GB of global memory, and 48 K of shared memory using the CUDA parallel computing architecture. Similar to many other computational problems where GPUs are used to accelerate algorithms in parallel, our implementation essentially decomposes the enumeration into many disjoint subspaces, which are deployed as threads to the GPU. Figure 5 illustrates the workflow of the GPGPU implementation. The Host (CPU) generates a set of K subpermutations P_m^N of size $m < N$ that comply with the Costas property. The set is then passed to the Device (GPU), where for each subpermutation a thread is generated to complete the exploration, that is, each thread determines all (if any) Costas arrays that begin with its given subpermutation. While the threads are executing, the Host is generating the next set of K subpermutations. When all threads complete, the results are passed to the Host, and the next set of K subpermutations is transferred to the GPU.

Two quite similar versions of Algorithm 1 run in the Host and each of the threads of the GPU. In the Host, Algorithm 1 is used to generate all subpermutations of length M compliant with the Costas property. As each subpermutation is found it is added to an array of size K of the data type shown in Algorithm 2 . When the array is full it is copied to the GPU global memory and the K CUDA threads are deployed to process the copied subpermutations.

Each CUDA thread runs a version of Algorithm 1 that takes one of the subpermutations as P_{init} and copies any found Costas arrays back to the GPU global memory. When all the GPU threads are done, the found Costas arrays of size

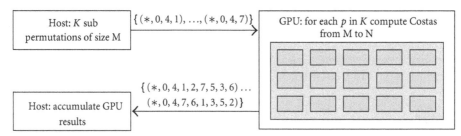

FIGURE 5: Simplified workflow of the GPGPU implementation. The Host generates a list of subpermutations, the GPU completes the search for the full permutations, then sends them back to the Host. The process repeats until no more subpermutations exist.

```
typedef struct{
    char counter;
    char subcostas[M];
    char costas[MAX_COSTAS_PT][N–M];
} CostasData;
```

ALGORITHM 2: The array of K permutations used between the Host and GPU is an array of size K of type CostasData counter stores the number of Costas array of size N found in each thread of the GPU, subcostas stores one of the subpermutations of size M computed in the Host, and costas stores a maximum number of the remaining $(N–M)$ elements of the Costas arrays of size N found in each thread of the GPU.

N are copied to the Host. The number of subpermutations (K) to be passed to the GPU is determined by the number of cores of the GPU. In our experiments we obtained the best performance with K = number of cores × 128.

7. FPGA Design

Many FPGA implementations obtain their impressive performance by exploiting fine-grained parallelism through deep, custom pipelines. However, backtracking is in essence a serial process, that is, generates permutation, then evaluates, then accepts or backtracks. Given this scenario, we opted to implement a highly tuned, low-resource serial MPCA enumeration (MPCAEn) core that can be instantiated many times inside the FPGA. Hence, the acceleration provided by our design comes mainly from two factors: (a) the rapid generation of candidate permutations and their evaluation within each core and (b) the high number of cores working in parallel on subsets of the enumeration.

7.1. Backtracking Functionality and Array Evaluation. Figure 6 illustrates the basic blocks of our MPCAEn core. A shift register is used for constructing or reversing the candidate permutation. The candidate permutation is constructed by shifting left and concatenating a new digit in the right-most position. As a permutation is generated, its compliance with the Costas array definition is verified by the Costas evaluation block. If the candidate complies, the next permutation P_{m+1}^N is generated by shifting left and concatenating the lowest available digit to the right-most position. If not, then one of two cases may occur.

(1) There is an available digit d that is higher than the rightmost digit. In this case, the rightmost digit is substituted by d. For example, $(*, 0, 4, 1, 2, 6)$ is evaluated and does not comply. Since the available digits are 3, 5, and 7, then 6 is substituted by 7 to compose the next candidate permutation $(*, 0, 4, 1, 2, 7)$.

(2) There are no digits available higher than the rightmost digit. In this case the shift register is shifted right and the digit that is shifted out is added to the available digits. This is repeated until there is an available digit that is higher than the current rightmost digit, at which case we perform the substitution described in the first case. For example, $(*, 0, 4, 3, 7)$ is determined to not comply with the MPCA difference property; the available digits are $1, 2, 5,$ and 6 but none of them is higher than 7 so the permutation must backtrack to $(*, 0, 4, 3)$. The available digits are now $1, 2, 5, 6,$ and 7, thus 3 is substituted by 5 to form the next permutation $(*, 0, 4, 5)$.

Figure 7 illustrates the operation of the MPCA evaluation block. When a new digit is added to the current permutation, for example, p_4 in the figure, the differences between the new digit and the rest are computed. The negatives of the differences are also computed, since they might be used to update some of the difference matrices (as explained in Section 5.1). Depending on the index of the newly added digit, the encoder/mux block routes the results of the differences to the corresponding hash tables. For the example in the figure, the result from Diff$_2$ corresponds to $p_4 - p_2$, that is, $p_{(1,1)} - p_{(0,2)}$; thus it will update the hash table for the difference matrix $h(1, 2)$. When p_5 is added to the permutation, Diff$_2$ corresponds to $p_5 - p_3$, that is, $p(1,2) - p(1,0)$; thus its negative will be used to update the hash table for the difference matrix $h(0, 1)$.

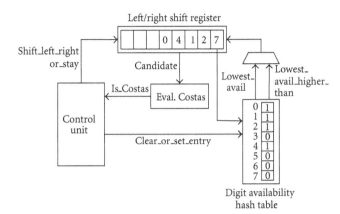

FIGURE 6: In the illustration, the permutation $(*, 0, 4, 1, 2, 7)$ has just been generated. The hash table keeps record of the digits that are in use in the current permutation (indicated by 1) and outputs two digits, the lowest available and the lowest available higher than the current input.

For 2DCAs, the deeper rows of the difference triangle are responsible for the detection of only a small percentage of the rejected arrays, as confirmed in [10, 11]. Our enumeration core for MPCAs is parameterizable in the number of distance vectors that are used to evaluate whether an array is an MPCA. The designer may choose to implement less than $(p^2 - 1)/2$ distance vectors to save FPGA resources. If so, the few false positives that will come out from the FPGA enumeration can be eliminated in software once they are communicated to the general purpose processor (GPP).

7.2. Resource Utilization and Core Organization. Figure 8 shows the amount of FPGA LUTs required by the MPCAEn core for $(\mathbb{Z}_5)^2$ and $(\mathbb{Z}_7)^2$, implementing various amounts of vector differences. LUTs are the most strained resource in the MPCAEn implementation (versus registers). The resource utilization results were obtained from the synthesis process using Xilinx ISE 11.5 targeting a Virtex5-XC5VLX330-2 FPGA. It was found through experimentation that keeping track of more than 7 differences for $(\mathbb{Z}_5)^2$ and 14 differences for $(\mathbb{Z}_7)^2$ did not significantly reduce enumeration times. The enumerators that were implemented for obtaining the results used those amounts of differences, for example, 7 for $(\mathbb{Z}_5)^2$ and 14 for $(\mathbb{Z}_7)^2$.

Since resource utilization per enumerator is low, multiple MPCAEn modules were instantiated in the FPGA as illustrated in Figure 9. The transfer of subpermutations and collection of results is performed by the transfer/collector module, which is connected through low-width data lines to the enumerators in order to save connection resources. MPCAs are so scarcely found during the enumeration that, regardless of the bandwidth between enumerators and transfer/collector module, these connections never become a bottleneck.

8. Results and Discussion

To compare GPU and FPGA performance, we implemented sizes 3×3, 5×5, and 7×7 of our MPCA enumeration designs in GPU (GeForce GTX 580) and FPGA (one Xilinx XC5VLX330-2 device of the four provided in a Convey HC-1 Server). Table 1 shows the number of found MPCAs starting with $(*, 0)$, the execution times for both designs as well as the growth rate as a function of p, and the speedup of FPGA versus GPU. Results for 3×3 and 5×5 are wall clock times while 7×7 is the worst case estimation of the run time based on sample runs.

We attribute the speedup mainly to the fact that the FPGA implementation was able to exploit the following two levels of parallelism, whereas the GPU could only make use of the highest level:

(1) *coarse-grained level* parallelism, which is achieved by splitting the solution space into multiple disjoint sets;

(2) *fine-grained* parallelism at the level of individual candidate evaluations, that is, the operations for the evaluation of each (sub)permutation are performed in parallel (as discussed in Section 7 and illustrated in Figure 7). An analogous, low-level technique could be used in general purpose processors by utilizing SIMD instructions. However, CUDA programs compile to the PTX instruction set, which does not contain SIMD instructions.

The GPU $(\mathbb{Z}_3)^2$ was greatly overshadowed by the data transfer times between FPGA/GPP; therefore, we only consider for fair comparisons the cases $(\mathbb{Z}_5)^2$ and $(\mathbb{Z}_7)^2$. For these larger cases we observe FPGA versus GPU speedups similar to those reported for 2DCAs in [11]. The enumeration of MPCAs exhibits a slower growth rate (approximately 3) per additional permutation digit as compared to the reported for two-dimensional Costas arrays (approximately 5) [8, 11]. We conjecture that the reason for the slower growth rate is that the conditions imposed in the MPCA definition are more strained, thus eliminating more candidate subpermutations earlier than the case of 2D Costas arrays.

All enumerated MPCAs turned out to be either Welch Costas constructions as presented in [13] or their symmetries introduced in [7], that is, no spurious MPCAs were found similar to some sizes of 2DCAs. These results support the conjecture that MPCAs (of all sizes and dimensions) are fully characterized by multidimensional Welch Costas arrays along with their symmetries.

9. Conclusions

In this work, we presented designs for the enumeration of multidimensional periodic Costas arrays in GPUs and FPGAs. Also, we introduced several MPCA symmetries and showed how they are used in our designs to significantly prune the search space. Both GPU and FPGA implementations rely on the concurrent exploration of multiple disjoint areas of the search space. In the GPU implementation, hundreds of threads are deployed to complete the search using the many GPU cores. For the FPGA, a multidimensional periodic Costas arrays enumeration core was designed taking into consideration pruning techniques while maintaining a low use of logic resources. Multiple cores were instantiated

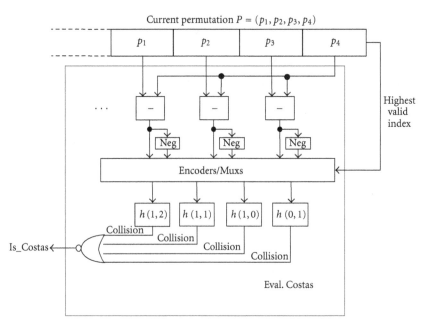

FIGURE 7: Detail of the Costas evaluation block.

TABLE 1: Experimental results for MPCA enumerations.

N	GPU			FPGA		Speedup
	MPCAs found[†]	Time (secs)	Growth rate[*]	Time (secs)	Growth rate	FPGA versus GPU
$(\mathbb{Z}_3)^2$	12	3.626	—	$1.24e-4$	—	29241
$(\mathbb{Z}_5)^2$	80	20389	1.72	662	2.63	30.76
$(\mathbb{Z}_7)^2$	336[‡]	1.87e14	3.15	7.42e14	3.18	25.21

[†] MPCAs starting with $(*; 0)$. As explained in Section 5, the rest of the MPCAs can be obtained using symmetries.
[*] Growth rate is computed as:
$$(p_{(n+1)}^2 - p_{(n)}^2)\sqrt{T(\mathbb{Z}_{P_{(n+1)}})^2/T(\mathbb{Z}_{P_{(n)}})^2}.$$
[‡] Lower bound of MPCAs based on Welch Costas construction and symmetries presented in [13].

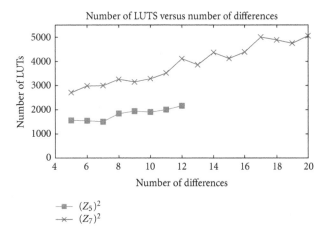

FIGURE 8: LUT utilization by the Costas enumeration module for various differences in the evaluation block. The target device is a XC5VLX330-2, which contains 207360 LUTs.

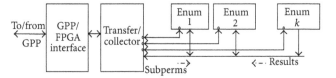

FIGURE 9: FPGA design. The transfer/collector (T/C) block receives a set of subpermutations from the GPP and schedules them among the various MPCA enumerators. Whenever an enumerator finds an MPCA it is sent back to the T/C and back to the GPP for validation.

multiple cores allowed the FPGA implementation to achieve speedups of up to 30× over the GPU. The implementations completed the first reported enumeration for MPCAs. Furthermore, the MPCA properties and symmetries discovered throughout the process help improve our understanding of these new structures.

Acknowledgments

Dr. R. A. Arce-Nazario was partially supported by NSF Grant number CNS-0923152. Dr. J. R. Ortiz-Ubarri was partially

in the FPGA to provide further acceleration. The fine grained parallelism utilized to evaluate and progress the exploration, coupled with the additional concurrency provided by the

supported by the UPR-RP FIPI funds. Thanks are due to Glen Edwards of Convey Computer for his engineering support in the HC1 implementations and Jonathan Vélez for his help in the GPU implementations.

References

[1] O. Moreno and J. Ortiz-Ubarri, "Group permutable constant weight codes," in *Proceedings of the IEEE Information Theory Workshop*, Dublin, Ireland, September 2010.

[2] O. Moreno and A. Tirkel, "Multi-dimensional arrays for watermarking," in *Proceedings of the IEEE International Symposium on Information Theory*, Saint-Petersburg, Russia, August 2011.

[3] K. Drakakis, "Higher dimensional generalizations of the Costas property," in *Proceedings of the 42nd Annual Conference on Information Sciences and Systems (CISS '08)*, pp. 1240–1245, Princeton, NJ, USA, March 2008.

[4] J. Ortiz-Ubarri and O. Moreno, "Three-dimensional periodic optical orthogonal code for OCDMA systems," in *Proceedings of the IEEE Information Theory Workshop*, pp. 170–174, October 2011.

[5] J. Costas, "Medium constraints on sonar design and performance," *FASCON Convention Record*, pp. 68A–68L, 1975.

[6] K. Drakakis, F. Iorio, and S. Rickard, "The enumeration of Costas arrays of order 28 and its consequences," *Advances in Mathematics of Communications*, vol. 5, no. 1, pp. 69–86, 2011.

[7] J. Ortiz-Ubarri, O. Moreno, A. Z. Tirkel, R. A. ArceNazario, and S. W. Golomb, "Algebraic symmetries of generic (m+1) dimensional periodic costas arrays," *IEEE Transactions on Information Theory*. In press.

[8] K. Drakakis, F. Iorio, S. Rickard, and J. Walsh, "Results of the enumeration of Costas arrays of order 29," *Advances in Mathematics of Communications*, vol. 5, no. 3, pp. 547–553, 2011.

[9] K. Drakakis, F. Iorio, and S. Rickard, "The enumeration of Costas arrays of order 28 and its consequences," *Advances in Mathematics of Communications*, vol. 5, no. 1, pp. 69–86, 2011.

[10] J. Devlin and S. Rickard, "Accelerated Costas array enumeration using FPGAs," in *Proceedings of the 42nd Annual Conference on Information Sciences and Systems (CISS '08)*, pp. 1252–1257, Princeton, NJ, USA, March 2008.

[11] R. Arce-Nazario and J. Ortiz-Ubarri, "Enumeration of Costas arrays using GPUs and FPGAs," in *Proceedings of the International Conference on Reconfigurable Computing and FPGAs*, pp. 462–467, 2011.

[12] K. Drakakis, "On the generalization of the Costas property in higher dimensions," *Advances in Mathematics of Communications*, vol. 4, no. 1, pp. 1–22, 2010.

[13] O. Moreno, A. Tirkel, S. Golomb, and K. Drakakis, "Multi-dimensional periodic Costas arrays over elementary Abelian groups," Preprint.

11

A Protein Sequence Analysis Hardware Accelerator Based on Divergences

Juan Fernando Eusse,[1] **Nahri Moreano,**[2] **Alba Cristina Magalhaes Alves de Melo,**[3] **and Ricardo Pezzuol Jacobi**[4]

[1] *Electrical Engineering Department, University of Brasilia, Brasilia, DF 70910-900, Brazil*
[2] *School of Computing, Federal University of Mato Grosso do Sul, Campo Grande, MS 79070-900, Brazil*
[3] *Computer Science Department, University of Brasilia, Brasilia, DF 70910-900, Brazil*
[4] *UnB Gama School, University of Brasilia, Gama, DF 72405-610, Brazil*

Correspondence should be addressed to Ricardo Pezzuol Jacobi, jacobi@unb.br

Academic Editor: Khaled Benkrid

The Viterbi algorithm is one of the most used dynamic programming algorithms for protein comparison and identification, based on hidden markov Models (HMMs). Most of the works in the literature focus on the implementation of hardware accelerators that act as a prefilter stage in the comparison process. This stage discards poorly aligned sequences with a low similarity score and forwards sequences with good similarity scores to software, where they are reprocessed to generate the sequence alignment. In order to reduce the software reprocessing time, this work proposes a hardware accelerator for the Viterbi algorithm which includes the concept of divergence, in which the region of interest of the dynamic programming matrices is delimited. We obtained gains of up to 182x when compared to unaccelerated software. The performance measurement methodology adopted in this work takes into account not only the acceleration achieved by the hardware but also the reprocessing software stage required to generate the alignment.

1. Introduction

Protein sequence comparison and analysis is a repetitive task in the field of molecular biology, as is needed by biologists to predict or determine the function, structure, and evolutionary characteristics of newly discovered protein sequences. During the last decade, technological advances had made possible the identification of a vast number of new proteins that have been introduced to the existing protein databases [1, 2]. With the exponential growth of these databases, the execution times of the protein comparison algorithms also grew exponentially [3], and the necessity to accelerate the existing software rose in order to speed up research.

The HMMER 2.3.2 program suite [4] is one of the most used programs for sequence comparison. HMMER takes multiple sequence alignments of similar protein sequences grouped into protein families and builds hidden Markov models (HMMs) [5] of them. This is done to estimate

statistically the evolutionary relations that exist between different members of the protein family, and to ease the identification of new family members with a similar structure or function. HMMER then takes unclassified input sequences and compares them against the generated HMMs of protein families (profile HMM) via the Viterbi algorithm (see Section 2), to generate both a similarity score and an alignment for the input (query) sequences.

As the Viterbi routine is the most time consuming part of the HMMER programs, multiple attempts to optimize and accelerate it have been made. MPI-HMMER [6] explores parallel execution in a cluster as well as software optimizations via the Intel-SSE2 instruction set. Other approaches like SledgeHMMER [7] and "HMMER on the Sun Grid" [8] provide web-based search interfaces to either an optimized version of HMMER running on a web server or the Sun Grid, respectively. Other approaches such as ClawHMMER [9] and GPU-HMMER [10] implement GPU parallelization of the Viterbi algorithm, while achieving a better cost/benefit relation than the cluster approach.

Studies have also shown that most of the processing time of the HMMER software is spent into processing poor scoring (nonsignificant) sequences [11], and most authors have found useful to apply a first-phase filter in order to discard poor scoring sequences prior to full processing. Some works apply heuristics [12], but the mainstream focuses on the use of FPGA-based accelerators [3, 11, 13–16] as a first-phase filter. The filter retrieves the sequence's similarity score and, if it is acceptable, instructs the software to reprocess the sequence in order to generate the corresponding alignment.

Our work proposes further acceleration of the algorithm by using the concept of divergence in which full reprocessing of the sequence after the FPGA accelerator is not needed, since the alignment only appears in specific parts of both the profile HMM model and the sequence. The proposed accelerator outputs the similarity score and the limits of the area of the dynamic programming (DP) matrices that contains the optimal alignment. The software then calculates only that small area of the DP matrices for the Viterbi algorithm and returns the same alignment as the unaccelerated software.

The main contributions of this work are threefold. First, we propose the Plan7-Viterbi divergence algorithm, which calculates the area in the Plan7-Viterbi dynamic programming matrices that contains the sequence-profile alignment. Second, we propose an architecture that implements this algorithm in hardware. Our architecture not only is able to generate the score for a query sequence when compared to a given profile HMM but also generates the divergence algorithm coefficients in hardware, which helps to speed up the subsequent alignment generation process by software. To the best of our knowledge, there is no software adaptation of the divergence algorithm to the Viterbi-Plan7 algorithm nor a hardware implementation of that adaptation. Finally, we propose a new measurement strategy that takes into account not only the architecture's throughput but also reprocessing times. This strategy helps us to give a more realistic measure of the achieved gains when including a hardware accelerator into the HMMER programs.

This work is organized as follows. In Section 2 we clarify some of the concepts of protein sequences, protein families, and profile HMMs. In Section 3 we present the related work in FPGA-based HMMER accelerators. Section 4 introduces the concept of divergences and their use in the acceleration of the Viterbi algorithm. Section 5 shows the proposed hardware architecture. Section 6 presents the metrics used to analyze the performance of the system. In Section 7 we show implementation and performance results, and we compare them with the existing works. Finally, in Section 8 we summarize the results and suggest future works.

2. Protein Sequence Comparison

2.1. Protein Sequences, Protein Families, and Profile HMMs. Proteins are basic elements that are present in every living organism. They may have several important functions such as catalyzing chemical reactions and signaling if a gene must be expressed, among others. Essentially, a protein is a chain of amino acids. In the nature, there are 20 different amino acids, represented by the alphabet $\Sigma = \{A, C, D, E, F, G, H, I, K, L, M, N, P, Q, R, S, T, V, W, Y\}$ [17].

A protein family is defined to be a set of proteins that have similar function, have similar 2D/3D structure, or have a common evolutionary history [17]. Therefore, a newly sequenced protein is often compared to several known protein families, in search of similarities. This comparison usually aligns the protein sequence to the representation of a protein family. This representation can be a profile, a consensus sequence, or a signature [18]. In this paper, we will only deal with profile representations, which are based on multiple sequence alignments.

Given a multiple-sequence alignment, a profile specifies, for each column, the frequency that each amino acid appears in the column. If a sequence-profile comparison results in high similarity, the protein sequence is usually identified to be a member of the family. This identification is a very important step towards determining the function and/or structure of a protein sequence.

One of the most accepted probabilistic models to do sequence-profile comparisons is based on hidden Markov models (HMMs). It is called profile HMM because it groups the evolutionary statistics for all the family members, therefore "profiling" it. A profile HMM models the common similarities among all the sequences in a protein family as discrete states; each one corresponding to an evolutionary possibility such as amino acid insertions, deletions, or matches between them. The traditional profile HMM architecture proposed by Durbin et al. [5] consisted of insert (I), delete (D), and match (M) states.

The HMMER suite [4], is a widely used software implementation of profile HMMs for biological sequence analysis, composed of several programs. In particular, the program *hmmsearch* searches a sequence database for matches to an HMM, while the program *hmmpfam* searches an HMM database for matches to a query sequence.

HMMER uses a modified HMM architecture that in addition to the traditional M, I, and D states includes flanking states that enable the algorithm to produce global or local alignments, with respect to the model or to the sequence, and also multiple-hit alignments [4, 5]. The Plan7 architecture used by HMMER is shown in Figure 1. Usually, there is one match state for each consensus column in the multiple alignment. Each M state aligns to (emits) a single residue, with a probability score that is determined by the frequency in which the residues have been observed in the corresponding column of the multiple alignment. Therefore, each M state has 20 probabilities for scoring the 20 amino acids.

The insertion (I) and deletion (D) states model gapped alignments, that is, alignments including residue insertions and deletions. Each I state also has 20 probabilities for scoring the 20 amino acids. The group of M, I, and D states corresponding to the same position in the multiple alignment is called a node of the HMM. Beside the emission

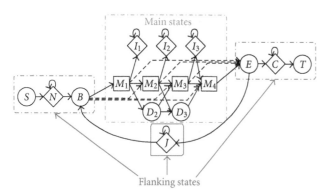

FIGURE 1: Plan7 architecture used by HMMER [3].

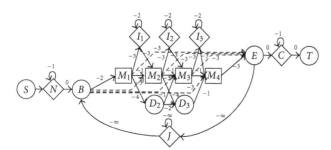

FIGURE 2: A profile HMM with 4 nodes and the transition scores.

probabilities, there are transition probabilities associated to each transition from one state to another.

2.2. Viterbi Algorithm. Given a HMM modeling a protein family and a query sequence, HMMER computes the probability that the sequence belongs to the family, as a similarity score, and generates the resulting alignment if the score is sufficiently good. To do so, it implements a well-known DP algorithm called the Viterbi algorithm [19]. This algorithm calculates a set of score matrices (corresponding to states M, I, and D) and vectors (corresponding to states N, B, E, C, and J) by means of a set of recurrence equations. As a result, it finds the best (most probable) alignment and its score for the query sequence with the given model.

Equations (1) show the Viterbi algorithm recurrence relations for aligning a sequence of length n to a profile HMM with k nodes. In these equations, $M(i, j)$ is the score of the best path aligning the subsequence $s_1 \ldots s_i$ to the submodel up to state M_j and $I(i, j)$ and $D(i, j)$ are defined similarly. The emission probability of the amino acid s_i at $state_1$ is denoted by $em(state_1, s_i)$, while $tr(state_1, state_2)$ represents the transition cost from $state_1$ to $state_2$. The similarity score of the best alignment is given by $C(n) + tr(C, T)$.

Plan7-Viterbi algorithm recurrence equations, for a profile HMM with k nodes and sequence s of length n are as follows;

$$M(i, 0) = I(i, 0) = D(i, 0) = -\infty \quad \forall 1 \le i \le n,$$

$$M(0, j) = I(0, j) = D(0, j) = -\infty \quad \forall 0 \le j \le k,$$

$$M(i, j) = em\left(M_j, s_i\right)$$

$$+ \max \begin{cases} M(i - 1, j - 1) + tr\left(M_{j-1}, M_j\right) \\ I(i - 1, j - 1) + tr\left(I_{j-1}, M_j\right) \\ D(i - 1, j - 1) + tr\left(D_{j-1}, M_j\right) \\ B(i - 1) + tr\left(B, M_j\right) \end{cases}$$

$$\forall 1 \le i \le n,$$

$$I(i, j) = em\left(I_j, s_i\right)$$

$$+ \max \begin{cases} M(i - 1, j) + tr\left(M_j, I_j\right) \\ I(i - 1, j) + tr\left(I_j, I_j\right) \end{cases}$$

$$\forall 1 \le j \le k,$$

$$D(i, j) = \max \begin{cases} M(i, j - 1) + tr\left(M_{j-1}, D_j\right) \\ D(i, j - 1) + tr\left(D_{j-1}, D_j\right), \end{cases}$$

$$N(0) = 0,$$

$$N(i) = N(i - 1) + tr(N, N), \quad \forall 1 \le i \le n,$$

$$B(0) = tr(N, B),$$

$$B(i) = \max \begin{cases} N(i) + tr(N, B) \\ J(i) + tr(J, B) \end{cases}$$

$$\forall 1 \le i \le n,$$

$$E(i) = \max_{1 \le j \le k} \left(M(i, j) + tr\left(M_j, E\right)\right) \quad \forall 1 \le j \le k,$$

$$J(0) = -\infty,$$

$$J(i) = \max \begin{cases} J(i - 1) + tr(J, J) \\ E(i) + tr(E, J) \end{cases} \quad \forall 1 \le i \le n,$$

$$C(0) = -\infty,$$

$$C(i) = \max \begin{cases} C(i - 1) + tr(C, C) \\ E(i) + tr(E, C) \end{cases} \quad \forall 1 \le i \le n.$$

$$similarity\_score = C(n) + tr(C, T).$$

$$(1)$$

Figure 2 illustrates a profile HMM with 4 nodes representing a multiple-sequence alignment. The transition scores are shown in the figure, labeling the state transitions. The emission scores for the M and I states are shown in Table 1.

Table 2 shows the score matrices and vectors computed by the Viterbi algorithm, while aligning the query sequence ACYDE to the profile HMM given in Figure 2. The best alignment has the similarity score of 25 and corresponds to

TABLE 1: Emission scores of amino acids for match and insert states of profile HMM of Figure 2.

State	A	C	D	E	F, I, L, M, V, W	G, K, P, S	H, Q, R, T	Y
M_1	7	-1	-1	1	-1	2	1	-1
M_2	-1	9	-1	1	-1	2	1	-1
M_3	-1	-1	8	2	-1	2	1	-1
M_4	-1	-1	3	9	-1	2	1	-1
I_1	-1	-1	0	1	-1	0	1	2
I_2	-1	-1	0	1	-1	0	1	2
I_3	-1	-1	0	1	-1	0	1	2

TABLE 2: Score matrices and vectors of the Viterbi algorithm for the comparison of the sequence ACYDE against the profile HMM of Figure 2.

	N	B	M					I					D					E	J	C
			0	1	2	3	4	0	1	2	3	4	0	1	2	3	4			
—	0	0	$-\infty$	$-\infty$	$-\infty$	$-\infty$	$-\infty$	$-\infty$	$-\infty$	$-\infty$	$-\infty$	$-\infty$	$-\infty$	$-\infty$	$-\infty$	$-\infty$	$-\infty$	$-\infty$	$-\infty$	$-\infty$
A	-1	-1	$-\infty$	-5	-4	-4	-4	$-\infty$	$-\infty$	$-\infty$	$-\infty$	$-\infty$	$-\infty$	$-\infty$	1	-1	-3	2	$-\infty$	2
C	-2	-2	$-\infty$	-4	13	-1	-3	$-\infty$	1	-8	-8	-8	$-\infty$	$-\infty$	-8	9	7	10	$-\infty$	10
Y	-3	-3	$-\infty$	-5	-3	11	7	$-\infty$	1	12	2	-4	$-\infty$	$-\infty$	-9	-7	7	8	$-\infty$	9
D	-4	-4	$-\infty$	-6	-3	17	13	$-\infty$	-1	10	8	6	$-\infty$	$-\infty$	-10	-7	13	14	$-\infty$	14
E	-5	-5	$-\infty$	-5	-3	9	25	$-\infty$	-2	9	15	24	$-\infty$	$-\infty$	-9	-7	5	25	$-\infty$	25

the path $(S,-) \rightarrow (N,-) \rightarrow (B,-) \rightarrow (M1,A) \rightarrow (M2,C) \rightarrow (I2,Y) \rightarrow (M3,D) \rightarrow (M4,E) \rightarrow (E,-) \rightarrow (C,-) \rightarrow (T,-)$.

3. Related Work

The function that implements the Viterbi algorithm in the HMMER suite is the most time consuming of the *hmmsearch* and *hmmpfam* programs of the suite. Therefore, most works [3, 11, 13–16, 20] focus on accelerating its execution by proposing a pre-filter phase which only calculates the similarity score for the algorithm. Then, if the similarity score is good, the entire query sequence is reprocessed to produce the alignment.

In general, FPGA-based accelerators for the Viterbi algorithm are composed of processing elements (PEs), connected together in a systolic array to exploit parallelism by eliminating the *J* state of the Plan7 Viterbi algorithm (Section 2.2). Usually, each node in the profile HMM is implemented by one PE. However, since the typical profile HMMs contain more than 600 nodes, even the recent FPGAs cannot accommodate this huge number of processing elements. For this reason, the entire sequence processing is divided into several passes [3, 11, 13, 14].

First-in first-out memories are included inside the FPGA implementation to store the necessary intermediary data between passes. Transition and emission probabilities for all the passes of the HMM are preloaded into block memories inside the FPGA to hide model turn around (transition probabilities reloading) when switching between passes. These memory requirements impose restrictions on the maximum PE number that can fit into the device, the maximum HMM size, and the maximum sequence size.

Benkrid et al. [13] propose an array of 90 PEs, capable of comparing a 1024 element sequence with a profile HMM containing 1440 nodes. They eliminate the *J* state dependencies in order to exploit the dynamic programming parallelism and calculate one cell element per clock cycle in each PE, reporting a maximum performance of 9 GCUPS (giga cell updates per second). Their systolic array was synthesized into a Virtex 2 Pro FPGA with a 100 MHz clock frequency.

Maddimsetty et al. [11] enhance accuracy by reducing the precision error induced by the elimination of the *J* state and proposes a two-pass architecture to detect and correct false negatives. Based on technology assumptions, they report an estimated maximum size of 50 PEs at an estimated clock frequency of 200 MHz and supposing a performance of 5 to 20 GCUPS.

Jacob et al. [3] divide the PE into 4 pipeline stages, in order to increase the maximum clock frequency up to 180 MHz and the throughput up to 10 GCUPS. Their work also eliminates the *J* state. The proposed architecture was implemented in a Xilinx Virtex 2 6000 and supports up to 68 PEs, a HMM with maximum length of 544 nodes, and a maximum sequence size of 1024 amino acids.

In Derrien and Quinton [16], a methodology to implement a pipeline inside the PE is outlined, based on the mathematical representation of the algorithm. Then a design space exploration is made for a Xilinx Spartan 3 4000, with maximum PE clock frequency of 66 MHz and a maximum performance of about 1.3 GCUPS.

Oliver et al. [14] implement the typical PE array without taking into account the *J* state when calculating the score. They obtain an array of 72 PEs working at a clock rate of 74 MHz, and an estimated performance of 3.95 GCUPS.

In [20] a special functional unit is introduced to detect when the *J* state feedback loop is taken. Then a control unit updates the value for state *B* and instructs the PEs to recalculate the inaccurate values. The implementation was made in a Xilinx Virtex 5 110-T FPGA with a maximum of 25 PEs and operating at 130 MHz. The reported performance is 3.2 GCUPS. No maximum HMM length or pass number is reported in the paper.

Takagi and Maruyama [21] developed a similar solution for processing the feedback loop. The alignment is calculated speculatively in parallel, and, when the feedback loop is taken, the alignment is recalculated from the beginning using the feedback score. With a Xilinx XC4VLX160 they could implement 100 PEs for profiles not exceeding 2048 nodes, reaching speedups up to 360 when compared to an Intel Core 2 Duo, 3.16 Ghz, and 4 GB RAM, when no recalculation occurs, and with a corresponding speed-up reduction otherwise.

Walters et al. [15] implement a complete Plan7-Viterbi algorithm in hardware, by exploiting the inherent parallelism in processing different sequences against the same HMM at the same time. Their PE is slightly more complex than those of other works as it includes the *J* state in the score calculation process. They include hardware acceleration into a cluster of computers, in order to further enhance the speedup. The implementation was made in a Xilinx Spartan 3 1500 board with a maximum of 10 PEs per node and a maximum profile HMM length of 256. The maximum clock speed for each PE is 70 MHz, and the complete system yields a performance of 700 MCUPS per cluster node, in a cluster comprised of 10 worker nodes. As any of the other analyzed works, its only output is the sequence score, and for the trace back, a complete reprocessing of the sequence has to be done in software.

Like all the designs discussed in this section, our design does not calculate the alignment in hardware, providing the score as output. Nevertheless, unlike the previous FPGA proposals, our design also provides information that can be used by the software to significantly reduce the number of cells contained in the DP matrices that need to be recalculated. Therefore, beside the score, our design outputs also the divergence algorithm information that will be used by the software to determine a region in the DP matrices where the actual alignment occurs. In this way, the software reprocessing time can be reduced, and better overall speedups can be attained.

Our work also proposes the use of a more accurate performance measurement that includes not only the time spent calculating the sequence score and divergence but also the time spent while reprocessing the sequences of interest, which gives a clearer idea of the real gain achieved when integrating the accelerator to HMMER.

4. Plan7-Viterbi Divergence Algorithm

The divergence concept was first introduced by Batista et al. [22], and it was included into an exact variation of the Smith-Waterman algorithm for pairwise local alignment of DNA sequences. Their goal was to obtain the alignment of huge biological sequences, handling the quadratic space, and time complexity of the Smith-Waterman algorithm. Therefore, they used parallel processing in a cluster of processors

to reduce execution time and exploited the divergence concept to reduce memory requirements. Initially, the whole similarity matrix is calculated in linear space. This phase of the algorithm outputs the highest similarity score and the coordinates in the similarity matrix that define the area that contains the optimal alignment. These coordinates were called superior and inferior divergences. To obtain the alignment itself using limited memory space, they recalculate the similarity matrix, but this time only the cells inside the limited area need to be computed and stored.

A direct adaptation of the original divergence concept to the Plan7-Viterbi algorithm is not possible because the recurrence relations of the Smith-Waterman and Plan7-Viterbi are totally distinct. The Smith-Waterman algorithm with affine gap calculates three DP matrices (E, F, D), but the inferior and superior divergence could be inferred from only one matrix (D) [22]. In the Plan7-Viterbi algorithm (Section 2.2), the inferior and superior divergence information depend on matrices M, I, D and vectors C, E. For this reason, we had to generate entirely new recurrence relations for divergence calculation. This resulted in a new algorithm, which we called the Plan7-Viterbi divergence algorithm. The recurrence equations for the M State of the proposed algorithm are shown in (3) and (4).

Also, the Smith-Waterman divergence algorithm provides a band in the DP matrix, where the alignment occurs, which is limited by the superior and inferior divergences [22]. We observed that the alignment region could be further limited if the initial and final rows are provided, in addition to the superior and inferior divergence information. Therefore, we also extended the divergence concept to provide a polygon that encapsulates the alignment, instead of two parallel lines, as it was defined in the Smith-Waterman divergence algorithm [22]. In the following paragraphs, we describe the Plan7-Viterbi divergence algorithm.

Given the DP matrices of the Viterbi algorithm, the limits of the best alignment are expressed by its initial and final rows and superior and inferior divergences (IR, FR, SD, and ID, resp.). The initial and final rows indicate the row of the matrices where the alignment starts and ends (initial and final element of the sequence involved in the alignment). The superior and inferior divergences represent how far the alignment departs from the main diagonal, in up and down directions, respectively. The main diagonal has divergence 0, the diagonal immediately above it has divergence -1, the next one -2, and so on. Analogously, the diagonals below the main diagonal have divergences $+1$, $+2$, and so on. These divergences are calculated as the difference $i - j$ between the row (i) and column (j) coordinates of the matrix cell. Figure 3 shows the main ideas behind the Plan7-Viterbi divergence algorithm.

Given a profile HMM with k nodes and a query sequence of length n, the figure shows the DP matrices M, I, D (represented as only one matrix, for clarity) of the Viterbi algorithm. The best alignment of the sequence to the HMM is a path (shown in a thick line) along the cells of the matrices. The initial and final rows of the alignment are 3 and 7, respectively, while the alignment superior and inferior divergences are -3 and 0, respectively. These limits

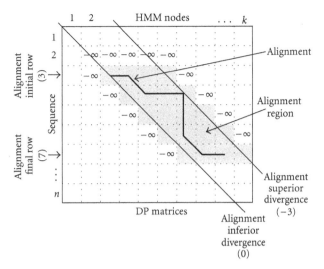

FIGURE 3: Divergence concept: alignment limits, initialized cells (with $-\infty$), and alignment region, for a HMM with k nodes and a sequence of length n.

determine what we define as the alignment region (AR), shown in shadow in the figure.

The AR contains the cells of the score matrices M, I, and D that must be computed in order to obtain the best alignment. The other Viterbi algorithm DP vectors are also limited by IR and FR, as well. The alignment limits are calculated precisely, leaving no space to error, in a sense that computing only the cells inside the AR will produce the same best alignment as the unbounded (not limited to the AR) computation of the whole matrices.

The Plan7-Viterbi Divergence Algorithm (Plan7-Viterbi-DA) works in two main phases. The first phase is inserted into a simplified version of the Viterbi algorithm which eliminates data dependencies induced by the J state. In this phase, we compute the similarity score of the best alignment of the sequence against the profile HMM, but we do not obtain the alignment itself. We also calculate the limits of the alignment, while computing the similarity score. These limits are computed as new DP matrices and vectors, by means of a new set of recurrence equations. The alignment limits IR, SD, and ID are computed for the M, I, D, E, and C states. The FR limit is computed only for the C state.

The Viterbi algorithm in (1) has the recurrence equation (2) for the M state score computation:

$$M(i, j) = \mathrm{em}\left(M_j, s_i\right)$$

$$+ \max \begin{cases} M(i - 1, j - 1) + \mathrm{tr}\left(M_{j-1}, M_j\right) \\ I(i - 1, j - 1) + \mathrm{tr}\left(I_{j-1}, M_j\right) \\ D(i - 1, j - 1) + \mathrm{tr}\left(D_{j-1}, M_j\right) \\ B(i - 1) + \mathrm{tr}\left(B_{j-1}, M_j\right). \end{cases} \quad (2)$$

Let Sel_M assume the values 0, 1, 2 or 3, depending on the result of the maximum operator in (2). If the argument selected by the maximum operator is the first, second, third,

or fourth one, then Sel_M will assume the value 0, 1, 2, or 3, respectively. Then, the alignment limits IR, SD, and ID, concerning the score matrix M, are defined by the recurrence equations in (6).

Recurrence equations for the alignment limits IR, SD, and ID, concerning the score matrix M, for $1 \le i \le n$ and $1 \le j \le k$:

$$\mathrm{IR}_M(i, j) = \begin{cases} \mathrm{IR}_M(i - 1, j - 1), & \text{if } \mathrm{Sel}_M = 0 \\ \mathrm{IR}_I(i - 1, j - 1), & \text{if } \mathrm{Sel}_M = 1 \\ \mathrm{IR}_D(i - 1, j - 1), & \text{if } \mathrm{Sel}_M = 2 \\ i, & \text{if } \mathrm{Sel}_M = 3, \end{cases}$$

$$\mathrm{SD}_M(i, j) = \begin{cases} \mathrm{SD}_M(i - 1, j - 1), & \text{if } \mathrm{Sel}_M = 0 \\ \min(i - j, \mathrm{SD}_I(i - 1, j - 1)), & \text{if } \mathrm{Sel}_M = 1 \\ \min(i - j, \mathrm{SD}_D(i - 1, j - 1)), & \text{if } \mathrm{Sel}_M = 2 \\ i - j, & \text{if } \mathrm{Sel}_M = 3, \end{cases}$$

$$\mathrm{ID}_M(i, j) = \begin{cases} \mathrm{ID}_M(i - 1, j - 1), & \text{if } \mathrm{Sel}_M = 0 \\ \max(i - j, \mathrm{ID}_I(i - 1, j - 1)), & \text{if } \mathrm{Sel}_M = 1 \\ \max(i - j, \mathrm{ID}_D(i - 1, j - 1)), & \text{if } \mathrm{Sel}_M = 2 \\ i - j, & \text{if } \mathrm{Sel}_M = 3. \end{cases}$$
$$(3)$$

The alignment limits IR, SD, and ID, related to the score matrices I and D and vector E, are defined analogously, based on the value of Sel_I, Sel_D, and Sel_E, determined by the result of the maximum operator of the Viterbi algorithm recurrence equation for the I, D, and E states, respectively. Given the recurrence equation for the C state's score computation in the Viterbi algorithm in (1), let Sel_C assume the values 0 or 1, depending on the result of the maximum operator in this equation. Equation (4) shows the recurrence equations that define the alignment limits IR, FR, SD, and ID, concerning the C score vector.

The first phase of the Plan7-Viterbi-DA was thought to be implemented in hardware because its implementation in software would increase the memory requirements and processing time as it introduces new DP matrices. Besides, the Divergence values computation does not create new data dependencies inside the Viterbi algorithm and can be performed in parallel to the similarity score calculation.

The second phase of the Plan7-Viterbi-DA uses the output data coming from the first one (similarity score and divergence values). If the alignment's similarity score is significant enough, then the second phase generates the alignment. To do this the software executes the Viterbi algorithm again for that sequence.

Nevertheless, it is not necessary to compute the whole DP matrices of the Viterbi algorithm, as we use the alignment limits produced by the first phase in order to calculate only the cells inside the AR of the DP matrices, thus saving memory space and execution time. Figure 4 illustrates

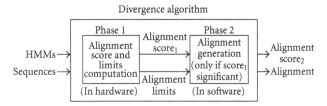

FIGURE 4: Phases of the Plan7-Viterbi-DA.

the high-level structure of the Plan7-Viterbi-DA and the interaction between its two phases.

Recurrence equations for the alignment limits IR, FR, SD, and ID, concerning the C score vector, for $1 \leq i \leq n$:

$$IR_C(i) = \begin{cases} IR_C(i-1), & \text{if } Sel_C = 0 \\ IR_E(i), & \text{if } Sel_C = 1, \end{cases}$$

$$FR_C(i) = \begin{cases} FR_C(i-1), & \text{if } Sel_C = 0 \\ i, & \text{if } Sel_C = 1, \end{cases}$$

$$\quad (4)$$

$$SD_C(i) = \begin{cases} SD_C(i-1), & \text{if } Sel_C = 0 \\ SD_E(i), & \text{if } Sel_C = 1, \end{cases}$$

$$ID_C(i) = \begin{cases} ID_C(i-1), & \text{if } Sel_C = 0 \\ ID_E(i), & \text{if } Sel_C = 1. \end{cases}$$

The Plan7-Viterbi-DA's second phase is implemented in software as a modification inside HMMER's Viterbi function used by the *hmmpfam* and *hmmsearch* programs. In this function, we need to initialize with $-\infty$ only the cells immediately above, to the left and to the right of the AR, as shown in Figure 3. The main loops are also modified in order to calculate only the cells inside the AR, using the alignment limits IR, FR, SD, and ID.

In the next section we propose a hardware implementation of the first phase of Plan7-Viterbi-DA.

5. HMMER-ViTDiV Architecture

The proposed architecture, called HMMER-ViTDiV, consists of an array of interconnected processing elements (PEs) that implements a simplified version of the Viterbi algorithm, including the necessary modifications to calculate the Plan7-Viterbi-DA presented in Section 4. The architecture is designed to be integrated to the system as a pre-filter stage that returns the similarity score and the alignment limits for a query sequence with a specific profile HMM. If the similarity score for the query sequence is significant enough, then the software uses the alignment limits calculated for the sequence inside the architecture and generates the alignment using the Plan7-Viterbi-DA. Each PE calculates the score for the j column of the DP matrices of the Viterbi algorithm and the alignment limits for the same column. Figure 5 shows the DP matrices antidiagonals and their relationship with each one of the PEs when the number of profile HMM nodes is equal

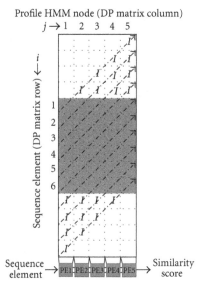

FIGURE 5: PE to DP matrices correspondence when the HMM number of nodes is less or equal to the number of PEs.

to the number of implemented PEs inside the architecture. In the figure, the arrows show the DP matrices anti-diagonals, cells marked with I correspond to idle PEs, and shaded cells correspond to DP cells that are being calculated by their corresponding PE. The systolic array is filled gradually as the sequence elements are inserted until there are no idle PEs left, and then, when sequence elements are exiting, it empties until there are no more DP cells to calculate.

Since the size of commercial FPGAs is currently limited, today we cannot implement a system with a number of PEs that is equal to one of the largest profile HMM in sequence databases (2295) [2]. We implemented a system that divides the computation into various passes, each one computing a band of size N of the DP matrices, where N is the maximum number of PEs that fits into the target FPGA. In each pass the entire sequence is fed across the array of PEs and the scores are calculated for the current band. Then the output of the last PE of the array is stored inside FIFOs, as it is the input to the next pass and will be consumed by the first PE. Figure 6 presents the concept of band division and multiple passes.

As shown in Figure 6, in each pass the PE acts as a different node of the profile HMM and has to be loaded with the corresponding transition and emission probabilities that are required by the calculations. Also, we note that the system does not have to wait for the entire sequence to be out of the array in one pass to start the next pass, and the PEs can be in different passes at a given time.

Two RAM memories per PE are included inside the architecture to store and provide the transition and emission probabilities for all passes. Two special sequence elements are included in the design to ease the identification of the end of a pass (@) and the end of the sequence processing (*). A controller is implemented inside each PE to identify these two characters, increment or clear the pass number, and signal the transition and emission RAM memories as their address offset depends directly on the pass number.

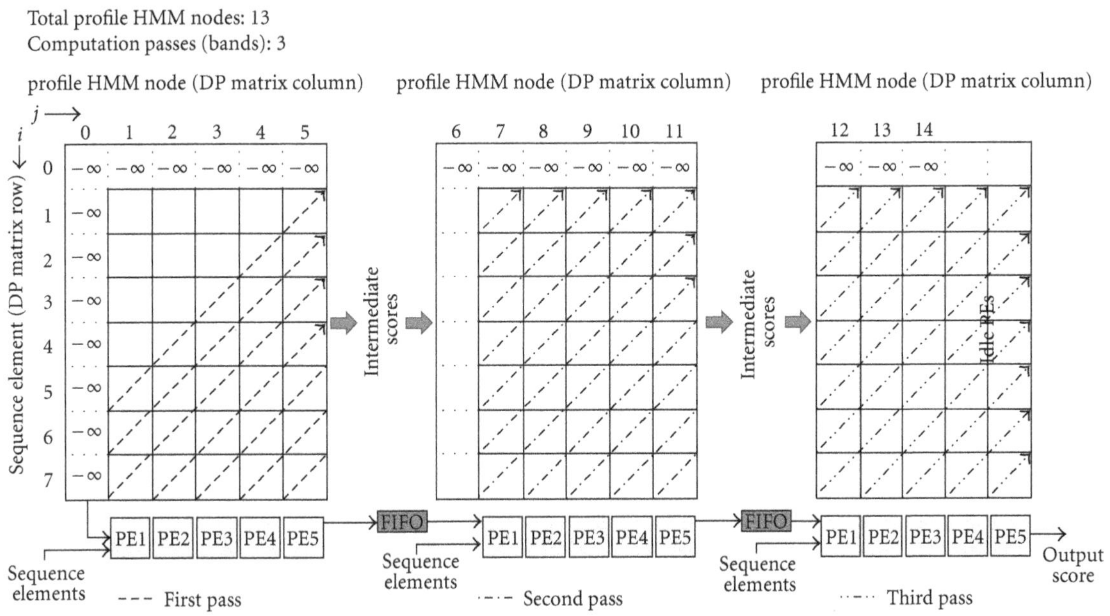

Total profile HMM nodes: 13
Computation passes (bands): 3

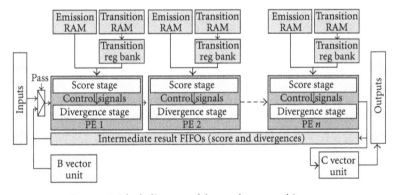

FIGURE 6: PE to DP matrices correspondence for HMMs with more nodes than the number of PEs (band division and multiple passes).

FIGURE 7: Block diagram of the accelerator architecture.

An input multiplexer had to be included to choose between initialization data for the first pass and intermediate data coming from the FIFOs for the other passes.

A transition register bank had also to be included to store the 9 transition probabilities used concurrently by the PE. This bank is loaded in 5 clock cycles by a small controller inside the transition block RAM memory. Figure 7 shows a general diagram of the architecture.

As illustrated in Figure 7, the PE consists of a score stage which calculates the M, I, D, and E scores and a Plan7-Viterbi divergence stage which calculates the alignment limits for the current sequence. Additional modules are included for the B and C score vector calculations which were placed outside the PE array in order to have an easily modifiable and homogeneous design.

5.1. Score Stage.
This stage calculates the scores for the M, I, D, and E states of the simplified Viterbi algorithm (without the J state). Each PE represents an individual HMM node, and calculates the scores as each element of the sequence

passes through. The PE's inputs are the scores calculated for the current element in a previous HMM node, and the PE's outputs are the scores for the current sequence element in the current node. The score stage of the PE uses (a) 16-bit saturated adders which detect and avoid overflow or underflow errors by saturating the result either to 32767 or to -32768 and (b) modified maximum units which not only return the maximum of its inputs but also the index of which of them was chosen. Finally, the score stage consists also of 8 16-bit registers used to store the data required by the DP algorithm to calculate the next cell of the matrix. Figure 8 shows the operator diagram of the score stage. The 4-input maximum unit was implemented in parallel in order to reduce the critical path of the system and thus increase the operating frequency.

5.2. Plan7-Viterbi Divergence Stage.
This stage calculates the alignment limits for the current query sequence element. The stage inputs are the previous node alignment limits for the current query sequence element, and the outputs are

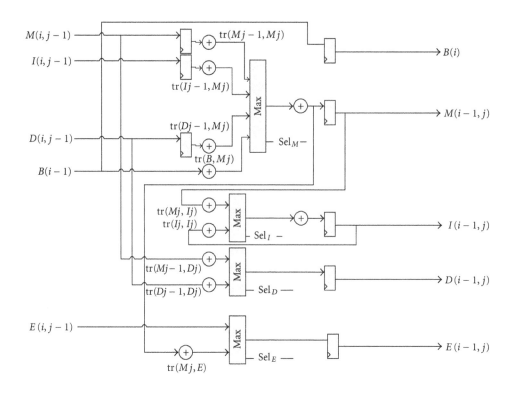

FIGURE 8: Score stage for the architecture's PE.

the calculated alignment limits for the current element. The outputs depend directly on the score stage of the PE and are controlled by the Sel_M, Sel_I, Sel_D, and Sel_E signals. The divergence stage also requires the current sequence element index, in order to calculate the alignment limits. Figure 9 shows the Plan7-Viterbi-DA implementation for the M and E states.

Figures 10 and 11 show the Plan7-Viterbi-DA implementation for the I and D states, respectively. The Base J parameter is the position of the PE in the systolic array, and the #PE parameter is the total number of PEs in the current system implementation. These parameters are used to initialize the divergence stage registers according to the current pass and ensure that the limits are calculated correctly. The divergence stage is composed of (a) 2 input maximum and minimum operators, (b) 4 and 2 input multiplexers, in which the selection lines are connected to the control signals coming from the score stage, and (c) 16-bit registers, which serve as temporal storage for the DP data that is needed to calculate the current divergence DP cell.

5.3. B and C Score Vector Calculation Units. The B score Vector calculation unit is in charge of feeding the PE array with the B score values. This module is placed left of the first PE, and it is connected to the $B(i-1)$ input of it. It has to be initialized for the first iteration with the $tr(N,B)$ transition probability for the current profile HMM by the control software. For other iterations, it adds the $tr(N,N)$ probability to the previous values and feeds the output to the

first PE. As discussed in Sections 2 and 4, the Plan7-Viterbi-DA does not generate modifications to the B calculation unit. Figure 12 shows its hardware implementation.

The C calculation unit is in charge of consuming the E output provided by the last PE of the array and generating the output similarity score for the current element of the query sequence (the score for the best alignment up to this sequence element). Since the Plan7-Viterbi-DA introduces the calculation of the limits for the best alignment in this state of the Viterbi algorithm, the score stage of the C unit also delivers the control signal (Sel_C) for the multiplexers of the divergence stage. Figure 13 shows the C state calculation unit, including the score and divergence stages.

6. Proposed Performance Measurement

In order to assess the proposed architecture's performance we used two approaches. The first uses the cell updates per second (CUPS) metric, which is utilized by the majority of the previous works [3, 11, 13–16, 20] and measures the quantity of DP matrix cells that the proposed architecture is capable of calculating in one second. We chose this metric in order to compare the performance of our system to the other proposed accelerators. The weakness of the CUPS approach is that it does not consider the reprocessing time and therefore the alignment generation for unaccelerated software, providing an unrealistic measure of the achieved acceleration when integrating the hardware to HMMER.

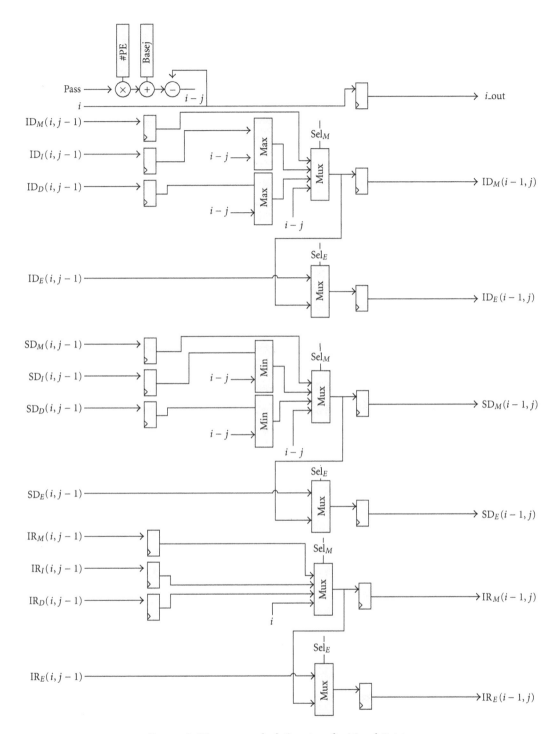

FIGURE 9: Divergence calculating stage for M and E states.

The second approach measures the execution times of the unaccelerated software when executing a predefined set of sequence comparisons. Then compares it to the execution time of the accelerated system when executing the same set of experiments, to obtain the real gain when integrating a hardware accelerator and the Plan7-Viterbi-DA.

Let S_t be the total number of query sequences in the test set, P_t the total number of profile HMMs in the test set, $t_{s(i,j)}$ the time the unaccelerated *hmmsearch* takes to compare the query sequence S_i to the profile HMM P_j, $t_{\mathrm{rep}(i,j)}$ the time the Plan7-Viterbi-DA takes to reprocess the significant query sequence S_i and the profile HMM P_j, $t_{\mathrm{con}(i,j)}$ the time spent in communication and control tasks inside the accelerated system, and $t_{h(i,j)}$ the time the hardware accelerator takes to execute the comparison between the query sequence S_i and the profile HMM P_j.

Then (5), (6), and (7) show the total time spent by unaccelerated HMMER (T_{ss}), the total time spent by the

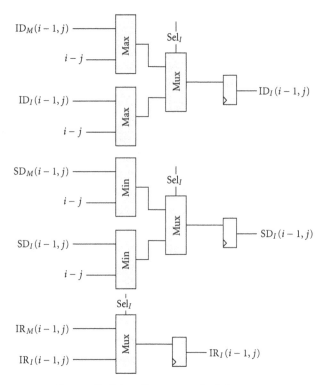

FIGURE 10: I state divergence calculating stage.

accelerated system (T_{sa}), and the achieved performance gains (G). The times $t_{s(i,j)}$, $t_{h(i,j)}$, $t_{\text{rep}(i,j)}$, and $t_{\text{con}(i,j)}$ are obtained directly from HMMER, the implemented accelerator, and the software implementing the Plan7-Viterbi-DA and will be shown in the following sections:

$$T_{ss} \longleftarrow \sum_{i=1}^{S_t} \sum_{j=1}^{P_t} t_{s(i,j)}, \tag{5}$$

$$T_{sa} \longleftarrow \sum_{i=1}^{S_t} \sum_{j=1}^{P_t} \left(t_{h(i,j)} + t_{\text{rep}(i,j)} + t_{\text{con}(i,j)} \right), \tag{6}$$

$$G \longleftarrow \frac{T_{ss}}{T_{sa}}. \tag{7}$$

7. Experimental Results

The proposed architecture not only enhances software execution by applying a pre-filter to the HMMER software but also provides a means to limit the area of the DP matrices that needs to be reprocessed, by software, in the case of significant sequences. Because of this, the speedup of the solution must be measured by taking into account the performance achieved by the hardware pre-filter as well as the saved software processing time by only recalculating the scores inside the alignment region. Execution time is measured separately for the hardware by measuring its real throughput rate (including loading time and interpass delays) and for software by computing the savings when calculating the scores and the alignment of the divergence-limited region of the DP matrices (Figure 3).

Experimental tests were conducted over all the 10340 profile HMMs for the PFam-A protein database [2]. Searches were made using 4 sets of 2000 randomly sampled protein sequences from the UniProtKB/SwissProt protein database [1] and only significantly scoring sequences were considered to be reprocessed in software. To find out which sequences from the sequence set were significant, we utilized a user-defined threshold and relaxed it to include the greatest possible number of sequences [11]. The experiments were done several times to guarantee the repeatability of them and the stability of the obtained data.

7.1. Implementation and Synthesis Results. The complete system was implemented in VHDL and mapped to an Altera Stratix II EP2S180F1508C3 device. Several configurations were explored to maximize the number of HMM nodes, the number of PEs, and the maximum sequence length. In order to do design space exploration, we developed a parameterizable VHDL code, in which we can modify the PE word size, the number of PEs of the array, and the size of the memories.

For the current implementation, we obtained a maximum frequency of 67 MHz after constraining the design time requirements in the Quartus II tool to optimize the synthesis for speed instead of area. Further works will include pipelining the PE to achieve better performance in terms of clock frequency. Table 3 shows the synthesized configurations and their resource utilization.

7.2. Unaccelerated HMMER Performance. To measure the *hmmsearch* performance in a typical work environment

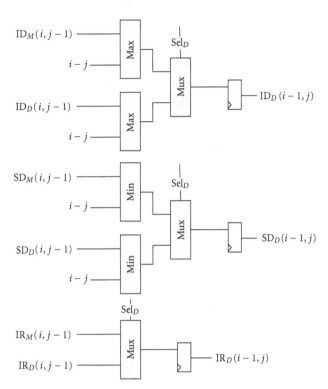

FIGURE 11: *D* state divergence calculating stage.

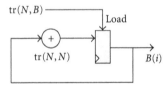

FIGURE 12: *B* score vector calculation unit (see Section 2).

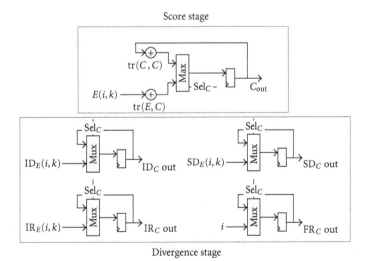

FIGURE 13: *C* vector calculation unit.

TABLE 3: Area and performance synthesis results.

NO. of PEs	Max. passes	Max. HMM nodes	Max. sequence size	Combinational ALUs	Dedicated registers	Memory bits	% Logic	Max. clock frequency (MHz)
25	25	625	8192	31738	18252	2609152	25	71
50	25	1250	8192	59750	35294	3121152	49	71
75	25	1875	8192	93132	52520	3663152	75	69
85	27	2295	8192	103940	59285	5230592	84	67

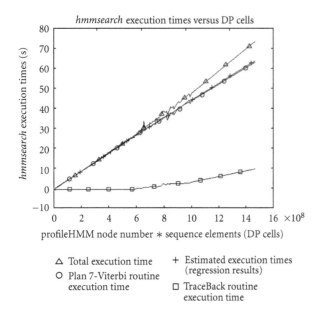

△ Total execution time   + Estimated execution times
                                      (regression results)
O Plan 7-Viterbi routine   □ TraceBack routine
   execution time   execution time

FIGURE 14: Unaccelerated *hmmsearch* performance for the test set.

we used a platform composed of an Intel Centrino Duo processor running at 1.8 GHz, 4 GB of RAM memory, and a 250 GB hard drive. HMMER was compiled to optimize execution time inside a Kubuntu Linux distribution. We also modified the *hmmsearch* program in order to obtain the execution times only for the Viterbi algorithm, as it was our main target for acceleration.

The characterization of HMMER was done by executing the entire set of tests (4 sets of 2000 randomly sampled sequences compared against 10340 profile HMMs) in the modified *hmmsearch* program. This was done to obtain an exact measure of the execution times of the unaccelerated software and to make its characterization when executing in our test platform. Figure 14 shows the obtained results for the experiments.

The line with triangular markers represents the total execution time of the *hmmsearch* program including the alignment generation times, the line with circular markers represents the execution time only for the Viterbi algorithm, the line with square markers represents the time consumed by the program when generating the alignments, and the line with the plus sign markers corresponds to the expected execution times obtained via the characterization expression shown in (8).

Let l_i be the number of amino acids in sequence S_i and let m_j be the number of nodes in the profile HMM P_j. Then the time to make the comparison between the profile HMM and the query sequence ($t_{s(i,j)}$) was found to be accurately represented by (8) which was found by making a least-squares regression on the data plotted in the circle-marked line of Figure 14:

$$t_{s(i,j)} \longleftarrow -1.3684 * 10^{-18} \left(m_j l_i \right)^2 + 4.3208 * 10^{-8}$$
$$* \left(m_j l_i \right) - 0.1160. \tag{8}$$

Even though we ran our tests with all the profile HMMs in the PFam-A database [2], we chose to show results only for 6 representative profile HMMs that include the smallest and the largest of the database, due to space limitations. Table 4 shows the estimated execution time obtained with (8) and its error percentage when compared to the actually measured execution times. We can calculate the number of average cell updates per second (CUPS) as the total number of elements of the entire data set sequences times the number of nodes of the profiles in the set divided by the complete execution time of the processing. We obtained a performance of 23.157 mega-CUPS for HMMER executing on the test platform.

7.3. Hardware Performance. We formulated an equation for performance prediction of the proposed accelerator, taking into account the possible delays, including systolic array data filling and consuming, profile HMM probabilities loading into RAM memories, and probability reloading delays when switching between passes. In order to validate the equation's results, we developed a test bench to execute all the test sets. I/O data transmission delays from/to the PC host were not considered into the formula due to the fact that, in platforms such as the XD2000i [23], data transmission rates are well above the maximum required for the system (130 MBps).

Let m_i be the number of nodes of the current HMM, S_j the size of the current query sequence being processed, n the number of PEs in hardware, f the maximum system frequency, T_{hw} the throughput of the system (measured in CUPS), and $t_{h(i,j)}$ the time the accelerator takes to process one sequence set. Then T_{hw} and $t_{h(i,j)}$ are fully described by (9) and (10), where $25n\lceil m_i/n \rceil$ are the number of cycles spent loading the current HMM into memory, n are the array filling number of cycles, $(S_j + 6)\lceil m_i/n \rceil$ are the cycles spent while processing the current sequence, 3 are the cycles spent loading the special transitions, and $S_j m_i$ are number of cells

TABLE 4: Modified *hmmsearch* performance results.

Sequence set elements	Number of HMM nodes	Measured time (total)	Measured time (Viterbi only)	Estimated time (Viterbi only)	Error (%)
	788	23.40	23.28	22.871	1.75
	10	0.40	0.35	0.1810	48.2
687406	226	6.55	6.47	6.5635	1.42
	337	9.85	9.8	9.8199	0.2
	2295	74.49	64.09	64.6425	0.8
	901	26.32	26.25	26.1199	0.4
	788	24.34	23.48	23.2158	1.12
	10	0.47	0.41	0.1853	54.1
697407	226	6.68	6.66	6.6602	0.003
	337	9.88	9.83	9.9634	1.35
	2295	78.87	62.89	65.5334	4.2
	901	27.55	25.96	26.4938	2.05
	788	24.40	23.37	23.3082	0.264
	10	0.42	0.38	0.1865	50.92
700218	226	6.76	6.72	6.6873	0.486
	337	10.26	9.84	10.0037	1.663
	2295	81.23	62.25	65.7849	5.678
	901	27.41	26.33	26.5989	1.021
	788	25.42	24.03	23.7193	1.293
	10	0.42	0.37	0.1919	48.13
712734	226	6.82	6.77	6.8083	0.565
	337	10.09	10.01	10.1832	1.730
	2295	81.07	63.81	66.8985	4.840
	901	27.46	26.82	27.0665	0.919

* Execution times are all expressed in seconds.

that the unaccelerated algorithm will have to calculate to process the current sequence with the current HMM:

$$T_{hw}$$

$$= \frac{\sum_{i=1}^{\#Seqs} \sum_{j=1}^{\#HMMs} S_i m_j}{\sum_{j=1}^{\#HMMs} \left[\left(\sum_{i=1}^{\#Seqs} (S_i + 6) \lceil m_j/n \rceil \right) + 25n \lceil m_j/n \rceil + n - 2 \right]} \\ * f,$$

(9)

$$t_{h(i,j)} = \frac{(S_i + 6) \lceil m_j/n \rceil + 25n \lceil m_j/n \rceil + n - 2}{f}.$$

(10)

We made the performance evaluation for the 4 proposed systolic PE arrays (25, 50, 75, and 85 PEs) and found out that the two characteristics that greatly influence the performance of the array are the quantity of PEs implemented in the array and the number of nodes of the profile HMM we are comparing the sequences against.

Table 5 shows the obtained performances for all the array variations when executing the comparisons for our 4 sets of sequences against the 6 profile HMM subsets. The best result for each case is shown in bold. From the table we can see that performance increases significantly with the number of

implemented PEs. Also we can observe that the system has better performance for profile HMMs whose node number is an exact multiple of the array node number. This is due to the fact that, when a PE does not correspond to a node inside the profile HMM, its transition and emission probabilities are set to minus infinity in order to stop that PE to modify the previously calculated result and only forward that result, thus wasting a clock cycle and affecting performance.

Figures 15 and 16 show the variations in the accelerator performance with the implemented PE number and the profile HMM node number, as seen from the experimental results.

From Figure 16 we can see that, as the performance varies according with profile HMM node number, there is an envelope curve around the performance data which shows the maximum and minimum performances of the array when varying the number of the HMM nodes.

7.4. Reprocessing Stage Performance (with Plan7-Viterbi-DA). When aligning different sequences with profile HMMs it is unlikely to find two alignments that are equal. Due to this fact, we cannot predict beforehand what will be the performance of the reprocessing stage as the divergence limits for every alignment are likely to be different. To make

TABLE 5: Hardware performance results.

Sequence set elements	Number of HMM nodes	25 PEs		50 PEs		75 PEs		85 PEs	
		T_{hw} (GCUPS)	t_h (sec)	T_{hw} (GCUPS)	t_h (sec)	T_{hw} (GCUPS)	t_h (sec)	T_{hw} (GCUPS)	t_h (sec)
687406	788	1.7468	0.3101	3.4903	0.1552	4.9293	0.1068	5.4203	0.0971
	10	0.7093	0.0097	0.7086	0.0097	0.6880	0.0097	0.6877	0.0097
	226	1.6031	0.0969	3.2033	0.0485	3.8876	0.0388	5.1815	0.0291
	337	1.7075	0.1357	3.4118	0.0679	4.6377	0.0485	5.7949	0.0388
	2295	**1.7695**	0.8915	**3.5358**	0.4462	**5.0942**	0.3010	**5.8468**	0.2622
	901	1.7274	0.3586	3.3607	0.1843	4.7691	0.1262	5.6341	0.1068
697407	788	1.7468	0.3146	3.4904	0.1574	4.9295	0.1083	5.4205	0.0985
	10	0.7093	0.0098	0.7086	0.0098	0.6880	0.0099	0.6877	0.0099
	226	1.6031	0.0983	3.2033	0.0492	3.8878	0.0394	5.1817	0.0296
	337	1.7075	0.1376	3.4119	0.0689	4.6379	0.0492	5.7952	0.0394
	2295	**1.7695**	0.9045	**3.5359**	0.4527	**5.0944**	0.3053	**5.8471**	0.2660
	901	1.7274	0.3638	3.3608	0.1870	4.7693	0.1280	5.6344	0.1084
700218	788	1.7468	0.3159	3.4905	0.1581	4.9296	0.1088	5.4206	0.0989
	10	0.7093	0.0099	0.7086	0.0099	0.6880	0.0099	0.6877	0.0099
	226	1.6031	0.0987	3.2034	0.0494	3.8878	0.0396	5.1818	0.0297
	337	1.7075	0.1382	3.4120	0.0692	4.6379	0.0494	5.7953	0.0396
	2295	**1.7695**	0.9081	**3.5359**	0.4545	**5.0945**	0.3066	**5.8472**	0.2671
	901	1.7274	0.3652	3.3608	0.1877	4.7693	0.1286	5.6345	0.1088
712734	788	1.7468	0.3215	3.4906	0.1609	4.9298	0.1107	5.4209	0.1007
	10	0.7093	0.0100	0.7086	0.0101	0.6880	0.0101	0.6878	0.0101
	226	1.6031	0.1005	3.2035	0.0503	3.8880	0.0403	5.1821	0.0302
	337	1.7075	0.1407	3.4121	0.0704	4.6382	0.0503	5.7956	0.0403
	2295	**1.7695**	0.9244	**3.5360**	0.4626	**5.0947**	0.3120	**5.8475**	0.2719
	901	1.7274	0.3718	3.3609	0.1911	4.7696	0.1308	5.6348	0.1108

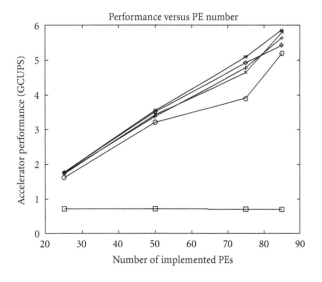

Profile HMM with

□ 10 nodes	× 788 nodes
○ 226 nodes	◇ 901 nodes
+ 337 nodes	* 2295 nodes

FIGURE 15: Performance versus number of PEs relation.

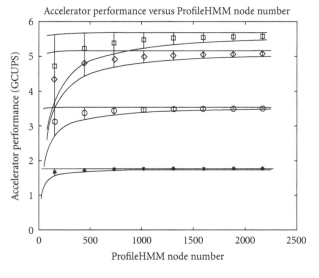

Array with

* 25 PEs	◇ 75 PEs
○ 50 PEs	□ 85 PEs

FIGURE 16: Performance versus number of HMM nodes envelope curves.

TABLE 6: Second-stage performance estimations.

Sequence set elements	Number of HMM nodes	Entire sequence set processing time in unaccelerated HMMER (sec)	Significant sequences reprocessing time with prefilter and unaccelerated HMMER (sec)	Divergence accelerated significant sequences reprocessing time (sec)
687406	788	23.40	0.234	0.0515
	10	0.40	0.004	0.0009
	226	6.55	0.0655	0.0144
	337	9.85	0.0985	0.0217
	2295	74.49	0.7449	0.1639
	901	26.32	0.2632	0.0579
697407	788	24.34	0.2434	0.0535
	10	0.47	0.0047	0.001
	226	6.68	0.0668	0.0147
	337	9.88	0.0988	0.0217
	2295	78.87	0.7887	0.1735
	901	27.55	0.2755	0.0606
700218	788	24.40	0.244	0.0537
	10	0.42	0.0042	0.0009
	226	6.76	0.0676	0.0149
	337	10.26	0.1026	0.0226
	2295	81.23	0.8123	0.1787
	901	27.41	0.2741	0.0603
712734	788	25.42	0.2542	0.0559
	10	0.42	0.0042	0.0009
	226	6.82	0.0682	0.015
	337	10.09	0.1009	0.0222
	2295	81.07	0.8107	0.1784
	901	27.46	0.2746	0.0604

an estimate of the performance of the second stage, we made a study in which we executed the comparison of the 20 top profile HMMs from the PFam-A [2] database with our 4 sets of query sequences to obtain both the similarity score and the divergence data for them. Then we built a graph plotting the similarity score threshold and the number of sequences with a similarity score greater than the threshold. From this graph we learned that less than 1% of the sequences were considered significant, even relaxing the threshold to include very bad alignments. With this information, we plotted the percentage of the DP matrices that the second stage of the system will have to reprocess in order to find out the worst case situation and make our estimations based on it. From Figure 17 we can see that, for the experimental data considered, in the worst case the divergence region only corresponds to 22% of the DP matrices.

To obtain the second-stage performance estimations for HMMER ($t_{\text{rep}(i,j)}$ in (6)), we obtained the percentage of significant sequences (p_s), multiplied it by the worst case percentage of the DP matrices that the second stage has to reprocess in order to generate the alignment (p_c), and then we multiplied it by the time the program *hmmsearch* takes to do the whole query sequence (S_i) comparison with a profile HMM (P_j). Equation (8) shows the expression

used to estimate the performance for the second stage. Table 6 presents the obtained results and also shows the comparison between the times the second stage will spend reprocessing the significant sequences with and without the Plan7-Viterbi-DA. As shown in Table 6, we obtained a performance gain up to 5 times only in the reprocessing stage.

$$t_{(\text{reg}(i,j))} = t * p_s * p_c \tag{11}$$

7.5. Total System Performance. In Section 6, we proposed two approaches to evaluate the performance for the system. For the first approach based in CUPS, we obtained a maximum system performance of up to 5.8 GCUPS when implementing a system composed by 85 PEs. This gives us a maximum gain of 254 times over the performance of unaccelerated HMMER software. For the second approach, as we obtained the individual processing times for every stage of the execution, we can determine the overall system performance by applying (6) to the results obtained in Tables 5 and 6. When including the Plan7-Viterbi divergence reprocessing stage, we got a maximum gain of up to 182 times the unaccelerated software, which still means a significant gain when comparing to unaccelerated HMMER. Table 7 presents the total execution time of the system and

TABLE 7: Total system performance and obtained performance gains.

Sequence set elements	Number of HMM nodes	Prefilter hardware execution time (sec)	Divergence second-stage execution time (sec)	Total time ($t_{sa(i,j)}$)	Unaccelerated HMMER execution time (sec)	Obtained gain
687406	788	0.0971	0.0515	0.1486	23.40	157.4697
	10	0.0097	0.0009	0.0106	0.40	37.7358
	226	0.0291	0.0144	0.0435	6.55	150.5747
	337	0.0388	0.0217	0.0605	9.85	162.8099
	2295	0.2622	0.1639	0.4261	74.49	**174.8181**
	901	0.1068	0.0579	0.1647	26.32	159.8057
697407	788	0.0985	0.0535	0.152	24.34	160.1316
	10	0.0099	0.001	0.0109	0.47	43.1193
	226	0.0296	0.0147	0.0443	6.68	150.7901
	337	0.0394	0.0217	0.0611	9.88	161.7021
	2295	0.2660	0.1735	0.4395	78.87	**179.4539**
	901	0.1084	0.0606	0.169	27.55	163.0178
700218	788	0.0989	0.0537	0.1526	24.40	159.8952
	10	0.0099	0.0009	0.0108	0.42	38.8889
	226	0.0297	0.0149	0.0446	6.76	151.5695
	337	0.0396	0.0226	0.0622	10.26	164.9518
	2295	0.2671	0.1787	0.4458	81.23	**182.2118**
	901	0.1088	0.0603	0.1691	27.41	162.0934
712734	788	0.1007	0.0559	0.1566	25.42	162.3244
	10	0.0101	0.0009	0.011	0.42	38.1818
	226	0.0302	0.015	0.0452	6.82	150.885
	337	0.0403	0.0222	0.0625	10.09	161.44
	2295	0.2719	0.1784	0.4503	81.07	**180.0355**
	901	0.1108	0.0604	0.1712	27.46	160.3972

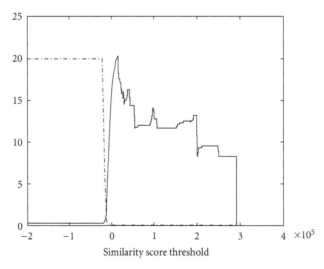

- - - Significant sequences/1000
——— DP matrices percentage needing to be reprocessed

FIGURE 17: Number of significant sequences and DP percentage that is required to reprocess in software versus similarity score threshold.

TABLE 8: Related work and comparison with our solution.

Reference	Number of PEs	Max. number of HMM nodes	Max. sequence size	Complete Plan7-Viterbi algorithm	Clock (MHz)	Performance (GCUPS)	Gain	FPGA
[3]	68	544	1024	N	180	10	190	Xilinx Virtex II 6000
[13]	90	1440	1024	N	100	9	247	Xilinx 2VP100
[11]	50	—	—	N	200	5 to 20	—	Not Synthesized
[14]	72	1440	8192	N	74	3.95	195	XC2V6000
[15]	10	256	—	Y	70	7	300	XC3S1500
[16]	50	—	—	N	66	1.3	50	Xilinx Spartan 3 4000
[20]	25	—	—	Y	130	3.2	56.8	Xilinx Virtex 5 110-T
Our work	**85**	**2295**	**8192**	*N*	**67**	**5.8**	**254 (182*)**	**Altera Stratix II EP2S180F1508C3**

*Including significant sequences reprocessing times.

shows the obtained performance gains. The table presents a summary of the execution time for each individual part of the system and calculates the performance gains with respect to the unaccelerated HMMER by applying (6).

Table 8 shows a brief comparison of this work with the ones found in the literature. We support longest test sequences and bigger profiles when compared with most works. As we include the divergence stage, we have to pay an area penalty, which limit the maximum number of PEs when compared with [13] and can affect the performance of the system. Nevertheless, we obtain additional gains from the divergence, a fact that justify the area overhead. Our architecture performs worse than complete Viterbi implementations such as the one presented in [15], but these cases are uncommon, and even if we relax the threshold for a sequence to be considered significant, the inclusion of the accelerator yields significant speedup.

8. Conclusions

In this paper, we introduced the Plan7-Viterbi-DA that enables the implementation of a hardware accelerator for the *hmmsearch* and *hmmpfam* programs of the HMMER suite. We proposed an accelerator architecture which acts as a pre-filtering phase and uses the Plan7-Viterbi-DA to avoid the full reprocessing of the sequence in software. We also introduced a more accurate performance measurement strategy when evaluating HMMER hardware accelerators, which not only includes the time spent on the pre-filtering phase or the hardware throughput but also includes reprocessing times for the significant sequences found in the process.

We implemented our accelerator in VHDL, obtaining performance gains of up to 182 times the performance of the HMMER software. We also made a comparison of the present work with those found in the literature and found that, despite the increased area, we managed to fit a considerable amount of PEs inside the FPGA, which are capable of comparing query sequences with even the largest profile HMM present in the PFam-A database.

For future works we intend to adapt the Plan7-Viterbi-DA to a complete version of the Plan7-Viterbi algorithm (including the *J* state) and make a pipelined version of the PE architecture, in order to further increase the performance gains achieved when integrating the array with the HMMER software.

Acknowledgments

The authors would like to acknowledge the CNPq, the National Microelectronics Program (PNM), the FINEP, the Brazilian Millennium Institute (NAMITEC), the CAPES, and the Fundect-MS for funding this work.

References

[1] The Universal Protein Resource—UniProt, June 2009, http://www.uniprot.org/.

[2] Sanger's Institute PFAM Protein Sequence Database, May 2009, http://pfam.sanger.ac.uk/.

[3] A. C. Jacob, J. M. Lancaster, J. D. Buhler, and R. D. Chamberlain, "Preliminary results in accelerating profile HMM search on FPGAs," in *Proceedings of the 21st International Parallel and Distributed Processing Symposium, (IPDPS '07)*, Long Beach, Calif, USA, March 2007.

[4] "HMMER: biosequence analysis using profile hidden Markov models," 2006, http://hmmer.janelia.org/.

[5] R. Durbin, S. Eddy, A. Krogh, and G. Mitchison, *Biological Sequence Analysis Probabilistic Models of Proteins and Nucleic Acids*, Cambridge University Press, New York, NY, USA, 2008.

[6] R. Darole, J. P. Walters, and V. Chaudhary, "Improving MPI-HMMER's scalability with parallel I/O," Tech. Rep. 2008-11, Department of Computer Science and Engineering, University of Buffalo, Buffalo, NY, USA, 2008.

[7] G. Chukkapalli, C. Guda, and S. Subramaniam, "SledgeHMMER: a web server for batch searching the Pfam database," *Nucleic Acids Research*, vol. 32, supplement 2, pp. W542–W544, 2004.

[8] "HMMER on the sun grid project," July 2009, http://www.psc.edu/general/software/packages/hmmer/.

[9] D. R. Horn, M. Houston, and P. Hanrahan, "ClawHMMER: a streaming HMMer-search implementation," in *Proceedings of the ACM/IEEE Supercomputing Conference, (SC '05)*, November 2005.

[10] GPU-HMMER, July 2009, http://www.mpihmmer.org/userguideGPUHMMER.htm.

[11] R. P. Maddimsetty, J. Buhler, R. D. Chamberlain, M. A. Franklin, and B. Harris, "Accelerator design for protein sequence HMM search," in *Proceedings of the 20th Annual International Conference on Supercomputing (ICS '06)*, pp. 288–296, New York, NY, USA, July 2006.

[12] "BLAST: Basic Local Alignment Search Tool," September 2009, http://blast.ncbi.nlm.nih.gov/.

[13] K. Benkrid, P. Velentzas, and S. Kasap, "A high performance reconfigurable core for motif searching using profile HMM," in *Procedings of the NASA/ESA Conference on Adaptive Hardware and Systems (AHS '08)*, pp. 285–292, Noordwijk, The Netherlands, June 2008.

[14] T. F. Oliver, B. Schmidt, Y. Jakop, and D. L. Maskell, "High speed biological sequence analysis with hidden Markov models on reconfigurable platforms," *IEEE Transactions on Information Technology in Biomedicine*, vol. 13, no. 5, pp. 740–746, 2009.

[15] J. P. Walters, X. Meng, V. Chaudhary et al., "MPI-HMMER-boost: distributed FPGA acceleration," *Journal of VLSI Signal Processing Systems*, vol. 48, no. 3, pp. 223–238, 2007.

[16] S. Derrien and P. Quinton, "Parallelizing HMMER for hardware acceleration on FPGAs," in *Proceedings of the International Conference on Application-specific Systems, Architectures and Processors (ASAP '07)*, pp. 10–17, Montreal, Canada, July 2007.

[17] L. Hunter, *Artificial Intelligence and Molecular Biology*, MIT Press, 1st edition, 1993.

[18] D. Gusfield, *Algorithms on Strings, Trees and Sequences: Computer Science and Computational Biology*, Cambridge University Press, 1997.

[19] L. R. Rabiner, "A tutorial on hidden Markov models and selected applications in speech recognition," *Proceedings of the IEEE*, vol. 77, no. 2, pp. 257–286, 1989.

[20] Y. Sun, P. Li, G. Gu et al., "HMMer acceleration using systolic array based reconfigurable architecture," in *Proceedings of the ACM/SIGDA International Symposium on Field Programmable Gate Arrays (FPGA '09)*, p. 282, New York, NY, USA, May 2009.

[21] T. Takagi and T. Maruyama, "Accelerating hmmer search using FPGA," in *Proceedings of the19th International Conference on Field Programmable Logic and Applications (FPL '09)*, pp. 332–337, Prague Czech Republic, September 2009.

[22] R. B. Batista, A. Boukerche, and A. C. M. A. de Melo, "A parallel strategy for biological sequence alignment in restricted memory space," *Journal of Parallel and Distributed Computing*, vol. 68, no. 4, pp. 548–561, 2008.

[23] XtremeData Inc., July 2009, http://www.xtremedata.com/.

12

Cellular Automata-Based Parallel Random Number Generators Using FPGAs

David H. K. Hoe, Jonathan M. Comer, Juan C. Cerda, Chris D. Martinez, and Mukul V. Shirvaikar

Department of Electrical Engineering, The University of Texas at Tyler, TX 75799, USA

Correspondence should be addressed to David H. K. Hoe, dhoe@uttyler.edu

Academic Editor: Dionisis Pnevmatikatos

Cellular computing represents a new paradigm for implementing high-speed massively parallel machines. Cellular automata (CA), which consist of an array of locally connected processing elements, are a basic form of a cellular-based architecture. The use of field programmable gate arrays (FPGAs) for implementing CA accelerators has shown promising results. This paper investigates the design of CA-based pseudo-random number generators (PRNGs) using an FPGA platform. To improve the quality of the random numbers that are generated, the basic CA structure is enhanced in two ways. First, the addition of a superrule to each CA cell is considered. The resulting self-programmable CA (SPCA) uses the superrule to determine when to make a dynamic rule change in each CA cell. The superrule takes its inputs from neighboring cells and can be considered itself a second CA working in parallel with the main CA. When implemented on an FPGA, the use of lookup tables in each logic cell removes any restrictions on how the super-rules should be defined. Second, a hybrid configuration is formed by combining a CA with a linear feedback shift register (LFSR). This is advantageous for FPGA designs due to the compactness of the LFSR implementations. A standard software package for statistically evaluating the quality of random number sequences known as DIEHARD is used to validate the results. Both the SPCA and the hybrid CA/LFSR were found to pass all the DIEHARD tests.

1. Introduction

Cellular computing is touted as one of the new paradigms for future computational systems due to three key properties: simplicity, massive parallelism, and local interconnect [1]. Such systems have advantages over the traditional general-purpose processor in terms of high-speed parallel computation and fault tolerant capabilities. A variety of unique applications have been proposed and implemented using the cellular computational model including fault-tolerant self-healing architectures [2], cellular neural networks [3, 4], and pseudo-random number generators [5]. Cellular automata (CA), which consist of an array of locally interconnected, elementary processing elements, can be viewed as one form of a high-speed massively parallel machine. As CA are dynamical systems which evolve in discrete time and space, they are used to model a variety of physical and biological processes, including fluid dynamics, the immune system, the evolution of genetic regulatory networks, and urban traffic flow [6–10]. A CA-based architecture will likely form the basis for the development of ultra-high speed and compact quantum-based computers [11, 12]. However, the programming of a CA-based machine to compute complex problems is a challenging and unresolved issue [13–15]. Also noteworthy is the development of a cellular automata hardware emulator known as the Wolfram machine [16].

This paper investigates a specific application for CA-based computation: the implementation of a high-quality pseudo random number generator (PRNG) [5]. A good PRNG will produce a sequence of repeatable, but high-quality, random numbers based on an initial seed. This is in contrast to a true random number generator (TRNG) which produces an unrepeatable sequence of random numbers [17]. Both types of random number generators are needed, for example, for computer security applications, where a TRNG is used to seed a PRNG with a completely random number. In addition, PRNGs are required in a variety of areas including Monte Carlo simulations, on-chip self-test circuitry, and optimization methods such as simulated annealing and genetic algorithms.

Reconfigurable platforms such as field programmable gate arrays (FPGAs) have been investigated for implementing cellular computing machines [18–20]. As an FPGA consists of an array of reconfigurable logic cells, it provides an attractive platform for implementing CA-based computational structures. In this paper, the potential for using FPGAs to implement high-quality random number generators using cellular automata is explored.

In many hardware implementations, it is desirable to optimize performance of the PRNGs in terms of speed, area, and power dissipation, while producing high-quality random numbers. For example, due to advances in very large scale integration (VLSI) processing technology, the complexity of integrated circuit designs now make it feasible, and even necessary, to place self-test circuits on the chip itself. The hardware overhead introduced by a built-in self-test (BIST) module should be a small portion of the overall circuit. A common method for implementing a PRNG for self-testing circuits is a linear feedback shift register (LFSR), since it can be compactly constructed from a series of cascaded flip-flops and a few XOR gates. However, for certain tests involving stuck-open faults that can convert a combinational circuit to a sequential one, the correlation between adjacent numbers in a test vector sequence should be minimized. Due to the shifting properties of the LFSR, it is known to have problems with detecting sequential faults [21]. Wolfram suggested in 1986 that cellular automata (CA) could be used for efficiently generating random numbers due to the use of nearest neighbor interconnectivity and regularity in their physical layout [5]. Subsequent research has demonstrated that heterogeneous CA, which are composed of two linear functions, are more suited for test vector generation for BIST than LFSRs and the homogeneous CAs originally proposed by Wolfram [22].

Advances in VLSI technology have also made it possible to implement complex digital systems on FPGAs. Because FPGA designs can be optimized for a given application, they often have superior performance in terms of speed and power dissipation over generic integrated circuit designs and microprocessor-based implementations. As an example, for an application involving signal processing for radio astronomy, an FPGA-based system built using a 130 nm process technology was compared with a DSP fabricated with a comparable technology and a microprocessor fabricated from a 90 nm technology. The FPGA system had 10 times the throughput compared with the DSP design and 4 times the throughput of the microprocessor-based system [23]. Similar improvements are reported by others [24, 25]. For this reason, FPGAs are increasingly being used in areas formerly dominated by application specific integrated circuits (ASICs), such as embedded system design and digital signal

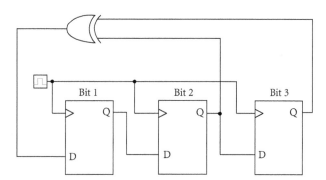

FIGURE 1: Schematic of a maximal length 3-bit linear feedback shift register.

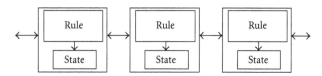

FIGURE 2: A one-dimensional nearest neighbor cellular automata.

processing applications. Hence, there is a need to explore the implementation of PRNGs on FPGAs.

An FPGA typically consists of an array of logic cells that can be arbitrarily connected through programmable interconnect. Each logic cell usually consists of a programmable lookup table (LUT), a flip-flop, and several multiplexers. The structure of the FPGA has an impact on the optimal design of PRNGs that will differ from a VLSI implementation. For example, a Xilinx FPGA has the ability to convert selected LUTs into shift registers. As such, a 52-bit LFSR can be efficiently implemented using only four logic cells [26]. By contrast, it takes at least one logic cell to implement each CA cell. For this reason, it is interesting to explore the construction of a PRNG that combines a CA with an LFSR. Another configuration of interest is a CA that updates its own internal rules based upon the states of cells in its neighborhood as proposed in [27]. While an efficient VLSI design restricts the possible rules that can be implemented in order to minimize the number of logic gates used, the use of LUTs removes this constraint in an FPGA design. The object of this paper is to investigate the quality of the random numbers that can be produced using the aforementioned designs while considering the amount of resources required when implemented on an FPGA. The widely used statistical tests implemented in the DIEHARD program are used to evaluate the quality of the random numbers [28]. The Xilinx Spartan-3E FPGA is the reconfigurable platform used in this study.

This paper is organized as follows. Section 2 provides some background on the design of LFSRs and CAs as well as describing the relevant previous work in this area. Section 3 on research method describes the PRNG configurations that are evaluated and the simulation strategy used. Section 4 contains the results and a discussion of their implementation. Conclusions and future work are given in Section 5.

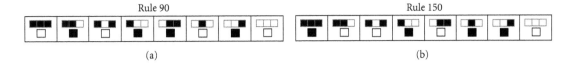

FIGURE 3: Graphical representations of CA rules "90" and "150" [6].

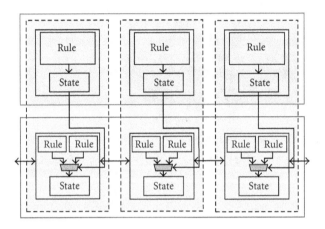

FIGURE 4: Schematic of the self-programmed cellular automata (SPCA).

2. Background and Previous Work

This section overviews the design of linear feedback shift registers (LFSRs) and cellular automata (CA), followed by a review of related works that have utilized LFSRs and CA for generating random numbers.

An LFSR consists of a shift register where selected outputs, known as taps, are fed into an XOR gate. In an LFSR using external feedback, the output of the XOR gate is then fed into the input of the shift register, as illustrated in Figure 1. Internal feedback LFSRs will place XOR gates between selected flip-flops that form the shift register. The location of the taps determines the pattern generated by the LFSR. An LFSR is said to have maximal length if it can generate a pattern which is $2^n - 1$ before repeating, where n is the length of the shift register. While the LFSR can be compactly implemented in both VLSI and FPGA designs, the shifting operation produces a high degree of correlation between adjacent bits.

A cellular automata can be viewed as a state machine consisting of an array of cells which hold their current states. The CA will evolve in discrete timesteps, where the next state of each cell is determined by the states of the cells in its "neighborhood" according to some specified rule. A common configuration is a one dimensional CA with binary state values, and a neighborhood consisting of the cell's own state and those of its immediate neighbors, as depicted in Figure 2.

Such a one-dimensional CA can be represented as an array of n cells, $\{s_1(t), s_2(t), \ldots, s_n(t)\}$, where $s_i(t)$ represents

the binary state of the ith cell at time t. As an example of an update rule for the one dimensional CA, consider

$$s_i(t+1) = s_{i+1}(t) \oplus s_{i-1}(t). \tag{1}$$

In this case, the current state of the ith cell is determined by taking the exclusive-OR of its two immediate neighbors. A pictorial representation of how this rule is encoded is illustrated in Figure 3, where the top row represents the eight possible configurations for a three-cell neighborhood and the bottom row represents the next state for the cell of interest. Since the eight bits in the bottom row represent a value of 90 in decimal, this update rule is dubbed rule "90" [6].

The current state of the ith cell can be included in the update rule that uses the exclusive-OR operations, as represented by (2):

$$s_i(t+1) = s_{i+1}(t) \oplus s_i(t) \oplus s_{i-1}(t). \tag{2}$$

In this case, the binary representation of the rule results in a value of 150 in decimal, and hence, (2) represents the CA rule "150." While higher dimensions and state values can be used, this paper will focus on one-dimensional CA with each state represented by a single bit.

As noted by Hortensius et al., if different rules are used in each cell (heterogeneous CA), higher quality random numbers can be generated from a CA than if a uniform (homogeneous) rule is applied to all cells [22]. Combinations of rules 90 and 150 were found to produce good random numbers with maximal length suitable for BIST. These rules are popular since they can be generated using XOR gates, where analysis in $GF(2)$ can be used to determine maximal length CA. The use of time and site spacing was shown to further decorrelate adjacent bits. Further work on hybrid 90/150 CA for generating self-test circuitry was carried out by Nandi et al. [29].

Guan and Tan proposed a one-dimensional CA where the rule in each cell changes dynamically based upon the states of the cells within a new neighborhood of three cells [27]. Dubbed "self-programmable cellular automata" (SPCA), the rules are switched between 90 and 165 or 150 and 105. These rules were selected because they can be easily implemented with XOR gates. The SPCA is diagramed in Figure 4. A "super-rule" is used to determine how the rules within the CA are switched, based on neighboring cells which can be up to a distance of three cells away. The use of the super-rule can help avoid the patterns that occur when cells have static rules. These patterns are indicative of low-quality random number sequences because they give rise to recurring structures (e.g., the "triangle pattern" seen in Figure 5(a)).

Each cell in the SPCA can be thought of as having a hierarchical structure (i.e., a "super rule" and a "rule state"),

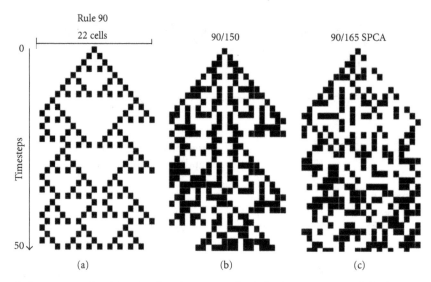

FIGURE 5: Space-time evolution patterns for: (a) a simple rule-90 CA, (b) a hybrid 90/150 CA, and (c) the SPCA using rules 90/165 and super-rule 90. All are initialized with a single bit in the center.

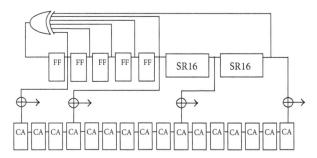

FIGURE 6: Schematic of a hybrid CA/LFSR FPGA implementation. SR16 represent the LUT-based 16-bit shift registers. Combined with the flip-flops (FFs), it forms a 37-bit LFSR.

which together control the lower parts: two rules and a state. This type of CA may also be thought of as two interlinked parallel CA (Figure 4), one of which (the "lower" CA) depends on the other (the "upper" CA) to decide which of its two internal rules is to be used in the next timestep. But the upper CA also depends on the states of the lower CA to determine its own states. The neighborhoods of the upper and lower CA need not be the same.

During each timestep, two things happen simultaneously in each cell: the "upper" cell checks its neighborhood and applies its rule to determine and update its next state, while the "lower" cell checks its neighborhood and the state of the upper cell and then applies the appropriate rule to its inputs and updates its new state. Because these events happen simultaneously, the lower cell always uses the rule indicated by the upper cell during the previous timestep, not the currently updating state of the upper cell. The use of the upper CA to switch the rules of the lower CA provides an additional randomizing effect. An inspection of the space-time diagram for a hybrid 90/150 CA and the SPCA, shown

in Figure 5, reveals the improved quality of the random numbers generated from the latter.

In [27], SPCA of lengths from 16 to 24 bits were found that could pass all the statistical tests using the DIEHARD program. This paper investigates the implementation of the SPCA on FPGAs where it should be noted that the use of LUTs allows more flexibility in the choice of rule selection.

Tkacik proposed a random number generator which combines the outputs of a CA with an LFSR [30]. A 37 bit CA was combined with a 43-bit LFSR. This maximal length configuration combined 32 bits from the CA and LFSR to produce a maximal length RNG. It was found that the LFSR and CA must be clocked at different frequencies to create a sequence of numbers that can pass all the DIEHARD tests. Figure 6 depicts the version implemented on FPGAs in our work. The last bit of the LFSR and CA can be combined in an XOR gate to produce a single random bit in order to generate maximal site spacing. In the design depicted in Figure 6, three additional internal nodes from the LFSR and CA are combined with XOR gates to generate four bits each clock cycle. The advantage of this site spacing [22], as we shall see, is that a sequence of random numbers can be produced that passes all of the DIEHARD tests without clocking the LFSR and CA at different rates. This technique makes use of site spacing in order to avoid any correlation between neighboring bits. It does, however, lead to decreased throughput (only up to 4 bits per timestep) which is undesirable because it may take several cycles to generate a multibit random number. In [30], Tkacik states the maximal length of a combined CA and LFSR is $2^{m+n} - 2^m - 2^n + 1$ for an m-sized CA and an n-sized shift register. This is true if the cycle lengths of the individual CA and LFSR are relatively prime. A 37 bit shift register and 16 bit cellular automata represent one example of a maximal length CA/LFSR configuration that was studied in this work (Figure 6).

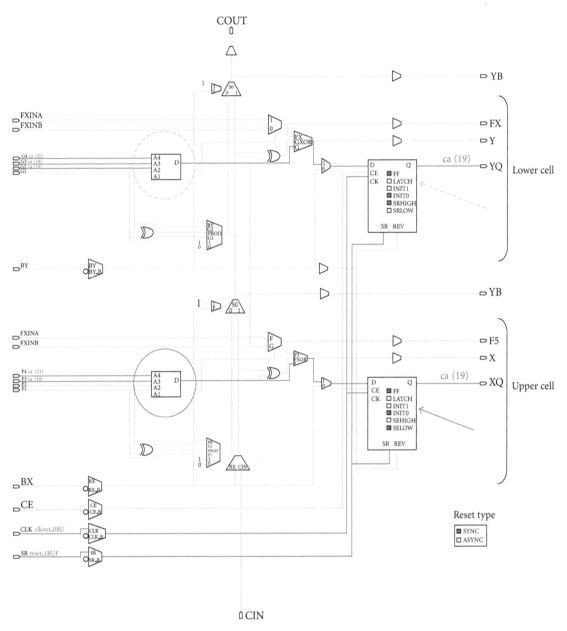

FIGURE 7: FPGA editor view of the hard macro used to form an SPCA cell showing the lower and upper cells.

3. PRNGs Implemented on FPGAs

This section describes the various CA configurations that were considered for implementation on FPGAs and the simulation method used to determine the quality of random numbers that were produced by each design.

Two programs were written in C to simulate the two PRNGs: SPCA and the hybrid LFSR/CA. These simulations output the states of the various components of the PRNGs, allowing analysis and confirmation of the hardware output. The Linux command diff was used to compare the output files from the simulations to the test data obtained from logic analyzer measurements.

Logisim was used as a secondary simulator to confirm the results of the C program. The usefulness of Logisim lies in its graphical representation of the simulation, which makes some flaws more obvious and easier to fix than in C code. C code, however, is itself sometimes easier to debug and is much faster. With the diff command, the outputs from Logisim, C, and the FPGA hardware were all able to be automatically compared. A combination of VHDL code and hard macros were used to implement these PRNGs on an FPGA. The hard macro used to form the SPCA cell is shown in Figure 7. One whole cell is contained in this hard macro, which uses one slice on the Spartan 3E FPGA. Both of the theoretical upper and lower cells are included in this macro. The dashed circle and arrow constitute the "lower" cell, and the solid circle and arrow constitute the "upper" cell. The circles are lookup tables (LUTs). These process the inputs from neighboring cells, applying the desired rule and

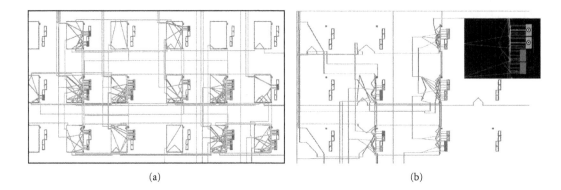

(a)   (b)

FIGURE 8: (a) The FPGA editor snapshot showing the layout of the 22-cell SPCA, using 30 slices (small, colored boxes). (b) The FPGA editor view of a portion of the CA + LFSR implementation. The inset shows a pair of hard macros used to realize the CAs.

outputting the new cell state. The flip-flops (FFs) that hold the cell's state and super-rule state are indicated with dashed and solid arrows, respectively.

Our SPCA uses rules 90 and 165 for the lower cells and rule 90 for the super-rule. The upper cells have a neighborhood of -2, $+1$. We have simulated this CA using a C program and confirmed with a Logisim simulation.

One of the limitations of the design in [27] is that the PRNG was designed for a VLSI implementation. Therefore, pairs of rules that can be implemented with minimal overhead were chosen. However, since our PRNGs will be implemented on FPGAs, we are not subject to the same types of overhead. As the basic logic unit in the Spartan 3E FPGA is a 4-input LUT, it takes up the same area whether it is implementing a logical AND, an XOR, or a more complicated rule or pair of rules. Therefore, all 256 rules or any pair of these rules are available at the same cost in overhead.

A pair of rules can be implemented in a 4-input LUT because three inputs can be used for the neighborhood (left neighbor, cell's own state, right neighbor) and the fourth input can be used to consider the state of the super rule—that is, to select which rule to use. If the rule selector is 0, rule 90 is applied to the other three inputs; but if the rule selector is 1, rule 165 is applied. As with the case of the SPCA, an LFSR is easily implemented using a 4-input LUT. In this case, the look-up table is configured as a 16-bit shift register. The LUT is configured as an addressable shift register rather than with fixed values and is referred to as a Shift Register LUT 16-bit (SRL16). The SRL16 allows for very efficient and compact FPGA implementations of LFSRs.

As previously noted, a hybrid LFSR + CA PRNG consisting of two state machines which are relatively prime in their cycle lengths will generate a sequence equal to $2^{n+m} - 2^n - 2^m + 1$ [30]. The advantage of this hybrid approach for FPGA implementation is the possible design tradeoffs. An LFSR by itself does not produce a good random sequence but can be compactly implemented on an FPGA. By comparison, a CA consumes more FPGA resources but provides good pseudorandom sequences due to the absence of adjacent bit correlations. The objective here is to create a new PRNG that possesses the CA's randomness and the LFSR's compactness.

A 16 cell heterogeneous CA consisting of a mixture of rules 90 and 150 was utilized as the baseline design. The rules were arranged to yield a maximal length pattern as described in [22]. This PRNG was implemented on an FPGA and was verified to run properly. Usage of hard macros allowed each cell to fit in one slice. This baseline PRNG failed many of the DIEHARD tests as shown in Table 4. A similar 22-cell hybrid CA was also simulated for comparison with the 22-cell SPCA. This CA too failed most of the DIEHARD tests as expected (Table 4).

4. Performance Evaluation

This section evaluates the FPGA PRNG implementations in terms of the quality of the random numbers, hardware resources utilized, throughput, and test results. The taps required to implement the various LFSRs in this study were obtained from [26] and are summarized in Table 1.

4.1. Overhead. The different CA combinations for the SPCA and CA/LFSR hybrid that were synthesized on an FPGA and associated resource usage are summarized in Table 2. When synthesized on a Xilinx Spartan 3E FPGA, a 52-bit LFSR requires 4 slices (3 flip-flops and 5 LUTs) while a 16 cell CA requires 16 slices (16 flip-flops and 16 LUTs). The 22-bit SPCA requires 30 slices (44 flip-flops and 60 LUTs). The SPCA is larger because it uses one slice per cell (1 bit) while the LFSR takes advantage of the compact 16 bit shift-register implementation in a single LUT (i.e., half a slice).

Figure 8(a) shows the FPGA editor view of the SPCA. Each colored box is a cell or some auxiliary circuit such as a multiplexer for initializing the SPCA.

Figure 8(b) shows the view of the LFSR + CA combination. The inset highlights the bulls-eye marking that indicates a slice containing the hard macro for implementing one cell of the cellular automaton.

4.2. Quality of the Generated Random Numbers. The DIEHARD suite of statistical tests was run on all the configurations listed in Tables 3 and 4. The tables also summarize

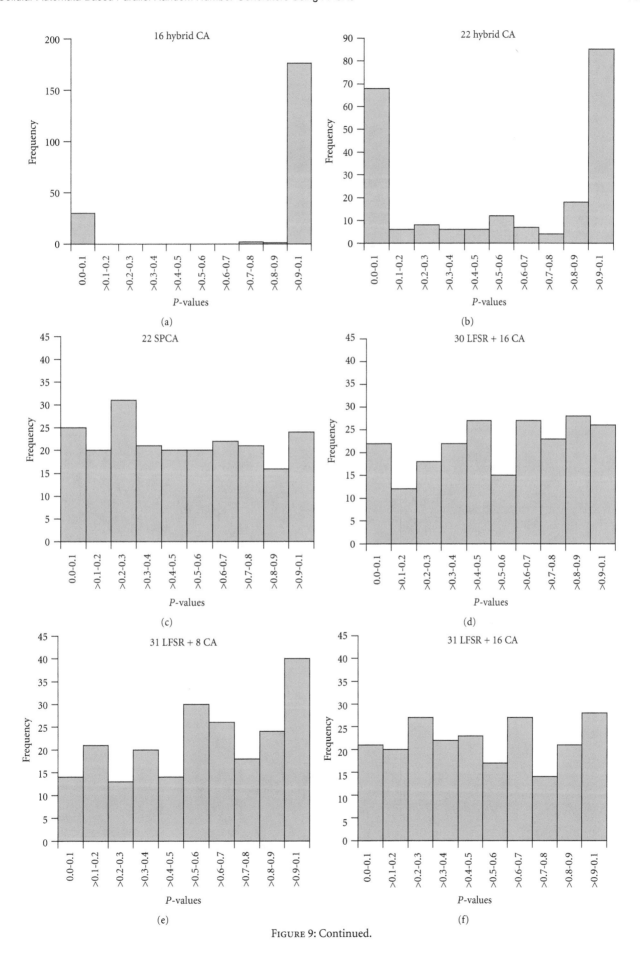

FIGURE 9: Continued.

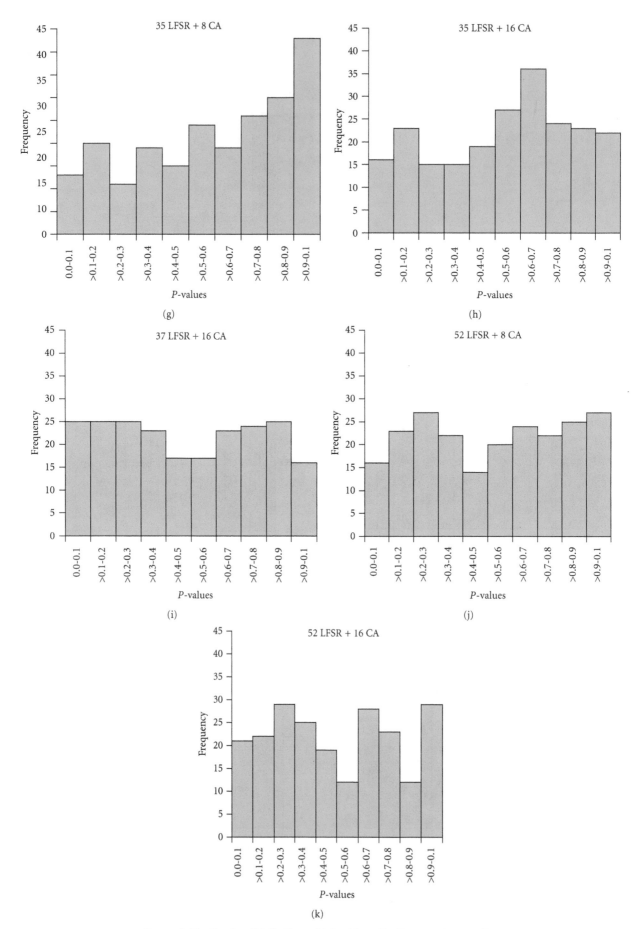

FIGURE 9: The *P*-value distributions obtained from the DIEHARD test results.

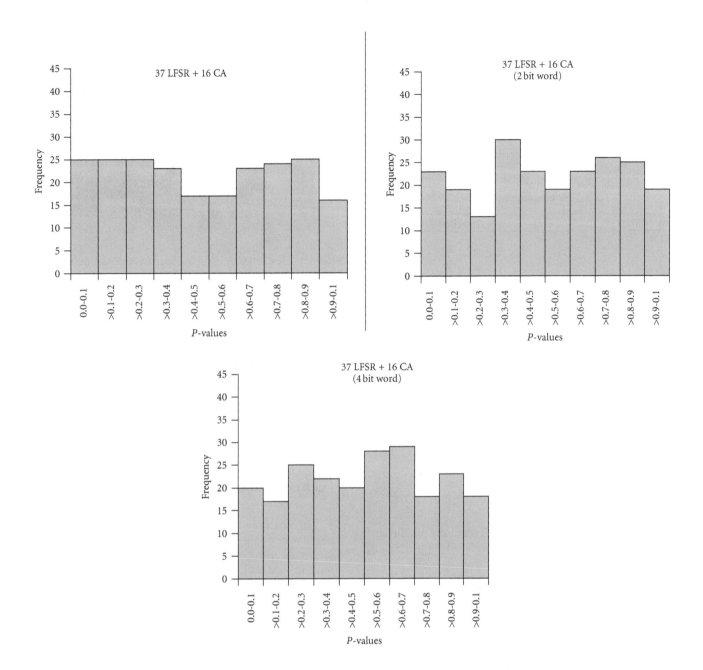

FIGURE 10: *P*-value distributions for the hybrid 37LFSR + 16CA with 2 and 4 bit outputs per time step. The previous result for the single bit version is listed again on the left for comparison.

the test results. The names of the tests are listed in Table 5 (for more details on each test, see [28]). Any test that returns a *P*-value equal to "1.000" or "0.000" is considered to have failed and is represented with an "F" on the table. A test with up to two *P*-values equal to "0.999" or "0.001" is said to barely pass and is represented with a "BP." Any test with at least three *P*-values equal to "0.999" or "0.001" is said to barely fail and is represented with a "BF." Otherwise, the test is said to pass (represented with a "P").

The results for maximum site spacing techniques are discussed first, followed by the maximum throughput results.

As for the various LFSR + CA configurations where only 1 bit is generated per clock cycle (i.e., the maximum site spacing case), the 37 bit LFSR + 16 bit CA and the 52 bit LFSR + 8 bit CA produced the best results, passing all 18 tests. An intriguing result is that the 52 bit LFSR + 8 bit CA performed slightly better than the 52 bit LFSR + 16 CA.

As can be seen from Table 4, a hybrid CA by itself is insufficient to pass all the DIEHARD tests. As for techniques with maximum throughput, the SPCA was simulated with twenty different initial seed patterns for the on-off states of the CA. Ten seeds were nonrandom, orderly patterns such as

TABLE 1: LFSR taps.

LFSR	Taps
30	30, 6, 4, 1
31	31, 28
35	35, 33
37	37, 5, 4, 3, 2, 1
52	52, 39

TABLE 2: FPGA resource utilized by the CAs.

Configuration	LUTs	Flip-Flops	Slices
8 CA	8	8	8
16 CA	16	16	16
31 LFSR	4	3	3
35 LFSR	4	4	4
52 LFSR	5	3	4
30 LFSR + 16 CA	21	19	19
31 LFSR + 8 CA	13	11	11
31 LFSR + 16 CA	21	19	19
35 LFSR + 8 CA	13	12	12
35 LFSR + 16 CA	21	20	20
37 LFSR + 16 CA	21	22	23
52 LFSR + 8 CA	13	11	12
52 LFSR + 16 CA	22	19	20
22 SPCA	60	44	30

FIGURE 11: Test setup showing the Spartan 3E FPGA development board connected to a Tektronix TLA 7012 logic analyzer.

greater throughput for the LFSR + CA, more than just the last bits were XORed to generate the output. The number of bits that could be XORed was limited however, because the shift register bits inside the compact LUT cannot be accessed. Therefore, only bits that were tapped out or that could not be placed in a LUT were used to XOR with bits from the CA. In two different variations of the 37 LFSR + 16 CA, throughput was increased to 2 and 4 bits per timestep. These PRNGs still pass all DIEHARD tests (Table 6). As seen in Figure 10, all the P-value distributions remained relatively level.

4.4. Test Results and Comparisons with Related Works. The designs were implemented on a Xilinx Spartan-3E FPGA and were tested using a Tektronix TLA 7012 logic analyzer, as shown in Figure 11.

In the SPCA design, each cell was programmed to assume an initial state when an onboard switch was in the "on" position. This initial condition allowed the SPCA to be set and held at an initial state, allowing for consistent readings. After setting up the initial cell states in the FPGA, four million timesteps were read, with the FPGA running at 50 MHz. Because the logic analyzer connection to the FPGA board only had 16 pins, the FPGA was programmed to use an onboard switch to multiplex the output pins between the first 16 cells of the 22 SPCA and the last 16 cells. In order to get all 22 states, the FPGA was run twice, starting from the same initial states each time. On the first run, the states of the first 16 cells were read out: on the second run, the states of the latter 16 cells were read. The 10-cell overlap between these two sets of data helped confirm that they did indeed coincide. This method was used three times to generate three sets of data from the FPGA. All three sets of data matched the simulation. The LFSR + CA has also been successfully implemented, matching the simulation.

The hybrid LFSR + CA design could operate at a speed of 110 MHz with a power dissipation of 89 mW while the SPCA design had a maximum operating frequency of 115 MHz and a power dissipation of 103 mW. In terms of throughput, the

all-on, alternating on/off, a single cell on in the middle, and so forth. Six of ten of these simulations failed DIEHARD using our standards and two barely passed.

Ten random initial seed patterns were also utilized. These random seeds have an unpatterned set of on/off states with approximately equal numbers of on and off states. Five of these simulations failed DIEHARD by our standards, one barely passed, and the remaining four passed all the DIEHARD tests.

In sum, the SPCA has much greater throughput than the LFSR + CA, while the LFSR + CA is not sensitive to the initial seed values for passing all the DIEHARD tests.

According to DIEHARD, an "ideal" PRNG should have a uniform distribution of P-values. Figure 9 compares the P-value distributions for different PRNGs tested using the DIEHARD test suite. PRNG configurations that failed DIEHARD tests tend to contain a high frequency of P-values in the 0.9 to 1.0 range as seen for the 35LFSR + 8CA and for the two baseline hybrid CA. PRNG configurations that passed all tests such as the 37LFSR + 16CA contain P-values that are more equally distributed across the range [0,1).

4.3. Tradeoffs between Throughput and Quality of the Random Numbers Generated. After these results were obtained, it was considered whether a better balance between throughput and quality of randomness could be found. In order to achieve a

TABLE 3: DIEHARD results for LFSR + CA maximum site spacing.

Configuration	1	2	3	4	5	6	7	8	9	10	11	12	13	14	15	16	17	18
30 LFSR + 16 CA	P	P	P	P	P	P	P	P	P	P	BP	P	P	BP	P	P	P	P
31 LFSR + 8 CA	P	P	P	P	P	P	F	P	P	P	BP	P	P	P	P	P	P	P
31 LFSR + 16 CA	P	P	P	P	P	P	P	P	P	P	P	P	P	BP	P	P	P	P
35 LFSR + 8 CA	P	P	P	P	BP	P	F	P	P	P	BP	P	F	P	P	P	P	P
35 LFSR + 16 CA	P	P	P	P	P	P	P	P	P	P	BP	P	P	P	P	P	P	P
37 LFSR + 16 CA	P	P	P	P	P	P	P	P	P	P	P	P	P	P	P	P	P	P
52 LFSR + 8 CA	P	P	P	P	P	P	P	P	P	P	P	P	P	P	P	P	P	P
52 LFSR + 16 CA	P	P	P	P	P	P	P	P	BP	P	BP	P	P	P	P	P	P	P

TABLE 4: DIEHARD results for hybrid CA and SPCA optimized for throughput.

	1	2	3	4	5	6	7	8	9	10	11	12	13	14	15	16	17	18
16 CA (90/150)	—	F	F	F	F	F	F	F	F	F	F	F	F	F	F	F	F	F
22 CA (90/150)	F	F	F	F	F	P	F	F	F	F	F	P	F	P	P	P	P	P
22 SPCA	P	P	P	P	P	P	P	P	P	P	P	P	P	P	P	P	P	P

TABLE 5: DIEHARD tests.

1	Birthday spacings
2	Overlapping 5-Permuatation
3	Binary rank 31 ∗ 31
4	Binary rank 32 ∗ 32
5	Binary rank 6 ∗ 8
6	Bitstream
7	OPSO
8	OQSO
9	DNA
10	Count-the-1's
11	Count-the-1's 2
12	Parking lot
13	Minimum distance
14	3D Spheres
15	Squeeze
16	Overlapping sums
17	Runs
18	Craps

LFSR + CA design can output 440 Mb/sec while the SPCA can deliver 2530 Mb/sec. The SPCA has a significantly higher throughput since it outputs all 22 bits in one clock cycle, while the hybrid LFSR + CA design outputs a maximum of 4 bits per clock cycle. The previous designs by Guan and Tan [27] and Tkacik [30] were implemented on custom integrated circuit processes instead of FPGAs, so a direct comparison is not feasible. It can be observed that the SPCA design by Guan reported an estimated throughput of 3510 Mb/sec for his 20 bit SPCA design [27]. Given that these design simulations targeted a 0.35 μm CMOS process and that the Spartan-3E FPGA used in our design is built from a 90 nm CMOS process, the comparable throughput numbers are consistent with the differences in performances typically experienced between ASIC and FPGA implementations [31].

5. Conclusions

Cellular automata represent a basic form of a high-speed massively parallel computation engine. Such forms of cellular computing can be implemented on current reconfigurable platforms, such as FPGAs, and will form the basis for quantum computers developed for emerging nanotechnologies. This paper has evaluated the performance of CA-based PRNGs suitable for implementation on FPGAs. Synthesis results for the Xilinx Spartan 3E FPGA give a good idea of the relative resources required for each configuration. The LFSR + CA combination uses less overhead than the SPCA, due to use of the compact LUT implementation of the LFSR. The DIEHARD suite of statistical tests was used to evaluate the quality of the random numbers produced from each configuration. It was found that the 37 bit LFSR + 16 bit CA and the 52 bit LFSR + 8 bit CA and the SPCA with random initial seeds passed all the tests. There is a large gap in throughput between the LFSR + CA and the SPCA. This is due to the inaccessibility of bits that are inside the compact LUT used for the LFSR. In order for more bits to be accessible, the LFSR must be split up, increasing the overhead. The SPCA, however, has a high throughput since the state of every cell can be used. Although the states of the theoretical upper CA in the SPCA could be used to double throughput, this technique was avoided because it could compromise usefulness in an encryption setting [27].

In the future, we will attempt to add more throughput to the LFSR + CA and also explore the aspect of maximum cycle length. The LFSR + CA combination can pack a large number of states in a small space using the current design

TABLE 6: DIEHARD results for modified throughput LFSR + CA and SPCA.

37 LFSR + 16 CA (2 bit word)	P	P	P	P	P	P	P	P	P	P	P	P	P	P	P	P	P
37 LFSR + 16 CA (4 bit word)	P	P	P	P	P	P	P	P	P	P	P	P	P	P	P	P	P

of FPGAs. This large quantity of states could give the LFSR + CA a very long cycle length. In the work reported here, the SPCA has the best throughput, the LFSR + CA has the smallest overhead, and both can produce quality random numbers.

References

[1] M. Sipper, "Emergence of cellular computing," *Computer*, vol. 32, no. 7, pp. 18–26, 1999.

[2] Z. Zhang, Y. Wang, S. Yang, R. Yao, and J. Cui, "The research of self-repairing digital circuit based on embryonic cellular array," *Neural Computing and Applications*, vol. 17, no. 2, pp. 145–151, 2008.

[3] L. O. Chua and L. Yang, "Cellular neural networks: theory," *IEEE Transactions on Circuits and Systems*, vol. 35, no. 10, pp. 1257–1272, 1988.

[4] C. Schwarzlmüeller and K. Kyamakya, "Implementing a CNN Universal Machine on FPGA: state-of-the-art and key challenges," in *Proceedings of the International Symposium on Theoretical Engineering (ISTET '09)*, pp. 1–5, June 2009.

[5] S. Wolfram, "Random sequence generation by cellular automata," *Advances in Applied Mathematics*, vol. 7, no. 2, pp. 123–169, 1986.

[6] S. Wolfram, *A New Kind of Science*, Wolfram Media, 2002.

[7] B. Chopard and M. Droz, *Cellular Automata Modeling of Physical Systems*, Cambridge University Press, 1998.

[8] J. Mata and M. Cohn, "Cellular automata-based modeling program: synthetic immune system," *Immunological Reviews*, vol. 216, no. 1, pp. 198–212, 2007.

[9] L. Schramm, Y. Jin, and B. Sendhoff, "Redundancy creates opportunity in developmental representations," in *Proceedings of the IEEE Symposium on Artificial Life (ALIFE '11)*, pp. 203–210, April 2011.

[10] O. K. Tonguz, W. Viriyasitavat, and F. Bai, "Modeling urban traffic: a cellular automata approach," *IEEE Communications Magazine*, vol. 47, no. 5, pp. 142–150, 2009.

[11] L. R. Hook IV and S. C. Lee, "Design and simulation of 2-D 2-dot quantum-dot cellular automata logic," *IEEE Transactions on Nanotechnology*, vol. 10, no. 5, pp. 996–1003, 2011.

[12] H. Cho and E. E. Swartzlander, "Adder designs and analyses for quantum-dot cellular automata," *IEEE Transactions on Nanotechnology*, vol. 6, no. 3, pp. 374–383, 2007.

[13] M. Mamei, A. Roli, and F. Zambonelli, "Emergence and control of macro-spatial structures in perturbed cellular automata, and implications for pervasive computing systems," *IEEE Transactions on Systems, Man, and Cybernetics Part A*, vol. 35, no. 3, pp. 337–348, 2005.

[14] S. Nichele and G. Tufte, "Trajectories and attractors as specification for the evolution of behaviour in cellular automata," in *Proceedings of the 6th IEEE World Congress on Computational Intelligence (WCCI '10)*, pp. 1–8, July 2010.

[15] H. Kanoh and S. Sato, "Improved evolutionary design for rule-changing cellular automata based on the difficulty of

problems," in *Proceedings of the IEEE International Conference on Systems, Man, and Cybernetics (SMC '07)*, pp. 1243–1248, October 2007.

[16] L. Fortuna, M. Frasca, A. S. Fiore, and L. O. Chua, "The wolfram machine," *International Journal of Bifurcation and Chaos*, vol. 20, no. 12, pp. 3863–3917, 2010.

[17] S. Srinivasan, S. Mathew, R. Ramanarayanan et al., "2.4GHz 7mW all-digital PVT-variation tolerant True Random Number Generator in 45nm CMOS," in *Proceedings of the 24th Symposium on VLSI Circuits (VLSIC '10)*, pp. 203–204, June 2010.

[18] T. Kobori, T. Maruyama, and T. Hoshino, "A cellular automata system with FPGA," in *Proceedings of the 9th Annual IEEE Symposium on Field-Programmable Custom Computing Machines*, pp. 120–129, 2001.

[19] P. A. Mudry, F. Vannel, G. Tempesti, and D. Mange, "CON-FETTI: a reconfigurable hardware platform for prototyping cellular architectures," in *Proceedings of the 21st International Parallel and Distributed Processing Symposium (IPDPS '07)*, pp. 1–8, March 2007.

[20] S. Murtaza, A. G. Hoekstra, and P. M. A. Shot, "Performance modeling of 2D cellular automata on FPGA," in *Proceedings of the International Conference on Field Programmable Logic and Applications (FPL '07)*, pp. 74–78, August 2007.

[21] K. Furuya and E. J. McCluskey, "Two-pattern test capabilities of autonomous TPG circuits," in *Proceedings of the International Test Conference*, pp. 704–711, October 1991.

[22] P. D. Hortensius, R. D. McLeod, W. Pries, D. M. Miller, and H. C. Card, "Cellular automata-based pseudorandom number generators for built-in self-test," *IEEE Transactions on Computer-Aided Design of Integrated Circuits and Systems*, vol. 8, no. 8, pp. 842–859, 1989.

[23] P. H. W. Leong, "Recent trends in FPGA architectures and applications," in *Proceedings of the 4th IEEE International Symposium on Electronic Design, Test and Applications (DELTA '08)*, pp. 137–141, January 2008.

[24] A. DeHon, "Density advantage of configurable computing," *Computer*, vol. 33, no. 4, pp. 41–49, 2000.

[25] J. Sun, G. Peterson, and O. Storaasli, "Sparse matrix-vector multiplication design on FPGAs," in *Proceedings of the 15th Annual IEEE Symposium on Field-Programmable Custom Computing Machines (FCCM '07)*, pp. 349–351, April 2007.

[26] M. George and P. Alfke, "Linear Feedback Shift Registers in Virtex Devices," *Xilinx Application Note XAPP210 (v1.3)*, 2007.

[27] S. U. Guan and S. K. Tan, "Pseudorandom number generation with self-programmable cellular automata," *IEEE Transactions on Computer-Aided Design of Integrated Circuits and Systems*, vol. 23, no. 7, pp. 1095–1101, 2004.

[28] G. Marsaglia, Diehard, 1996, http://stat.fsu.edu/~geo/diehard.html.

[29] S. Nandi, B. Vamsi, S. Chakraborty, and P. P. Chaudhuri, "Cellular automata as a BIST structure for testing CMOS circuits," *IEE Proceedings*, vol. 141, no. 1, pp. 41–47, 1994.

[30] T. E. Tkacik, "A hardware random number generator," in *Proceedings of the Cryptographic Hardware and Embedded Systems (CHES '02)*, vol. 2523 of *Lecture Notes in Computer Science*, pp. 450–453, 2003.

[31] I. Kuon and J. Rose, "Measuring the gap between FPGAs and ASICs," *IEEE Transactions on Computer-Aided Design of Integrated Circuits and Systems*, vol. 26, no. 2, pp. 203–215, 2007.

13

Exploration of Uninitialized Configuration Memory Space for Intrinsic Identification of Xilinx Virtex-5 FPGA Devices

Oliver Sander, Benjamin Glas, Lars Braun, Klaus D. Müller-Glaser, and Jürgen Becker

Institute for Information Processing Technology (ITIV), Karlsruhe Institute of Technology (KIT),
Engesserstr. 5, 76131 Karlsruhe, Germany

Correspondence should be addressed to Oliver Sander, sander@kit.edu

Academic Editor: Claudia Feregrino

SRAM-based fingerprinting uses deviations in power-up behaviour caused by the CMOS fabrication process to identify distinct devices. This method is a promising technique for unique identification of physical devices. In the case of SRAM-based hardware reconfigurable devices such as FPGAs, the integrated SRAM cells are often initialized automatically at power-up, sweeping potential identification data. We demonstrate an approach to utilize unused parts of configuration memory space for device identification. Based on a total of over 200,000 measurements on nine Xilinx Virtex-5 FPGAs, we show that the retrieved values have promising properties with respect to consistency on one device, variety between different devices, and stability considering temperature variation and aging.

1. Introduction

Identification of devices is a primitive that plays a crucial role for a number of applications, including authentication of devices and protection against cloning of devices (cocalled *product piracy*) or intellectual property. IDs which are stored in nonvolatile memory can often be easily cloned or modified. Hence approaches have been published to overcome the aforementioned drawbacks. They are usually based on unique physical properties of the single chip. For example, such properties are caused by manufacturing process variations. The two main approaches in this context are physical fingerprinting and the use of physical uncloneable functions (PUFs). Former strives to identify a given circuit directly by physical characteristics latter use physical characteristics to perform a challenge-response authentication.

A promising technique used for both approaches is to observe the state of uninitialized SRAM cells. When voltage above a certain threshold is applied to an SRAM cell its initial unstable state will change to one of two possible stable states "0" or "1". The probability for each stable state is heavily dependant on small variations originated during the CMOS fabrication process causing slight deviation in threshold voltage inside the cells. The probability varies between

different cells even inside a single chip thus representing a characteristic initial memory content on power-up for each device. Depending on the probability distribution the major part of the memory content is stable for most of the power-ups. Other bits having a probability around 50% show a power-up behaviour similar to random noise. Assuming a high rate of stable data the memory content can be used to provide high quality identification data that is very hard to reproduce deliberately.

Considering SRAM-based field-programmable gate arrays (FPGAs), configuration memory or BRAM cells can potentially be used to retrieve fingerprints from uninitialized SRAM cells. Nevertheless this technique depends on the availability of SRAM that is not automatically initialized to a designated fixed value at device power-up. As a random configuration might well lead to short circuits and therefore damage the device physically, many vendors enforce the clearing of configuration memory by an unavoidable initialization phase on power-up. This is the case, for example, for the Xilinx Virtex-5 series FPGAs considered in this contribution. Certainly not all parts of the configuration are so critical. Initializing SRAM cells on power-up to a fixed value might consume additional area on the chip. Due to area efficiency, there is some chance for certain regions in configuration memory without this kind of reset-on-powerup procedure. The challenge is to find possibilities for secure hardware identification without having to implement and configure complex additional logic on the device.

In this work we present a method to retrieve identification data from the configuration memory space using readouts from presumably unused and therefore uninitialized hidden address ranges. Besides description of the method and the used tools we give statistical data from our measurements on a population of Virtex-5 devices indicating the potential to use the memory region for identification purposes. Moreover we demonstrate a straightforward methodology to generate reference keys that allow for robust identification of devices.

The remainder of this paper is structured as follows. Section 2 gives an overview of some related publications. The situation and identification approach and the data measurement basics are given in Section 3. The methods for data examination are presented in Section 4. Section 5 presents the analysis results from the measurements that are interpreted in Section 6. Also open points and potential applications are discussed in Section 6. In Section 7 we give some examples of possible security applications. Specific properties and benefits of the used memory region are considered in Section 8. The paper is concluded in Section 9.

2. Related Work

As previously mentioned there exist two main approaches for physical identification of CMOS devices which have received considerable attention in recent years. An introduction to PUFs can be found, for example, in [1–4], and a collection of related publications is given in [5]. For FPGAs also the use of flip flops is presented in [6, 7]. PUFs implementation as proposed in [6] is possible but it requires a specific configuration of the device.

In the following we will focus on physical fingerprinting based on SRAM cells. The use of fabrication process-related variations of CMOS gates for identification has been widely examined. Excellent identification properties show dedicated circuits as in [8]. The use of SRAM cells (see, e.g., [9], patent [10]) comes at the cost of more noisy data but with the benefit of not requiring extra space on the chip. To extract IDs and cryptographic keys from this noisy data, various mechanisms like fuzzy extraction [11] have been proposed. Finally a preliminary version of this work was previously published in [12].

3. FPGA Configuration Memory and Proposed Approach

On many current FPGA devices the used configuration memory is initialized to a defined value at startup, rendering the SRAM cells useless for device identification by physical fingerprinting. We look at the Xilinx Virtex-5 series [13] as representatives of this kind of devices. The challenge is to find

TABLE 1: Frame address register description (Xilinx Virtex-5).

Address type	Bit index	description
Block type	[23:21]	Used in Virtex-5: 000 up to 011.
Top_B bit	20	Selects between top and bottom
Row address	[19:15]	Selects the current row
Column address	[14:7]	Selects a major column
Minor address	[6:0]	Selects a frame

areas in the configuration memory which are not initialized due to not being critical for the chip integrity.

In first experiments we found, that the SRAM configuration cells are reliably set to zero on device power up and can therefore not be used for identification of a single device. Even the BRAM blocks where random content poses no direct threat to the physical device are reliably zeroed out.

As a solution approach we looked at parts of the configuration memory address space that are not used for configuration and are therefore possibly not included in the initialization process. It turned out that readout of address ranges reserved for additional future block types other than configurable logic, BRAMs, special frames and non-configuration frames yielded device-specific data that can serve for identification. We therefore looked at the address regions officially not used, that is, the addresses starting with a "1" in bit 23 (see Table 1).

3.1. Structure of Configuration Memory. Configuration memory in Xilinx Virtex-5 devices is organized in frames as smallest configurable units. All frames have an identical, fixed length of 1312 bits, split into 41 words of 32 bits [14]. Each frame can be addressed individually using a 24-bit address written to the Frame Address Register (FAR) of the device. The FAR is divided into five subfields as described in Table 1. Over several interfaces like JTAG and SelectMAP, frames can be written for configuration and the content can also be read out for verification.

As can be seen, the three most significant bits [23:21] are designated for identifying the block type. The block types used in the Virtex-5 series [14] are Interconnect and block configuration (000), Block RAM content (001), Interconnect and Block Special Frames (010), and Block RAM Non-Configuration Frames (011). Not (officially) used is the complete address range starting with MSB 1 ($1xx$).

3.2. Tooling. For readouting the configuration memory we used the 1149.1 JTAG [15] configuration interface and the readout procedure given by Xilinx [14]. A PC was connected via Digilent USB programming cable to the FPGA board. Based on the Digilent Port Communications Utility (DPCUTIL) [16] Library and API we created a tool for directly reading and writing configuration registers and data frames based on C#. Besides simple JTAG access the tool allows multiple readbacks and generation of some additional data thus providing the basis of our statistical analysis. For writing complete bitstreams to program the devices we used the standard Xilinx Suite v10.1, the associated programming cables, and the iMPACT tool.

4. Examination

In this section we give some figures about the collected data. Examination results based on this data are given in Section 5.

We looked at a total of nine Xilinx XC5VLX110T devices [17], integrated in Digilent XUPV5-LX110T Evaluation Platforms [18]. In the following we denote the devices with letters $A, \ldots, I$. Since the substructure of the address space outside the area used for configuration is not public, we used the autoincrementation of the FAR to determine valid addresses. It turned out that at least 96 kbit of nontrivial data could be read out from an unconfigured device within a certain memory region. A block of ten consecutive frames (13,120 bit) was chosen for closer investigation. In this paper, we refer to this data stream consisting of 10 frames of data. Each time we perform a readout of the device, we read these 10 frames.

For statistical examination for each device $X \in (A, \ldots, H)$ two measurement series of 10,000 readouts $\Theta_X = (\vartheta_X^1, \ldots, \vartheta_X^{10,000})$ each were collected, one series from the unconfigured device (Θ_X^i) and one from the programmed device $(\overline{\Theta}_X^i)$. So a total of 160,000 data streams (each consists of 10 frames) could be used for statistics and creating master identification keys. In addition, test data $T_X = (\tau_X^1, \ldots, \tau_X^{100})$, resp., $\overline{T}_X = (\overline{\tau}_X^1, \ldots, \overline{\tau}_X^{100})$ of 100 readouts was collected from every board setup, that is, a total of 1,600 test streams. Eventually for the exploration of temperature stability we made another 40000 measurements for three selected boards D, H, and I which were exposed to a wide temperature range.

For ideal identification of devices it would be optimal to have a bijective mapping from an ID to a physical device and vice versa. The examination of the measurement data was therefore done looking in two directions. First the correlation and consistency of the different measurements on one board were investigated, to get a unique mapping from a device to an ID. From each measurement series a reference data stream as master identification key was created that serves as a candidate for device representation. In a second step the results from different boards were compared aiming for an injective mapping from one ID to one specific device. Validation of the identification process was performed using the test data sets and the reference IDs. The results are given in the following paragraphs.

5. Results

5.1. Similarity and Reference Keys. First we look at the conformity of different readouts from the very same device X to map each device to an ID. Therefore we used 10,000 readouts to create a frequency distribution of zeros and ones of every bit in the data stream for each FPGA. Figures 1 and 2 show the results for two single devices. The other devices showed similar figures.

The measurement reveals a distinct accumulation of bits showing constantly the same value. As can be seen in Table 2

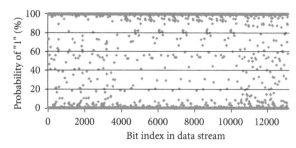

FIGURE 1: Probability of bit value "1" over 10 k measurements on device D.

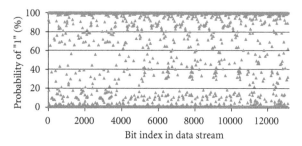

FIGURE 2: Probability of bit value "1" over 10 k measurements on device F.

the number of ones dominates the number of zeros by a factor of 1.7. The portion of flipping bits is below ten percent ranging from 7.2% to 9.7% with a mean value of 8.4% over the devices under consideration (see Figure 3). The distribution of zeros and ones is pretty similar for different devices (Figure 3). For the very same device—configured or unconfigured—the numbers are not identical but relatively close to each other. These differing results for one device are more probably caused by temperature variances than by the fact of configuration dependencies.

Figure 4 depicts the total amount of constant bits observed over a variable number of compared readouts for different devices. The measurements show that more than 90% of all bits are constant over all compared readouts. We therefore notice a distinctive coherence of measurements from one device.

To quantify this coherence we compared the single data streams with a reference stream ρ to get a measurable deviation value. To achieve this we used the probability distribution to generate a reference data stream ρ of the measurement, setting each bit to the value with the higher probablity of occurrence according to the measured data. ρ therefore represents the bitwise rounded mean of all measured streams.

We then determined the Hamming Distance (HD) of every readout to this reference key. Figure 5 shows the respective distribution for one device. The readouts from one board show a close cross-correlation. For device D the Hamming distances show an expectancy value of 99, equivalent to only 0.75% of the total data, and a standard deviation of 7.4. Device F gives an expectancy value of 137 (1.0%) with a standard deviation of 9.1. All HD values

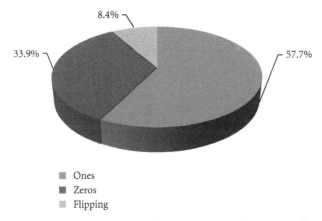

FIGURE 3: Mean occurrences of constant ones and zeros as well as flipping bits of Table 2.

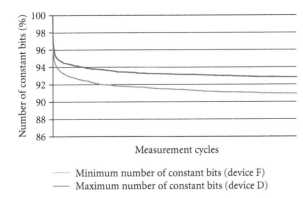

FIGURE 4: Percentage of constant bits over 10,000 measurements for two devices, that represent the maximum (device D) and minimum (device F) over all devices. All other values reside in the area between the two curves.

TABLE 2: Number of constant zeros, ones, and flipping bits.

Device	Ones		Zeros		Flipping	
A	7798	59,4%	4238	32,3%	1084	8,3%
$\overline{A}$	7744	59,0%	4190	31,9%	1186	9,0%
B	7698	58,7%	4435	33,8%	987	7,5%
$\overline{B}$	7661	58,4%	4414	33,6%	1045	8,0%
C	7388	56,3%	4676	35,6%	1056	8,0%
$\overline{C}$	7325	55,8%	4642	35,4%	1153	8,8%
D	7702	58,7%	4479	34,1%	939	7,2%
$\overline{D}$	7638	58,2%	4432	33,8%	1050	8,0%
E	7626	58,1%	4350	33,2%	1144	8,7%
$\overline{E}$	7566	57,7%	4357	33,2%	1197	9,1%
F	7517	57,3%	4418	33,7%	1185	9,0%
$\overline{F}$	7491	57,1%	4352	33,2%	1277	9,7%
G	7498	57,1%	4577	34,9%	1045	8,0%
$\overline{G}$	7418	56,5%	4543	34,6%	1159	8,8%
H	7537	57,4%	4543	34,6%	1040	7,9%
$\overline{H}$	7460	56,9%	4552	34,7%	1108	8,4%

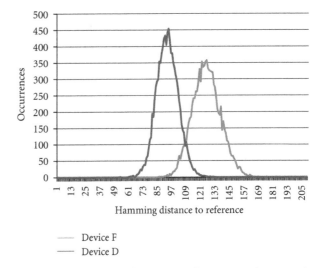

FIGURE 5: Distribution of Hamming distances to the respective reference streams for unconfigured devices D and F and 10,000 measurements each.

computed from all devices resided in an interval of [53–208]. The analyses of the measurement series from the other devices are in between the two extremal values given.

So far, the compared values were originated from unconfigured devices and directly measured after startup. For identification of the device, the key data should be independent from the content of the address ranges of configuration memory that are used for programming the device. Therefore, also the programmed device was examined. Figure 6 depicts the HD values of readouts of a programmed board in relation to the reference key determined on the same board in unconfigured state.

The values read out from the configured board show a slightly higher deviation from the reference but are still within a mean deviation of well below 1% of the total data stream. This is also the case for the other examined devices (see also Table 3). So all data streams from one board show a great mutual similarity. To verify the usability of the proposed approach, we compare in a next step data from different devices.

5.2. Distinction and Identification. For unique identification, the mapping of a given ID value to a device is necessary.

Here the difference between readouts of different boards is the crucial property. A first indicator is the difference between the computed reference keys. Table 3 shows the mutual Hamming distances of all reference keys.

The table shows a very close correlation between the measurements of the same device, meaning that only a slight dependency on the configuration state can be determined. In contrast, HD values between different devices are all near 6000, meaning a 45% deviation and therefore near to the expected value of 50% for pure random streams. A closer look at the streams revealed some bits that are constantly zero over all measurements of all devices, which in combination with the slight nonuniform distribution of ones and zeroes (see Table 2) may account for the lower absolute deviation.

TABLE 3: Mutual Hamming distances of reference streams from unconfigured devices A...G and configured devices $\overline{A}$...$\overline{G}$.

Device	A	$\overline{A}$	B	$\overline{B}$	C	$\overline{C}$	D	$\overline{D}$	E	$\overline{E}$	F	$\overline{F}$	G	$\overline{G}$	H	$\overline{H}$
A	0	90	5903	5918	6161	6151	6020	6024	6089	6118	6201	6201	5981	5973	6073	6100
$\overline{A}$	90	0	5897	5912	6157	6147	6008	6012	6101	6130	6199	6199	5975	5967	6047	6072
B	5903	5897	0	87	6268	6276	5967	5963	5990	6011	6050	6048	6118	6128	5952	5969
$\overline{B}$	5918	5912	87	0	6283	6291	5972	5968	5965	5980	6077	6075	6103	6113	5949	5964
C	6161	6157	6268	6283	0	74	6339	6343	6054	6053	6170	6176	6266	6250	6012	6027
$\overline{C}$	6151	6147	6276	6291	74	0	6315	6319	6032	6031	6146	6152	6262	6246	6014	6029
D	6020	6008	5967	5972	6339	6315	0	78	5991	6010	6165	6159	5989	5991	5979	6000
$\overline{D}$	6024	6012	5963	5968	6343	6319	78	0	5997	6016	6135	6129	5977	5979	5993	6014
E	6089	6101	5990	5965	6054	6032	5991	5997	0	113	6088	6092	6032	6024	6042	6079
$\overline{E}$	6118	6130	6011	5980	6053	6031	6010	6016	113	0	6101	6105	6041	6033	6039	6080
F	6201	6199	6050	6077	6170	6146	6165	6135	6088	6101	0	30	6194	6198	6108	6135
$\overline{F}$	6201	6199	6048	6075	6176	6152	6159	6129	6092	6105	30	0	6188	6192	6098	6125
G	5981	5975	6118	6103	6266	6262	5989	5977	6032	6041	6194	6188	0	58	6080	6077
$\overline{G}$	5973	5967	6128	6113	6250	6246	5991	5979	6024	6033	6198	6192	58	0	6086	6085
H	6073	6047	5952	5949	6012	6014	5979	5993	6042	6039	6108	6098	6080	6086	0	119
$\overline{H}$	6100	6072	5969	5964	6027	6029	6000	6014	6079	6080	6135	6125	6077	6085	119	0

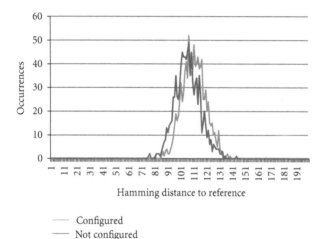

— Configured
— Not configured

FIGURE 6: Distribution of Hamming distances to the device D reference stream ρ_D (generated from the unconfigured device data Θ_D) for 1000 test data streams from the unconfigured ($T_X = (\tau_X^1, \ldots, \tau_X^{1000})$) and configured ($\overline{T}_X = (\overline{\tau}_X^1, \ldots, \overline{\tau}_X^{1000})$) device each.

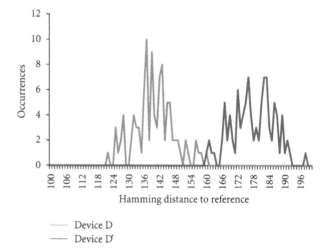

— Device D
— Device D′

FIGURE 7: Enlarged presentation of the Hamming distance distribution of T_D relative to ρ_D and $\overline{\rho}_D$.

devices are very similar and also provide recognition rates of 100% using very simple threshold algorithms.

5.3. Temperature Stability. So far all measurements have been made at standard laboratory conditions including a regular temperature of app. 25°C. In diverse applications the temperature of the FPGA may vary in some range around this temperature. In order to ensure applicability of our approach some independability of temperatures must be proven. For this we selected three different boards D, F, and I and exposed these to different temperatures ranging from $-30°C$ to $+80°C$ in a climate chamber.

The first experiment conducted was to determine the variation of the fingerprint at different temperatures. This was done by reading back the device 1000 times and building a master bitstream out of this measurement. Then each

Figure 8 shows the comparison of the test value set from device D with all reference strings. Two distinctive peak clusters are visible in the chart. Two peaks with relatively small average Hamming weights of about 160 originate from the comparison with the two reference sets ρ_D (unconfigured) and $\overline{\rho}_D$ (configured) from the same board D (see Figure 7 for an enlarged view). The remaining 14 peaks belong to reference values of the other devices and are clustered in a narrow interval around an HD of 6000. Figures 7 and 9 detail the two interesting intervals rescaled for better visibility.

The charts show a clear separation of matching and non-matching devices with differences in the Hamming distance of more than an order of magnitude. The results for the other

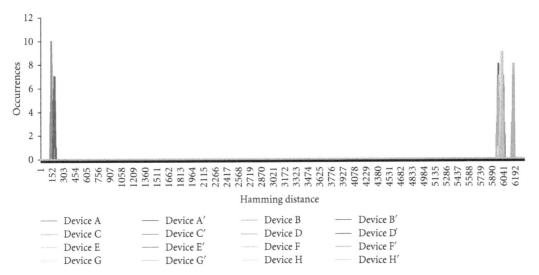

FIGURE 8: Distribution of Hamming distances of test set $T_D = (\tau_D^1, \ldots, \tau_D^{100})$ to all reference values ρ_X and $\overline{\rho}_X$ for $X \in \{A, \ldots, G\}$.

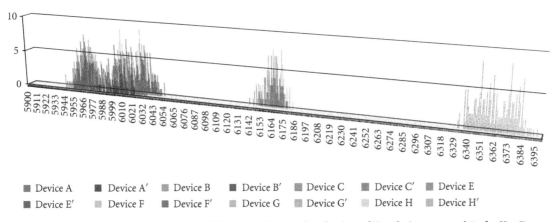

FIGURE 9: Enlarged presentation of the Hamming distance distribution of T_D relative to ρ_X and $\overline{\rho}_X$ for $X \neq D$.

bitstream is compared to the master. Representative results are depicted in Figures 10, 11, and 12 for the mean value of 20°C and both extrema −30°C and +80°C. The mean hamming distance varies for about 40 bits depending on the temperature, what is quite a moderate value, having in mind a nonmatching HD of about 6000. Moreover for different temperatures the curves look quite similar. Interestingly there is no common temperature-dependent behavior. While in Figure 11 the standard temperature has the smallest variation and the lowest temperature the highest one, the situation changes for the second board, where the lowest temperature has the lowest variation and the highest temperature the highest one. Actually this is the behavior we expected before our experiments. However the situation reverses for board D in Figure 12. So we can only conclude that there is some slight variation with different temperatures.

In our second experiment we compared the measurements taken at different temperatures to the reference bitstream generated from the readbacks at 20°C. The results for Board H are depicted in Figure 13. Results for

other boards look similar. Obviously the comparison shows optimum results for 20°C. For all other measurements we get a rising hamming distance with greater temperature differences for both measurements. Again the form of the curves remains similar which again means the variance of the hamming distances are almost equal. The maximum hamming distance goes up to around 300 for the highest and lowest temperatures which is very moderate compared to non matching hamming distances.

The third experiment is a temperature sweep, starting at 85°C and cooling down to −30°C. This process took about 40 min, and 4800 measurements were taken with 500 ms between each measurement. Out of all measurements a master bitstream was built and the hamming distance for each readback calculated. The results are shown in Figure 14. At the beginning the hamming distance is around 350, goes down to 120 at approximately 0°C, and then goes up again with even more decreasing temperature. The blue line shows the chip temperature which is around 5 to 10° higher than the surrounding temperature for an unconfigured Virtex-5 device.

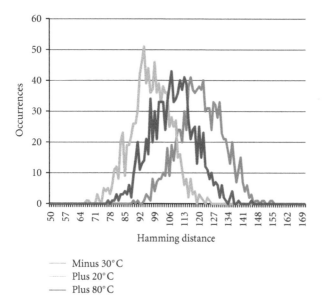

FIGURE 10: Hamming distance of single readback and master bitstream of board H at different temperatures.

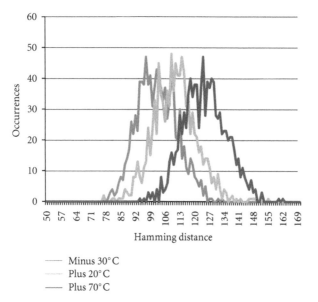

FIGURE 11: Hamming distance of single readback and masterbitstream of board I at different temperatures.

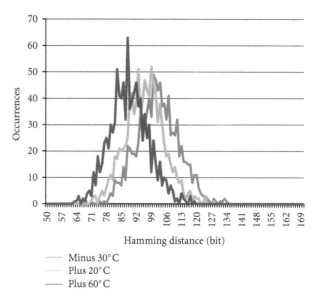

FIGURE 12: Hamming distance of single readback and masterbitstream of board D at different temperatures.

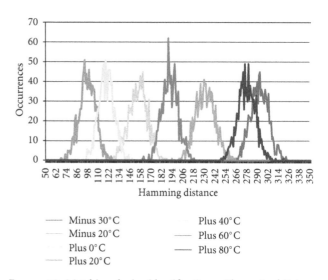

FIGURE 13: Matching device identification with master bitstream generated at 20°C and identification readback temperature range from −30°C to +80°C (1 k measurements at each temperature step).

One can conclude that our device identification mechanism shows slight temperature dependency, which does not influence the identification process. In a final experiment we used the 20°C master bitstreams for non matching devices at different temperatures. For such non matching devices the temperature has almost no influence, resulting in a deviation of about 20 in the hamming distance. Related to an absolute hamming distance of around 6000 this is neglectable. So finally device recognition is feasible for a wide temperature range.

5.4. Aging. Another important aspect is device aging. Again, we have to point out we do not know what information exactly is read from the device by our methodology. However

we did a readback for different devices with a time difference of one year. The master bitstream generated one year ago was applied to the readback. Figure 15 shows the result for device H. One can see a slight deviation between both devices. The difference might be based on some aging of the device, but also slight deviations in the environment cannot be completely ruled out. However this effect is relatively small and does not affect the identification mechanism presented in this paper.

6. Discussion

The examination shows a very high correlation within data streams from a single device. Test data revealed deviations from the reference master around 1% of the total data

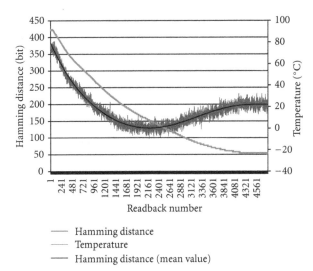

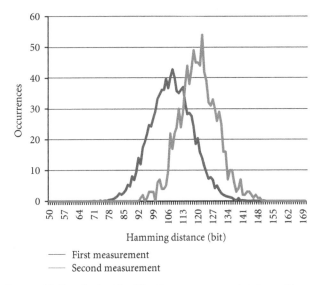

FIGURE 14: 4800 hamming distance measurements taken during temperature sweep from 85°C to −30°C environmental temperature. The blue curve shows the chip temperature.

FIGURE 15: Two device identification measurements taken with one year between 1st and 2nd measurement.

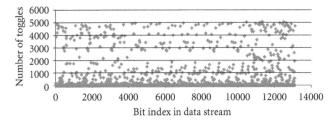

FIGURE 16: Number of single bit value changes for the different bit indices over 10,000 measurements on device D.

stream. On the other hand comparison to reference keys from other devices resulted in HD values corresponding to a deviation in more than 40% of the bits enabling a reliable identification of the device being read out. In addition the identification technique needs no configuration on the device and therefore no area on the configurable fabric or other hardware resources. We therefore believe that the method can be used to securely and reliably identify physical devices.

An open issue is the question where the data originates from in the first place. Since the address space is not used officially on the devices it could as well be omitted. So it is possible that the readback retrieves data from memory locations that are in fact used for some purpose. On the other side there are the distinct differences between different instances of the same device model and the Hamming

distances near the expectancy values for random strings. This seems to be unlikely for deliberately configured data. Nevertheless we are so far not able to determine the precise origin of the readout data. In addition the data shows slight repetitive patterns as can be seen in Figures 1 and 2 that have to be analysed to get valid statements about the number of usable identification bits.

Moreover the question arises whether the data could also be used to generate random numbers. Here not the constant but the variable bits are crucial for the quality. Figures 1 and 2 already show that the data have different distribution depending on the bit index. Figure 16 shows in addition the number of value changes over the measured set of data streams for the different bit indices.

The variety of behaviours of the different bits could be seen as an indication that an extraction of random numbers could be possible, but further analysis and postprocessing of the data is needed to get reliable results.

7. Security Applications

There are several possible applications for the described SRAM-based PUFs. Since the PUF consists of memory values, it is easy to evaluate also for an attacker. Hence it should be possible to create the memory response without the specific device but only a readout of the memory. A security application therefore has to make sure that the PUF is actually evaluated and not replayed values are used. One possibility for that is guaranteed direct physical access to the device. This is utilized in two applications examplarily looked at in the following: product piracy protection and IP protection.

For the first use case, the initial memory content is read out at production of the device and an adequate error correcting coding mechanism is applied to create a stable fingerprint. This fingerprint is then used to create a manufacturer certificate for the device, for example, by signing a hash value of the fingerprint with a manufacturer-specific secret key. This certificate is then delivered together with the device to the customer who is then able to verify whether he acquired a genuine device since a manufacturer of bogus devices is neither able to create valid certificates for his device nor to clone the PUF-fingerprints for the cloned units. Since the fingerprinting does not rely on memory regions used for configuration the verification can be performed even during operation without interruption and without need to restart the device.

Possible applications for the considered identification mechanism are not restricted to external evaluation of a device but could as well be used inside a configuration bitstream itself. This is considered in the second use case for IP protection. Since the configuration memory is accessible from the fabric through the common ICAP interface, a configured bitstream could easily use the available information to identify the device it is configured on and perhaps react accordingly. A straightforward application would be to bind a configuration to a specific device. To show feasibility we implemented the basic functionality.

Using an ICAP interface connected to a MicroBlaze System we were able to read out the identifying data from within the device, getting similar results as when using the external JTAG access. By comparing the data with a reference string stored in the configuration bitstream, the design can verify whether it is run on a predefined device. If a mismatch is detected, an internal enforcement mechanism can, for example, disable the design or reduce functionality, building a reliable copy protection mechanism for hardware configuration IP.

8. Specific Properties of the Memory Region

When the identification is used for policy enforcement and copy protection, circumventing the identification could be of interest for possible attackers. In the classical use case using memory cells for identification it has to be guaranteed that the cells are read out before any influence on the contents is possible, since the memory cells can easily be written with arbitrary values. In contrast to that we observed that writing on the considered addresses was not possible over the examined interfaces—the readout values were not changeable by write attempts. This is a major benefit in contrast to general memory cells.

In addition, since the used cells are outside the memory space used for configuration, we assume that they are not used for programming a design to the chip. The identification should therefore work also for configured devices during runtime and for partial bitstreams having no control and no information about the contents of the surrounding chip area or even about their own placing on the area as long as they have access to the ICAP interface. So no area has to be reserved for the identification and no constraints for placement and routing are imposed by the approach.

9. Conclusion and Further Work

For the challenge of identifying physical devices of Xilinx Virtex-5 FPGA family we examined configuration memory readouts from address ranges that are assumedly not used in the series. We chose an address range reserved for future block types to read out data and compared the readouts mutually from one device and between devices. Results showed a strong coherence of different streams from the same device and strong deviations between devices. This holds true also for a wide temperature range. Moreover we showed device identification is feasible after one year of aging. We therefore assume the data suitable for identification of physical devices. The method opens identification possibilities for FPGA series where other SRAM-based approaches fail because of enforced initialization to defined values at startup.

To proof reliable identification some future work is necessary. So far it is not clear how long the potential key sequences are and in what ratio they include real identification information and noise. It could also be investigated, whether it is also applicable to devices of other series.

Acknowledgments

The authors acknowledge support by Deutsche Forschungs-gemeinschaft and Open Access Publishing Fund of Karlsruhe Institute of Technology.

References

[1] B. Gassend, D. Clarke, M. van Dijk, and S. Devadas, "Silicon physical random functions," in *Proceedings of the 9th ACM Conference on Computer and Communications Security (CCS '02)*, pp. 148–160, ACM, New York, NY, USA, November 2002.

[2] B. Gassend, D. Lim, D. Clarke, M. van Dijk, and S. Devadas, "Identification and authentication of integrated circuits," *Concurrency and Computation: Practice and Experience*, vol. 16, no. 11, pp. 1077–1098, 2004.

[3] J. Guajardo, S. S. Kumar, G.-J. Schrijen, and P. Tuyls, "Fpga intrinsic pufs and their use for ip protection," in *Proceedings of the 9th International Workshop on Cryptographic Hardware and Embedded Systems (CHES '07)*, pp. 63–80, Springer, Berlin, Germany, 2007.

[4] P. Tuyls and B. Skoric, "Strong authentication with physical unclonable functions," in *Security, Privacy, and Trust in Modern Data Management*, M. Petkovic and W. Jonker, Eds., Data-Centric Systems and Applications, pp. 133–148, Springer, Berlin, Germany, 2007.

[5] R. Maes, "PUF Bibliography," 2010, http://www.rmaes.ulyssis .be/pufbib.php/.

[6] R. Maes, P. Tuyls, and I. Verbauwhede, "Intrinsic pufs from flip-flops on reconfigurable devices," in *Proceedings of the 3rd Benelux Workshop on Information and System Security (WISSec '08)*, p. 17, Eindhoven, NL, USA, 2008.

[7] S. S. Kumar, J. Guajardo, R. Maes, G. J. Schrijen, and P. Tuyls, "The butterfly PUF protecting IP on every FPGA," in *Proceedings of the IEEE International Workshop on Hardware-Oriented Security and Trust (HOST '08)*, pp. 67–70, June 2008.

[8] Y. Su, J. Holleman, and B. Otis, "A1.6pJ/blt 96% stable chip-ID generating circuit using process variations," in *Proceedings of the 54th IEEE International Solid-State Circuits Conference (ISSCC '07)*, pp. 406–611, San Francisco, Calif, USA, February 2007.

[9] D. E. Holcomb, W. P. Burleson, and K. Fu, "Power-up SRAM state as an identifying fingerprint and source of true random numbers," *IEEE Transactions on Computers*, vol. 58, no. 9, pp. 1198–1210, 2009.

[10] S. Chaudhry, P. A. Layman, J. G. Norman, and J. R. Thomson, "Electronic fingerprinting of semiconductor integrated circuits," US patent 6,738,294, Agere Systems Inc., 2002.

[11] Y. Dodis, R. Ostrovsky, L. Reyzin, and A. Smith, "Fuzzy extractors: how to generate strong keys from biometrics and

other noisy data," *SIAM Journal on Computing*, vol. 38, no. 1, pp. 97–139, 2008.

[12] O. Sander, B. Glas, L. Braun, K. Müller-Glaser, and J. Becker, "Intrinsic identification of xilinx virtex-5 fpga devices using uninitialized parts of configuration memory space," in *International Conference on Reconfigurable Computing and FPGAs (ReConFig '10)*, pp. 13–18, December 2010.

[13] Xilinx Inc., *UG190: Virtex-5 FPGA User Guide*, 2009, v5.2, November 2009.

[14] Xilinx Inc., *UG191: Virtex-5 FPGA Configuration User Guide*, 2009, v3.8, 14.08.2009.

[15] IEEE, "1149.1: IEEE Standard Test Access Port and Boundary-Scan Architecture," IEEE-SA Standards Board, IEEE Standard 1149.1-2001 (R2008), 2006.

[16] Digilent Inc., *DPCUTIL Programmer's Reference Manual*, 2007, doc 576-000, August 2007, http://www.digilentinc.com /Data/Software/Adept/DPCUTIL_Programmers_RM.pdf.

[17] Xilinx Inc., *DS100: Virtex-5 Family Overview. Product Specification, 2009, v5.0*, February 2009.

[18] Xilinx Inc., *UG347: ML505/ML506/ML507 Evaluation Platform: User Guide, 2009, v3.1.1*, October 2009.

14

Evaluation of Runtime Task Mapping Using the rSesame Framework

Kamana Sigdel,[1] Carlo Galuzzi,[1] Koen Bertels,[1] Mark Thompson,[2] and Andy D. Pimentel[2]

[1] *Computer Engineering Group, Technical University of Delft, Mekelweg 4, 2628 CD, Delft, The Netherlands*
[2] *Computer Systems Architecture Group, University of Amsterdam, Science Park 904, 1098 XH, Amsterdam, The Netherlands*

Correspondence should be addressed to Kamana Sigdel, k.sigdel@tudelft.nl

Academic Editor: Viktor K. Prasanna

Performing runtime evaluation together with design time exploration enables a system to be more efficient in terms of various design constraints, such as performance, chip area, and power consumption. rSesame is a generic modeling and simulation framework, which can explore and evaluate reconfigurable systems at both design time and runtime. In this paper, we use the rSesame framework to perform a thorough evaluation (at design time and at runtime) of various task mapping heuristics from the state of the art. An extended Motion-JPEG (MJPEG) application is mapped, using the different heuristics, on a reconfigurable architecture, where different Field Programmable Gate Array (FPGA) resources and various nonfunctional design parameters, such as the execution time, the number of reconfigurations, the area usage, reusability efficiency, and other parameters, are taken into consideration. The experimental results suggest that such an extensive evaluation can provide a useful insight both into the characteristics of the reconfigurable architecture and on the efficiency of the task mapping.

1. Introduction

In recent years, reconfigurable architectures [1, 2] have received an increasing attention due to their adaptability and short time to market. Reconfigurable architectures use reconfigurable hardware, such as Field Programmable Gate Array (FPGA) [3, 4] or other programmable hardware (e.g., Complex Programmable Logic Device (CPLD) [5], reconfigurable Datapath Array (rDPA) [6]). These hardware resources are frequently coupled with a core processor, typically a General Purpose Processor (GPP), which is responsible for controlling the reconfigurable hardware. Part of the application's tasks is executed on the GPP, while the rest of the tasks are executed on the hardware. In general, the hardware implementation of an application is more efficient in terms of performance than a software implementation. As a result, reconfigurable architectures enhance the whole application through an implementation of selected application kernels onto the reconfigurable hardware, while preserving the flexibility of the software execution with the GPP at the same time [7, 8]. The design of such architectures is subject to numerous design constraints and requirements,

such as performance, chip area, power consumption, and memory. As a consequence, the design of heterogeneous reconfigurable systems imposes several challenges to system designers such as hardware-software partitioning, Design Space Exploration (DSE), task mapping, and task scheduling.

Reconfigurable systems can evolve under diverse conditions due to the changes imposed either by the architecture, by the applications, or by the environment. A reconfigurable architecture can evolve under different conditions, for instance, processing elements shutdown in order to save power, or additional processing elements are added in order to meet the execution deadline. The application behavior can change, for example, due to the dynamic nature of the application-application load changes due to the arrival of sporadic tasks. In such systems, the design process becomes more sophisticated as all design decisions have to be optimized in terms of runtime behaviors and values. Due to changing runtime conditions with respect to, for example, user requirements or having multiple simultaneously executing applications competing for platform resources, design time evaluation alone is not enough for any kind of architectural exploration. Especially in the case of partially dynamic reconfigurable architectures that are subject to changes at the runtime, design time exploration and task mapping are inadequate and cannot address the changing runtime conditions. Performing runtime evaluation enables a system to be more efficient in terms of various design constraints, such as performance, chip area, and power consumption. The evaluation carried at runtime can be more precise and can evaluate the system more accurately than at design time. Nevertheless, such evaluations are typically hard to obtain due to the enormous size and complexity of the search space generated by runtime parameters and values.

In order to benefit from both design time and runtime evaluations, we developed a modeling and simulation framework, called rSesame [9], which allows the exploration and the evaluation of reconfigurable systems at both design time and runtime. With the rSesame framework, designers can instantiate a model that can explore and evaluate any kind of reconfigurable architecture running any set of streaming applications from the multimedia domain. The instantiated model can be used to evaluate and compare various characteristics of reconfigurable architectures, hardware-software partitioning algorithms, and task mapping heuristics. In [10], we used the rSesame framework to perform runtime exploration of a reconfigurable architecture. In [11], we proposed a new task mapping heuristic for runtime task mapping onto reconfigurable architectures based on hardware configurations reuse. In this paper, we present an extension of the work presented in [10, 11]. In particular, we present an extensive evaluation and comparison of various task mapping heuristics from the state of the art (including the heuristics we presented in [11]) both at design time and at runtime using the rSesame framework. More specifically, the main contributions of this paper are the following:

(i) a detailed case study using the rSesame framework for mapping different runtime task mapping heuristics from the state of the art (including the runtime task mapping heuristics in [11]). For this case study, we use an extended MJPEG application and a reconfigurable architecture;

(ii) an extensive evaluation of the different heuristics for a given reconfigurable architecture. This evaluation is performed by considering different number of FPGA resources for the same reconfigurable architecture model;

(iii) a thorough comparison of the aforementioned heuristics under different resource conditions using various nonfunctional design parameters, such as execution time, number of reconfiguration, area usage, and reusability efficiency. The comparison is done both at design time as well as at runtime.

The rest of the paper is organized as follows. Section 2 provides the related research. Section 3 discusses the rSesame framework, which is used as a simulation platform for evaluating task mapping at runtime, while Section 4 presents a detailed case study using the different heuristics. In Section 5, a detailed analysis and evaluation of the task mapping at runtime using the rSesame framework is presented. Finally, Section 6 concludes the paper.

2. Related Work

Task mapping can be performed in two mutual nonexclusive ways: at design time and at runtime. The task mapping performed at the design time can generally be faster, but it may be less accurate as the runtime behavior of a system is mostly captured by using offline (static) estimations and predictions. Examples of techniques for task mapping at design time are dynamic programming [12], Integer Linear Programming (ILP) [13], simulated annealing [14, 15], tabu search [16], genetic algorithm [17, 18], and ant colony optimization [19].

In another way of performing task mapping, the reconfigurable system is evaluated for any changes in the runtime conditions and the task mapping is performed at runtime based on those conditions. Under such scenario, the changes in the system are considered and the task mapping is performed accordingly. In [20], the authors present a simple approach for runtime task mapping in which a mapping module evaluates the most frequently executed tasks at runtime and maps them onto a reconfigurable hardware component. However, this work [20] focuses on the lower level and it targets only loop kernels. A similar approach for high-level runtime task mapping is presented in [21] for multiprocessor System on Chip (SoC) containing fine-grain reconfigurable hardware tiles. This approach details a generic runtime resource assignment heuristic that performs fast and efficient task assignment. In [22], the authors define the dynamic coprocessor management problem for processors with an FPGA and provide a mapping to an online optimization based on the cumulative benefit heuristic, which is inspired by a commonly used accumulation approach in online algorithm work.

In the same way, the study in [23] presents runtime resource allocation and scheduling heuristic for the multi-threaded environment, which is based on the status of the reconfigurable system. Correspondingly, [24] presents a dynamic method for runtime task mapping, task scheduling and task allocation for reconfigurable architectures. The proposed method consists of dynamically adapting an architecture to the processing requirement. Likewise, the authors in [25, 26] present an online resource management for heterogeneous multiprocessor SoC systems, and the authors in [27] present a runtime mapping of applications onto a heterogeneous reconfigurable tiled SoC architecture. The approach presented in [27] proposes an iterative hierarchical approach for runtime mapping of applications to a heterogeneous SoC. The approach presented in [28] consists of a mapper, which determines a mapping of application(s) to an architecture, using a library at runtime. The approach proposed by authors in [29] performs mapping of streaming applications, with real-time requirements, onto a reconfigurable MPSoC architecture. In the same way, Faruque et al. [30] present a scheme for runtime-agent-based distributed application mapping for on-chip communication for adaptive NoC-based heterogeneous multiprocessor systems.

There are few attempts which combine design time exploration together with runtime management and try to evaluate the system at both stages [21, 31]. However, these methodologies are mostly restricted to the MPSoC domain and do not address the reconfigurable system domain. Unlike existing approaches that are either focused on design time or on runtime task mapping, we are focused on exploring and evaluating reconfigurable architectures at *design time* as well as at *runtime* during early design stages.

3. rSesame Framework

The rSesame [9] framework is a generic modeling and simulation infrastructure, which can explore and evaluate reconfigurable systems at early design stages both at design time and at runtime. It is built upon the Sesame framework [32]. The rSesame framework can be efficiently employed to perform DSE of the reconfigurable systems with respect to hardware-software partitioning, task mapping, and scheduling [10]. With the rSesame framework, an application task can be modeled either as a hardware (HW), or as a software (SW), or as a *pageable* task. A HW (SW) task is always mapped onto the reconfigurable hardware component (microprocessor), while a *pageable* task can be mapped on either of these resources. Task assignment to the SW, HW, and pageable categories is performed at design time based on the design time exploration of the system. At runtime, these tasks are mapped onto their corresponding resources based on time, resources, and conditions of the system.

The rSesame framework uses the Kahn Process Network (KPN) [33] at the granularity of coarse-grain tasks for application modeling. Each KPN process contains functional application code instrumented with annotations that generate read, write, and execute events describing the actions of the process. The generated traces are forwarded onto the architecture layer using an intermediate mapping layer, which consists of Virtual Processors (VPs) to schedule these traces. Along with the VPs, the mapping layer contains a Runtime Mapping Manager (RMM) that deals with the runtime mapping of the applications on the architecture. Depending on current system conditions, the RMM decides where and when to forward these events. To support its decision making, the RMM employs an arbitrary set of user-defined policies for runtime mapping, which can simply be plugged in and out of the RMM. The RMM also collaborates with other architectural components to gather architectural information. The architecture layer in the framework models the architectural resources and constraints. These architectural components are constructed from generic building blocks provided as a library, which contains components for processors, memories, on-chip network components, and so forth. As a result, any kind of reconfigurable architecture can be constructed from these generic components. Beside the regular parameters, such as computation and communication delays, other architectural parameters like reconfiguration delay and area for the reconfigurable architecture can also be provided as extra information to these components.

The rSesame framework provides various useful design parameters to the designer. These include the total execution time (in terms of simulated cycles), area usage, number of reconfigurations, percentage of reconfiguration, percentage of HW/SW execution, and reusability efficiency. These design parameters are described in more detail in the following.

3.1. Execution Time. The execution time is recorded in terms of simulated clock cycles. The SW execution time is the total number of cycles when all the tasks are mapped only on the GPP. The HW execution time is recorded when the tasks are mapped onto the FPGA. The speedup is calculated as a ratio of these two values.

3.2. Percentage of HW and SW Execution Time. The percentage of HW (SW) execution is computed as the total percentage of the execution time contributed by the FPGA (GPP) for HW (SW) execution of an application. Similarly, the percentage of reconfiguration time represents the percentage of the total execution time spent in reconfigurations. This provides an indication on the total time spent in the computation and in the reconfiguration. These values are calculated as follows.

The percentage of SW execution time is given by

$$\text{SW Exec}(\%) = \frac{\sum_{i=1}^{N} \#\text{SWEx}(T_i) \cdot T_{\text{SW}(i)}}{\text{TotalExecTime}} \cdot 100, \quad (1)$$

where $\#\text{SWEx}(T_i)$ is the total number of SW executions counted by the model for task T_i, $T_{\text{SW}(i)}$ is the software execution latency for task T_i, and TotalExecTime is the total simulated execution time.

The percentage of HW execution time is given by

$$\text{HW Exec.}(\%) \leq \frac{\sum_{i=1}^{N} \#\text{HWEx}(T_i) \cdot T_{\text{HW}(i)}}{\text{TotalExecTime}} \cdot 100, \quad (2)$$

where $\#\text{HWEx}(T_i)$ is the total number of HW executions counted for task T_i by the model, $T_{\text{HW}(i)}$ is the hardware execution latency for task T_i, and TotalExecTime is the total execution cycles incurred while running an application onto the given reconfigurable architecture.

Note that, the HW execution percentage can only be given here as an upper bound, since the execution of tasks on the FPGA can be performed in parallel. The metric calculated here is an accumulated value. The simulator, however, can give the actual value. A similar equation holds for the time spent reconfiguring, which is given as a percentage of the total execution time as follows:

$$\text{Recon}(\%) \leq \frac{\sum_{i=1}^{N} \#\text{Recon}(T_i) \cdot T_{\text{Recon}(i)}}{\text{TotalExecTime}} \cdot 100, \quad (3)$$

where $\#\text{Recon}(T_i)$ is the number of times T_i is configured, $T_{\text{Recon}(i)}$ is the reconfiguration delay of T_i, and TotalExecTime represents the total execution cycles incurred while running an application onto the given reconfigurable architecture.

3.3. Number of Reconfigurations. The number of reconfigurations is recorded as the total number of reconfigurations incurred during the execution of an application onto the given architecture. This provides an indication on how efficiently the reconfiguration delay is avoided, while mapping tasks onto the FPGA. For example, the mapping of task A, task B, and then task A again on the FPGA requires 3 reconfigurations, while by changing this mapping sequence to task A, task A and then task B, only 2 reconfigurations are required.

3.4. Time-Weighted Area Usage. The weighted area usage factor is a metric that computes how much area is used throughout the entire execution of an application on a particular architecture. This provides an indication on how efficiently the FPGA area is utilized. This metric is calculated as follows:

$$\text{Area Usage(\%)} = \frac{\sum_{i=1}^{N} \text{Area}(T_i) \cdot T_{\text{HW}(i)} \cdot \#\text{HWEx}(T_i)}{\text{TotalExecTime} \cdot \text{Area(FPGA)}} \cdot 100, \tag{4}$$

where $\text{Area}(T_i)$ is the area occupied by task T_i on the FPGA, $T_{\text{HW}(i)}$ is the hardware execution latency of T_i, $\#\text{HWEx}(T_i)$ is the total number of HW executions counted by the model for task T_i, Area(FPGA) is the total area available on the FPGA, and TotalExecTime is the total execution time of the application.

3.5. Reusability Efficiency. A task execution onto the FPGA has two phases: the *configuration phase*, where its configuration data that represents a task is loaded onto the FPGA, and the *running phase*, where the task is actually processing data. In an ideal case, a task can be configured onto the FPGA only once and it is executed in all other cases. Nonetheless, this is not always possible as the FPGA has limited area. The Reusability Efficiency (RE) is the ratio of the reconfiguration time that is saved due to the hardware configuration reuse to the total execution time of any task. The RE of a task can be defined as follows:

$$\text{RE}_{\text{task}} = \frac{(\#\text{HWEx} - \#\text{Recon}) \cdot T_{\text{Recon}}}{\#\text{HWEx} \cdot T_{\text{HW}} + \#\text{SWEx} \cdot T_{\text{SW}} + \#\text{Recon} \cdot T_{\text{Recon}}}, \tag{5}$$

where $\#\text{HWEx}$, $\#\text{SWEx}$, and $\#\text{Recon}$ are the number of HW executions, SW executions, and reconfigurations of a task, respectively. Similarly, T_{HW}, T_{SW}, and T_{Recon} are the corresponding hardware, software, and reconfigurable latencies.

The RE of a task indicates the percentage of the total time saved by a task when multiple reconfigurations are avoided or, in other words, a task configuration is reused. The numerator in (5) represents the time that is saved when a mapping of a task is reused, and the denominator represents the total execution time. The total RE for an application can be calculated as the summation of the numerator in (5) for all N tasks divided by the total execution time for the whole application as follows:

$$\text{RE}_{\text{App}} \leq \frac{\sum_{i=1}^{N} (\#\text{HWEx}(i) - \#\text{Recon}(i)) \cdot T_{\text{Recon}(i)}}{\text{TotalExecTime}}. \tag{6}$$

Note that the RE calculated in this way for the whole application can only be given here as an upper bound, since the execution of tasks on the reconfigurable hardware can be performed in parallel. A higher RE can obtain a higher speedup. To study this relation, we use the RE as an evaluation parameter to study the behavior of each task.

4. Case Study

We use the rSesame framework as a simulation platform for performing extensive evaluation of the various task mapping heuristics from the state of the art. In order to perform this case study, we constructed a Molen model using the rSesame framework for mapping an extended MJPEG application (see Section 4.2) onto the Molen reconfigurable architecture [34] (see Section 4.1). The Molen model is used to evaluate the different task mapping heuristics under consideration. We incorporated these heuristics as strategies for the Molen model to perform runtime task mapping of the extended MJPEG application onto the Molen architecture. We conducted an evaluation of these task mapping heuristics based on various system attributes recorded from the model.

The rSesame framework allows easy modification and adjustment of individual components in the model, while keeping other parts intact. As a result, the framework allows designers to experiment with different kinds of runtime task mapping heuristics. The considered heuristics have variable complexity in terms of their implementation and the nature of their execution. In the original context, they were used at different system stages, ranging from the lower architecture level to Operating System (OS), and the higher application levels. These heuristics are used as a strategy to perform runtime mapping decisions in the model. They are taken from literature, and have been adapted to fit in the framework. In the following, we discuss these heuristics in more detail.

4.1. As Much As Possible Heuristic (AMAP). AMAP tries to maximize the use of FPGA resources (such as area) as much as possible, and it performs task mapping based on resource availability. In this case, tasks are executed on the FPGA if the latter has enough resource to accommodate them; otherwise, they are executed on the GPP. This straightforward heuristic can be used as a simple resource management strategy in various domains.

Algorithm 1 presents the pseudocode that describes the functionality of the AMAP heuristic for performing runtime mapping of a task T_i. The heuristic chooses to execute task T_i onto the FPGA if there are sufficient resources (e.g., area in Algorithm 1) for T_i (line 3 to 6 in Algorithm 1). In all other conditions, tasks are executed on the GPP (line 7 to 9 in Algorithm 1).

```
(1) HW ← set of tasks mapped onto the FPGA
(2) SW ← set of tasks mapped onto the GPP
(3) if T_i.area ≤ area then
(4)    {T_i is mapped onto FPGA}
(5)    HW = HW ∪ T_i
(6)    area = area − T_i.area
(7) else
(8)    {Map T_i onto the GPP}
(9)    SW = SW ∪ T_i
(10) end if
```

ALGORITHM 1: Pseudocode for the As Much As Possible heuristic (AMAP) for mapping task T_i.

```
(1) HW ← set of tasks mapped onto the FPGA
(2) SW ← set of tasks mapped onto the GPP
(3) if T_i.area ≤ area then
(4)    if CB(T_i) > (T_SW(i) − T_HW(i)) then
(5)       {T_i is mapped onto the FPGA}
(6)       HW = HW ∪ T_i
(7)       area = area − T_i.area
(8)    end if
(9) else
(10)    {Not enough area, swap the mapped tasks.}
(11)    while area ≤ T_j.area and j ∈ HW do
(12)       if CB(T_i) - (T_SW(i) − T_HW(i)) > CB(Tj) then
(13)          area = area + T_j.area
(14)       end if
(15)    end while
(16)    if T_i.area ≤ area then
(17)       {T_i is mapped onto the FPGA}
(18)       HW = HW ∪ T_i
(19)       area = area − T_i.area
(20)    else
(21)       {Map T_i onto the GPP}
(22)       SW = SW ∪ T_i
(23)    end if
(24) end if
```

ALGORITHM 2: Pseudocode for the cumulative benefit heuristic (CBH) for the mapping on task T_i.

4.2. Cumulative Benefit Heuristic (CBH).

CBH maintains a cumulative benefit (CB) value for each task that represents the amount of time that would have been saved up to that point if the task had always been executed onto the FPGA. Mapping decisions are made based on these values and on the available resources. For example, if the available FPGA resources are not sufficient to load the current task, other tasks can be swapped if the CB of the current task is higher than that of the to-be-swapped-out set. Huang and Vahid [22] used this heuristic for dynamic coprocessor management of reconfigurable architectures at architecture level.

Algorithm 2 presents the pseudocode that describes the functionalities of CBH for performing runtime mapping of a task T_i. If resources, such as area slices, are available

```
(1) T ← set of all tasks.
(2) while T ! = ∅ and area ≤ Total_area do
(3)    Select T_i with maximum frequency count
(4)    if area + T_i.area ≤ Total_area then
(5)       map T_i onto the FPGA
(6)       area = area + T_i.area
(7)    else
(8)       map T_i onto the GPP
(9)    end if
(10)    Remove T_i from T
(11) end while
(12) Map rest of the tasks from T onto the GPP
```

ALGORITHM 3: Pseudocode for the Interval Based Heuristics (IBH) for the mapping on task T_i.

in the FPGA, then T_i is executed onto the FPGA only if the CB of T_i is larger than its loading time defined by the difference between $T_{SW(i)}$ and $T_{HW(i)}$, where $T_{SW(i)}$ and $T_{HW(i)}$ are the software and the hardware latencies of task T_i, respectively (line 3 to 8 in Algorithm 2). In other cases, when the FPGA lacks current capacity for executing the task, the heuristic searches for a subset of FPGA-resident tasks, such that removing the subset yields sufficient resources in the FPGA to execute the current task. The condition, however, is such that all the tasks in the subset must have smaller CB value than the current task (line 9 to 18 in Algorithm 2). If such a subset is not attained, then the current task is executed by the GPP (line 19 to 22 in Algorithm 2).

4.3. Interval-Based Heuristic (IBH).

In IBH, the execution is divided into a sequence of time slices (intervals) for mapping and scheduling. At the beginning of each interval, a task is examined for its execution. In each interval, the execution frequency of each task is counted, and the mapping decisions are made based on the frequency count of the previous intervals, such that tasks with the highest frequency count are mapped onto the FPGA. In [23], this heuristic is used for resource management in a multithreaded environment at OS level.

Algorithm 3 presents the pseudocode that describes the functionalities of the IBH heuristic for performing runtime mapping in each interval for a set T of tasks. Working from the highest to the lowest frequency count, each task $T_i \in T$ that satisfies the current resource conditions is selected for FPGA execution. The area constraint is updated accordingly before considering the next task. This process continues until the FPGA is full or until there is no task left in T (line 2 to 6 in Algorithm 3). If the FPGA current capacity is not enough for executing any task from T, then these tasks are executed with the GPP (line 8 to 12 in Algorithm 3). As it can be seen in Algorithm 3, tasks are executed onto the FPGA based on frequency count, but other mapping criteria, such as speedup, can also be used.

4.4. Reusability-Based Heuristic (RBH).

RBH is based on the hardware configuration reuse concept, which tries to avoid

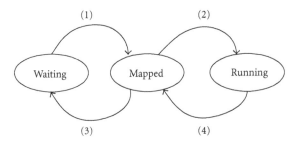

FIGURE 1: A finite-state machine (FSM) showing the different states of a task.

the reconfiguration overhead by reusing the configurations, which are already available on the FPGA. The basic idea of the heuristic is to avoid reconfiguration as much as possible, in order to reduce the total execution time. Especially in case of application domains, such as streaming and networking, where certain tasks are executed in a periodic manner, for example, on the basis of pixel blocks or entire frames, hardware configuration reuse can easily be exploited. To take advantage of such characteristics of streaming applications, we proposed this heuristic in [11].

For certain tasks that are mapped onto the FPGA, RBH preserves them in the FPGA after their execution. These tasks are not removed from the hardware, so that their hardware configurations can be reused when the task is re-executed. Reusing hardware configurations multiple times can significantly avoid reconfiguration overhead; thus, performance can be considerably improved. Unfortunately, preserving hardware configurations is not possible for all tasks. For this reason, the heuristic tries to preserve hardware configurations for selected tasks. For example, tasks that have higher reconfiguration delay and occur more frequently in the system have priority on being preserved in the FPGA.

We define three states for a task as shown in Figure 1: a waiting state, a mapped state, and a running state. A task is in the waiting state if it waits to be mapped. A task is in the mapped state if it is already configured onto the FPGA, but it is not being executed; however, it may be re-executed later. A task is in the running state when the task is actually processing data. Figure 1 depicts a finite-state machine (FSM) showing the different states of a task, where the numbers 1 to 4 refer to the following state transitions:

(1) area becomes available or task dependency ends;

(2) task execution starts;

(3) other tasks need to be executed;

(4) task execution finishes, but the task may re-execute.

It should be noted that the mapped state has a reconfiguration delay associated with it. If a task transits from a waiting state to a running state, this delay is considered. However, if the task is already in the mapped state, its hardware configuration is saved in the FPGA and this delay is ignored. Thus, when the task needs to be re-executed, it can immediately start processing without reconfiguration. The performance can be significantly improved by avoiding the former transition.

Algorithm 4 presents the pseudocode that describes the functionality of the RBH heuristic for performing runtime mapping of a task T_i. If T_i is already configured, then it starts directly processing data (line 1 to 4 in Algorithm 4). However, if T_i is not currently available in the FPGA, then the task is evaluated for its speedup. If resources are available, T_i is executed onto the FPGA only if there is a performance gain (line 5 to 10 in Algorithm 4). The performance gain in this case is measured in terms of speedup. The speedup for each task is measured at runtime by using the following equation:

$$\text{Speedup} =$$

$$\begin{cases} \dfrac{T_{\text{SW}}}{T_{\text{HW}}} & t = 0, \\[2ex] \dfrac{T_{\text{SW}} \cdot (\#\text{HWEx} + \#\text{SWEx})}{\#\text{SWEx} \cdot T_{\text{SW}} + \#\text{HWEx} \cdot T_{\text{HW}} + \#\text{Recon} \cdot T_{\text{Recon}}} & t > 0, \end{cases} \tag{7}$$

where #HWEx, #SWEx, and #Recon are the number of HW executions, SW executions, and reconfigurations of a task, respectively. Similarly, T_{HW}, T_{SW}, and T_{Recon} are the corresponding hardware, software, and reconfigurable latencies, and t is the execution time-line. When the application execution starts, $t = 0$. The heuristic maintains a profiling count of HW executions, SW executions, and reconfigurations for all tasks. Each time a task is executed, these counters for that task are updated. For instance, if a task is executed with the GPP, its SW count is incremented, and if the task is executed on the FPGA, its HW count is incremented. Similarly, the reconfiguration count of a task is incremented when a task is (re)configured. These count values for each task are accumulated from all the previous executions. As a result, they reflect the execution history of a task. The speedup calculated with these count values indicates the precise speedup of a task up to that point of execution.

If the available resources are not enough in the FPGA, a set of tasks from the FPGA is swapped to accommodate T_i in the FPGA. The task swapping, in this case, is done based on two factors: (a) speedup and (b) reconfiguration-to-execution ratio (RER). In the first step, a candidate set of tasks from the FPGA is selected, in such a way that these tasks are less beneficial than the current task in terms of speedup (line 12 to 16 in Algorithm 4). The speedup in this case is also calculated by using (7). In the second step, the candidate set is examined for its RER ratio, such that tasks with the lowest RER values are swapped first (line 17 to 21 in Algorithm 4). The RER value for each task is computed as follows:

$$\text{RER} = \frac{T_{\text{Recon}}}{T_{\text{HW}}} \cdot \text{Exec\_Freq}, \tag{8}$$

where Exec_Freq is the average execution frequency of the task in its past history. The execution frequency of a task can be simply computed from the execution profile of each task with respect to the total execution count of that application as follows:

$$\text{Exec}_{\text{Freq}} = \frac{\#\text{HWEx}}{\sum_{i=1}^{N} \text{HW}_i \text{Ex}}, \tag{9}$$

```
(1)   {Task already mapped onto the FPGA, do not configure.}
(2)   if Tᵢ == MAPPED then
(3)      Tᵢ.state ← RUNNING;
(4)   else
(5)      if area ≥ Tᵢ.area then
(6)         if Speedup(Tᵢ) > 1 then
(7)            {Task not mapped onto the FPGA, configure it.}
(8)            configure(Tᵢ);
(9)            Tᵢ.state ← RUNNING;
(10)        end if
(11)     else
(12)        for All tasks Tⱼ onto the FPGA do
(13)           if SpeedUp(Tⱼ) < SpeedUp(Tᵢ) then
(14)              candidateSet = candidateSet ∪ Tⱼ
(15)           end if
(16)        end for
(17)        while area ≤ Tᵢ.area do
(18)           Select Tₖ ∈ candidate Set with lowest RER
(19)           removeSet = removeSet ∪ Tₖ
(20)           area = area + Tₖ.area;
(21)        end while
(22)        if Tᵢ.area ≤ area then
(23)           for All task Tₘ ∈ removeSet do
(24)           Tₘ.state = WAITING;
(25)              end for
(26)           {Task not mapped onto the FPGA, configure it.}
(27)           configure(Tᵢ);
(28)           Tᵢ.state ← RUNNING;
(29)           end if
(30)        end if
(31)     end if
```

ALGORITHM 4: Pseudocode for the Reusability Based Heuristics (RBH) for the mapping on task T_i.

where the numerator represents the number of times a task is executed on the FPGA. The denominator represents the total hardware execution count of the entire application, and N represents the total number of tasks in the application.

A task with a high RER value indicates that it has high reconfiguration-per-execution delay, and it has executed frequently, in its history in the system, making it a probable candidate for future execution. The heuristic makes a careful selection while removing tasks from the FPGA. By preserving tasks with high RER values as long as possible in the FPGA, we try to avoid the reconfiguration of the frequently executed tasks. We would like to stress the fact that the speedup value computed using (7) is not a constant factor. This value is continuously updated based on the execution profile of the task at runtime. Hence, mapping tasks onto the FPGA based on such value represents the precise system behavior at that instance of time. Note that the RBH is a generic heuristic, and it is not restricted to one type of resource or to one type of architecture. To perform runtime mapping decisions considering multiple resources (such as memory or DSP slices) for different architectural components, the parameters defining the heuristic can be easily customized, hence making it a flexible approach.

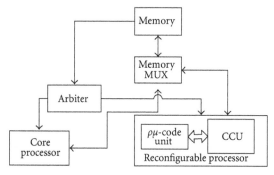

FIGURE 2: The machine organization of the Molen reconfigurable architecture. The architecture consists of a General Purpose Processor (GPP) and a Reconfigurable Processor (RP), which are coordinated by an arbiter.

4.4.1. The Molen Architecture. Figure 2 depicts the machine organization of the Molen polymorphic processor that is established on the basis of the tightly coupled coprocessor architectural paradigm [34, 35]. It consists of two different kinds of processors: the core processor that is a GPP and a Reconfigurable Processor (RP), such as an FPGA.

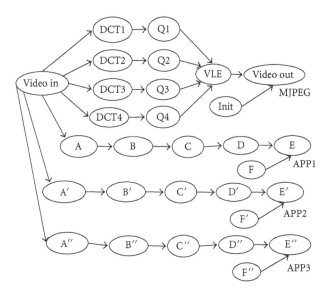

FIGURE 3: The Motion-JPEG (MJPEG) application model considered for the case study. The MJPEG application is extended by injecting sporadic applications in each frame.

TABLE 1: Available area (in slices) for different FPGAs from the Xilinx Virtex4 FX family [36].

Hardware	Area (slices)
XC4VFX12	5472
XC4VFX20	8544
XC4VFX40	18624
XC4VFX60	25280
XC4VFX100	42176
XC4VFX140	63168

The reconfigurable processor is further subdivided into the reconfigurable microcode ($\rho\mu$-code) unit and a *Custom Computing Unit* (CCU). The CCU is executed on the FPGA, and it supports additional functionalities, which are not implemented in the core processor. In order to speed up the program execution, parts of the code running on a GPP can be implemented on one or more CCUs.

The GPP and the RP are connected to an arbiter. The arbiter controls the coordination of the GPP and the RP by directing instructions to either of these processors. The code to be mapped onto the RP is annotated with special `pragma` directives. When the arbiter receives the `pragma` instruction for the RP, it initiates an "*enable reconfigurable operation*" signal to the reconfigurable unit, gives the data memory control to the RP, and drives the GPP into a waiting state. When the arbiter receives an "*end of reconfigurable operation*" signal, it releases the data memory control back to the GPP and the GPP can resume its execution. An operation executed by the RP is divided into two distinct phases: `set` and `execute`. In the `set` phase, the CCU is configured to perform the supported operations, and in the `execute` phase the actual execution of the operation is performed. The decoupling of `set` and `execute` phase allows the `set` phase to be scheduled well ahead of the `execute` phase and thereby hiding the reconfiguration latency.

4.4.2. The Application Model. We extend a Motion-JPEG (MJPEG) encoder application to use it as an application model for this case study. The corresponding KPN is shown in Figure 3. The frames are divided into blocks, and each task performs a different function on each block as it is passed from task to task. MJPEG operates on these blocks (partially) in parallel. A random number (0 to 3) of applications (APP1 to APP3) is injected in each frame of the MJPEG application in order to create a dynamic application

behavior. These applications are considered as sporadic ones, which randomly appear in the system and compete with MJPEG for the resources. In this case study, we want to evaluate task mapping under different resource conditions; therefore we use only one application as a benchmark for comparing different heuristics. Nevertheless, the rSesame framework allows to evaluate any number of applications, architectures, and task mapping heuristics.

4.4.3. Experimental Setup. As discussed before, for this case study, we consider a model instantiated from the rSesame framework for the Molen reconfigurable architecture. The model instantiated for this case study consists of 30 CCUs allowing each task to be mapped onto one CCU. Note that the number of CCUs is a parameter that can be defined based on the number of pageable and HW tasks. For this case study, we consider all tasks as pageable to fully exploit the runtime mapping by deciding *where* and *when* to map them at runtime depending on the system condition. The model allows dynamic partial reconfiguration and, therefore, if the FPGA cannot accommodate all tasks at once, the latter can be executed after runtime reconfiguration.

We study and evaluate different task mapping heuristics from various domains by considering, for the same architecture model, different FPGA sizes. We consider six FPGAs from the Xilinx Virtex-4 FX family [36], namely, XC4VFX12, XC4VFX20, XC4VFX40, XC4VFX60, XC4VFX100, and XC4VFX140. These FPGAs have different available area (slices) as shown in Table 1. As a result, they are used to evaluate the runtime task mapping under different resource conditions. Note that, in this case study, we have used area as one dimensional space. Nevertheless, rSesame can evaluate any other types and numbers of architectural parameter. We assume that the Processor Local Bus (PLB) of these FPGAs is 4 bytes wide, and the Internal Configuration Access Port (ICAP) functions at 100 MHz; thus, its configuration speed is considered at 400 MB/sec [37].

We use estimated values of the computational latency, the area occupancy (on the FPGA), and the reconfiguration delay for each CCU. The computational latency values for the GPP model are initialized using the estimates obtained from literature [38, 39] (non-Molen specific).

We estimated area occupancy for each process mapped onto the CCU using the Quipu model [40]. Quipu establishes a relation between hardware and software, and it

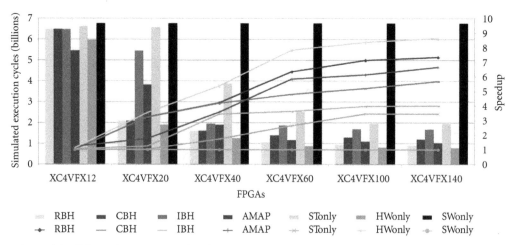

FIGURE 4: Comparison of the different heuristics tested in the proposed case study under different FPGAs conditions in terms of simulated execution time with corresponding application speedup. The application performance is proportional to the FPGA size. HWonly mapping has the best performance followed by RBH, AMAP, CBH, and IBH. STonly has the worst performance.

predicts FPGA resources from a C-level description of an application using Partial Least Squares Regression (PLSR) and Software Complexity Metrics (SCMs). Kahn processes contain functional C-code together with annotations that generate events such as read, execute, and write. As a result, Quipu can estimate area occupancy of each Kahn process. Such estimations are accepted while exploring systems at very early design stages with rSesame. In later design stages, other more refined models can be used to perform more accurate architectural explorations.

Based on the reconfiguration delay of each FPGA and the estimated area of each Kahn process, we computed the reconfiguration delay of each CCU using the following equation:

$$T_{\text{Recon}} = \frac{\text{CCU\_slices}}{\text{FPGA\_slices}} \cdot \frac{\text{FPGA\_bitstream}}{\text{ICAP\_bandwidth}}, \quad (10)$$

where CCU_slices is the total number of area slices a CCU requires, FPGA_slices is the total number of slices available on a particular FPGA, FPGA_bitstream is the bitstream size in MBs of the FPGA, and ICAP_bandwidth is the ICAP configuration speed. As a final remark, we assume that there is no delay associated with the runtime mapping, such as task migration and context switching.

5. Heuristics Evaluation

In this section, we provide a detailed analysis of the experimental results and their implications for the aforementioned case study. We conducted a wide variety of experiments on the above-mentioned task mapping heuristics with the Molen architecture by considering various FPGAs of different sizes. We evaluated and compared these heuristics based on the following parameters:

(i) the execution time,

(ii) the number of reconfigurations,

(iii) the percentage of hardware/software executions,

(iv) the reusability efficiency.

The detailed description of these parameters has been provided in Section 3. In the rest of this section, we discuss the evaluation results by using these parameters in more detail.

5.1. Execution Time. Figure 4 depicts the results of running different task mapping heuristics for mapping an extended MJPEG application onto the Molen architecture with various FPGAs of different sizes. The primary *y*-axis (left) in the graph represents the application execution time measured for each heuristic. The software-only (SWonly) execution is measured when all the tasks are mapped onto the GPP. Similarly, the hardware-only (HWonly) execution is measured when all the tasks are mapped onto the FPGA. In HWonly, tasks are forced to be executed on the FPGA. However, if the task does not fit on the entire FPGA, the task is executed on the GPP. The static execution (STonly) is measured when only design time exploration is performed. In STonly execution, a fixed set of hardware tasks is considered for the FPGA mapping and this set does not change during the application runtime. For this experiment, tasks considered as fixed hardware are DCT1–DCT4 and Q1–Q4. The secondary *y*-axis (right) in Figure 4 represents the application speedup for each heuristic compared to the SWonly execution. The *x*-axis lists different types of FPGAs, which are ranked (from left to right) based on their sizes, such that XC4VFX12 has the smallest number of area slices and XC4VFX140 has the largest number of area slices (see Table 1). Several observations in terms of FPGA resources and speedup for different heuristics can be made from Figure 4.

A first observation that can be noticed from Figure 4 is that the application performance is proportional to the FPGA size to a certain degree: the bigger the available area in the FPGA, the higher the application performance. In the case of XC4VFX12, there is no significant performance gain

TABLE 2: The performance increase in different heuristics with the corresponding area increase in the FPGA. There is no linear relation between the area and the corresponding performance improvement.

Heuristics	Performance increase (%)	
	XC4VFX12 ⇒ XC4VFX20 (54% slice increase)	XC4VFX100 ⇒ XC4VFX140 (33% slice increase)
HWonly	67.9	3.14
STonly	0.69	0.007
AMAP	30	7.7
IBH	15	0.87
CBH	67	8.5
RBH	70	2.8

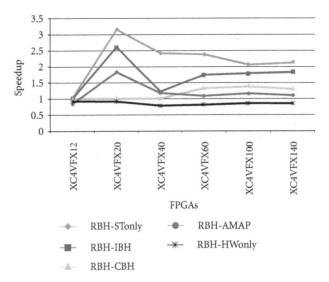

FIGURE 5: The performance increase of the RBH compared to HWonly, STonly, IBH, CBH, and AMAP. RBH performs better than AMAP under all resource conditions except XC4VFX12. RBH performs better than STonly, IBH, and CBH under all resource conditions.

by using any heuristic compared to the software execution. As there is a limited area, only few tasks can be mapped onto the FPGA; thus, performance is limited. Nevertheless, there is a notable performance improvement with the other FPGAs.

Secondly, while comparing the results of different heuristics for different FPGAs in Figure 4, we observe that there is no linear relation between the FPGA area and the corresponding performance. For instance, although XC4VFX20 has 54% more slices than XC4VFX12, the corresponding increase in the application performance is 67.9%, in the case of HWonly, as shown in Table 2. Similarly, there is 33% increase in area slices while comparing XC4VFX140 with XC4VFX100 in Table 1. Nevertheless, there is considerably lower increase in the performance in this case, as compared to the former case. The performance increase associated with the corresponding area increase in XC4VFX12 and XC4VFX20 as compared to XC4VFX100, and XC4VFX140 respectively, in case of different heuristics is reported in Table 2. The table depicts that there is no linear increase in the performance with area increase. This becomes obvious as the performance increase in an application is bounded by the degree of parallelism in that application. The use of more resources does not always guarantee a better application performance.

Another observation that can be made from Figure 4 is in terms of application performance of each heuristic. As it can be seen from the figure, STonly has the worst application performance, and HWonly has the best application performance. HWonly executes *all* tasks on the FPGA. As a result, it has approximately up to 9 times better performance than SWonly. STonly executes a fixed set of tasks on the FPGA, and mapping optimizations cannot be performed at runtime and, as a result, it has only upto 3 times better performance than SWonly. On the other hand, with runtime heuristics such as AMAP, IBH, CBH, and RBH, the task mapping is performed at runtime. When the application behavior changes due to the arrival of a sporadic application, task mapping is optimized, and better performance can be obtained in latter cases. This can be clearly seen in the figure,

where the performance of the other heuristics, such as RBH, CBH, IBH, and AMAP, are bounded by HWonly and STonly.

While comparing the application performance of RBH against the other heuristics, we observe that RBH provides the best performance. RBH outperforms IBH under all resource conditions. RBH performs similar to CBH in the case of XC4VFX12, XC4VFX20, and XC4VFX40, while it performs better than CBH for the rest of the FPGAs. Task mapping is highly influenced by the task selection criteria and the FPGA size. CBH chooses a task with the highest SW/HW latency difference and executes that task in FPGA. RBH also maps tasks based on the speedup factor, but the major difference is in the way this value is calculated. RBH calculates the speedup value at runtime taking into account the past execution history, while with CBH, the SW/HW value is calculated statically. This difference significantly influences the performance of these heuristics. The performance increase of the RBH as compared to HWonly, STonly, IBH, CBH, and AMAP is reported in Figure 5. As it can be inferred from the figure, the performance improvement of the RBH compared to AMAP shows an irregular behavior. The RBH performs 10% worse than AMAP for XC4VFX12. However, the improvement significantly increases for XC4VFX20. For XC4VFX40, the improvement suddenly decreases to 10%. The improvement is regained for XC4VFX60 and stays identical for XC4VFX100 and XC4VFX140. AMAP performs task mapping based on the area availability in an ad hoc manner, in the sense that it tries to map as many tasks as possible at once. However, the RBH performs a selective task mapping based on the task speedup and the hardware configuration reuse. When area is limited, as in the case of XC4VFX12, not many hardware configurations can be preserved in the FPGA. Thus, configuration reuse cannot

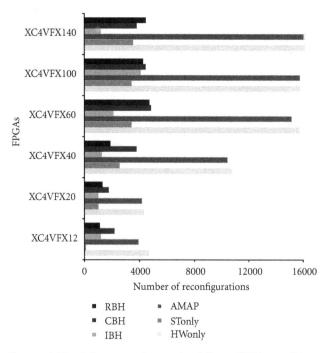

FIGURE 6: Heuristics comparison under different FPGAs conditions in terms of number of reconfigurations. There is a direct relation between the number of reconfigurations and the FPGA area.

be exploited with the RBH. As a result, AMAP performs better than RBH. With the increase in area, many hardware configurations can be preserved in the FPGA. Consequently, the RBH performs better than AMAP.

5.2. Number of Reconfigurations. Figure 6 depicts an overview of the number of reconfigurations for different heuristics, by considering different FPGAs. Several observations can be made from Figure 6 in terms of FPGA resources and the number of reconfigurations for the different heuristics. Only few tasks can be executed on the FPGA with limited area slices, contributing to the small reconfiguration counts. When the area slices increase, more tasks can be executed onto the FPGA, and, hence, reconfiguration counts increase. Nevertheless, the reconfiguration count is greatly influenced by the mapping strategies used. As it can be inferred from Figure 6, HWonly has relatively higher reconfigurations as compared to other heuristics. With HWonly, *all* tasks are executed to the FPGA, and hence, they are configured frequently. In large FPGAs, there is a possibility for CCUs to save and reuse their configurations and, hence, to avoid their reconfiguration. Therefore, reconfigurations saturate with large FPGAs. Similarly, STonly has a relatively low number of reconfigurations with small FPGAs, such as XC4VFX12 and XC4VFX20. The reconfiguration count increases in case of XC4VFX40 and XC4VFX60, and, then, it stays constant in all other cases. STonly executes a fixed set of HW tasks in all cases; since the number of HW task is constant, the reconfiguration also saturates.

We can observe from Figure 6 that AMAP has significantly higher reconfiguration counts unlike the other heuristics. AMAP performs task mapping based on the area availability in an adhoc manner, in the sense that any task can be mapped onto the FPGA. This leads to a significant increase in reconfiguration counts. It is worth noticing that the application performance in case of AMAP does not decrease drastically with the higher reconfiguration numbers. We may expect a significant performance decrease due to massive reconfigurations. The reconfiguration latency considered for a task is relatively small compared to the HW execution latency. Despite the larger number of reconfigurations, the performance can be considerably improved with the HW execution in such cases. Similarly, in the case of CBH, the reconfiguration counts are lower in smaller FPGAs due to lower hardware executions. This number increases with large FPGAs. There are no significant changes in the reconfiguration counts with the increase in area slices once sufficient area is available.

The number of reconfigurations for IBH is somewhat lower compared to the other heuristics, such as AMAP, CBH, and RBH under all FPGA conditions. This is not due to an efficient algorithm, which tries to optimize the reconfiguration delay, rather it is the effect of limited HW execution. In case of IBH, the mapping decision is changed only in the beginning of each interval, and the mapping behavior is fixed within an interval. Thus, a fixed set of tasks is mapped onto the FPGA during such an interval. This limits the hardware execution percentage, and hence, the reconfigurations. On the other hand, RBH reuses the hardware configurations to reduce the total number of reconfigurations. As a result, we observe a lower number of reconfigurations in case of RBH compared to CBH and AMAP in Figure 6. Note that IBH and STonly have lower reconfigurations than RBH as a consequence of their lower hardware execution. Nonetheless, RBH has a better reconfiguration-to-HW-execution ratio as compared to IBH and STonly, making the former better in terms of performance.

5.3. Percentage of Hardware Execution, Software Execution, and Reconfiguration. Figure 7 shows the comparison between different task mapping heuristics in terms of hardware execution, software execution and reconfiguration measured using (1), (2), and (3), respectively. The x-axis in the graph is stacked as 100%, and it shows the contribution of hardware execution, software execution, and reconfiguration to the total execution time. We observe that in few FPGAs the percentage of execution is greater than 100%. The hardware execution percentage measured in (1) is provided as an upper bound to address the parallel execution possibility of the FPGA. As a result, its value can go beyond the 100% limitation.

A first observation that can be made from Figure 7 is in terms of execution percentage and FPGA area. The limited area slices in the FPGA confines the HW execution percentage in smaller FPGAs. The hardware execution percentage increases considerably with more area slices, but this increase is not linear. As it can be seen from the figure, hardware

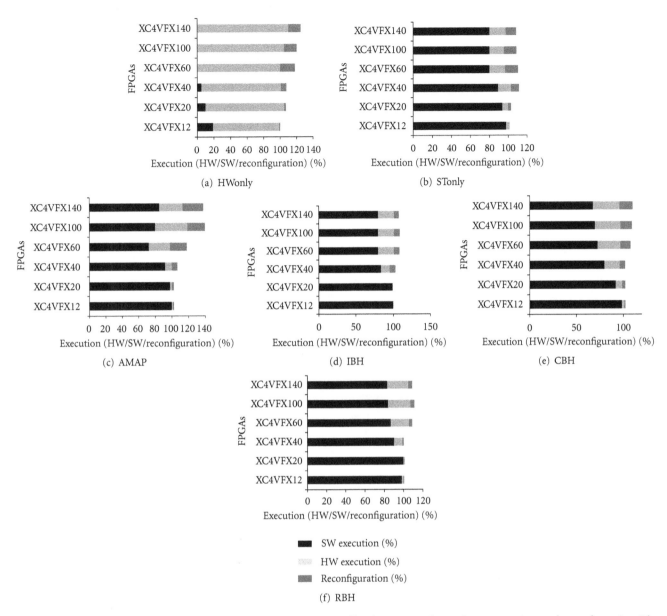

FIGURE 7: The comparison of different heuristics based on percentage of hardware execution, software execution, and reconfiguration. The hardware execution percentage is low in smaller FPGAs, and it increases considerably with more area slices.

execution percentage somewhat saturates with large FPGAs, such as XC4FX100 and XC4FX140. This observation is valid for all the runtime mapping heuristics including STonly and HWonly.

With HWonly mapping, *all* tasks are forced to be executed to the FPGA. However, if the task does not fit on the entire FPGA, then the task is executed with the GPP. Therefore, in Figure 7, we observe certain percentage of software execution with small FPGAs, but, with larger FPGA, there is only HW execution and the corresponding reconfiguration. With smaller FPGAs, almost no tasks are executed in hardware and, as a result, STonly has very minimal hardware execution (if any) and, therefore, the less reconfigurations. With the larger FPGAs, STonly has a relatively good but constant hardware execution and

reconfiguration percentage, since it executes a fixed set of tasks on the FPGA.

While comparing the runtime heuristics, such as AMAP, CBH, IBH, and RBH, we can observe that AMAP has the best hardware execution percentage in larger FPGAs, followed by RBH and CBH. CBH and RBH somehow show similar behavior in terms of hardware execution percentage. However, in case of reconfiguration percentage, they do not follow the same trend. The reconfiguration is somewhat linear to the hardware execution in case of CBH. However, RBH does not show any linear increase in reconfiguration with hardware execution. RBH performs task mapping based on configuration reuse and, as a result, tries to avoid reconfiguration with more hardware executions. This behavior of RBH heuristic is apparent in the figure, especially

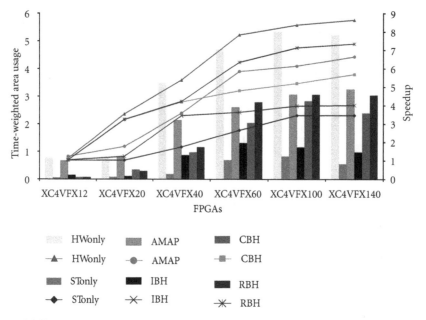

FIGURE 8: The comparison of different heuristics in terms of time-weighted area usage against speedup under different FPGAs conditions. The HWonly has the most time-weighted area usage, followed by the other runtime heuristics AMAP, CBH, IBH, and RBH.

in the case of moderate to large FPGAs, such as XC4FX60, XC4FX100, and XC4FX140. IBH follows a behavior similar to STonly in terms of software and hardware execution, as it also executes a fixed set of tasks on the FPGA.

By mapping more tasks onto the FPGA, the application can be accelerated, but it also has reconfiguration overhead. The efficiency of the mapping heuristics lies in finding the best mapping while minimizing the number of reconfigurations. Nevertheless, in Figure 7, we see almost a linear contribution of the reconfiguration overhead to the total execution time in all heuristics, except in RBH. This phenomenon is highly influenced by the policy implemented for task mapping. Another observation that can be made from the figure is the contribution of the hardware execution, SW execution, and reconfiguration to the total execution time. The figure shows that the GPP executes most of the application and the FPGA computes only less than 40% of the total application. This is due to the architectural restrictions of the Molen architecture. The GPP and the RP run in a mutual exclusive way, due to the processor/coprocessor nature of the architecture. This influences the mapping decision, which, in turn, contributes to the low hardware execution rates. This significantly increases the total execution time. Another reason for the lower percentage of hardware execution is due to the lower hardware latency for each task. The execution percentage is calculated as the ratio of execution latency of all tasks to the total execution time of an application. The hardware latency is comparatively lower than the SW latency for each task. Therefore, the corresponding hardware execution contribution is always lower compared to the percentage of SW execution.

5.4. Time-Weighted Area Usage. Figure 8 depicts an average time-weighted area usage measured using Equation (4) for

different heuristics under different FPGA devices. The primary y-axis (left) in the graph represents the time-weighted area usage measured for each heuristic. The secondary y-axis (right) in the figure represents the application speedup for each heuristic compared to the SWonly execution. Several observations can be made from Figure 8 in terms of FPGA resources and time-weighted area usage of different heuristics. The first observation that can be made from the figure is in terms of time-weighted area usage and the hardware resource. As it can be seen from the figure, the time-weighted area usage is directly impacted by the number of area slices in the FPGA. With the limited area slices in small FPGAs, few tasks are executed in the FPGA, contributing to a smaller number of hardware executions. This, in turn, contributes to the lower area usage. With sufficient area slices, there is a considerable number of hardware executions and, hence, the area usage is high. Nonetheless, there is no linear relation between the time-weighted area usage and the available FPGA area. In XC4VFX140, the area usage is relatively low compared to XC4FX100, despite the fact that area slices are greater in the former. The area usage measured is the time-weighted factor, and it depends on the hardware execution, the total FPGA area and the total execution time, as shown in Equation (4). The increase in the area slices, with no significant increase in hardware executions, contributes to the lower area usage in the former case.

As it can be inferred from Figure 8, HWonly has the highest time-weighted area usage under all FPGA conditions. HWonly executes *all* tasks onto the FPGA and, as a result, the cost of using FPGA in this case is higher than all the other heuristics. STonly, however, has the lowest area usage due to its lower number of hardware executions and, therefore, its corresponding performance is also very poor. Similarly, AMAP has higher area usage compared to other heuristics, such as CBH, IBH, and RBH, under all FPGA conditions, except XC4VFX60. AMAP performs task mapping based on area availability. As a matter of fact, it has a relatively higher number of hardware executions compared to the other heuristics and, therefore, it consumes additional area. RBH, on the other hand, has less time-weighted area usage. While comparing AMAP and RBH, we can observe that RBH performs somewhat better than AMAP in terms of performance. This implies that RBH reuses the hardware configuration already present in the FPGA to avoid reconfiguration overhead and, as a result, it can give better performance with the same amount of hardware resources as required by AMAP. Likewise, CBH has a comparable percentage of time-weighted area usage, but it lags behind in terms of speedup as compared to RBH. However, IBH has a considerably low percentage of area usage, as it also has lower hardware executions due to the constantly executed HW task set, and hence it also has lower performance. We can summarize that HWonly has the best performance but consumes more hardware resources. STonly has the lowest area usage but straggles behind in terms of performance. A tradeoff in terms of performance and resources can be obtained with task mapping at runtime, which performs selective task mapping onto the FPGA at runtime.

Another compelling observation that can be made from Figure 8 is about the lower value of the time-weighted area usage. The Molen architecture is based on processor/coprocessor paradigm. As a result, the GPP and the RP run in a mutual exclusive. This contributes to the lower number of hardware executions, which consequently increases the total execution time. Thus, these two factors significantly contribute to the low value of area usage. The area usage can be increased either by mapping more tasks onto the FPGA or by operating the RP and the GPP in parallel.

5.5. Reusability Efficiency. Figure 9 depicts the reusability efficiency (RE_{Task}) recorded for all CCUs using Equation (5) for different heuristics under different FPGA conditions. Several observations can be made from the figure in terms of FPGA area and the RE_{Task} of each CCU. Firstly, we observe that the CCU reuse is significantly affected by the number of area slices in the FPGA. Small FPGAs, such as XC4VFX12 and XC4VFX20, have many CCUs with RE_{Task} value zero. A CCU has an RE_{Task} value of zero under the following conditions:

(i) when a CCU is always mapped onto the GPP

(ii) when a CCU is configured every time it is executed on the FPGA.

With few resources in the FPGA, only a limited number of tasks can be executed to the FPGA. Additionally, in such cases, hardware configurations cannot be preserved for future reuse. As a result, CCUs have an RE_{Task} value of zero. Moreover, in this case, CCUs that are reused have a very small size in terms of area. With the increase in number of slices in the FPGA, more CCUs are reused. Medium-sized FPGAs, such as XC4VFX40 and XC4VFX60, reuse more CCUs compared to smaller FPGAs, but, in such cases, the reuse percentage is still low. With the larger FPGAs such as XC4VFX100 and XC4VFX140, more CCUs are reused with large RE_{Task} value.

As it can be inferred from Figure 9, HWonly has the best RE_{Task} for many CCUs in large FPGAs, such as XC4VFX100 and XC4VFX140. HWonly executes all the tasks on the FPGA and, as a result, it has high hardware execution count. However, with small FPGAs, all the tasks are configured, due to area restrictions, and there is no configuration reuse. On the other hand, with larger FPGAs, more configurations are saved and reused and, as a consequence, many CCUs have a considerably high RE_{Task} value. Similarly, STonly always maps a set of fixed tasks onto the FPGA. Out of these tasks, only a few number of small tasks can be reused. We notice that these CCUs have a relatively higher RE value compared to the ones reused with the AMAP heuristic in the figure. AMAP has higher HW execution percentage as compared to IBH and CBH. As a matter of fact, many tasks are reused in case of AMAP, but the reuse percentage of these CCUs is low. AMAP has no fixed pattern for task execution and, as a result, any task can be executed in FPGA. Therefore, the reusability is rather distributed among many CCUs. CBH, on the other hand, follows a specific policy for task execution in FPGA and hence executes a fixed set of selected task. As a result, a set of selected tasks is reused. Similar behavior is observed in the case of CBH. As it also executes a set of specific task within an interval, same tasks are reused (if any).

Likewise, from Figure 9, we observe that the RE_{Task} of RBH is better than that of other runtime heuristics for many CCUs. The impact of this hardware configuration reuse, in case of RBH, can be directly seen in terms of performance gain in Figure 4, where RBH has better speedup than the other heuristics. From Figure 10, we also observe that, for few tasks, RE_{Task} decreases when FPGA resources increase. With larger FPGAs, more tasks can fit onto the FPGA. As a result, these tasks are also mapped onto the FPGA, thus, over writing the saved configurations of other tasks. RE_{Task} for few tasks decreases in the FPGAs with moderate size. With the abundant resources, the hardware configuration can be saved for more tasks, and RE_{Task} increases again.

Note that STonly, AMAP, CBH, and IBH do not map the task based on the hardware configuration reuse. The reuse obtained in the case of STonly, AMAP, CBH, and IBH is a default value determined based on the arrival of the application task. If a CCU is already configured on the FPGA when its corresponding task arrives, the task can be executed without reconfiguration. However, the RBH reuses more hardware configurations than the other heuristics on top of the default value obtained.

Figure 10 depicts the total RE_{app} recorded using Equation (6) for different heuristics under different resource conditions. In the figure, we again observe that the reusability increases when using larger FPGAs. HWonly executes *all* the tasks in FPGA and, therefore, there can be a possibility that many of these tasks are reused when sufficient area is available, resulting into higher RE_{app}. STonly has almost a constant RE_{app} in larger FPGA, since it executes a constant set of tasks in FPGA. While comparing runtime heuristics, such as AMAP, CBH, IBH, and RBH, we can observe that

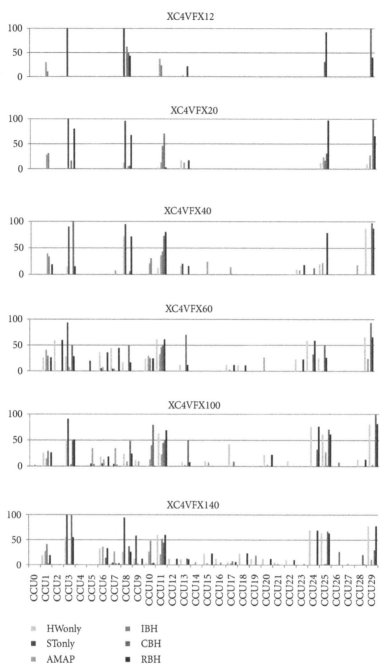

FIGURE 9: Reusability efficiency (RE_{Task}) of CCUs for different heuristics under different FPGA conditions. The CCU reuse is significantly affected by the number of area slices in the FPGA.

since the RBH has more CCUs reused than other heuristics, as shown in Figure 7(f), RBH has a better RE_{app} value than other heuristics in all resource conditions but XC4VFX12. Since XC4VFX12 has less area, all the heuristics have approximately the same value for RE_{app}. RE_{app} is the accumulation of the time saved due to hardware configuration reuse of each CCU. If all CCUs obtain the same value of the RE for a task mapping heuristic, then the application RE_{app} depends on the corresponding total execution time of that heuristics.

6. Observations and Conclusions

In this paper, we evaluated the task mapping of application(s) onto reconfigurable architectures under different resource conditions. We thoroughly evaluated various task mapping heuristics from the state of the art with the rSesame framework for a reconfigurable architecture with different FPGA resources using an extended MJPEG application. Based on the evaluation discussed in the previous sections, we can summarize the following conclusions.

    (i) The comparison of different FPGAs shows that with very limited resources (in case of small FPGAs), the

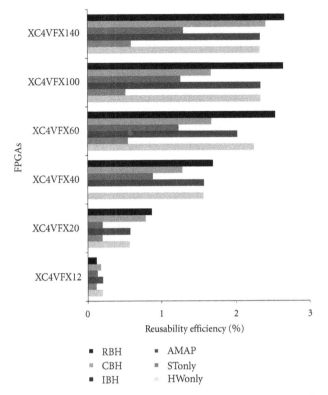

FIGURE 10: Heuristics comparison under different FPGAs conditions in terms of application reusability efficiency (RE$_{app}$). RBH has better RE$_{app}$ compared to other heuristics.

number of tasks that can be mapped onto the FPGA is low. Consequently, these tasks are mapped onto the GPP. This leads to a poor application performance.

(ii) More resources (in case of moderate/higher FPGAs) imply more tasks mapped onto the FPGA. Consequently, we can obtain better application performance.

(iii) Runtime mapping provides better performance in case of dynamic application/architecture conditions. If the application behavior is well known in advance, design time mapping can give equal performance.

(iv) Mapping all the tasks onto the FPGA gives better performance, but it consumes more hardware resources. Runtime mapping performs task mapping based on the runtime system conditions. As a matter of fact, with the runtime mapping, a tradeoff can be obtained in terms of performance and resources.

(v) Comparing different heuristics, in case of limited resources conditions (small FPGAs), the adhoc task mapping of AMAP performs better compared to CBH, IBH, and RBH. Due to limited resources, the careful task selection with RBH, CHB, and IBH cannot be fully exploited in such cases.

(vi) The reuse of hardware configurations is better in case of sufficient resource conditions (medium-to-large FPGAs). As a result, the configuration reuse can be

well exploited. Additionally, the RBH provides better application performance than AMAP and CBH.

(vii) In case of abundant resource conditions (very large FPGAs), the performance saturates due to application constraints. Under such scenarios, all the heuristics have similar performances.

Acknowledgments

This research is partially supported by Artemisia iFEST Project (Grant 100203), Artemisia SMECY (Grant 100230), FP7 Reflect (Grant 248976).

References

[1] K. Compton and S. Hauck, "Reconfigurable computing: a survey of systems and software," *ACM Computing Surveys*, vol. 34, no. 2, pp. 171–210, 2002.

[2] T. J. Todman, G. A. Constantinides, S. J. E. Wilton, O. Mencer, W. Luk, and P. Y. K. Cheung, "Reconfigurable computing: architectures and design methods," *IEE Proceedings—Computers and Digital Techniques*, vol. 152, no. 2, pp. 193–207.

[3] S. Hauck, "The roles of FPGA's in reprogrammable systems," *Proceedings of the IEEE*, vol. 86, no. 4, pp. 615–638, 1998.

[4] R. J. F. Stephen, D. Brown, and J. Rose, *Field-Programmable Gate Arrays*, vol. 180 of *The Springer International Series in Engineering and Computer Science*, Kluwer Academic Publishers, 1992.

[5] Xilinx Corporation, *Coolrunner-II CPLDs Family Overview*, September 2008.

[6] R. W. Hartenstein and R. Kress, "A datapath synthesis system for thereconfigurable datapath architecture," in *Proceedings of the Asia andSouth Pacific Design Automation Conference (ASP-DAC '95)*, pp. 479–484, September 1995.

[7] S. Vassiliadis and D. Soudris, *Fine- and Coarse-Grain Reconfigurable Computing*, vol. 16, Springer, Berlin, Germany, 2007.

[8] N. S. Voros and and K. Masselos, *System-Level Design of Reconfigurable Systems-on-Chip*, Springer, Berlin, Germany, 1st edition, 2005.

[9] K. Sigdel, M. Thompson, C. Galuzzi, A. D. Pimentel, and K. Bertels, "rSesame —a generic system-level runtime simulation framework for reconfigurable architectures," in *Proceedings of the International Conference on Field-Programmable Technology (FPT '09)*, pp. 460–464, 2009.

[10] K. Sigdel, M. Thompson, C. Galuzzi, A. D. Pimentel, and K. Bertels, "Evaluation of runtime task mapping heuristics with rSesame—a case study," in *Proceedings of the Design, Automation and Test in Europe Conference and Exhibition (DATE '10)*, pp. 831–836, deu, March 2010.

[11] K. Sigdel, C. Galuzzi, K. Bertels, M. Thompson, and A. D. Pimentel, "Runtime task mapping based on hardware configuration reuse," in *Proceedingsof the International Conference on Reconfigurable Computing and FPGAs (ReConFig '10)*, pp. 25–30, 2010.

[12] P. V. Knudsen and J. Madsen, "PACE: a dynamic programming algorithm for hardware/software partitioning," in *Proceedings of the 4th International Workshop on Hardware/Software Co-Design (Codes/CASHE '96)*, pp. 85–92, March 1996.

[13] M. Kaul and R. Vemuri, "Design-space exploration for block-processing based temporal partitioning of run-time reconfigurable systems," *Journal of VLSI Signal Processing Systems for*

Signal, Image, and Video Technology, vol. 24, no. 2, pp. 181–209, 2000.

[14] B. Miramond and J. M. Delosme, "Design space exploration for dynamically reconfigurable architectures," in *Proceedings of the Design, Automation and Test in Europe (DATE '05)*, pp. 366–371, March 2005.

[15] B. Miramond and J. M. Delosme, "Decision guide environment for design space exploration," in *Proceedings of the 10th IEEE International Conference on Emerging Technologies and Factory Automation (ETFA '05)*, pp. 881–888, September 2005.

[16] L. Y. Li and M. Shi, "Software-hardware partitioning strategy using hybrid genetic and Tabu search," in *Proceedings of the International Conference on Computer Science and Software Engineering (CSSE '08)*, vol. 4, pp. 83–86, 2008.

[17] B. Mei, P. Schaumont, and S. Vernalde, "A hardware-software partitioning and scheduling algorithm for dynamically reconfigurable embedded systems," in *Proceedings of the Annual Workshop on Circuits, Systemsand Signal Processing (ProRISC '00)*, pp. 1–8, November 2000.

[18] C. Haubelt, S. Otto, C. Grabbe, and J. Teich, "A system-level approachto hardware reconfigurable systems," in *Proceedings of the Asia and South Pacific Design Automation Conference (ASP-DAC '05)*, pp. 298–301, 2005.

[19] G. Wang, W. Gong, and R. Kastner, "Application partitioning on programmable platforms using the ant colony optimization," *Embedded Computing*, vol. 2, no. 1, pp. 119–136, 2006.

[20] G. Still, R. Lysecky, and F. Vahid, "Dynamic hardware/software partitioning: a first approach," in *Proceedings of the Design AutomationConference (DAC '03)*, 2003.

[21] V. Nollet, P. Avasare, H. Eeckhaut, D. Verkest, and H. Corporaal, "Run-time management of a MPSoC containing FPGA fabric tiles," *IEEE Transactions on Very Large Scale Integration (VLSI) Systems*, vol. 16, no. 1, pp. 24–33, 2008.

[22] C. Huang and F. Vahid, "Dynamic coprocessor management for FPGA-enhanced compute platforms," in *Proceedings of the International Conference on Compilers, Architecture and Synthesis for Embedded Systems (CASES '08)*, pp. 71–78, 2008.

[23] W. Fu and K. Compton, "An execution environment for reconfigurable computing," in *Proceedings of the 13th Annual IEEE Symposium on Field-Programmable Custom Computing Machines (FCCM '05)*, pp. 149–158, April 2005.

[24] F. Ghaffari, M. Auguin, M. Abid, and M. B. Jemaa, "Dynamic and on-line design space exploration for reconfigurable architectures," *Transactions on High-Performance Embedded Architectures and Compilers*, vol. 4050, pp. 179–193, 2007.

[25] A. Kumar, B. Mesman, B. Theelen, H. Corporaal, and H. Yajun, "Resource manager for non-preemptive heterogeneous multiprocessor system-on-chip," in *Proceedings of the IEEE/ACM/IFIP Workshop on Embedded Systems for Real Time Multimedia (ESTIMEDIA '06)*, pp. 33–38, October 2006.

[26] O. Moreira, J. J. D. Mol, and M. Bekooij, "Online resource management in a multiprocessor with a network-on-chip," in *Proceedings of the ACM Symposium on Applied Computing (SAC '07)*, pp. 1557–1564, March 2007.

[27] L. T. Smit, J. L. Hurink, and G. J. M. Smit, "Run-time mapping of applications to a heterogeneous SoC," in *Proceedings of the International Symposium on System-on-Chip (SoC '05)*, pp. 78–81, November 2005.

[28] L. T. Smit, G. J. M. Smit, J. L. Hurink, H. Broersma, D. Paulusma, and P. T. Wolkotte, "Run-time mapping of applications to a heterogeneous reconfigurable tiled system on chip architecture," in *Proceedings of the IEEE International Conference on Field-Programmable Technology (FPT '04)*, pp.

421–424, December 2004.

[29] P. K. F. Hölzenspies, G. J. M. Smit, and J. Kuper, "Mapping streaming applications on a reconfigurable MPSoC platform at run-time," in *Proceedings of the International Symposium on System-on-Chip (SOC '07)*, pp. 74–77, November 2007.

[30] M. A. A. Faruque, R. Krist, and J. Henkel, "ADAM: run-time agent-based distributed application mapping for on-chip communication," in *Proceedings of the 45th Design Automation Conference (DAC '08)*, pp. 760–765, June 2008.

[31] C. Ykman-Couvreur, E. Brockmeyer, V. Nollet, T. Marescaux, F. Catthoor, and H. Corporaal, "Design-time application exploration for MPSoC customized runtime management," in *Proceesings of InternationalSymposium on System-on-Chip (SOC '05)*, pp. 66–69, 2005.

[32] A. D. Pimentel, C. Erbas, and S. Polstra, "A systematic approach to exploring embedded system architectures at multiple abstraction levels," *IEEE Transactions on Computers*, vol. 55, no. 2, pp. 99–111, 2006.

[33] G. Kahn, "The semantics of a simple language for parallel programming," in *Proceedings of the IFIP Congress*, vol. 74, 1974.

[34] S. Vassiliadis, S. Wong, G. N. Gaydadjiev, K. L. M. Bertels, G. Kuzmanov, and E. M. Panainte, "The MOLEN polymorphic processor," *IEEE Transactions on Computers*, vol. 53, no. 11, pp. 1363–1375, 2004.

[35] S. Vassiliadis, G. N. Gaydadjiev, K. Bertels, and E. M. Panainte, "The Molen programming paradigm," in *Proceeding of the International workshopon Systems, Architectures, Modeling and Simulation (SAMOS '03)*, pp. 1–30, July 2003.

[36] Xilinx Corporation, "Virtex-4 family overview (V3.0)".

[37] Xilinx DS86, "LogiCORE IP XPS HWICAP (v5.00a)," 2010.

[38] H. Nikolov, M. Thompson, T. Stefanov et al., "Daedalus: toward composable multimedia MPSoC design," in *Proceedings of the 45th annual Design Automation Conference (DAC '08)*, pp. 574–579, 2008.

[39] A. D. Pimentel, M. Thompson, S. Polstra, and C. Erbas, "Calibration of abstract performance models for system-level design space exploration," *Journal of Signal Processing Systems*, vol. 50, no. 2, pp. 99–114, 2008.

[40] R. Meeuws, Y. Yankova, K. Bertels, G. Gaydadjiev, and S. Vassiliadis, "A quantitative prediction model for hardware/software partitioning," in *Proceedings of the International Conference on Field Programmable Logic and Applications (FPL '07)*, pp. 735–739, August 2007.

15

Configurable Transmitter and Systolic Channel Estimator Architectures for Data-Dependent Superimposed Training Communications Systems

E. Romero-Aguirre,[1] R. Parra-Michel,[1] Roberto Carrasco-Alvarez,[2] and A. G. Orozco-Lugo[3]

[1] *Department of Electrical Engineering, CINVESTAV-GDL, 45019 Zapopan, JAL, Mexico*
[2] *Department of Electronic Engineering, UDG-CUCEI, 44430 Guadalajara, JAL, Mexico*
[3] *Department of Electrical Engineering, CINVESTAV-DF, 07630 Mexico City, DF, Mexico*

Correspondence should be addressed to E. Romero-Aguirre, eromero@gdl.cinvestav.mx

Academic Editor: René Cumplido

In this paper, a configurable superimposed training (ST)/data-dependent ST (DDST) transmitter and architecture based on array processors (APs) for DDST channel estimation are presented. Both architectures, designed under full-hardware paradigm, were described using Verilog HDL, targeted in Xilinx Virtex-5 and they were compared with existent approaches. The synthesis results showed a FPGA slice consumption of 1% for the transmitter and 3% for the estimator with 160 and 115 MHz operating frequencies, respectively. The signal-to-quantization-noise ratio (SQNR) performance of the transmitter is about 82 dB to support 4/16/64-QAM modulation. A Monte Carlo simulation demonstrates that the mean square error (MSE) of the channel estimator implemented in hardware is practically the same as the one obtained with the floating-point golden model. The high performance and reduced hardware of the proposed architectures lead to the conclusion that the DDST concept can be applied in current communications standards.

1. Introduction

Presently, there is need to develop communications systems capable of transmitting/receiving various types of information (data, voice, video, etc.) at high speed. Nevertheless, designing these systems is always an extremely difficult task, and, therefore, the system must be broken down into several stages each with a specific task. The complexity of each stage is higher when the system operates in a wireless environment because the additional challenges that should be facing due to the complex nature of the channel and its susceptibility to several types of interference.

As it is not possible to avoid the influence of the channel on a transmitted data sent through it, an option is to characterize the channel parameters with enough precision so that their effects can be reverted in the receiver. For that reason, channel estimation stage is a key part of any reliable wireless system because a correct channel estimation leads to a reduction of the bit error rate (BER). The channel estimator must deal with multiple phenomenas, such as multipath propagation and frequency Doppler (due to the mobility of the users). In order to deal with these problems, current communication standards specify the transmission of pilot signals which are known in the receiver, allowing an ease estimation of the communication channel. The way of transmitting such pilot signals can be classified in to two major branches: pilot-assisted transmission (PAT)—where pilot and data signals are multiplexed in time, frequency, code, space, or in a combination of the mentioned domains—and implicit training (IT), a technique proposed recently where the pilot signal is hidden in the data transmitted. PAT is the technique implemented in actual standards, such as WiMAX, WiFi, and Bluetooth. It presents the advantage that pilots and data relies on orthogonal subspaces allowing a simple separation of them in the receiver; however, it is necessary to decrease the available bandwidth for data in order to transmit the pilot signal. On the other hand, IT overcomes this problem because all the time, data and pilot signal are transmitted;

nevertheless, it leads to a transmission of such signals into nonorthogonal subspaces. Despite the aforementioned, IT has been recognized as a feasible alternative for future communication standards [1].

The simplest form to carry out IT is to add (superimpose) the pilot signal to the data. This approach is known as superimposed training (ST), first proposed in [2] and enhanced by diverse authors whose results are summarized in [3, Ch. 6]. In [4–8] was presented a refinement of ST known as data-dependent superimpose training (DDST), this technique makes it possible to null the interference of data during the estimation process via the addition of a new training sequence, which depends on the transmitted data, together with the data and the ST sequence.

Because of the benefits that ST/DDST offer, it is necessary to develop efficient implementations of these algorithms. Although these techniques have been widely studied, to this point, there exist few reported practical implementations in the literature. In fact, almost all of them are approximations based on floating point and software. In [9], the algorithms are programmed in a digital signal processor (DSP) for a low-rate communication system, while in [10] the proposed implementation is developed into an embedded microprocessor with hardware accelerators inside of a FPGA. At ReConFig 2011, we have presented a full-hardware architecture—with high throughput, low hardware consumption, and high degree of reusability—for the channel estimation stage of an ST/DDST receiver [11]. Its novelty consisted in that a systolic array processors (AP) was used for performing the entire estimation process instead of two separated signal processing modules. In this paper, we present a extended version of that paper, where a hardware-efficient architecture for configurable ST/DDST transmitter that supports 4/16/64-QAM constellations is used to complement the results presented in [11], because now, all transmitted data—in each Monte Carlo trial—are generated by the proposed transmitter hardware instead of the transmitter simulation model programmed in Matlab.

The rest of the paper is organized as follows. Section 2 presents the system model being considered, the ST/DDST transmitter structure, the channel estimation algorithm, and the cyclic mean reformulation onto systolic APs. Section 3 describes in detail the full-hardware architectures for the configurable ST/DDST transmitter. Section 4 proposes an architecture based on SA processor for the DDST channel estimator. In Section 5, the performance evaluation of the proposed architectures is carried out. Conclusions are set down in Section 6.

Notation 1. Lowercase (uppercase) bold letters denote column vectors (matrices). Operators $(\mathbf{A})^H$, $(\mathbf{A})^T$, and $(\mathbf{A})^{-1}$, denote the Hermitian, transpose, and inverse operations of matrix $\mathbf{A}$. $\mathbf{1}_n$ represents a column vector of length n with all its elements equal to one; similarly, $\mathbf{0}_n$ represents an all-zeros column vector of length n. $\mathbf{I}_n$ is the identity matrix of size $n \times n$. $[\mathbf{a}]_k$ denotes the kth element of vector $\mathbf{a}$. $[\mathbf{a}]_{m:n}$ denotes a vector conformed with the elements of $\mathbf{a}$ as follows: $[[\mathbf{a}]_m, [\mathbf{a}]_{m+1}, \ldots, [\mathbf{a}]_n]^T$. $\otimes$ represents Kronecker product. Finally, $E(\cdot)$ represents the expectation operator.

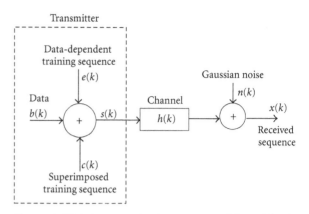

FIGURE 1: Digital communication system model considered.

2. System Model

This section is devoted to introduce the DDST algorithm mentioned previously. Suppose a single carrier, baseband communication system based on DDST as the one presented in Figure 1. The transmitted signal $x(k)$ conformed to the sum of the data sequence $b(k)$, the training sequence $c(k)$ and the data-dependent training sequence $e(k)$. The index k helps to enumerate the samples of such signals which are transmitted at a rate equal to $1/T$. $c(k)$, is a periodic sequence with period equal to P and power equal to σ_c^2 [12]. It is assumed that the data sequence is a zero-mean, stationary stochastic process with power equal to σ_b^2, where the symbols of such process come from a equiprobable alphabet. The sequence $e(k)$ is constructed as mentioned in [5]. $s(k)$ is propagated through the communication channel $h(k)$ whose time impulse response conformed to the convolution of the system filters and the propagation medium impulse responses (all of them assumed to be time-invariant). Such channel can be modeled as a finite impulse response (FIR) filter with L time-invariant coefficients as much. Finally, the distorted signal by the channel is contaminated with the noise $n(k)$ for conforming the received signal $x(k)$. $n(k)$ is a zero-mean white Gaussian noise, which possess variance equal to σ_n^2. The transmission of blocks of N symbols, which is preceded by a cyclic prefix of length $CP \geq L$ is assumed. Perfect block synchronization, which allows to fix $P = L$ it is also assumed. For ease of implementation, it is assumed that N is a multiple of P and P is a power of two.

Thus, the received signal after removing the cyclic prefix can be expressed in a matrix form as follows:

$$\mathbf{x} = \mathbf{H}(\mathbf{b} + \mathbf{c} + \mathbf{e}) + \mathbf{n}, \tag{1}$$

where $\mathbf{H}$ is a circulant matrix whose first row is given by $[\mathbf{h}^T, \mathbf{0}_{N-L}^T]$, where $\mathbf{h}$ is a vector containing the coefficients of the channel impulse response (CIR). Similarly, $\mathbf{x}$, $\mathbf{b}$, $\mathbf{c}$, $\mathbf{e}$, and $\mathbf{n}$ are vectors equal to $[\mathbf{x}]_k = x(k)$, $[\mathbf{b}]_k = b(k)$, $[\mathbf{c}]_k = c(k)$, $[\mathbf{e}]_k = e(k)$, and $[\mathbf{n}]_k = n(k)$, respectively, with $0 \leq k \leq N - 1$.

2.1. Digital Transmitter with ST/DDST Included. Figure 2 depicts the discrete-time baseband block diagram of the

Configurable Transmitter and Systolic Channel Estimator Architectures for Data-Dependent Superimposed Training
Communications Systems

183

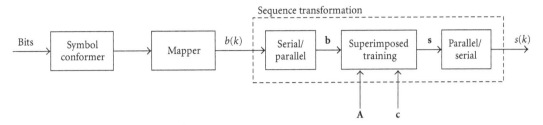

FIGURE 2: Block diagram of the digital baseband (data-dependent) superimposed training transmitter.

(data-dependent) superimposed training transmitter. This is a modified version of the IT transmitter presented in [3]. From Figure 2, it can be noted that the key component of the transmitter is the sequence transformation block. It serves to implicitly embed the training sequences onto data sequence **b** by the affine transformation expressed as

$$s = Ab + c, \tag{2}$$

where **s** represent the complex baseband discrete-time transmitted signal, **A** is a precoding matrix, and **c** refers to vector obtained by replicating N_P times one period of the training signal c_{OCI} of size P, that is,

$$c = 1_{N_P} \otimes c_{OCI}, \tag{3}$$

where $N_P = N/P$, $[c_{OCI}]_n = c_{OCI}(n)$ and such sequence is given by [12]:

$$c_{OCI}(n) = \sigma_c e^{j(\pi/P)(n(n+v))} \tag{4}$$

with $v = 1$ when P is odd, $v = 2$ if P is even, and $n = 0, \ldots, P - 1$.

The precoding matrix allows to modify the training technique according to

$$\text{Training} = \begin{cases} A = I_N, & c \neq 0 \text{ for ST,} \\ A = I_N - G, & c \neq 0 \text{ for DDST} \end{cases} \tag{5}$$

with

$$G = \frac{1}{N_p}(1_{N_P \times 1} \otimes K), \tag{6a}$$

$$K = 1_{1 \times N_P} \otimes I_P, \tag{6b}$$

where **G** and **K** are matrices of sizes $N \times N$ and $P \times N$, respectively.

In the DDST case, the N-length vector **e** containing the data-dependent sequence (DDS) can be obtained from (2) and using (5)–(6b) as follows:

$$e = Gb. \tag{7}$$

2.2. Channel Estimation Using DDST. It is possible to observe that due to the periodicity of $c(k)$, $s(k)$ will have a periodic signal embedded with a period equal to P. Taking advantage of this characteristic, an estimated of the cyclic mean of the received signal is utilized for performing the

estimate of the channel. Such cyclic mean estimator can be defined as:

$$y = Jx, \tag{8}$$

where **y** is a column vector of length P whose elements are the estimated coefficients of the cyclic mean of **x** and **J** given by

$$J = \frac{1}{N_P}\left(1_{N_P}^T \otimes I_P\right). \tag{9}$$

According to [4], the estimation of the CIR is given by

$$\hat{h} = \Gamma y, \tag{10}$$

where $\hat{h}$ is a vector containing the estimated CIR coefficients, Γ is a matrix formed by the first L rows of C^{-1}, and C is a circulant matrix of size $P \times P$ formed by vector $[c(0), c(1), \ldots, c(P-1)]^T$.

2.3. Cyclic Mean Algorithm Using Array Processors and Partitioning. The next analysis describes how the cyclic mean is obtained using a systolic array that computes a matrix-vector multiplication (MVM). Consider (8), where it is not possible to perform directly the MVM operation due to the Kronecker product involved. To avoid this cumbersome operator, the same equation can be reformulated as follows:

$$y = \frac{1}{N_P}(\aleph 1_{N_P}), \tag{11}$$

where $\aleph$ is a matrix of size $P \times N_P$ which is defined as follows:

$$\aleph = \begin{bmatrix} [x]_0 & [x]_P & [x]_{2P} & \cdots & [x]_{(N_P-1)P} \\ [x]_1 & [x]_{P+1} & [x]_{2P+1} & \cdots & [x]_{(N_P-1)P+1} \\ [x]_2 & [x]_{P+2} & [x]_{2P+2} & \cdots & [x]_{(N_P-1)P+2} \\ \vdots & \vdots & \vdots & & \vdots \\ [x]_{P-1} & [x]_{2P-1} & [x]_{3P-1} & \cdots & [x]_{N_PP-1} \end{bmatrix}. \tag{12}$$

An architecture based on AP for computing (11) would be impractical from the point of view of hardware consumption because it will need N_P processor elements (PEs). This problem is known as *problem-size-dependent array* where the algorithm requires a systolic AP whose size depends on the complexity of the problem to be solved. However, it is possible to map the cyclic mean algorithm to a systolic AP of a smaller size using the partitioning method [13, Ch. 12]. Considers $\aleph$ to be partitioned in blocks of size chosen to match a systolic array size P then (12) becomes

$$\aleph = \left[\mathbf{B}_0 \mid \mathbf{B}_1 \mid \cdots \mid \mathbf{B}_{(N_P/P)-1}\right], \qquad (13)$$

where

$$\mathbf{B}_i = \begin{bmatrix} [\mathbf{x}]_{iP^2} & [\mathbf{x}]_{iP^2+P} & \cdots & [\mathbf{x}]_{iP^2+(P-1)P} \\ [\mathbf{x}]_{iP^2+1} & [\mathbf{x}]_{iP^2+P+1} & \cdots & [\mathbf{x}]_{iP^2+(P-1)P+1} \\ [\mathbf{x}]_{iP^2+2} & [\mathbf{x}]_{iP^2+P+2} & \cdots & [\mathbf{x}]_{iP^2+(P-1)P+2} \\ \vdots & \vdots & & \vdots \\ [\mathbf{x}]_{iP^2+P-1} & [\mathbf{x}]_{iP^2+2P-1} & \cdots & [\mathbf{x}]_{iP^2+P^2-1} \end{bmatrix}, \qquad (14)$$

$$\text{for } i = 0, \ldots, \frac{N_P}{P} - 1.$$

In similar way, $\mathbf{1}_{N_P}$ is partitioned in N_P/P unitary vectors $\mathbf{1}_P$. Substituting (13) in (11), the cyclic mean with *partitioning* is concisely expressed as

$$\mathbf{y} = \frac{1}{N_P}\left(\mathbf{B}_0\mathbf{1}_P + \mathbf{B}_1\mathbf{1}_P + \cdots + \mathbf{B}_{N_P/P-1}\mathbf{1}_P\right). \qquad (15)$$

Therefore, the array of PEs will process one pair of $\mathbf{B}$ and $\mathbf{1}_P$ blocks after another in a sequential manner together with partial results.

3. A Configurable ST/DDST Transmitter Architecture

Considering the explained in Section 2.1, the architecture shown in Figure 3 is proposed for the transmitter. It is composed of the five hardware modules: the symbol adecuator, the mapper, the data sequence transformer, the Tx_control, and the Tx_AGU. The reconfigurability feature of the architecture allows to switch between two operating modes: ST or DDST, in order to send data blocks with a cyclic prefix attached. In both modes, the transmitter hardware supports 4/16/64-QAM constellations.

In the next subsections, additional details about the main transmitter modules will be described.

3.1. Symbol Adecuator. The design of this module is widely conditioned by the features of the mapper. By early account, a key aspect exploited in the mapper design, it consists of the fact that the 4-QAM and 16-QAM constellations are contained in Grey-coded 64-QAM one, as shown in Figure 4. For that reason, the symbol adecuator is necessary because not all the same point-numbers in the three constellations are mapped to the same complex symbol output. For example, while the point number 2 of the 4-QAM constellation is mapped to $-1 + j$ symbol, 16-QAM will map this point number to $3 - 3j$ and 64-QAM will map to $3 + 5j$.

3.2. Mapper. As stated in Section 3.1, in the mapper design is only required the 64-QAM constellation. In this work,

a memory-efficient scheme is proposed to build that constellation, whose eight possible values $(1, 3, 5, 7, -1, -3, -5,$ and $-7)$ of the I and Q axes are stored in the *constellation LUT*. Additionally, the mapper has to normalize the complex symbols based on two criteria: the constellation order and power assigned to each of the sequences involved. Thus, a normalization constant *Norm_Mapp_Cte* that combines the two criteria is given by

$$Norm\_Mapp\_Cte = \sigma_b \times Norm\_QAM\_Cte, \qquad (16)$$

where

$$Norm\_QAM\_Cte = \begin{cases} \dfrac{1}{\sqrt{2}}, & \text{for 4-}QAM, \\[2mm] \dfrac{1}{\sqrt{10}}, & \text{for 16-}QAM, \\[2mm] \dfrac{1}{\sqrt{42}}, & \text{for 64-}QAM, \end{cases} \qquad (17)$$

with

$$\sigma_b^2 + \sigma_c^2 = 1 \quad \text{for ST}, \qquad (18a)$$

$$\sigma_{b+e}^2 + \sigma_c^2 = 1 \quad \text{for DDST}. \qquad (18b)$$

The mapper architecture designed is depicted in Figure 5. The *constellation LUT* was implemented with a dual-port ROM with eight memory locations, depth. On the contrary, in the *normalization LUT*, the ROM depth was 16 locations.

3.3. Data Sequence Transformer. The data sequence transformer is the greater complexity module of the transmitter. Thus, its design was broken down into three submodules, whose individual architectures are described in the following paragraphs.

3.3.1. Training Sequence Generator. Analyzing (4), it can be noticed that the parameters σ_c^2, N, and P, needed to generate the training sequence, are known in advance and they remain constants during the transmitter operating. Hence, the P values of the training sequence can be calculated off-line, quantized, and stored in an LUT. This LUT is read N_P times in order to expand the training sequence length, as indicated in (3), and it can be superimposed, element by element, with the data sequence by the complex adder.

3.3.2. ST Cyclic Prefix Insertion Submodule. There are several problems to arise because of the way in which the prefix cyclic is generated and its position where it is attached in the ST sequence.

  (i) Since the prefix cyclic conformed to the last P data of the sequence ST, it can only be generated from this sequence until it has been completely processed.

  (ii) Given that, in all the $N + P$ data to be transmitted, the first P data correspond to the cyclic prefix, it is necessary to use a memory buffer in order to store the remaining N data (ST sequence) and, thus, prevent data loss.

Configurable Transmitter and Systolic Channel Estimator Architectures for Data-Dependent Superimposed Training Communications Systems

185

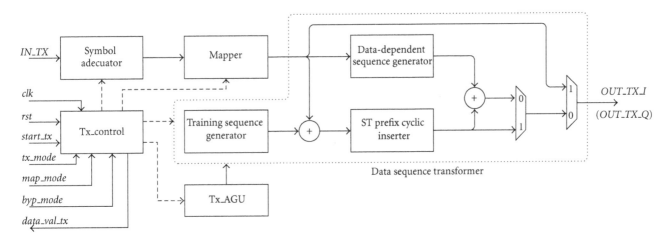

FIGURE 3: Digital architecture of the configurable ST/DDST transmitter.

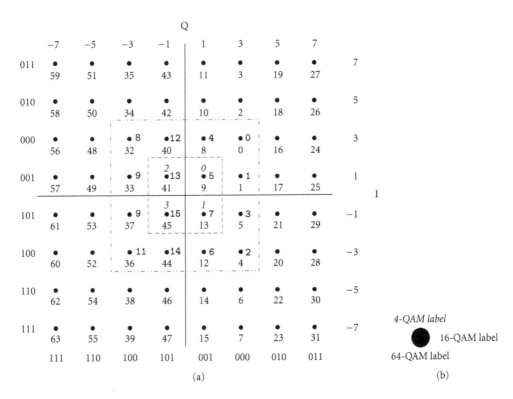

FIGURE 4: Grey-coded 64-QAM constellation used in the mapper module. (a) The 4-QAM and 16-QAM constellations are delimited with a dashed lines; (b) label guide for identifying the constellation point number.

A dual-port RAM (*RAM_CP*) of depth N was used for the ST cyclic prefix insertion submodule designing. The *RAM_CP* have two independent address buses one for data reading (*addr_rd_st_cp*) and one for data writing (*addr_wr_st_cp*). This feature allows to read and write data simultaneously to/from the *RAM_CP*. The process for generating and attaching a cyclic prefix in the ST sequence can be summarized in the following steps (Figure 6).

(I) When the $(N - P + 1)$th datum is stored in *RAM_CP*, the previous datum stored is addressed by *addr_rd_st* bus.

(II) During P clock cycles, the ST sequence storing and reading take place in the *RAM_CP*.

(III) The ST sequence storing in the *RAM_CP* is stopped. However, the data reading will continue for N cycles.

3.3.3. Data-Dependent Sequence Generator. The operation of this submodule is based on (6a)–(7), which implies to compute two high-demand processing operations: an MVM and the Kronecker product. Moreover, similar to the cyclic prefix insertion case, the DDS can only be generated from data sequence $b(k)$ until it has been completely processed.

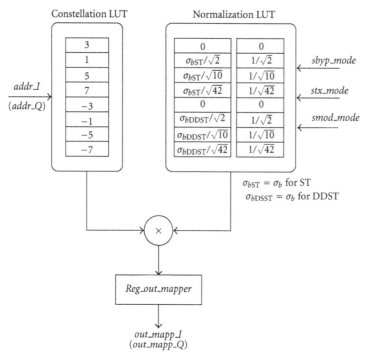

FIGURE 5: Hardware-efficient 4/16/64-QAM mapper with ST/DDST incorporated.

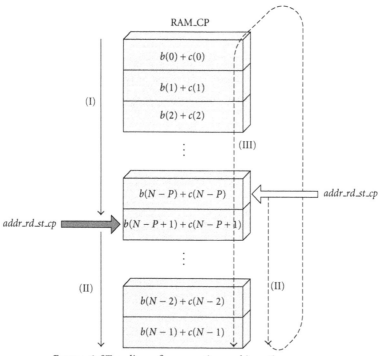

FIGURE 6: ST cyclic prefix generation and insertion process.

In consequence, the following adaptations should be made to the original equations in order to ease its mapping-to-hardware process.

(I) The $b(k)$ sequence is rearranged into a matrix of size $P \times N_P$, according to

$$\left[\mathbf{B}^T\right]_{i,j} = [\mathbf{b}]_{iP+j} = b(iP+j)$$

for $i = 0,\ldots,N_P - 1$, $j = 0,1,\ldots,P - 1$.

$$(19)$$

(II) The mean of the each rows of the matrix $\mathbf{B}$ is obtained.

(III) The P mean results are replicated N_P+1 times in order to obtain the $\mathbf{e}$ vector and P data for DDST cyclic prefix purposes.

Figure 7 shows the hardware architecture of DDS generator. Its novel design avoids the $b(k)$ sequence rearranging by the loop-back shift register lb_delay_dds. This register

Configurable Transmitter and Systolic Channel Estimator Architectures for Data-Dependent Superimposed Training
Communications Systems

187

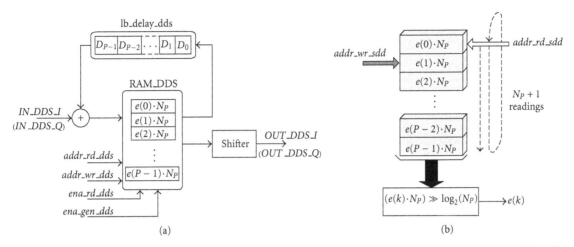

FIGURE 7: Data-dependent sequence generator submodule. (a) Simplified architecture; (b) pictorial representation of the $e(k)$ sequence generation.

generates a P symbol delay in order to align the data for each **B** matrix row. So, the data rows can be added "on the fly" by the complex adder without the data input stream is stopped. The sum results are stored in the *RAM_DDS*, after its entire contents are read $N_P + 1$ times and each datum is divided by N_P in the *shifter* block. Finally, the results are sent to the DDS generator outputs.

4. Systolic Channel Estimator Architecture

This section introduces an architecture for the DDST-based channel estimation process. Its design is based on MVM operation, which is carried out in a systolic way into AP. The main idea in the system design is to reuse the same systolic array for computing the cyclic mean of the received data. The proposed architecture, called in this paper "systolic DDST channel estimator" (SYSDCE) is depicted in Figure 8(a). Four functional units can be identified: a modified systolic matrix-vector multiplier (MSYSMVM), a data input feeder (DATINF), an inverse C look-up table (ICLUT), and a control unit (CU). Broadly speaking, the SYSDCE operation can be divided into three phases: input sequence storage, cyclic mean compute, and CIR estimate.

As soon as the *start* signal is asserted, an $N + P$ data samples (vector **x** and cyclic prefix, resp.) can be read from the input port *IN*. After excluding the samples corresponding to the cyclic prefix, the rest of samples are rearranged and stored in the memory bank of DATINF. When this process is finished, the CU configures the MSYSMVM unit and during N_P cycles it reads P parallel data per cycle from DATINF and computes the cyclic mean **y**. Once this phase is finished, the obtained vector **y** together with ICLUT data are fed to the MSYSMVM again for performing the product expressed in (10). Finally, after $P + 1$ cycles, the *done* flag is asserted and one by one the coefficients of the channel estimated $\hat{\mathbf{h}}$ are sent to the bus *H_OUT*. It is worth mentioning that the SYSDCE can be configured to compute only the cyclic mean if *mode* input control signal has been set to zero. In this case, the *cm_flag* out is asserted to indicate that valid results are available in *CM_OUT* bus. Thus, the channel estimator is prepared for another data sequence processing. A deeper explanation about each component of the SYSDCE architecture will be given in the subsections.

4.1. Modified Systolic Matrix-Vector Multiplier (MSYSMVM). The fundamental operation to perform by SYSDCE is a matrix-vector multiplication which is high time-processing demanding. The hardware design for solving this operation is the most critical part in the architecture. The obvious strategy for accelerating MVM consists in computing as many operations as possible, with the penalty of a great consumption of FPGA resources. Therefore, this paper proposes a modification of the systolic MVM presented in [14, Ch. 3] in order to obtain a good performance with reasonable resources consumption. This modification allows to compute the cyclic mean using *partitioning* method with the same systolic array reported. Figure 8(b) shows the processor element (PE), which is the atomic digital signal processing module in MSYSMVM. It processes three flows: the data flow from the ICLUT or DATINF, the input registers values, and the data produced by the previous adjacent PE.

In the MSYSMVM design was considered that the number of PEs needed (AP size) is P, which matches with the dimensions of matrix $\mathbf{\Gamma}$ and vector **y**, respectively. The projection vector $\mathbf{d} = \begin{bmatrix} 1 & 0 \end{bmatrix}^T$ (see details in [14]) was used with a vector schedule $\mathbf{s} = \begin{bmatrix} 1 & 1 \end{bmatrix}^T$. The pipelining period for this design is equal to 1 and the computing time for the full MVM is $2P - 1$ clock periods.

For computing the cyclic mean using the MSYSMVM module, the original structure of PE was modified with an additional multiplexer. For that reason, the PE can perform all trivial multiplications by bypassing the data from the input of the complex multiplier directly to the complex adder.

4.2. Data Input Feeder (DATINF). Similar to almost any systolic array, the MSYSMVM needs the data, which will be fed to each of its PEs to be given in a defined order before

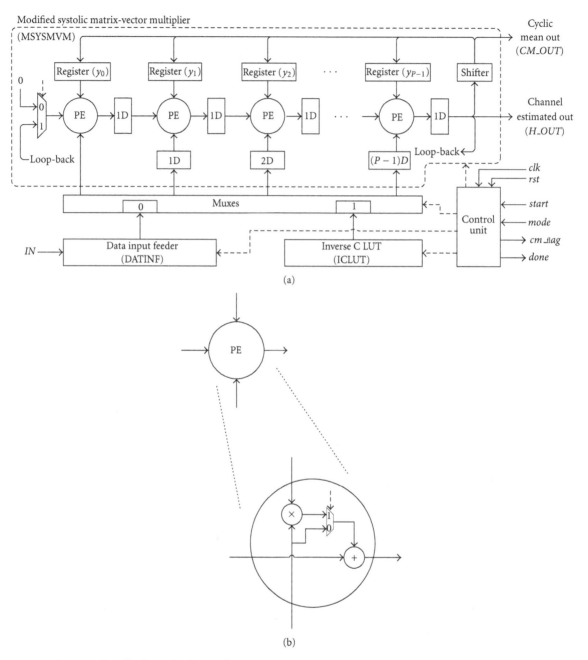

FIGURE 8: Systolic channel estimator for DDST receiver. (a) Simplified architecture; (b) the PE module.

processing it. In the proposed approach, the module DATINF is responsible for performing this task. It is made up of an array of P memories, each with a depth of N_P, organized as a memory bank as shown in Figure 9. DATINF reads $N + P$ data from IN bus; it identifies and removes the first P data corresponding to CP. Subsequently, this module rearranges this sequence (correspondence to $x(k)$) in N_P/P blocks of size $P \times P$ in order to form $\mathbf{B}_0, \mathbf{B}_1, \ldots, \mathbf{B}_{N_P/P}$. Therefore, the N stored data can be viewed as a $N_P \times P$ matrix, where each individual memory in the bank stores one column of each block and the blocks are stored consecutively one after another, as depicted in Figure 9.

Each datum of the input sequence $\mathbf{x}$ has associated three addresses that define its location inside the memory bank:

block number (blk_num), memory number (mem_num), and memory address (mem_addr). The DATINF must generate these addresses using the following expressions:

$$blk\_num = \left\lfloor \frac{k \times N_P}{N \times P} \right\rfloor, \quad k = 0, 1, \ldots, N - 1, \quad (20\text{a})$$

$$mem\_num = \left\lfloor \frac{k \times N_P - blk\_num \times N \times P}{N} \right\rfloor, \quad (20\text{b})$$

$$mem\_addr = (k \bmod P) + (P \times blk\_num), \quad (20\text{c})$$

where k is the kth element of $\mathbf{x}$ and $\lfloor \cdot \rfloor$ denotes the *floor* operator.

Configurable Transmitter and Systolic Channel Estimator Architectures for Data-Dependent Superimposed Training Communications Systems

189

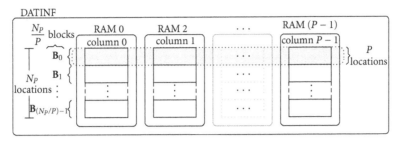

FIGURE 9: Data block organization in the DATINF.

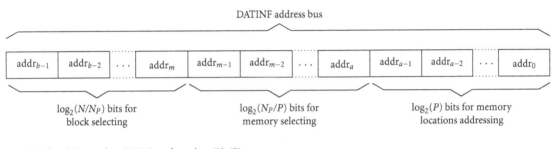

$b = \log_2(N), m = \log_2(N/N_P),$ and $a = \log_2(N_P/P)$

FIGURE 10: Hard-wired addressing for memory bank.

In order to minimize the hardware consumption, a "hard-wired" addressing approach was built for the memory bank. As shown in Figure 10, the $\log_2(N)$ bits corresponding to the DATINF *address bus* are split into three parts. The first $\log_2(N/N_P)$ most significant bits (MSB) are used for block selecting, the next $\log_2(N_P/P)$ MSB are used to select a particular memory in the bank and the remaining $\log_2(P)$ bits are used to individually address each of the locations in the selected memory.

4.3. Inverse C Look-Up Table (ICLUT). The values of the circulant matrix $\mathbf{C}^{-1}$ are constants that can be precomputed once off-line and stored in a LUT. Only the values of the first column are necessary because the remaining columns are shifted versions of the first one. Consequently, the ROM location's number required for the LUT is just P. If traditional design is used, then the LUT will be designed with a multiport ROM of P locations, but it will be synthesized by the employed compiler tool as an array of P single-port ROMs. Therefore, the number of memory locations is increased to P^2. A novel solution was designed with an array of P registers operating as a circular buffer. This is called "inverse C lookup table" (ICLUT) and it saves $P(P-1)$ memory locations. The first row values of $\mathbf{C}^{-1}$ are stored in the registers. Next, one rotation is applied in each tick of the clock to change the register's outputs, as indicated in Figure 11.

5. Results

In this section, the proposed architectures are evaluated. First, the hardware utilization and throughput of the ST/DDST transmitter implementation are presented. After, its functional performance from the point of the signal-to-quantization-noise ratio (SQNR) is analyzed. Next, the FPGA resources consumption and throughput of the SYSDCE implementation are obtained. Finally, the SYSDCE functional results specified in terms of the MSE of the channel estimated and SQNR performance are carried out by Monte Carlo simulations and using the transmitter hardware in DDST mode.

5.1. Implementation and Simulation of the Transmitter. The configurable ST/DDST transmitter architecture was implemented in RTL level using Verilog hardware description hardware. It is able to transmits ST or DDST data blocks of length N with $CP = P$. The power of training sequence is set to $0.2\sigma_s^2$ with a period $P = 8$. The configurable transmitter was synthesized and targeted in Xilinx Virtex-5 XC5VLX110T FPGA. Default settings and no "user constraints" were selected in the EDA tool Xilinx ISE v11. No IP core o predesigned component were used. All signals are represented in signed fixed-point two's complement, and nonrounding scheme was considered.

Table 1 summarizes the synthesis results for the proposed ST/DDT transmitter. Analyzing this table, it can be noted a operating frequency of 160 MHz with a symbolic FPGA resource utilization. So, it is clear that excellent area-frequency balance is achieved.

On the other hand, it is difficult to compare directly the proposed transmitter and channel estimator with the others previously presented in [9, 10] because of the differences in technology, paradigms used, and testing conditions. In

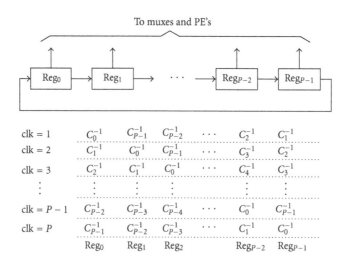

FIGURE 11: Simplified architecture of inverse C look-up table (ICLUT) and its corresponding outputs values.

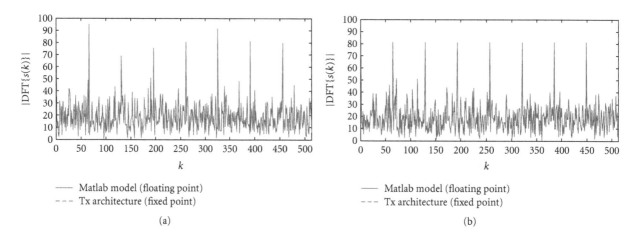

(a)

(b)

FIGURE 12: Discrete Fourier transform of the $s(k)$ sequence generated by the transmitter architecture. (a) ST mode; (b) DDST mode.

TABLE 1: Synthesis results of the ST/DDST transmitter.

FPGA resource	Used	Available	Utilization
Frequency	160.12	MHz	—
Slice registers	141	69120	<1%
Slice LUTs	437	69120	<1%
Fully used LUT-FF pairs	134	444	30%
IOBs	46	640	7%
BRAMs	4	148	2%

[9], DDST communication system was implemented under full-software philosophy in TMS320C6713 DSP with a 300 MHz external clock. A hybrid software-hardware FPGA implementation of the DDST receiver is described in [10]. In both DDST implementations mentioned, the comparison against our transmitter was not possible. In the former because the transmitter was full-software based and the latter only the DDST receiver was implemented.

The transmitter operating validity is presented in Figure 12. The first graph (Figure 12(a)) shows clearly that the transmitter hardware has embedded the training sequence $c(k)$ into $b(k)$. It can be noted that the data sequence energy is spread in all frequency components. In contrast, the training sequence energy are only concentrated in P equispaced frequency components. Similar behavior occurs in the DDST mode (Figure 12(b)), but now the pilots signals also have the same energy. This is unequivocal proof that the transmitter architecture is properly superimposing $c(k)$ and $e(k)$ into $b(k)$.

The SQNR obtained for 100 Monte Carlo trials is monitored, in order to quantify the difference between the $s(k)$ sequence obtained with the hardware transmitter compared with the floating-point transmitter golden model. Thus, the histogram of Figure 13 represents concisely the results of this test. The most of the occurrence are concentrated in 84 dB.

5.2. Implementation and Simulation of the Channel Estimator.

The SYSDCE architecture was implemented using the same considerations and design parameters of the transmitter.

Configurable Transmitter and Systolic Channel Estimator Architectures for Data-Dependent Superimposed Training Communications Systems

191

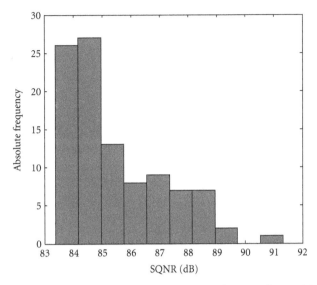

FIGURE 13: SQNR performance histogram of the ST/DDST architecture for 100 Monte Carlo trials.

TABLE 2: Synthesis results of the SYSDCE.

Input length (without CP)	(N)	512
Frequency	(MHz)	115.247
Slice registers	(69120)	1370 (1%)
Slice LUTs	(69120)	2587 (3%)
Fully used LUT-FF pairs	(3348)	609 (18%)
Block RAMs	(148)	8 (5%)
DSP48Es	(64)	32 (50%)

Also, the systolic channel estimator was synthesized and targeted in the same FPGA.

Table 2 summarizes the synthesis results for the proposed estimator. The values in the parenthesis in each feature indicate the total of corresponding available resources in the FPGA. The results in Table 1 reveal a frequency operation of 115.247 MHz with a minimal consumption (except DSP48Es) with respect to the total resources of the FPGA.

Againly, it was not possible to compare the SYSDCE against the existent approaches. In [10], the module corresponding to the channel estimation, only the arithmetic mean was accelerated by a dedicated coprocessor. In this work, the input sequence length was assumed (but it did not explicitly mentioned) to be $N = 512$ symbols. The MVM operation described in (9) was implemented in software. Also, no results—from the point of view of the mean square error (MSE) in the channel estimated or SQNR performance—are presented.

Other important parameter of the proposed estimator is the number of cycles required for performing the tasks estimation. Particularly, the cyclic mean requires

$$\text{cycles}_{\hat{\gamma}} = (N + P) + (N_P + P - 1). \tag{21}$$

The first term in (21) corresponds to the input storage phase and the second to the N_P/P MVM operations involved in the cyclic mean task. Furthermore, the number of cycles required for the CIR estimator is

$$\text{cycles}_{\hat{h}} = \text{cycles}_{\hat{\gamma}} + 2P - 1. \tag{22}$$

Consider the set of metrics listed in Table 3 to compare the performance of the SYSDCE system. The processing time (PT) is the time elapsed from the beginning of cyclic mean or channel estimation process until its computing has finished. The throughput (TP) per area is another useful metric, a higher value of this ratio indicates that the system implementation is better. As can be seen from Table 3, the proposed architecture provides a better performance compared to the arithmetic mean coprocessor used in [10].

The validity of the provided architectures is granted by comparing their results with the floating-point simulation golden model programmed in Matlab, in terms of channel estimation error versus signal-to-noise ratio (SNR). Thereby, the following scenario (similar to that used in [6]) was considered. The hardware transmitter was configured in DDST mode, in order to send data blocks of $N = 512$ symbols obtained from a 4 QAM constellation. The channel is randomly generated at each Monte Carlo trial and it is assumed to be Rayleigh with length $L = 8$. The power of training sequence is set to $0.2\sigma_s^2$ with a period P equal to L.

Figure 14 shows the MSE of channel estimated, which is averaged over 300 Monte Carlo simulations for each value of SNR. Note that the MSE of the hardware estimator is too close to the theoretical line [4] and almost indistinguishable with respect to the golden model. On the other hand, Figure 15 presents the probability density function (PDF) of the SYSDCE hardware, obtained for the same Monte Carlo trials. Analyzing such PDF, it can be noted that the fixed-point performance in average is about 68 dB in terms of SQNR.

TABLE 3: Channel estimator throughputs comparison.

Channel estimator	Input length	Cycles/estimation	CT (us)	TP (MS/s)	TP/area (MS/s/slices)
SYSDCE (cyclic mean mode)	512	591	5.128	101.40	25.625e3
SYSDCE (channel estimator mode)	512	606	5.258	98.91	24.996e3
Arithmetic mean coprocessor in [10]	512	2238	20	26.39	NA

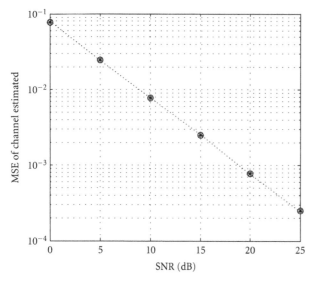

..... Theoretical
* SYSDCE architecture (fixed point)
O Matlab simulation (floating point)

FIGURE 14: MSE performance of the SYSDCE hardware for 300 Monte Carlo trials.

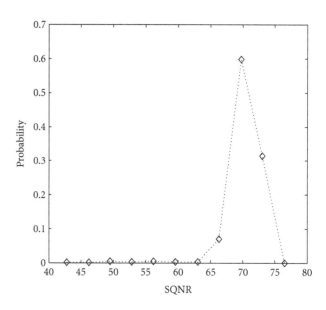

FIGURE 15: SQNR probability density function of SYSDCE architecture for 300 Monte Carlo trials.

6. Conclusions

In this paper, digital architectures for transmitter and channel estimation stages of the ST/DDST communications systems have been presented. These architectures represent the first implementations under the full-hardware philosophy for a wireless systems based on ST/DDST. Both architectures present high throughput and reduced FPGA resources consumption, achieving a good trade-off between performance and area utilization. The proposed transmitter architecture is configurable enough to generate two types of training using three constellation orders. In the SYSDCE hardware, it is possible to observe a great flexibility and reusability because the same systolic array is used for two different tasks (operations): cyclic mean and channel estimation. Also, the SYSDCE design can be easily modified (by means of partitioning strategy) for processing channels of different lengths. The validity and performance of these approaches have been verified by Monte Carlo simulations, where an SQNR of 82 dB and 68 dB in average are achieved for the transmitter and the SYSDCE, respectively. At the same time both architectures present a insignificant differences in the performance results when they are compared with their respective floating-point golden models. The provided results show that ST/DDST concepts can be effectively utilized in current and future wireless communications standards.

Acknowledgments

This work was supported by PROMEP ITSON-92, CONACYT-181962, and Mixbaal 158899 Research Grants.

References

[1] A. Goljahani, N. Benvenuto, S. Tomasin, and L. Vangelista, "Superimposed sequence versus pilot aided channele estimations for next generation DVB-T systems," *IEEE Transactions on Broadcasting*, vol. 55, no. 1, pp. 140–144, 2009.

[2] B. Farhang-Boroujeny, "Pilot-based channel identification: proposal for semi-blind identification of communication channels," *Electronics Letters*, vol. 31, no. 13, pp. 1044–1046, 1995.

[3] S. Haykin and K. J. Ray Liu, *Handbook on Array Processing and Sensor Networks*, John Wiley & Sons, New York, NY, USA, 2009.

[4] E. Alameda-Hernandez, D. C. McLernon, A. G. Orozco-Lugo, M. M. Lara, and M. Ghogho, "Frame/training sequence synchronization and DC-offset removal for (data-dependent) superimposed training based channel estimation," *IEEE Transactions on Signal Processing*, vol. 55, no. 6, pp. 2557–2569, 2007.

Configurable Transmitter and Systolic Channel Estimator Architectures for Data-Dependent Superimposed Training
Communications Systems

193

[5] M. Ghogho and A. Swami, "Improved channel estimation using superimposed training," in *Proceedings of the IEEE 5th Workshop on Signal Processing Advances in Wireless Communications (SPAWC '04)*, pp. 110–114, July 2004.

[6] M. Ghogho, D. McLernon, E. Alameda-Hernandez, and A. Swami, "Channel estimation and symbol detection for block transmission using data-dependent superimposed training," *IEEE Signal Processing Letters*, vol. 12, no. 3, pp. 226–229, 2005.

[7] O. Longoria-Gandara, R. Parra-Michel, M. Bazdresch, and A. G. Orozco-Lugo, "Iterative mean removal superimposed training for siso and mimo channel estimation," *International Journal of Digital Multimedia Broadcasting*, vol. 2008, Article ID 535269, 9 pages, 2008.

[8] R. Carrasco-Alvarez, R. Parra-Michel, A. G. Orozco-Lugo, and J. K. Tugnait, "Enhanced channel estimation using superimposed training based on universal basis expansion," *IEEE Transactions on Signal Processing*, vol. 57, no. 3, pp. 1217–1222, 2009.

[9] V. Najera-Bello, *Design and construction of a digital communications system based on implicit training [M.S. thesis]*, CINVESTAV-IPN, 2008.

[10] F. Martín del Campo, R. Cumplido, R. Perez-Andrade, and A. G. Orozco-Lugo, "A system on a programmable chip architecture for data-dependent superimposed training channel estimation," *International Journal of Reconfigurable Computing*, vol. 2009, Article ID 912301, 10 pages, 2009.

[11] E. Romero-Aguirre, R. Parra-Michel, R. Carrasco-Alvarez, and A. G. Orozco-Lugo, "Architecture based on array processors for data-dependent superimposed training channel estimation," in *Proceeding of the International Conference on Reconfigurable Computing and FPGAs (RECONFIG '11)*, pp. 303–308, December 2011.

[12] A. G. Orozco-Lugo, M. M. Lara, and D. C. McLernon, "Channel estimation using implicit training," *IEEE Transactions on Signal Processing*, vol. 52, no. 1, pp. 240–254, 2004.

[13] N. Petkov, *Systolic Parallel Processing*, Elsevier Science, New York, NY, USA, 1992.

[14] S. Kung, *VLSI Array Processors*, Prentice Hall, New York, NY, USA, 1985.

16

The "Chimera": An Off-The-Shelf CPU/GPGPU/FPGA Hybrid Computing Platform

Ra Inta, David J. Bowman, and Susan M. Scott

The Centre for Gravitational Physics, Department of Quantum Science, The Australian National University, Canberra, ACT 0200, Australia

Correspondence should be addressed to Ra Inta, ra.inta@anu.edu.au

Academic Editor: Thomas Steinke

The nature of modern astronomy means that a number of interesting problems exhibit a substantial computational bound and this situation is gradually worsening. Scientists, increasingly fighting for valuable resources on conventional high-performance computing (HPC) facilities—often with a limited customizable user environment—are increasingly looking to hardware acceleration solutions. We describe here a heterogeneous CPU/GPGPU/FPGA desktop computing system (the "Chimera"), built with commercial-off-the-shelf components. We show that this platform may be a viable alternative solution to many common computationally bound problems found in astronomy, however, not without significant challenges. The most significant bottleneck in pipelines involving real data is most likely to be the interconnect (in this case the PCI Express bus residing on the CPU motherboard). Finally, we speculate on the merits of our Chimera system on the entire landscape of parallel computing, through the analysis of representative problems from UC Berkeley's "Thirteen Dwarves."

1. Computationally Bound Problems in Astronomical Data Analysis

Many of the great discoveries in astronomy from the last two decades resulted directly from breakthroughs in the processing of data from observatories. For example, the revelation that the Universe is expanding relied directly upon a newly automated supernova detection pipeline [1], and similar cases apply to the homogeneity of the microwave background [2] and strong evidence for the existence of dark matter and dark energy [3]. Most of these discoveries had a significant computational bound and would not have been possible without a breakthrough in data analysis techniques and/or technology. One is led to wonder the astounding discoveries that could be made without such a computational bound.

Many observatories currently have "underanalyzed" datasets that await reduction but languish with a prohibitive computational bound. One solution to this issue is to make use of distributed computing, that is, the idle CPUs of networked participants, such as the SETI@HOME project [4]. It is clear that a number of common data analysis techniques are common across disciplines. For example, LIGO's Einstein@HOME distributed computing project, designed to search gravitational wave data for spinning neutron stars, recently discovered three very unusual binary pulsar systems in Arecibo radio telescope data [5].

These are far from the only "underanalyzed" datasets from existing observatories, and this situation is expected to only compound as we look forward to an ever increasing deluge of data. For example, the Square Kilometer Array is expected to produce about an exa-byte *a day* [6] (to put this into perspective, it is estimated that *all* the stored information created by humanity is roughly 300 EB [7]); just for fairly basic operation, this alone will require to be close to the projected computing power of the world's single most powerful computing system [8] at the expected 2020 date of "first light." There are a number of robotic survey telescopes either already, or scheduled soon to be, on-line to detect transient events, from near-Earth objects such as asteroids [9] to distant GRBs [10].

It should be obvious that many other sectors have exponentially growing appetites for computation, from military [11] through financial [12], even cinematic applications require the most powerful HPC systems [13]. Considering the common computational requirements of these systems, it is clear that a revolution in HPC technology is required in order to keep pace with projected needs.

2. Problems with Conventional Cluster-Based HPC Systems

Until very recently, the most powerful HPC systems (the "Top 500") were purely CPU based [8], although there is a very recent but significant shift towards the use of general-purpose graphical processor unit (GPU) coprocessing. However, many critics point out that the "Top 500" may not be representative of the true compute power of a cluster [14]. The negative corollary of the efficient compliance of CPUs with LINPACK is that the resulting rigid instruction set can compromise performance when performing operations not heavily dependent on dense linear algebra. As we show in Section 6 below, this is, only one feature of many that are vital to problems involving parallel computation.

Because power consumption, and hence heat generation, is proportional to clock speed, processors have begun to hit the so-called "speed wall" (e.g., Intel cancelled their 4 GHz processor line because of heat dissipation issues [15]). Furthermore, there is a growing awareness of the monetary cost of powering traditional HPC systems: over half the lifetime cost of a modern supercomputer is spent on electrical power [16]. Indeed, many computing clusters are sited near large generation plants in order to save on power transport costs [17].

It is also easy to forget that the concept of a "general purpose" microprocessor is a relatively recent idea—for example, only since the introduction of the 486 processor have Intel not used a dedicated floating point coprocessor. Meanwhile, hardware accelerators have occupied specialized niches, such as video processing and high-speed DSP applications. The most commonly available of these accelerators are the (general-purpose) graphical processor unit (GPU) and the FPGA. Easing or circumventing many of the issues with CPU-based HPC is becoming an attractive prospect to a growing cadre of consumers. Currently promising teraflop/s performance with a low initial capital outlay and without need of a specialized power supply or cooling facility, both the GPU and the FPGA are viable alternatives to purchasing many CPU-based units. Until recently, the development time associated with these platforms was considered rather high, especially for the FPGA. However, the programming interfaces for both have become more user-friendly. Finally, the future appears bright for both accelerator classes, as both have performance growth well exceeding Moore's Law, and consequently, that of CPUs [18].

3. Comparisons between CPUs and Hardware Accelerators

The long-standing workhorse of the vast majority of data analysts is the general-purpose CPU. Because it is expected to perform a range of different tasks, CPU processor designs cannot afford to specialize. Although the processor clock speeds are fairly high, it can take many cycles to perform an intensive computation, because it will be scanning for interrupts, and so forth. CPUs are generally very good at performing a multitude of separate tasks at a moderate speed and are efficient at moderating/coordinating a range of slave devices. The performance and merits of these devices should be fairly familiar to the reader.

Because GPU platforms were designed to efficiently perform linear operations on vectors and matrices, a general rule of thumb is that any operations that require intensive linear calculations are best made on a GPU. Many embarrassingly parallel computations rely on linear algebraic operations that are a perfect match for a GPU. This, in addition to the amount of high level support, such as C for CUDA, means they have become adopted as the hardware accelerator of choice by many data analysts. For example, a comparison of the GPU-based CUDA-FFT against the CPU-based FFTW3 on gravitational wave data analysis showed a 4X speedup for one million, and 8X for four million, points; this exact approach can also be used to detect radio transients with synthetic aperture array radio telescopes [19]. An excellent analysis of a range of algorithms heavily used in astronomy with applications including imaging, gravitational lensing, and pulsar characterization, implemented on GPUs, is given in [20].

FPGAs, on the other hand, of course, represent an entirely different approach to computing altogether. Because of their unrivalled computing flexibility, it can be difficult for the data analyst, used to a rigid instruction set-based processor, to be entirely comfortable with the low level required to construct an analysis pipeline. The majority of the applications in astronomy have been in instrumentation and data capture, such as the FPGA-based digital cross-correlator for synthetic aperture array radio telescopes [21, 22] or spectrometers [23]. However, there is a small but growing base of analysts willing to adopt an FPGA-based hardware acceleration solution, with applications including detection of gamma-ray pulsars [24]. There are a number of FPGA-based HPC facilities such as Janus [25] and Maxwell [26], and companies such as Starbridge, Inc. and Pico Computing, Inc. [11] offering FPGA computing solutions. A good survey of the state of FPGA-based HPC is given in [27].

Determining the relative strengths of each hardware acceleration class is highly algorithm (and data-type) dependent. There are many comparisons in the literature between FPGA, GPU and CPU, implementations of the same algorithms, ranging from random number generation [28] (where at 260 Gsample/s, FPGAs were found to be faster by a factor of 15 and 60 over a contemporaneous GPU and CPU resp.), video processing [29] (where FPGAs may have a significant advantage over GPUs when multiplying arrays of rank four or higher), convolution [30] (FPGAs are advantageous because of their pipelining and streaming abilities) to MapReduce [26, 31] (where the former show that GPUs considerably out-perform FPGAs and the latter show that an FPGA implementation of Quasi-Random Monte Carlo outperforms a CPU version by two orders of magnitude and beats a contemporaneous GPU by a factor of three), and least squares applications [32] (an FPGA implementation is slightly worse than that for a GPU, which is in turn slightly worse than a CPU, for large matrices). Some more general overviews are given in [33, 34]. However, one must be careful not to generalize performance without consideration of the detailed technical specifications of the components. Both FPGA and GPU platform designs are in a state of unprecedented flux, and hence relative performance benchmarks are likely to change also. This caveat notwithstanding there are a number of distinctions amongst each hardware platform intrinsic to the underlying design features.

With the above considerations in mind, we present here a system that attempts to exploit the innate advantages of all three hardware platforms, in order to attack problems with a computational bound that would benefit from a mixed hardware subsystem "heterogeneous" approach.

4. The "Chimera" Heterogeneous CPU/GPU/FPGA Computing Platform

We originally conceived a platform that would exploit the advantages of both FPGA and GPU accelerations *via* a high-speed backplane interconnect system [35]. A schematic is shown in Figure 1.

There are a number of platforms that implement a heterogeneous FPGA/GPU/CPU system. The "Quadro-Plex Cluster" [36] is a sophisticated sixteen node cluster with two 2.4 GHz AMD Opteron CPUs, four nVidia Quadro FX5600 GPUs, and one Nallatech H101-PCIX FPGA in each node, with a thread management design matching that of the GPUs. However, it does not yet appear to implement a combination of FPGAs *and* GPGPUs within an algorithmic pipeline, which is essential for our applications. Also, the FPGA architecture was designed to mirror that of the microprocessor, including full double precision support, which in general will not optimize the potential performance of the FPGA. The "Axel" [37] system is a configuration of sixteen nodes in a Nonuniform Node Uniform System (NNUS) cluster, each node comprising an AMD Phenom Quad-core CPU, an nVidia Tesla C1060, and a Xilinx Virtex-5 LX330 FPGA. From the perspective of Axel, our proposed platform would conform to the Uniform Node Nonuniform System (UNNS) configuration, or perhaps an optimized version of each node within an Axel-type cluster. There is a "desktop supercomputer" comprising a single CPU, GPU, and FPGA [38], used to model coupled resonator optical waveguides, although unfortunately the architecture and configuration of this system is unclear. Finally, there is a fledgling system that proposes to use a combination of GPUs and FPGAs for cryptoanalytic problems [39], although to date the applications have only been tested on GPUs.

We also would like the system to be scalable if possible, although the focus of this paper is the combined heterogeneity of the hardware accelerators in a single-node architecture. The main problems we are concerned with here feature embarrassingly parallel analysis pipelines, and so extrapolation to a cluster system ought to be relatively straight forward. The granularity of this system is dictated by the particular algorithm being used; the most coarse-grained

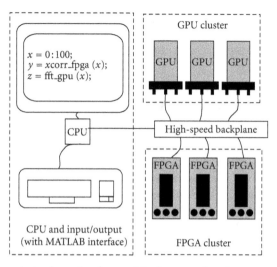

FIGURE 1: A schematic of our original concept for a heterogeneous CPU/GPGPU/FPGA system.

TABLE 1: Description of subsystem hardware configuration for the "Chimera" heterogeneous CPU/GPGPU/FPGA computing platform used here.

Subsystem	Vendor	Model
CPU	Intel	i7 Hexacore
GPGPU	nVidia	Tesla C2070
FPGA	Altera	Stratix-IV

pipelines will be those with a large reliance on GPU-based resources.

Finally, a significant constraint was an inexpensive initial outlay, which immediately restricted us to commercial-off-the-shelf (COTS) components. Table 1 lists the components of the heterogeneous system we describe here, which we call "Chimera," after the mythical Greek beast with a head of a goat, a snake, and a lion on the same body.

Aside from the actual CPU, FPGA, and GPU components, perhaps the most important element in this system is the high-speed backplane or interconnect. Because of COTS constraints, we eventually settled on the simplest solution, that is, that already residing as the northbridge system on the CPU motherboard. In this case, the interconnect protocol is Peripheral Component Interconnect express (PCIe) Gen 2.0, on an Intel DX58SO2 motherboard. Although the board has 2X PCIe 2.0 × 16 ports, only one 16 lane port is dedicated, the other is multiplexed with a third 8 lane slot. The maximum theoretical PCIe throughput, is therefore, 2×16 lane devices or 32 GB/s. These 32 PCIe lanes are routed to the I/O hub processor (the 82X58IOH, which we loosely term here a "northbridge") which implements Intel's Quick Peripheral Interconnect (QPI) protocol to the CPU. The QPI has a 25.6 GB/s point-to-point link to the CPU. In spite of the impressive performance of the motherboard we found, as expected, the PCIe bottleneck presented the most significant limitation to our computing model. We choose to ignore this limitation in what follows for several reasons.

(1) The limitation is algorithm dependant, in some cases (e.g., generation of pseudorandom numbers) large-data sets are developed and processed solely on-chip. In other cases, processing pipelines may be organized to avoid this bottleneck.

(2) FPGA devices, in particular, are provided with very high speed I/O connections allowing multiple FPGAs to process and reduce data-sets before passing them to the final, PCIe limited device.

(3) The purpose of the Chimera is to prove the concept of the hybrid computing model using low-cost COTS devices. Having established that a hybrid design is limited only by interconnect speed the way is open for faster and more expensive interconnect solutions.

The Altera Stratix-IV FPGAs reside on DE-530 development boards, with an 8-lane PCIe interface, while the Tesla C2070 has a 16-lane PCIe interface. The development environment for the FPGAs was Verilog and ModelSim, while that for the GPUs was C/C++ for CUDA and nVidia's SDK libraries. Because there is not yet a widely available communication protocol that allows FPGA-GPU communication without the mediation of a CPU, we are currently developing kernel modules for the PCIe bus. A primary goal of the Chimera system is to provide access to high-performance computing hardware for novice users. This inherently means providing an operating system (OS) with familiar signal processing tools (e.g., MATLAB). Running the OS is naturally a task exclusively handled by the CPU, but it presents some difficulties because the security layers of the OS will usually deny direct access to the FPGA and GPU hardware. In the case of the GPU, this problem is solved by the vendor (nVidia) provided drivers, but, for the FPGA, an alternative approach is necessary: custom driver development is necessary. We opted for a Linux-based OS because we feel it is much simpler to develop drivers than for proprietary OSs. Like all modern OSs, GNU/Linux implements a virtual memory environment that prevents "user" code from directly accessing memory and memory-mapped peripherals. In order to directly control system hardware, such as a PCIe device, it is necessary to write code that runs in "kernel" mode. Linux permits these "kernel modules" to be loaded and unloaded into the running kernel *via* the `insmod` and `rmmod` commands. This provides a straightforward means to share data between the FPGA and GPU devices on the PCIe bus, as well as the system memory. A schematic of this stack design is given in Figure 2.

It is also possible to rebuild the Linux kernel, thus incorporating the module into a custom Linux kernel. The kernel code then provides a bridge between the user code space and the FPGA hardware. As these kernel modules are still under development, and the bottleneck from the PCIe transfer is simple to calculate for the simple examples below, we consider here the subsystem performance only. Hence, the run-time and data-transfer systems are currently fairly primitive. In order to optimize performance, the parallel programming models are algorithm dependent, including the number of threads and how data is shared. Data transfer between the subsystem components currently has only limited

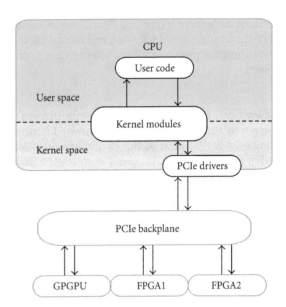

FIGURE 2: The software stack hierarchy of the Chimera system. The Linux kernel modules provide an interface between user-generated code and the PCIe bus and hardware components.

automation, and pipelines are mediated by the CPU, which is highly undesirable. However, we are in the process of building data transfer protocols (*via* the kernel modules) that depend upon the particular application but are implemented using a coherent level of abstraction.

Finally, this system was conceived with the explicit consideration of the significant trade-off between development time (especially associated with development of the FPGA related pipeline and PCIe modules) and performance. Hence, we consider only computing solutions that are likely to have a high reuse within the data analysis community.

5. Appropriate Algorithms for a Heterogeneous Computing System

As with most compute intensive problems, the implementation is extremely dependent on the underlying hardware and the most significant bottlenecks. Much consideration is required in the "technology mapping" from one system to another. For example, an important consideration for FPGA HPC applications is whether fixed or floating point calculations are required. Data analysts have become accustomed to assume that their pipeline requires single precision or more, without considering that this may actually *decrease* the absolute error of the calculation. It is also not entirely true that FPGAs perform poorly on floating point performance [40] (note that this is not necessarily the same as conforming exactly to the IEEE-754 single or double precision definition [41]; GPUs do not natively support denormals but now perform linear operations very well with most double precision calculations). Considering around 50% of FPGA logic can be consumed by tracking denormals, there are recent ingenious developments, optimizing floating point pipelines on FPGAs, such as Altera's "fused datapath" approach [42].

We consider here three important algorithms to attempt to illustrate the considerations required, and relative benefits of, mapping common problems to our heterogeneous computing system.

5.1. Monte Carlo Integration. The simplest illustration of the advantages of this system is the well-known Monte Carlo calculation of π (the ratio of the circumference of a circle to its diameter) [43]. This proceeds as follows. A large set of points (x, y) are created from pairs of random numbers, uniformly distributed between -1 and $+1$, such that they fall within a square of area $2 \times 2 = 4$ units^2. Each point is then checked to see if it lies within a circle of unit radius (equivalently solving the inequality $x^2 + y^2 < 1$). The ratio of the number of points satisfying this inequality to the total number of points then determines the ratio of the total area to the area of the circle. Yet the area of a circle of unit radius is π, so the ratio will yield a numerical estimate of $\pi/4$.

Because FPGAs have the unrivalled capacity to generate large quantities of uniformly distributed random numbers, and GPUs are vastly superior at taking squares (or square roots) over any other commonly available general purpose platform, it would be sensible if an FPGA were to generate the randomly placed points (in parallel), which were in turn directly given to a GPU to determine the placement of each point (i.e., within the circle or not). This calculation and how we anticipate performing it using a hybrid approach is depicted in Figure 3. We could implement a more sophisticated quasirandom version of this algorithm, that is, using a Halton, Sobol' or other low-discrepancy sequence [26, 43], but considering this a rather poor way to calculate π, we restrict ourselves here to uniform pseudorandom distributions for illustrative purposes.

The pseudorandom calculation of π was implemented entirely in the GPU and entirely in the FPGA. In both cases, two 32 bit unsigned integers ((x, y) pairs) were generated using a pseudorandom generator. These were squared and added and the result compared to unity. The limiting factor in the StratixIV530 FGPA was the available number of multiplier blocks which were necessary for the square operation. Our design required 5 DSP18 blocks per sampling module, allowing a total of ≈ 200 parallel units. Applying a conservative clock speed of 120 MHz, we achieved 24 giga-samples per second. Surprisingly, this is approximately an order of magnitude greater than our results for the GPU, which performed 100,000 trials in 47 μsec, giving ≈ 2.13 giga-samples per second. These results agree broadly with those in [26], in that the FPGA calculation of the entire pipeline is about an order of magnitude faster than the GPU implementation, and many many times faster than that by a comparable CPU.

This result ought to be surprising, *prima facie*, considering that the multiplication intensive calculations involved in testing whether the points lie within the unit circle ought to favor the GPU. However, one must remember that a considerable amount of effort went into an implementation optimized for the FPGA, including the avoidance of the costly square root operation. We expect the GPU to perform a lot better, in relative terms, when the function to be

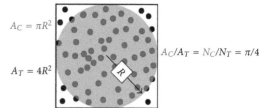

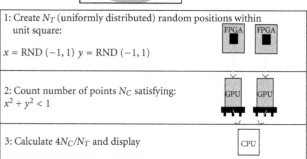

FIGURE 3: A schematic of Monte Carlo calculation of π, and how we expect to perform this calculation on a hybrid GPU/FPGA system.

integrated is more complicated than this extremely simple model. This argument, of course, ignores the fact that copying memory to devices takes far longer than these simple calculations (e.g., in the case of the GPU, about 42 times as long, at 2,118 μsec).

5.2. Normalized Cross-Correlation. Template matching is one of the most important tasks in signal processing and is often achieved by computing the cross-correlation (or "sliding-dot product") between the template and a search signal. For example, cross-correlation is a crucial operation for resolving images in synthetic aperture array-based observatories such as the Very Long Baseline Array or the proposed Square Kilometre Array (SKA) [44].

The point in the search signal with maximum correlation is considered the best match to the template. For discrete one-dimensional signals, we seek to find $\max(A \times B[t])$, where $A \times B[t] = \sum_T A[T] * B[T + t]$. Essentially, we are treating the template, and a template-sized window of the search signal, as vectors in N-dimensional space (where N is the length of the template) and computing their dot-product. The Pythagorean relationship shows that, for vectors of equal length, this is simply a measure of the angular relationship between them, since $\mathbf{A} \cdot \mathbf{B} = |\mathbf{A}| \cdot |\mathbf{B}| \cos \theta$.

Normalized cross-correlation (NCC) is so called because it divides the cross-correlation by the product of the magnitude of the vectors, thus calculating $\cos \theta$, regardless of the length of the vectors. NCC is widely applied in image processing, such as video compression, pattern recognition, and motion estimation where the signals are, of course, two-dimensional, real, and nonnegative. For image processing applications, the 2DNCC is given by (1):

$$\sum_X \sum_Y \frac{A[x, y] \cdot B[x + X, y + Y]}{\sqrt{A^2 B[X, Y]^2}}. \tag{1}$$

Assuming the pixel data in question is always an integer and, since $\sqrt{A^2 B^2} \leq A^2 B^2$, we can equally express (1) as (2):

$$\sum_X \sum_Y \frac{A[x,y] \cdot B[x+X, y+Y]}{A^2 B[X, Y]^2}, \qquad (2)$$

provided we are only interested in finding the peak of the NCC surface.

Computationally, there are many options to accelerate (2) [45]. For most real-world datasets, calculation of the numerator is faster if the Fourier shift theorem is applied and the (unnormalized) cross-correlation computed via the usual transform multiply and inverse transform approach (although it is important to remember that in order to prevent wrap-around pollution it is necessary to zero-pad both images to be size(A) + size(B) − 1). The multiply-intensive nature of this approach, combined with the all-but-essential use of floating-point data types, leads us to conclude that the numerator will be best computed with the GPU.

The ideal platform to calculate the denominator, however, is not so easily assured. As the image data is integral and the only operators are the sum and square, which are both closed under the set of integers, this would seem an ideal candidate for an FPGA. However, because $\mathbf{B}^2 \equiv \mathbf{B} \cdot \mathbf{B}$, it is also a task which might be well handled by a second GPU.

We evaluated the 2D NCC using a common image matching task. We exhaustively searched a 1024×768 pixel search image for an 8×8 template. In both cases, the pixels used were 16 bit unsigned greyscale integers. The numerator of (2) was calculated in the Fourier domain on the C2070 GPU and found to take 6.343 ms (≈ 158 frame/s). We then investigated two approaches to calculating the denominator: FPGA based, or using a second GPU. The FPGA implementation of the dot-product relied on the multiply-accumulate pipeline built into the DSP18 blocks in the StratixIV FPGA. Four DSP18s were required for each 8×8 dot-product block and, because very few of the FPGA's other resources were required, this was the limiting factor in determining the number of parallel units. For the StratixIV530 device, this allowed 256 dot-product modules to operate in parallel. As the DSP18 is a hard silicon block, the maximum clock speed was relatively high, at slightly over 400 MHz, giving a total value of roughly 10 giga-ops. For the search image size quoted, this would achieve ≈ 12.5 kframes/s. The GPU dot-product was profiled at one operation in about 1.4 nsec, or 715 Mop/s, corresponding to a frame rate of ≈ 894 frames/s.

Thus, in this implementation, ignoring the impact of the PCIe bottleneck, a hybrid system comprising a GPU working in tandem with an FPGA was found to achieve a better result than a system consisting of two GPUs. We would like to apply a similarly optimized algorithm to the correlation problem required by a synthetic aperture array observatory such as the VLBA or SKA [44].

5.3. Continuous Gravitational Wave Data Analysis. A much more complicated, and consequently useful, example is that related to the computationally bound problems found in gravitational wave data analysis. A number of mechanisms may cause rotating neutron stars to emit periodic distortions of space time (gravitational waves), which may be detected by ground-based gravitational wave observatories such as LIGO [46] or Virgo [47]. The data analysis pipeline is as follows: the data coming from the gravitational wave observatories is filtered, then template matching is applied. If no candidate is found, in order to determine the statistical upper limits, intensive Monte Carlo calculation of injections is required. This stage is so computationally intensive that it is often not fully implemented because of the prohibitive computational cost [48]. We estimate the Chimera platform will be able to provide these limits for approximately a dozen potential neutron star targets, including central objects in supernova remnants of unknown pulsation frequency. There are already GPU-based acceleration of similar pipelines used in gravitational wave data analysis; many FFTW3-based routines have been replaced with CUDA FFT, to enable low-latency detection of gravitational waves from coalescing neutron stars [19]. We see a similar pipeline as a natural application for the Chimera system we describe here, and we are in the process of implementing this.

5.4. Other Promising Algorithms. Many promising data analysis applications that are considered computationally expensive may be implemented rather simply using this type of heterogeneous hardware acceleration. For example, digital filter application is efficiently implemented on FPGA devices [49]. A number of promising analysis techniques based on compressed sensing [50] are considered computationally expensive. However, the most compute-intensive component, namely, the least-squares minimization routine, may be efficiently implemented on an FPGA via Cholesky decomposition [51–53].

6. Potential for Other Data Analysis Applications: Analysis via Berkeley's "Thirteen Dwarves"

Probably the most labor-intensive process involved in choosing the most appropriate platform weighting between the hardware accelerators in a heterogeneous system is that of identifying the most appropriate algorithms—especially their most efficient implementations—for a given pipeline and input/output constraints. Although we have identified a small number of algorithms here, it would be an interesting and valuable exercise to consider the possible classifications to determine which hardware acceleration combinations would be most appropriate.

In practice, there is a natural classification of problems merely by virtue of the similarity in computation and data movement through usage of the same software packages. Take, for example, FFTW/FFTW3 for spectral methods, or the dense linear algebra LAPACK/ScaLAPACK libraries. Indeed, the latter forms an important benchmark providing some measure of CPU performance (and possible entry into the popular "Top 500" list). However, we would like a more systematic approach to benchmark performance on parallel algorithms that are not necessarily strongly dependent on linear algebra.

In order to identify the likely future requirements of software and hardware design, Phil Colella identified seven parallel numerical methods important for science and engineering [54], known as "dwarves" (a reference to the Snow White fairy tale). This concept of a dwarf, as an "algorithmic method encapsulating a pattern of computation and/or communication," was further extended by the Department of Computer Science of UC Berkeley, to thirteen [55]. It is intended these "dwarves" comprise an algorithm classification system spanning the entire landscape of parallel computing for the foreseeable future ([55]; see Table 2). We see this approach as a promising means of determining the relative (dis)advantages of our Chimera system on other scientific problems. To our knowledge, this is the first attempt at the analysis of dwarf performance on systems heterogeneous at the hardware accelerator level.

The example of the Monte Carlo calculation of π above falls under the "MapReduce" Dwarf: the Mapper function is each trial point, while the reducer just aggregates the counts. From the Chimera perspective, the mapper functions are either performed on the FPGA (the simple example above) or split between the FPGAs and the GPU, while the reducer runs on the CPU. The normalized cross-correlation would be classified within the "Dense Matrix" dwarf. The much more complicated case of the full gravitational wave analysis pipeline largely falls under the "Spectral Methods" jurisdiction, along with that of "MapReduce."

It is clear that many dwarves naturally map to each of the separate hardware accelerators. For example, the "Dense Matrix" dwarf equivalently relates to LAPACK/ScaLAPACK performance on a problem such as principal component analysis of a dense structure. Here, we should expect different performance for floating and fixed point operations, and hence we expect the GPU to excel alone on floating point (at least for matrices of up to rank 4 [29]), while the FPGA will be extremely competitive for fixed point versions. The same argument applies for naïve implementations of the "Sparse Matrix" dwarf, we expect GPUs to have superior performance calculating a sparse PCA problem in floating point, while the FPGA ought to well on fixed point. The "Spectral" dwarf generally comprises an FFT-based computation, such as wavelet decomposition. It is difficult for any platform to beat the GPU CUFFT library, and hence the GPU will be superior in most implementations, although for large numbers of FFT points, FPGAs may be more appropriate [40].

On the other hand, "Combinational Logic" problems (dwarf 8) such as hashing, DES encryption, or simulated annealing, are extremely well suited for the logic-intensive FPGA. It is also clear the "Finite State Machine" dwarf (13), such as control systems, compression (e.g., the bzip2 function), or cellular automata, can be most easily optimized by an FPGA. For example, consider a simple implementation of a 4-bit TTL (Transistor-Transistor Logic) counter, requiring 4 XOR gates, 3 AND gates, and 4 1-bit registers, our Stratix-4 could produce $\approx 120\,\mathrm{k}$ operations per clock cycle, or roughly 36 peta-op/s.

What are not so clear are problems requiring conditional elements or communication between hardware accelerators that would require prohibitively costly transfers across the

TABLE 2: The "Thirteen Dwarves" of Berkeley. Each dwarf represents an "algorithmic method encapsulating a pattern of computation and/or communication," and this intended to be a comprehensive list of the major requirements of parallel computational problems for now into the short term.

	Dwarf	Examples/Applications
1	Dense Matrix	Linear algebra (dense matrices)
2	Sparse Matrix	Linear algebra (sparse matrices)
3	Spectral	FFT-based methods
4	N-Body	Particle-particle interactions
5	Structured Grid	Fluid dynamics, meteorology
6	Unstructured Grid	Adaptive mesh FEM
7	MapReduce	Monte Carlo integration
8	Combinational Logic	Logic gates (e.g., Toffoli gates)
9	Graph traversal	Searching, selection
10	Dynamic Programming	Tower of Hanoi problem
11	Backtrack/ Branch-and-Bound	Global optimization
12	Graphical Models	Probabilistic networks
13	Finite State Machine	TTL counter

back plane. The "N-Body" dwarf generally consists of calculations such as particle-particle interactions. A Barnes-Hut-based particle-particle N-Body model, as used for modelling astrophysical gravitating systems [56], would be able to calculate the changes in interaction on a GPU, while the memory-intensive cell (spatial position) data would be optimally handled by an FPGA. Although there is an implementation of an Ising "spin-flip" model on the Janus FPGA cluster [25], an example of a "Structured Grid" dwarf, a simple Ising model with a limited number of FPGAs would be better optimized using a GPU in addition.

The "Unstructured Grid" dwarf involves Adaptive Mesh Refinement, where calculations may be simplified by considering that only salient points in a space need be calculated, such as for adaptive finite element modelling (FEM) or computational fluid dynamics (CFD). The CPU will be useful in this case to tally changes in the mesh and co-ordinate calculations on salient mesh points using the FPGA and/or GPU.

Because of its conditional nature, "graph traversal" (including selection (Section 3.4, [43]), searching (Section 8.5, [43]) or decision trees) requires coordination from a CPU, and hardware acceleration is dependent on the particular application. "Dynamic Programming," such as the famous "Tower of Hanoi" problem, also requires CPU coordination, and also memory-intensive routines that are likely to benefit from an FPGA.

"Backtrack/Branch-and-Bound" problems, including search and global optimization problems, also depend on coordination from a CPU and again are generally memory intensive. "Graphical Models," such as Hidden Markov, probabilistic, neural, and Bayesian networks are also heavily dependent on coordination.

In light of these arguments, we summarize the most promising subsystem combination to apply for each dwarf

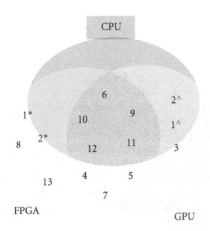

FIGURE 4: The most appropriate hardware acceleration subsystem combination for representative problems from the "Thirteen Dwarves" (Table 2). The *refers to fixed point, while ^ represents floating point calculations.

as a Venn diagram in Figure 4. Of course, this should be understood that the performance is heavily dependent on the particular implementation, generation of subsystem (including on-board memory, number of LUTs, etc.), and interconnect speed.

To characterize the performance of the Chimera system, we would like to analyze representative problems in each dwarf in the future using appropriate benchmark packages such as, for example, the "DwarfBench" package [57] or "Rodinia" [58]. Such a benchmark would be of use to researchers considering the benefits of this approach for their own work.

7. Discussion

We see a heterogeneous CPU/GPU/FPGA solution as a viable future platform for ameliorating some of the computationally bound problems in astronomy based on performance, initial outlay, and power consumption considerations. Because of the outstanding progress made in microprocessor technologies, most members of the astronomical and broader scientific community will not have considered the possibility of including an FPGA-based accelerator to their analysis pipelines; indeed the adoption of the GPU is relatively new within the data analysis community.

However, this solution is not without challenges. There is a significant investment required in development time. This begins with the "technology mapping" stage, which can require many hours for a modest pipeline, such as in Sections 5.1 and 5.2, each of which required considerable thought of how to distribute compute resources, including small-scale trials using MATLAB as a development environment, comprising one to two hours each. The GPU programming for these two examples took a total of about five hours, largely thanks to nVidia's comprehensive CUDA SDK support. However, because the degree of optimization of the FPGA pipelines meant the total amount of time spent "programming" was approximately forty to fifty hours, the

majority of which was spent in the synthesis/debugging phase using ModelSim. Although we have not yet implemented the example in Section 5.3—which requires the dynamic range given by floating point types—considerable development time was saved using Altera's DSP Builder, which interfaces easily with Mathworks' Simulink. Another issue to be aware of is that a high degree of hardware optimization generally means a trade-off in problem-size scalability. For example, in Section 5.1 example, the pairs of numbers (x, y) are each 32-bit and the cases under-/overflow are well known; a naïve scaling to, say, single precision floating point pairs would quickly reduce the number of parallel units on the FPGA. In example Section 5.2, if instead of an 8×8 template, we were to use 32×32 template, performance would scale very poorly because the limiting factor in performance is the number of DSP18 blocks on the StratixIV530 FPGA.

A promising advantage of this platform is the low power consumption. Taking the peak rated single precision performance of each subsystem gives 1.02 Tflop/s for the Tesla C2070, drawing a power of 228 W. This gives 4.3 Gflop/s/W, or 4.3 Gflop/J. Compare to the StratixIV, with 500 Mflop performance, drawing around 20 W at this performance, yielding roughly 25 Mflop/s/W. Perhaps more importantly, the FPGA draws virtually no power when not performing intensive calculations, unlike both the GPU and CPU systems.

Although we have shown the merits and challenges of a mixed system, the advantages are obvious for a diverse range of parallel computing tasks, as shown by analysis of Berkeley's "Thirteen Dwarves." This paper hopefully provides a blueprint for future researchers intending to perform computationally intensive investigations and are willing to embrace a heterogeneous computing platform.

Acknowledgments

The authors wish to thank the Australian National University and Altera Corporation for their generous support. R. Inta is supported by an Australian Research Council "Discovery" project and D. J. Bowman is supported by an Australian Research Council "Super Science" Project. They would like also to thank Martin Langhammer for helpful discussion, and the anonymous reviewers, whose suggestions greatly improved the manuscript.

References

[1] B. P. Schmidt, N. B. Suntzeff, M. M. Phillips et al., "The high-Z supernova search: measuring cosmic deceleration and global curvature of the universe using type Ia supernovae," *Astrophysical Journal*, vol. 507, no. 1, pp. 46–63, 1998.

[2] G. F. Smoot, C. L. Bennett, A. Kogut et al., "Structure in the COBE differential microwave radiometer first-year maps," *Astrophysical Journal*, vol. 396, no. 1, pp. L1–L5, 1992.

[3] D. N. Spergel, L. Verde, H. V. Peiris et al., "First-year Wilkinson Microwave Anisotropy Probe (WMAP) observations: determination of cosmological parameters," *Astrophysical Journal, Supplement Series*, vol. 148, no. 1, pp. 175–194, 2003.

[4] University of California, 2011, http://setiathome.berkeley.edu/.

[5] B. Knispel, B. Allen, J. M. Cordes et al., "Pulsar discovery by global volunteer computing," *Science*, vol. 329, no. 5997, p. 1305, 2010.

[6] T. Cornwell and B. Humphreys, "Data processing for ASKAP and SKA," 2010, http://www.atnf.csiro.au/people/tim.cornwell/presentations/nzpathwaysfeb2010.pdf.

[7] M. Hilbert and P. López, "The world's technological capacity to store, communicate, and compute information," *Science*, vol. 332, no. 6025, pp. 60–65, 2011.

[8] H. Meuer, E. Strohmaier, J. Dongarra, and H. Simon, "Top 500 supercomputers," 2011, http://www.top500.org/.

[9] LSST Corporation, "Large synoptic survey telescope," 2011, http://www.lsst.org/lsst/.

[10] The Australian National University, "The SkyMapper survey telescope," 2010, http://msowww.anu.edu.au/skymapper/.

[11] Pico Computing, Inc., "Using FPGA clusters for fast password recovery," 2010, http://www.scribd.com/doc/26191199/Using-FPGA-Clusters-for-Fast-Password-Recovery.

[12] C. Duhigg, "Stock traders find speed pays, in milliseconds," 2009, http://www.nytimes.com/2009/07/24/business/24trading.html.

[13] J. Ericson, "Processing Avatar," 2009, http://www.information-management.com/newsletters/avatar_data_processing-10016774-1.html.

[14] J. Jackson, "Supercomputing top500 brews discontent," 2010, http://www.pcworld.idg.com.au/article/368598/supercomputing_top500_brews_discontent/.

[15] N. Hasasneh, I. Bell, C. Jesshope, W. Grass, B. Sick, and K. Waldschmidt, "Scalable and partitionable asynchronous arbiter for micro-threaded chip multiprocessors," in *Proceedings of the 19th International Conference on Architecture of Computing Systems (ARCS '06)*, W. Grass, B. Sick, and K. Waldschmidt, Eds., vol. 3894 of *Lecture Notes in Computer Science*, pp. 252–267, Frankfurt, Germany, 2006.

[16] P. E. Ross, "A computer for the clouds," 2008, http://spectrum.ieee.org/computing/hardware/a-computer-for-the-clouds.

[17] M. Wehner, L. Oliker, and J. Shalf, "Low-power supercomputers (ieee spectrum)," 2009, http://spectrum.ieee.org/computing/embedded-systems/lowpower-supercomputers.

[18] K. Underwood, "FPGAs vs. CPUs: trends in peak floating-point performance," in *Proceedings of the 12th International Symposium on Field-Programmable Gate Arrays (FPGA '04)*, pp. 171–180, New York, NY, USA, February 2004.

[19] S. K. Chung, L. Wen, D. Blair, K. Cannon, and A. Datta, "Application of graphics processing units to search pipelines for gravitational waves from coalescing binaries of compact objects," *Classical and Quantum Gravity*, vol. 27, no. 13, Article ID 135009, 2010.

[20] B. R. Barsdell, D. G. Barnes, and C. J. Fluke, "Analysing astronomy algorithms for graphics processing units and beyond," *Monthly Notices of the Royal Astronomical Society*, vol. 408, no. 3, pp. 1936–1944, 2010.

[21] M. Bergano, F. Fernandes, L. Cupido et al., "Digital complex correlator for a C-band polarimetry survey," *Experimental Astronomy*, vol. 30, no. 1, pp. 23–37, 2011.

[22] L. De Souza, J. D. Bunton, D. Campbell-Wilson, R. J. Cappallo, and B. Kincaid, "A radio astronomy correlator optimized for the Xilinx Virtex-4 SX FPGA," in *Proceedings of the International Conference on Field Programmable Logic and Applications (FPL '07)*, pp. 62–67, August 2007.

[23] B. Klein, S. D. Philipp, I. Krämer, C. Kasemann, R. Güsten, and K. M. Menten, "The APEX digital fast fourier transform spectrometer," *Astronomy and Astrophysics*, vol. 454, no. 2, pp. L29–L32, 2006.

[24] J. Frigo, D. Palmer, M. Gokhale, and M. Popkin Paine, "Gamma-ray pulsar detection using reconfigurable computing hardware," in *Proceedings of the 11th IEEE Symposium Field-Programmable Custom Computing Machines*, pp. 155–161, Washington, DC, USA, 2003.

[25] F. Belletti, M. Guidetti, A. Maiorano et al., "Janus: an FPGA-based system for high-performance scientific computing," *Computing in Science and Engineering*, vol. 11, no. 1, Article ID 4720223, pp. 48–58, 2009.

[26] T. Xiang and B. Khaled, "High-performance quasi-Monte Carlo financial simulation: FPGA vs. GPP vs. GPU," in *Proceedings of the ACM Transactions on Reconfigurable Technology and Systems*, vol. 3, pp. 26:1–26:22, New York, NY, USA, 2010.

[27] M. Awad, "FPGA supercomputing platforms: a survey," in *Proceedings of the 19th International Conference on Field Programmable Logic and Applications (FPL '09)*, pp. 564–568, Prague, Czech Republic, 2009.

[28] D. B. Thomas, L. Howes, and W. Luk, "A comparison of CPUs, GPUs, FPGAs, and massively processor arrays for random number generation," in *Proceedings of the 7th ACM SIGDA International Symposium on Field-Programmable Gate Arrays (FPGA '09)*, pp. 63–72, Monterey, Calif, USA, 2009.

[29] B. Cope, P. Y. K. Cheung, W. Luk, and S. Witt, "Have GPUs made FPGAs redundant in the field of video processing?" in *Proceeding of the IEEE International Conference on Field Programmable Technology*, vol. 1, pp. 111–118, December 2005.

[30] B. Cope, "Implementation of 2D convolution on FPGA, GPU and CPU," Tech. Rep., Imperial College, London, UK, 2006.

[31] D. H. Jones, A. Powell, C. -S. Bouganis, and P. Y.K. Cheung, "GPU versus FPGA for high productivity computing," in *Proceedings of the International Conference on Field Programmable Logic and Applications (FPL '10)*, pp. 119–124, 2010.

[32] D. Yang, J. Sun, J. Lee et al., "Performance comparison of cholesky decomposition on GPUs and FPGAs," in *Proceedings of the Symposium Application Accelerators in High Performance Computing (SAAHPC '10)*, Knoxville, Tenn, USA, 2010.

[33] S. Che, J. Li, J. W. Sheaffer, K. Skadron, and J. Lach, "Accelerating compute-intensive applications with GPUs and FPGAs," in *Proceedings of the Symposium on Application Specific Processors (SASP '08)*, pp. 101–107, Anaheim, Calif, USA, 2008.

[34] S. J. Park, D. R. Shires, and B. J. Henz, "Coprocessor computing with FPGA and GPU," in *Proceedings of the Department of Defense High Performance Computing Modernization Program: Users Group Conference—Solving the Hard Problems*, pp. 366–370, Seattle, Wash, USA, 2008.

[35] R. Inta and D. J. Bowman, "An FPGA/GPU/CPU hybrid platform for solving hard computational problems," in *Proceedings of the eResearch Australasia*, Gold Coast, Australia, 2010.

[36] M. Showerman, J. Enos, A. Pant et al., "QP: a heterogeneous multi-accelerator cluster," in *Proceedings of the 10th LCI International Conference on High-Performance Cluster Computing*, vol. 7800, pp. 1–8, Boulder, Colo, USA, 2009.

[37] K. H. Tsoi and W. Luk, "Axel: a heterogeneous cluster with FPGAs and GPUs," in *Proceedings of the International Symposium on Field Programmable Gate Arrays (FPGA '01)*, pp. 115–124, Monterey, Calif, USA, 2010.

[38] E. J. Kelmelis, J. P. Durbano, J. R. Humphrey, F. E. Ortiz, and P. F. Curt, "Modeling and simulation of nanoscale devices with a desktop supercomputer," in *Proceedings of the Nanomodeling II*, vol. 6328, p. 62270N, 2006.

[39] W. Kastl and T. Loimayr, "A parallel computing system with specialized coprocessors for cryptanalytic algorithms," in *Proceedings of the Sicherheit*, pp. 73–83, Berlin, Germany, 2010.

[40] K. D. Underwood and K. S. Hemmert, *Reconfigurable Computing: The Theory and Practice of FPGA-Based Computing*, chapter 31, Morgan Kaufmann Publishers, Burlington, Mass, USA, 2008.

[41] K. Asanovic, "IEEE standard for binary floating-Point Arithmetic," Tech. Rep. ANSI/IEEE Std., IEEE Standards Board, The Institute of Electrical and Electronics, 1985.

[42] M. Langhammer, "Floating point datapath synthesis for FPGAs," in *Proceedings of the International Conference on Field Programmable Logic and Applications (FPL '08)*, pp. 355–360, Heidelberg, Germany, 2008.

[43] S. A. T. W. H. Press, W. T. Vettering, and B. P. Flannery, *Numerical Recipes in C: The Art of Scientific Computing*, Cambridge University Press, New York, NY, USA, 2nd edition, 1997.

[44] P. J. Napier, D. S. Bagri, B. G. Clark et al., "Very long baseline array," *Proceedings of the IEEE*, vol. 82, no. 5, pp. 658–672, 1994.

[45] D. Bowman, M. Tahtali, and A. Lambert, "Rethinking image registration on customizable hardware," in *Image Reconstruction from Incomplete Data VI*, vol. 7800 of *Proceedings of SPIE*, San Diego, Calif, USA, 2010.

[46] LIGO Scientific Collaboration, 2010, http://www.ligo.caltech.edu/.

[47] Virgo Scientific Collaboration, 2010, http://www.virgo.infn.it/.

[48] P. K. Patel, *Search for gravitational waves from a nearby neutron star using barycentric resampling*, Ph.D. thesis, California Institute of Technology, Pasadena, Calif, USA, 2011.

[49] D. Llamocca, M. Pattichis, and G. A. Vera, "Partial reconfigurable FIR filtering system using distributed arithmetic," *International Journal of Reconfigurable Computing*, vol. 2010, Article ID 357978, 14 pages, 2010.

[50] E. J. Candès, J. K. Romberg, and T. Tao, "Stable signal recovery from incomplete and inaccurate measurements," *Communications on Pure and Applied Mathematics*, vol. 59, no. 8, pp. 1207–1223, 2006.

[51] O. Maslennikow, V. Lepekha, A. Sergiyenko, A. Tomas, and R. Wyrzykowski, *Parallel Implementation of Cholesky LL^T—Algorithm in FPGA-Based Processor*, Springer, Berlin, Germany, 2008.

[52] D. Yang, H. Li, G. D. Peterson, and A. Fathy, "Compressed sensing based UWB receiver: hardware compressing and FPGA reconstruction," in *Proceedings of the 43rd Annual Conference on Information Sciences and Systems (CISS '09)*, pp. 198–201, Baltimore, Md, USA, 2009.

[53] A. Septimus and R. Steinberg, "Compressive sampling hardware reconstruction," in *Proceedings of the IEEE International Symposium on Circuits and Systems: Nano-Bio Circuit Fabrics and Systems (ISCAS '10)*, pp. 3116–3119, Paris, France, 2010.

[54] P. Colella, *Defining Software Requirements for Scientific Computing*, DARPA HPCS, 2004.

[55] K. Asanovic and U C Berkeley Computer Science Deptartment, "The landscape of parallel computing research: a view from Berkeley," Tech. Rep. UCB/EECS-2006-183, UC Berkeley, 2005.

[56] J. Barnes and P. Hut, "A hierarchical O(N log N) force-calculation algorithm," *Nature*, vol. 324, no. 6096, pp. 446–449, 1986.

[57] R. Palmer et al., "Parallel dwarfs," 2011, http://paralleldwarfs.codeplex.com/.

[58] S. Che, M. Boyer, J. Meng et al., "Rodinia: a benchmark suite for heterogeneous computing," in *Proceedings of the IEEE International Symposium on Workload Characterization (IISWC '09)*, pp. 44–54, Austin, Tex, USA, October 2009.

Permissions

The contributors of this book come from diverse backgrounds, making this book a truly international effort. This book will bring forth new frontiers with its revolutionizing research information and detailed analysis of the nascent developments around the world.

We would like to thank all the contributing authors for lending their expertise to make the book truly unique. They have played a crucial role in the development of this book. Without their invaluable contributions this book wouldn't have been possible. They have made vital efforts to compile up to date information on the varied aspects of this subject to make this book a valuable addition to the collection of many professionals and students.

This book was conceptualized with the vision of imparting up-to-date information and advanced data in this field. To ensure the same, a matchless editorial board was set up. Every individual on the board went through rigorous rounds of assessment to prove their worth. After which they invested a large part of their time researching and compiling the most relevant data for our readers. Conferences and sessions were held from time to time between the editorial board and the contributing authors to present the data in the most comprehensible form. The editorial team has worked tirelessly to provide valuable and valid information to help people across the globe.

Every chapter published in this book has been scrutinized by our experts. Their significance has been extensively debated. The topics covered herein carry significant findings which will fuel the growth of the discipline. They may even be implemented as practical applications or may be referred to as a beginning point for another development. Chapters in this book were first published by Hindawi Publishing Corporation; hereby published with permission under the Creative Commons Attribution License or equivalent.

The editorial board has been involved in producing this book since its inception. They have spent rigorous hours researching and exploring the diverse topics which have resulted in the successful publishing of this book. They have passed on their knowledge of decades through this book. To expedite this challenging task, the publisher supported the team at every step. A small team of assistant editors was also appointed to further simplify the editing procedure and attain best results for the readers.

Our editorial team has been hand-picked from every corner of the world. Their multi-ethnicity adds dynamic inputs to the discussions which result in innovative outcomes. These outcomes are then further discussed with the researchers and contributors who give their valuable feedback and opinion regarding the same. The feedback is then collaborated with the researches and they are edited in a comprehensive manner to aid the understanding of the subject.

Apart from the editorial board, the designing team has also invested a significant amount of their time in understanding the subject and creating the most relevant covers. They scrutinized every image to scout for the most suitable representation of the subject and create an appropriate cover for the book.

The publishing team has been involved in this book since its early stages. They were actively engaged in every process, be it collecting the data, connecting with the contributors or procuring relevant information. The team has been an ardent support to the editorial, designing and production team. Their endless efforts to recruit the best for this project, has resulted in the accomplishment of this book. They are a veteran in the field of academics and their pool of knowledge is as vast as their experience in printing. Their expertise and guidance has proved useful at every step. Their uncompromising quality standards have made this book an exceptional effort. Their encouragement from time to time has been an inspiration for everyone.

The publisher and the editorial board hope that this book will prove to be a valuable piece of knowledge for researchers, students, practitioners and scholars across the globe.

List of Contributors

Manuel Saldaña and Arun Patel
ArchES Computing Systems, 708-222 Spadina Avenue, Toronto, ON, Canada M5T 3A2

Hao Jun Liu and Paul Chow
The Edward S. Rogers Sr. Department of Electrical and Computer Engineering, University of Toronto, 10 King's College Road, Toronto, ON, Canada M5S 3G4

Hanaa M. Hussain, Khaled Benkrid, Ali Ebrahim and Ahmet T. Erdogan
School of Engineering, University of Edinburgh, King's Buildings, Mayfield Road, Edinburgh EH9 3JL, UK

Huseyin Seker
Bio-Health Informatics Research Group, Centre for Computational Intelligence, De Montfort University, Leicester LE1 9BH, UK

John M. McNichols and Eric J. Balster
Department of Electrical and Computer Engineering, University of Dayton, Kettering Laboratory, Room 341, 300 College Park, Dayton, OH 45469, USA

William F. Turri
University of Dayton Research Institute, 300 College Park, Dayton, OH 45469, USA

Kerry L. Hill
Air Force Research Laboratory Sensors Directorate, Wright-Patterson Air Force Base, OH, USA

Jones Y. Mori, Janier Arias-Garcia, Camilo Sánchez-Ferreira, Carlos H. Llanos and J. M. S. T. Motta
Faculty of Technology, University of Brasilia, 70910-900, Brasilia, DF, Brazil

Daniel M. Muñoz
Faculty of Gama, University of Brasilia, 72405-610, Brasilia, DF, Brazil

Andrew G. Schmidt, Neil Steiner and Matthew French
Information Sciences Institute, University of Southern California, 3811 North Fairfax Drive, Suite 200, Arlington, VA 22203, USA

Ron Sass
Reconfigurable Computing Systems Lab, ECE Department, UNC Charlotte, 9201 University City Boulevard, Charlotte, NC 28223, USA

Lu Wan and Deming Chen
ECE Illinois, University of Illinois at Urbana-Champaign, Urbana, IL 61801-2918, USA

Chen Dong
Magma Design Automation, Inc., San Jose, CA 95110, USA

Florent Bernard, Viktor Fischer, Crina Costea and Robert Fouquet
Laboratoire Hubert Curien, CNRS, UMR5516, Universit´e de Lyon, 42000 Saint-Etienne, France

Supriya Aggarwal and Kavita Khare
Department of Electronics and Communication Engineering, MANIT, Bhopal 462007, India

Gustavo Sanchez and Luciano Agostini
Group of Architectures and Integrated Circuits (GACI), Federal University of Pelotas (UFPEL), 96010-610 Pelotas, RS, Brazil

Felipe Sampaio and Sergio Bampi
Microelectronics Group (GME), Federal University of Rio Grande do Sul (UFRGS), 90040-060 Porto Alegre, RS, Brazil

Marcelo Porto
Group of Architectures and Integrated Circuits (GACI), Federal University of Pelotas (UFPEL), 96010-610 Pelotas, RS, Brazil
Microelectronics Group (GME), Federal University of Rio Grande do Sul (UFRGS), 90040-060 Porto Alegre, RS, Brazil

Rafael A. Arce-Nazario and José Ortiz-Ubarri
Department of Computer Science, University of Puerto Rico, R'io Piedras, San Juan, PR 00924, USA

Juan Fernando Eusse
Electrical Engineering Department, University of Brasilia, Brasilia, DF 70910-900, Brazil

Nahri Moreano
School of Computing, Federal University of Mato Grosso do Sul, Campo Grande, MS 79070-900, Brazil

Alba Cristina Magalhaes Alves de Melo
Computer Science Department, University of Brasilia, Brasilia, DF 70910-900, Brazil

Ricardo Pezzuol Jacobi
UnB Gama School, University of Brasilia, Gama, DF 72405-610, Brazil

David H. K. Hoe, Jonathan M. Comer, Juan C. Cerda, Chris D. Martinez and Mukul V. Shirvaikar
Department of Electrical Engineering, The University of Texas at Tyler, TX 75799, USA

Oliver Sander, Benjamin Glas, Lars Braun, Klaus D. Möller-Glaser and Jörgen Becker
Institute for Information Processing Technology (ITIV), Karlsruhe Institute of Technology (KIT), Engesserstr. 5, 76131 Karlsruhe, Germany

Kamana Sigdel, Carlo Galuzzi and Koen Bertels
Computer Engineering Group, Technical University of Delft, Mekelweg 4, 2628 CD, Delft, The Netherlands

Mark Thompson and Andy D. Pimentel
Computer Systems Architecture Group, University of Amsterdam, Science Park 904, 1098 XH, Amsterdam, The Netherlands

E. Romero-Aguirre and R. Parra-Michel
Department of Electrical Engineering, CINVESTAV-GDL, 45019 Zapopan, JAL, Mexico

Roberto Carrasco-Alvarez
Department of Electronic Engineering, UDG-CUCEI, 44430 Guadalajara, JAL, Mexico

A. G. Orozco-Lugo
Department of Electrical Engineering, CINVESTAV-DF, 07630 Mexico City, DF, Mexico

Ra Inta, David J. Bowman and Susan M. Scott
The Centre for Gravitational Physics, Department of Quantum Science, The Australian National University, Canberra, ACT 0200, Australia

Printed in the USA
CPSIA information can be obtained
at www.ICGtesting.com
JSHW051439221024
72173JS00006B/1521

9 781632 402882